Peter Nichols
Plays : One

**A Day in the Death of Joe Egg, The National Health,
Forget-me-not Lane, Hearts and Flowers, The Freeway**

In this new collection of Peter Nichols' work, all his earlier successes
are presented in the order in which they were written and staged.
The volume contains the first four stage plays: *A Day in the Death of
Joe Egg*, *The National Health*, *Forget-me-not Lane* and *The
Freeway*, as well as one of his original plays for television, *Hearts
and Flowers*. Each play is introduced by the author.

Peter Nichols was born in Bristol in 1927 and educated there at The
Grammar School and Old Vic Theatre School. After National
Service in India, Malaya and Hong Kong, he was an actor in
repertory and television for five years, then a teacher in London
schools. He has written some twenty original plays and adaptations
for television, six feature films and the following stage plays: *A Day
in the Death of Joe Egg*, *The National Health*, *Forget-me-not Lane*,
The Freeway, *Chez Nous*, *Privates on Parade*, *Born in the Gardens*,
Passion Play, *Poppy* and *A Piece of My Mind*. These have won four
Evening Standard Awards, a Society of West End Theatres Award
for Best Comedy and two Best Musical Awards. He was resident
playwright at the Guthrie Theatre, Minneapolis, where he co-
directed *The National Health*. He has also directed revivals of *Joe
Egg* and *Forget-me-not Lane* at Greenwich and the first production
of *Born in the Gardens* at Bristol. The 1985 Broadway revival of *Joe
Egg* won two Tonies. *Feeling You're Behind*, a first book of
memoirs, came out in 1984.

*The painting on the front cover is of the author's daughter, Abigail;
both this and the painting of the author on the back cover are by
Thelma Nichols (photographs by Fergus Greer).*

PETER NICHOLS

Plays: One

A Day in the Death of Joe Egg
The National Health
Forget-me-not Lane
Hearts and Flowers
The Freeway

Newly revised and
introduced by the author

Methuen Drama

Methuen Drama World Dramatists

This edition was first published in Great Britain in 1991
by Methuen Drama

SEP 2013

A Day in the Death of Joe Egg first published in 1967
by Faber and Faber Ltd, reprinted 1968, 1971, 1975, 1977, 1981 and 1981.
Copyright © 1967 by Peter Nichols

The National Health first published in 1970
by Faber and Faber Ltd, reprinted 1972, 1977, 1981, 1983 and 1988.
Copyright © 1970 by Peter Nichols

Forget-me-not Lane first published in 1971 by Faber and Faber Ltd,
revised in 1987 for first Methuen edition of *Nichols Plays: One*.
Copyright © 1971 by Peter Nichols

Hearts and Flowers first published in 1987 in first Methuen edition
of *Nichols Plays: One*. Copyright © 1987 by Peter Nichols

The Freeway first published in 1975 by Faber and Faber Ltd,
reprinted 1979. Copyright © 1975 by Peter Nichols

Introductions and selection copyright © 1991 by Peter Nichols

The author has asserted his moral rights

ISBN 0 413 64870 2

A CIP catalogue record for this book
is available at the British Library

Typeset by Rowland Phototypesetting Ltd, Suffolk
Transferred to digital printing 2002

Contents

Peter Nichols

A Chronology of First Performances

The Freeway (stage) National Theatre   1974
  Details this volume
Harding's Luck (stage adaptation of E. Nesbit novels)   1974
  Greenwich
The Common (tv) BBC-TV   1975
Privates on Parade (stage) RSC/Aldwych   1977
  In February 1978 at Piccadilly Theatre. In 1989 at
  the Roundabout Theatre, New York, with Jim Dale
  as Terri. In London it won *Evening Standard*,
  Society of West End Theatres and Ivor Novello
  awards and in New York a Critics Circle award. In
  1983 Handmade Films released a version with John
  Cleese as Flack.
Born in the Gardens (stage) Bristol Old Vic   1979
  Directed by author. Transferred to Globe Theatre,
  London, by Eddie Kulukundis in slightly revised
  production by Clifford Williams. BBC-TV:
  adaptation by author, 1968. Pub: Faber
Passion Play (stage) RSC/Aldwych   1981
  Longacre Theatre, New York, 1983 (as 'Passion').
  Rev: Leicester Haymarket and transferred to
  Wyndham's Theatre, London, 1984. At Théâtre des
  Champs-Elysées, Paris, as 'comédie passion'. Later
  Oslo, Brussels, Los Angeles, Washington, Seattle etc.
  Won Standard Best Play Award, 1983. Pub:
  Methuen, and in anthology 'Landmarks of Modern
  British Drama: The Seventies' Screenplay, Private
  View, 1990.
Poppy (stage musical) RSC/Barbican   1982
  Music by Monty Norman. Revised version opened at
  Adelphi Theatre, London, 1983. Society of West End
  Theatre Award, Best British Musical. Pub: Methuen
Feeling You're Behind (autobiography). Pub:
  Weidenfeld and Nicolson, 1984. Penguin, 1985
Film work, apart from screenplays of own plays – *Joe
  Egg*, *The National Health*, *Privates on Parade* – has
  included *Catch Us If You Can*, 1965, and *Georgy Girl*,

1966. Another dozen or so scripts of various kinds
remain unproduced, including two films, a sequence
of five for television (*See Me*), a stage anthology
of the works of Orwell and several stage plays.

For Michael Blakemore
who has been in turn my landlord,
friend, actor, critic and
editor, theatre and film
director, without whom . . .

Introduction

CASTING THE AUDIENCE

The only thing old Phoebe liked was when Hamlet patted his dog on the head. She thought that was funny and nice and it was. What I'll have to do is, I'll have to read that play. The trouble with me is, I always have to read that stuff by myself. If an actor acts it out, I hardly listen. I keep worrying about whether he's going to do something phoney every minute.

J. D. Salinger, *The Catcher in the Rye*

Who, apart from Holden Caulfield, reads plays? Actors, looking for parts or audition speeches. Credit-hungry American students. Critics charting a trend. Plays on the stage are plans for action. Apart from Shakespeare, they're not for reading – and how far would Holden have got with *Hamlet*? Actors often do bring something phoney, but without them – and a director and various designers – scripts are skeletal, mere propositions for an event, interesting but spare. Performers give them flesh and a sort of animation, but the real life of a play doesn't start until the public is let in: in other words, when the play becomes interplay. But who are these watchers? Why have they come? More to the point, why have they stopped coming? We can hardly blame them for not wanting to gather in discomfort with a lot of strangers to catch snatches of dialogue through a clamour of coughing, hawking, yawning, seat-creaking, paper crackling and demands of 'What did he say?' when they could have stayed home and watched something far better on the video. Even the first performance of deathless lines was probably punctuated by all this irrelevant din:–

> Absent thee from felicity awhile
> And in this harsh hrrm draw thy tschoo in what-did-he-say?

Yet without this bronchial congregation, drama is a ritual conducted in an empty church. Nabokov damned theatre for this very quality – 'stone-age rites and communal nonsense' – but in his youth (and mine) responses weren't encouraged. The audience was supposed to be as silent and anonymous as at a Soho strip-club. The ultimate show of this kind would be, I suppose, the exhibition where any sound from the voyeurs out front would break the trancelike concentration of the fornicators. It would be interesting to know whether these performers convince themselves that they're alone or only demand silence to stimulate the viewers by implying a sort of two-way mirror. A less rigid form of this was called naturalism, a purgative reform that became an inflexible genre. A direct appeal, an aside, any breach of the two-way mirror was seen as a sign that the playwright didn't know his job. Yet, of course, there was always interplay: actors responded to the audience, spoke in loud clear voices, waited for laughs, were arranged in pictures that told the story. At its best, this fashion made possible the irony and fatalism of Chekhov and Ibsen. We felt powerless to help these poor fools, mirror-images of ourselves, blundering to their doom. The interplay here was odd, tense, as between mortals and impotent gods. We felt for them but could do nothing. At the end, the actors came out smiling to remind us it had all been a game and we applauded that as much as their skill. No-one pointed out the absurdity of a style that otherwise ignored the audience. It would be some time before Joe Orton could make one character confide in another 'Just between these three walls'. It was a form ripe for television and that's what – in the 1950s – it became. The box in the corner is Strindberg's chamber drama, and we can advise and abuse the actors out loud as we never can in the theatre – or cinema. Films are shown to an audience but no-one must acknowledge that or they will risk the event I witnessed when, in the film version of the play *Alfie*, Michael Caine turned to the camera after learning that a girl-friend was pregnant.

'What shall I do now?' he asked.

'Get out the knitting-needles,' advised someone from the circle – but Michael Caine didn't bat an eye and went on with his next line.

At the time I was earning a living writing plays for television, keyhole naturalism in monochrome. I'd already thrown out a basketful of stage plays in other men's styles but never found my own. In the course of wondering what was left for theatre to do, I defined a rough approach to playwriting. I would try to find a role for the spectators. Straightforward in its early drafts, my first real stage play *A Day in the Death of Joe Egg* broke the mirror more and more as I revised it. The audience was shouted at, appealed to, confided in; some of the actors broke up or seemed to be improvising and at such moments it wasn't at all clear whom to trust. Either the actors or the characters or the author – probably all – were betraying the implicit licence the audience had granted them: to play the game of illusion by understood rules. But many works of fiction are also critical demonstrations and, if *Joe Egg* is a problem play, the problem is not only how to live with a handicapped child but how to describe that life (as the husband puts it) 'in a way that will prevent a sudden stampede to the exit-doors'. Its final draft became a criticism of its first. It's a play about a play.

In the ten or so stage plays I've written since, some thought has always been given to casting the audience, a method that works best when they're not allowed to settle comfortably into any one role. It's one way of accepting, while at the same time exploiting, the limitations of the form. The means are certainly spare, compared to films for instance, but capable of great variation, like those of any good game. Henry James, about to embark on his brief, disastrous playwriting career, wrote that 'one may use them, command them, squeeze them, lift them up and better them. As for the form itself, its honour and inspiration are in its difficulty.' There came a point when I began to feel this difficulty to be too attractive in itself. Trying to manage what James later called 'the hard meagreness of the theatrical form' can become an end, virtuosity for its own sake. I tired of the restrictions and wondered if perhaps my real bent was towards fiction, where scene and costume changes were so easy, weather so convincing and where you never missed a line because another reader coughed. In so many ways, too, my plays had been misplaced novels. But when I tried, I found the old problem of address had to be tackled again, though without the hard meagreness to help. Now that I could do anything, I could do nothing. Institutionalised, I ran back to my familiar cell. *Born in the Gardens* is a defence of life in a cage, and it occurs to me that most of my plays have been about captivity and many of the characters captives.

If that's my theme, my manner's been eclectic, mixing the box-set naturalism which was so common in my youth with bits and pieces from the sort of theatre I enjoyed more – Variety, revue, magic shows, concert parties and pantomimes. This has been thought of as my style, but of the ten plays in this collection (Plays One and Two), several do not break the two-way mirror in any way. Of course, *Hearts and Flowers* is for television, which hasn't developed a dramatic form of its own and probably never will. When I wrote my first play for the box, I hadn't even seen one. It wasn't hard to guess that it could only do small-scale films, mostly for talking heads. Television's been called tapwater, but in fact it's only the conduit through which the water flows.

For many years theatre was the best part of my life. These days I seldom go, not wanting to find myself at some play that pretends to ignore me. 'Communal nonsense' appeals to me more. I enjoy those parts of the event that more fastidious writers find tiresome – the audience assembling, intervals, curtain calls, even the accidents that aren't to do with art or entertainment. I wish I'd seen the performance of *The National Health* when someone in the stalls had a cardiac arrest and, from a stage full of actors robed and masked for a surgical operation, one had to ask, 'Is there a doctor in the house?'. The writing of scripts might well go on, even if all the theatres closed, because it is a spare, enjoyable and demanding form of composition, what Charles Wood calls 'our side of it'. Revivals and musicals are what the public wants; new plays are risky. Already they have more or less gone from The Great Dark Way. All that can make up for the bother and discomfort and high prices are the rare, small miracles and they will only happen when an event is caused that can't happen anywhere else. When our side of it meets theirs.

Peter Nichols
December 1990

A Day in the Death of Joe Egg

A Day in the Death of Joe Egg

A few months ago my wife and I returned to Glasgow for the first time for over twenty years and saw a play at the Citizens' Theatre, which now stands in a no-man's land of municipal demolition. The original Victorian foyer has given way to a light and airy hall but the auditorium of 1878, with its faultless acoustic, is more or less unchanged. We crouched at the back of the gods and heard every word. In the interval I found the circle seats we'd sat on in May 1967 for the first night of *A Day in the Death of Joe Egg*, an occasion which changed our lives.

The full story of how the play was written and how it arrived at last on that stage is told in my memoirs, *Feeling You're Behind*, a book which can be borrowed from libraries or bought second-hand. In its earlier form, the script had been turned down by an impressive list of theatre managers before being taken up by my friend Michael Blakemore, an actor in the process of becoming a director. He pushed it through against much resistance from the Theatre Board and The Lord Chamberlain. This was still a year before the abolition of stage censorship and every play had to be issued with a licence from St James's Palace, where one day we went to meet The Assistant Comptroller of the Queen's Household and his side-kick, a wing-commander.

The atmosphere was friendly, almost apologetic, with Nelson cigarettes on offer and tea promised soon. Michael praised the buildings. 'Aren't they agreeable?' said the Comptroller. 'As you know, the gateway is the only survival from Henry VIII's original palace which was built on the site of a mediaeval leper hospital. Many of your colleagues think it a very appropriate place to house the official censor.'

We all laughed.

'As you know,' said the wing-commander, 'it's not a job we particularly enjoy. Indeed, we support those among you who advocate its abolition. However, until that happy day, we are duty-bound to protect people from gratuitous unpleasantness.'

Which brought us to my play. For some time we fumigated the early scenes, horse-trading a 'sod off' here for a 'piss yourself' there, while prim women brought tea on a trolley, even providing the slice of lemon Michael preferred to milk.

'Now,' said the Comptroller at one point, 'how do we feel about "has he flashed it lately"? Ah, thank you, ladies. . . .'

It's an easy step from prude to philistine and they took it in their stride. To protect the feelings of spastics' parents and spastics themselves, they would prefer that the handicapped daughter should not be seen. Michael explained that I was myself such a parent or could not have written the play, and that, if the child was kept offstage, we should be back in Victorian melodrama, with something nasty locked up in the west wing, when our aim was to present the case as part of the everyday life of those who live it. This they understood, quite so, point taken. In that case, they would suggest the child be played not by an actress but a dummy. Till that I had been buttoning my lip but now my mouth fell open. A sort of life-size doll, they went on. Perhaps it might be workable – a marionette or puppet – or one of those things ventriloquists use, Archie Andrews sort of thing. Michael soon showed how this would be a crueller joke than any in the play and the principle of a visible actress was at last conceded *but* that now raised the matter of what a ten-year-old girl could be allowed to hear. For instance, the scene where the father suggested to the mother that they go to bed could not be done in the child's presence.

I pointed out that she was so mentally handicapped that she would not follow anything anyone said.

'The character, yes,' said the Comptroller, 'but not the child actress. The audience will know she's not really handicapped.'

'But she won't be a child either. She'll be at least fourteen,' said Michael, 'that's the youngest age the GLC allows.'

'But the audience won't know that.'

'Even though they'll know she's not a spastic?' I asked.

'We could not license a scene in which an ostensible child apparently heard one adult proposing sex to another.'

'I wonder would it be possible,' suggested the Wing-co., 'for the child to be pushed off in her wheelchair just before this conversation and brought back on again afterwards?'

'But,' said Michael, 'she'd be sitting in the wings behind a canvas flat. She'd hear every word.'

'Yes, but she wouldn't be *seen* to!'

This solution to their moral dilemma became a condition of the licence and was written in. I added stage directions and Michael staged it that way in Glasgow and, I believe, London. The first published edition of the script included it and companies across the world have done that business ever since without knowing why.

A few of the London producers who'd turned it down before came up for the first night at Glasgow and turned it down again. We all went home to England and I got on with my next television play. Ten days later my agent rang to say Memorial, Albert Finney's company, would transfer the show as it stood and that Ken Tynan had read it and would like to re-mount it at the National Theatre. The choice was mine. Of course, we went with Memorial and by July it was in London more or less intact, the best-staged and best-cast production of the play I've so far seen. It ran for four months, won the *Evening Standard* Best Play and John Whiting awards and never had a full house. The following year Finney took it to New York, replacing Joe Melia in the lead but agreeing to play only eleven weeks. We changed one word – 'fag' meaning cigarette – and it's still the least revised of all my plays. Its particular tone is of its time and updating the money, the political jokes or magazine titles would take the fish out of water only to have it die on the bank.

Our first daughter was three when I wrote it but lived on, in one of those mental hospitals mentioned in the play, till she was eleven. Two days after her death, we saw it performed by drama students and I felt a strong urge to stand up and announce the good news. Of course that would have been to trespass on territory that now belonged to the theatre. Her life and ours had gone on but the play she provoked had become common property and its autonomous existence, we sometimes felt, was more real than our own.

Its latest revivals have been in New York, where it won two Tonies, and Paris, where it played at the same theatre as it had over twenty years ago, but since that first short run, it has never again been seen in the West End.

A Day in the Death of Joe Egg was first performed at the Citizens' Theatre, Glasgow, on 9 May 1967, with the following cast:

BRI	Joe Melia
SHEILA	Zena Walker
JOE	Barbara Goldman
PAM	Carole Boyer
FREDDIE	Michael Murray
GRACE	Joan Hickson

Directed by Michael Blakemore

Later the same year it transferred to the Comedy, London, presented by Memorial Enterprises (Albert Finney, Michael Medwin), with Phyllida Law as Pam and John Carson as Freddie.

In 1968, it was performed at the Brooks Atkinson Theatre, New York with Albert Finney.

In Paris a version by Claude Roy, with Jean Rochefort and Marthe Keller was performed as *Un Jour dans la Mort de Joe Egg* at Gaieté Montparnasse, 1968.

The same year a production at the Berlin Festival by Schiller Theatre at Schlosspark.

Filmed by Columbia Pictures in 1972, with Alan Bates and Janet Suzman.

The author directed a revival at the Greenwich Theatre in 1972.

In 1985 another revival played at the Roundabout Theatre, New York, transferring to the Longacre Theatre.

In the 1980s, a revival at Long Wharf, New Haven, starring Richard Dreyfuss and Stockard Channing, directed by Arvin Brown; transferred to New York with Jim Dale.

ACT ONE

BRI *and* SHEILA.

BRI comes on without warning. Shouts at audience.

BRI. That's enough! (*Pause. Almost at once, louder.*) I said enough! (*Pause. Stares at audience. He is thirty-three but looks younger. Hardly ever at rest, acts being maladroit but the act is skilful. Clowning may give way to ineffectual hectoring and then self-piteous gloom.*)

Another word and you'll all be here till five o'clock. Nothing to me, is it? I've got all the time in the world. (*Moves across without taking his eyes off them.*) I didn't even get to the end of the corridor before there was such a din all the other teachers started opening their doors as much as to say what the hell's going on there's SOMEBODY'S TALKING NOW! (*Pause, stares again, like someone facing a mad dog.*) Who was it? You? You, Mister Man? . . . I did not *accuse* you, I *asked* you. Someone in the back row? (*Stares dumbly for some seconds. Relaxes, moves a few steps. Shrugs.*) You're the losers, not me. Who's that? (*Turns on them again.*) Right – hands on heads! Come on, that includes you, put the comb away. Eyes front and sit up. All of you, sit up! (*Puts his own hands on his head for a while, watching for a move, waiting for a sound, then takes them down. Suddenly roars.*) Hands on head and eyes front! YOU I'm talking to! You'll be *tired* by the time I've finished. Stand on your seat. And keep your hands on your heads. Never mind what's going on outside, that joker at the back. Keep looking out here. Eyes front, hands on heads.

Moves across.

Bell rings.

Who said MOVE? Nobody. Said move. Hands on heads . . . Next one to groan stands on the seat. We're going to have one minute's perfect silence before you go. (*Looks at his watch.*) If we have to wait till midnight. (*Stands watching for some seconds.*) That's nice. I like that. Now try to hold it just like that till I get to this machine-gun over here. (*Moves upstage, turning his back. Turns back at once.*) My fault, all right. Little joke. No more laughing. Eyes front, hands on heads. (*Waits for silence, looks at watch, moving across suddenly looks up, very cross again.*) Who was that? Whoever did – that – can open the window before we all get gassed . . . Wait a minute! Three of you? What are you – a group? One go – one nearest the window. All the others, eyes front, hands on heads. Right. (*Looks at watch.*) That characteristic performance from our friend near the window means we return to Go. (*Looks up sharply.*) Shall I make it *two* minutes? (*Looks down again. Ten seconds pass.*) We could have had this sooner. Then we shouldn't be wasting time sitting here when we might be . . . well . . . let's all – think – what we might be doing – 'stead of sitting here when the rest have all gone home – we could be . . .

Speaking quietly now, absently staring into space. Few more seconds pass. When he speaks again, it is as if in a reverie.

Yes – eyes front . . . hands on breasts . . . STOP the laughter! WHO wants to start another minute? (*Looks at watch then up again.*) And whatever the great joke is, whatever it is that has so tickled your Stone Age sense of humour – when all my efforts have failed . . . save it till you're outside. I'm going to get my coat from the staff-room now. And you will be as quiet as mice – no, fish – till I get back. All right? I don't want to hear a sound. Not a bubble. (*Goes off.*)

Lights up on set behind; Living-room.

Pleasant and comfortable, furnished with a gallant collection of junk-shop bargains and H.P. modern. Plain walls with two essential doors and one optional window. Door in upstage wall leads to hall and stairs, which can be seen when the door is opened. Door in other wall leads to kitchen. Bird in cage, fish in tank, plants in pots. Two paintings of cowboys are conspicuous.

SHEILA comes from kitchen with tea on a tray. She is thirty-five, generously built, serious and industrious. When dressed for society, she can be captivating. Puts down tray and runs back to kitchen door, pushing with her foot, keeping out an animal.

SHEILA. Back, back, no no.

Shuts the door and comes back. Door slams off. SHEILA starts pouring tea.

(*Shouts.*) Bri?

BRI (*off*). No.

SHEILA (*shouts*). Just got tea.

He comes on, approaches her, takes the offered kiss, then stands close looking at her. She goes back to pouring tea and offers him his cup. He doesn't take it, so she looks at his face. She screams, nearly spills tea.

What's that?

BRI. What?

SHEILA. On your face!

BRI. Where?

SHEILA. Near your eye.

BRI. What is it?

SHEILA. A black thing.

BRI. For Christ's sake –

SHEILA. A spider –

BRI. Shall I touch it?

SHEILA. A great black – get it off!

BRI. How?

SHEILA. Knock it off! (BRI *takes it off, smiling.*) Ugh!

He puts it on the back of his hand and shows her.

BRI. I confiscated it. (*She knocks it away angrily.*)

From Terry Hughes.

SHEILA. Vicious sod!

BRI. He *is*. For thirteen.

SHEILA. You, I mean.

BRI. In Religious Instruction.

SHEILA. It's not funny.

BRI. What I told *him*.

She has turned from him. He sees he has done wrong and now tries to make amends. Approaches from behind and kisses her neck.

SHEILA. Get away!

BRI. Oh, look –

SHEILA. Why d'you do it, Brian, honestly? You knew that would upset me and the first thing you do –

BRI. Sorry, love.

SHEILA. I even kissed you –

BRI. Sorry.

He takes and drinks the tea. So does she. He puts down cup and kisses her again. Then caresses her.

Oh, love, if you knew how I'd been thinking of you –

SHEILA. You'll spill this tea.

BRI. Let's go to bed, come on.

SHEILA. Ow! – don't –

BRI. What?

SHEILA. Your hands are cold, you've just come in –

BRI. Let's go to bed.

SHEILA. At quarter to five?

BRI. I came home early specially.

SHEILA. The usual time.

BRI. Yeah, but I was *going* to keep them in.

SHEILA. Who?

BRI. Four D.

SHEILA. Did you *say* you would?

BRI. Yes.

SHEILA. To them?

BRI. Yes.

SHEILA. Then why didn't you?

BRI. I kept imagining our bed, our room, your legs thrashing about –

SHEILA. When *are* you going to learn?

BRI. My tongue half-way down your throat –

He is at her again.

SHEILA. You must carry out your threats.

BRI. – train screaming into tunnel –

SHEILA. They'll never listen to you if you don't –

BRI. – waves breaking on rocky shore.

She moves out of his reach. Pause. He sips tea, winces.

Sugar. (*He helps himself.*)

SHEILA. You want bromide.

BRI. I want you. It's you I want.

Turns, makes a joke of it, pointing to her like the advert.

I want you. Kitchener, look. I want you.

She smiles. He sits and drinks.

SHEILA. You should have kept them in.

BRI. I did for a bit. Then I left them with their hands on heads and went to fetch my coat and suddenly couldn't face them any more, so I never went back. Wonder how long they sat there.

SHEILA. Brian –

BRI. Terry Hodges, Fatty Brent . . . Glazebrook, the shop steward – he's got a new watch. And of course Scanlon –

Shakes his head at the idea.

– the Missing Link. Pithecanthropus Erectus.

SHEILA. Has he flashed it lately?

BRI. Not at the teachers anyway.

SHEILA. Only that once.

BRI. That once was the only time it was reported.

SHEILA. Poor girl.

BRI. Some of the older women might keep quiet. Hope for more.

SHEILA. What happened to that girl?

BRI. Never heard of since.

SHEILA. Not surprising.

BRI. Shortest teaching career on record. Thirty-five minutes.

They drink.

No, I don't hate Scanlon any more. That's all a thing of the
past. I just stare at him and wonder – is he only a monster of
my own imagining? (*Mad Doctor voice comes on, not for the
last time.*) 'Certainly, Nurse, he strangled a little girl, but that
only means he's lonely. We must make him a mate.

SHEILA *smiles. He drinks again.* ·

No, you take this morning. I was on playground duty sipping
my Nescaff, dreaming of a sudden painless road accident that
would put an end to it all. Suddenly aware of the silence – too
quiet for comfort. Few of the wilder elements sniggering and
casting crafty glances. Whipped round in time to spot Scanlon
sidling into the girls' bog. Went to the door and shouted,
'That boy, out of it!' Saw this figure zipping up his flies in a
panic. Not Scanlon at all.

SHEILA. No!

BRI. No. This new supply teacher.

SHEILA. Oh, no.

BRI. Yes.

SHEILA. Funny that way?

BRI. Not a bit. He didn't know it was the girls'. Only *looks*
about twelve even from the front. Dresses like them too. Why
can't he wear the right bloody uniform – tweedy jacket and
leather elbows – so we'd know whose side he's on?

Pause again. He eats a biscuit.

SHEILA. Never mind. You break up in two days.

BRI. I broke up years ago.

Puts down cup. He embraces her. She disengages. He looks at his hands.

BRI. Shall I put my gloves on?

SHEILA. What's the point of starting *now*? Joe's home any minute.

BRI. Well?

SHEILA. Well! She's got to be fed, bathed, exercised, put to bed. You know that.

Pause.

BRI. She can wait.

SHEILA. What?

BRI. Well, can't she?

SHEILA. Why should she? (*Pause.*) Anyway my rehearsal's at seven and I promised to paint some scenery before that.

BRI moves away, kicks off shoes, sprawls in armchair. She gives him more tea.

I shouldn't be late but your dinner's in the oven. On automatic.

He takes out cigarette, finds matchbox is empty.

Take it out any time after seven. You'd never believe the job I had finding a miniature bottle of Kirsch. In the local off-licence they offered Spanish Van Rose instead. Luckily I was going into town so I got it there. I had to take those old clothes into the Unmarried Mothers. They were only collecting moths. What are you looking for?

BRI. Matches.

She gives them to him.

Collecting moths? The Unmarried Mothers?

SHEILA. The clothes. So I got the Kirsch at the same time. Oh, and all the wild-life's fed – the cats, the guinea-pigs, the goldfish, the stick-insects –

Pause.

BRI. The ginger-beer plant?

SHEILA. All the plants. Oh, remember not to let the cats in. I found a flea in here today again. And this afternoon I did my Oxfam collection and looked after Jenny's children while she got her coil fitted. (*Pause.*) Quite a day, one way or another. What are you thinking?

BRI. Wondering if we could have our guinea-pig fitted with a coil. Or guinea-sow, should it be? (*Scratches. Jumps out of the chair.*) I've got one now. (*Looks closely at chair for fleas.*)

SHEILA. If you've had a bad day, why don't you come with me?

BRI. Bad day? You ought to see the staffroom. Christmas Spirit nearly at breaking-point. Excuse me, I was under the impression that was my soap you're using – sod off! – I beg your pardon? – Sod off, matey – come outside and say that – grow up – no, I insist – come on – I sang: Great tidings of comfort and joy. But it fell on stony ground.

He sits on sofa, she sits beside him, takes his hand.

I said to my class, 'Right – Christmas decorations – paper-chains.' Deep voice from the back said, 'Kids' stuff.' I frowned at him and realised I'd never seen him before. Turned out he was the elder brother of one of the more backward boys. On the dole, he'd come in out of the cold, been sitting in classes all day, nobody'd noticed.

SHEILA. Did you throw him out?

BRI. What for? (*Smiles at recollection.*) When he brought me up his paper-chain, he said, 'You're not much good at teaching, are you, mate?'

SHEILA. Oh, I should have hit him.

BRI. He meant it nicely. (*Smokes.*) I must find something else.

SHEILA. Come with me to rehearsal. Do you good to get out, see some people.

BRI. What people? Freddie?

SHEILA. Plenty of whisky afterwards.

BRI. I should want the whisky first –

SHEILA. All right, first –

BRI. – if I had to talk to Freddie.

SHEILA. All right.

BRI. If I had to watch you caper about with muck on your face.

SHEILA. Shall I ring your mother and see if she's free?

BRI. Bloody hell! What a swinging prospect! My mother, Freddie –

SHEILA. I seem to remember –

BRI. And all that Kirsch bubbling away down there.

SHEILA. I seem to remember it was *you* introduced me to Freddie in the first place.

Doorbell rings.

BRI. There's Joe.

SHEILA. Remember that.

BRI *gets up and makes for door while* SHEILA *shouts.*

And at least I don't just sit about coining epigrams – wallowing in self-pity! At least I *do* something about it!

BRI. You and Freddie together, yes –

Goes off.

SHEILA (*shouts*). At least I try to make life work instead of –

Breaks off. Sighs deeply, almost as though doing an exercise in relaxation.

Honestly. (*Puts cups on tray and takes it off to kitchen.*) Get away from the door then you won't get stepped on.

Shuts it behind her.

Pause.

BRI *has left hall door open, showing hall and lower part of the stairs. He now comes back wheeling* JOE *in her invalid chair.*

JOE *is ten, physically normal but for the stiffness of her legs and arms. Her legs, at this stage, are covered with a blanket. She cannot support herself properly and has to be propped wherever she is put: for the most part, she lies supine. In her chair, she sits with the upper part of her body forward on the tray in front of her chair, as though asleep. Her face is pretty but vacant of expression, her voice feeble.*

BRI *pushes her to the centre of the stage. He carries a small grip marked BOAC.*

BRI. There we are then, lovely. Home again. (*Leaves her, puts down grip, looks at her.*) Safe and sound. You been a good girl?

JOE. A-aaah!

This is her closest approach to speech.

BRI. Really good?

JOE. Aaaah!

BRI. The lady in the bus said you'd been good. Sat by the driver, did you?

JOE. Aaaah!

BRI. There's a clever girl!

JOE. Aaaah!

BRI (*as though he understood*). Saw the Christmas trees?

JOE. Aaaah!

BRI. And the shops lit up?

JOE. Aaaah!

BRI. What d'you say? Saw *Jesus*? Where was he, where was Jesus, you poor softy?

SHEILA *comes back.*

JOE. Aaaah!

BRI. I see.

SHEILA. My great big beautiful darling home at last? (*Kneels by her chair.*) Got a great big beautiful kiss for Mummy?

Kisses her.

JOE. Aaaah!

SHEILA. I'm lovely, she says.

BRI. Mad, she says, but lovely.

SHEILA. She been a good girl, Dad? Did the lady say?

BRI. Very good, Mum. She sat by the driver.

SHEILA (*mock amazement*). Did you sit by the driver? Did you, lovely?

They act as parents do receiving home a child of two from the Infants' School.

BRI. Saw the Christmas trees, Mum.

SHEILA. Did you see the Christmas trees? *What* a clever girl!

BRI. And Jesus.

SHEILA. Jesus?

BRI. Bathed in light, in the sky.

SHEILA (*aside, to* BRI). She got a screw loose, Dad?

BRI. No, Mum.

SHEILA. Seeing Jesus?

BRI. On top the Electricity building.

SHEILA (*relieved*). Oh, yes! Thought she was off her chump for a minute, Dad.

BRI. Seeing Jesus in a dump like this? No wonder, Mum. But no, she's doing well, they say.

SHEILA. Daddy's pleased you're trying, love. What with your eleven-plus on the way.

BRI gives a short burst of laughter then resumes.

BRI. You want to get to a decent school.

SHEILA. I don't want to be shunted into some secondary modern slum, she says —

Kisses her again.

BRI. Like the one where Daddy works —

SHEILA. Share a room with forty or fifty council-house types and blackies.

BRI. No, I've had enough of them, she says, at the Spastics' Nursery. You want to go on to the Training Centre, help to make those ball-point pens.

Rummages in grip.

JOE. Aaaah!

SHEILA. I'm trying my hardest, she says.

BRI. You keep it up, my girl. Here's a note from Mrs —

SHEILA. From the Nursery?

BRI. A school report, Mum. (*Reads.*) 'Thank you for the present for Colin's birthday.' Which is Colin?

SHEILA. Little boy who had meningitis.

BRI. Never stops whimpering?

SHEILA. That's him.

BRI. Did you send him Many Happy Returns?

SHEILA. I sent a card. And a cuddly bunny.

BRI. It's the thought that counts. (*Reads.*) 'Quite a few of the
parents remembered and the kitchen ladies made a lovely cake
with seven candles and we held up Colin so he could see them
burning, then we all helped him blow them out.'

*Without looking at each other, they make the 'Aaah' sound of
a cinema audience being shown a new-born lamb.*

'The physiotherapist lady came and looked at us all today and
said Josephine's shoulders show signs of improvement. She
says keep on with the exercises.'

SHEILA. Do your homework like a good girl. Daddy help.

BRI (*to Joe*). *She* won't be able to help. She's going out for a bit
on the side.

SHEILA. Let me call your mother. Please.

BRI (*ignoring her, reading on*). Hullo, hullo, what's *this* I see?
What's this? 'She's had a few fits today but I think it must
have been the excitement over Colin's cake.'

Moves about, acting cross father. SHEILA *stops the comedy
and begins to be seriously concerned.*

SHEILA. Oh, dear, now why's that, I wonder?

BRI. Just you listen to me, my girl –

SHEILA. I thought we'd got them under control.

BRI. How are you to raise yourself above the general level if you
keep having fits?

SHEILA. This is the first for weeks – except an occasional *petit
mal*.

BRI. Those council-house types down there, what d'you think
they say? (*Goes into a heavy village rustic act.*) 'She puts it on,

a voice you could cut with a knife – Lady Bleedin' Muck and no mistake! But look at her, she's no better than the likes of us, just another raver.'

SHEILA. Poor kid, poor blossom.

Caresses JOE.

BRI. Spare the rod spoil the child, Mum.

SHEILA. I don't know why they've started.

BRI. Welfare State. Life's all too easy these days – free milk, show-jumping. Physiotherapy. Singing and candles. What singing and candles did we have at her age? Air-raids and clothing coupons and if we didn't like that, my mother used to say, 'That be all you're getting, my sonner.'

SHEILA. Hullo.

JOE's head has turned suddenly from right to left. Her body tenses. They watch silently. JOE remains staring towards her left. The right arm now stretches out as though commanding attention, the mouth begins to open and shut spasmodically, the eyes close, the head slowly and tensely returns from left to right. The legs are pulled up in the seizure. The opening and shutting of the mouth causes a distinct and explosive sucking sound.

SHEILA *takes the note from* BRI's *hand and reads it.*

That's great, that is. Explains it.

BRI. What?

SHEILA. They've run out of anti-convulsant suspension again.

BRI. Again?

SHEILA (*reading*). '. . . excitement over Colin's cake. Or perhaps because we've used up all her yellow medicine.'

BRI. Call themselves a day nursery.

SHEILA. How many times is this?

BRI. Why don't they keep a few spare bottles in the 'fridge? Nearly all the kids need it.

SHEILA. The amount they use, they should have it on draught.

She goes to kitchen. JOE's fit has now finished. She rests on the shelf. BRI is excited by SHEILA's suggestion.

BRI. Yes! Drawn to the nurseries and day-centres in barrels by a dirty great fleet of dray-horses. (*Acts commentator with awe-struck voice. Holds hand-mike.*) And here – in the City Pharmacy – you can stand – as I'm standing now – in the nerve-centre of this great operation of mercy – and watch the myriad craftsmen at their various chores.

SHEILA comes back with two bottles and a spoon. They kneel, one each side of JOE.

SHEILA. Give her the phenos.

BRI. Or something less trad?

She hands him a bottle, which he opens and from which he pours two pills. She shakes the other bottle.

Bit more in keeping with our forward-looking technological society? A central pumping station and a vast complex of underground culverts and sluice-gates.

SHEILA (*to JOE*). Soon be better, my flower.

BRI forces JOE's jaws apart and puts the pills into her mouth.

BRI. No, they'll never stand for it.

SHEILA. Who?

BRI. Bristol's ratepayers. Cost a fortune.

SHEILA. Here, my blossom, lovely orange.

She spoons it in, with BRI's help.

BRI. Too fond of the ceremonial, the bullshit.

SHEILA. There's a clever girl.

BRI *holds her jaw shut.*

BRI. New life to dying crafts. Horse-brasses in the sun, tang of the cooper's apron – (*Makes sound effects of horse-hooves, whinnying.*) Dagenham Girl Pipers.

SHEILA *stoppers the bottles. Kisses* JOE.

SHEILA. And for a special treat, Mummy got her favourite ice-cream for tea.

BRI *releases her jaws.*

BRI. Gone down now.

SHEILA. Tell Mummy – are you wet?

BRI *looks in the grip again.* SHEILA *puts her hand under* JOE's *blanket.*

Soaking.

BRI. This nappy's dry.

SHEILA (*indignant*). Honestly! They've started *doing* that again this week. Leaving the one I send in the bag and letting her sit like Joe Egg in the damp all day. Her parts get spreathed.

BRI. Perhaps she *was* dry before the fit.

SHEILA. She could hardly have gone all day without a wee.

BRI. No.

SHEILA (*looks at watch*). Will *you* change her? I must go and get ready.

BRI *throws nappy on* JOE's *chair-shelf, takes bottle from* SHEILA.

If she's spreathed, there's ointment in the cupboard.

He nods, with a cheesy smile.

And if I were you, I should put her on the kitchen floor to change her.

BRI. I'm not the new nannie.

Pause.

SHEILA. No. 'Course not but –

BRI. I've done it before. Once or twice. In the last ten years.

He wheels JOE *towards kitchen.*

SHEILA. Brian.

He turns.

Shall I call your mother?

BRI. What for?

SHEILA. So we can go out.

BRI. Tuesday night there's nowhere much to go. The zoo's shut. There's a Western at the Gaumont.

SHEILA. Come and see the rehearsal. Get drunk if you like. But not too drunk to bring me home and have me.

BRI (*pointing to* JOE). *Pas devant* –

SHEILA. What?

BRI. *Pas devant l'enfant.*

SHEILA. Aitch-ay-vee-ee me.

She comes forward. He leaves chair and meets her. She embraces him.

Seriously. Shall I?

He kisses her, buries his face in her hair, then emerges.

BRI. Hey, listen! What's it like with Freddie?

She stiffens, then struggles to break away but he holds her.

No, come on, you've told me about the others. Not all, of course –

SHEILA. Let go –

BRI. But a sampling – a cross-section –

SHEILA. I shall bite.

BRI. The ones that because of some exceptional feature stand out from the crowd.

SHEILA. They were all before I met you.

BRI. But Freddie's *now*.

SHEILA. Let go.

BRI. What's his speciality?

SHEILA. Even if he wanted to – which he doesn't –

BRI. You must think I'm soft –

SHEILA. – Freddie would run a mile from a breath of scandal, you know that!

BRI. No, but I mean – what's his gimmick?

SHEILA. Come and ask him –

BRI. For instance –

SHEILA. Why don't you?

BRI. – all your four Americans, you said, made you –

SHEILA. What? Where d'you get that?

BRI. What?

SHEILA. Four Americans.

BRI. Wrong?

SHEILA. Two Americans.

BRI. Oh.

SHEILA. One Canadian.

BRI. Ah. (*Releases her.*) Well. They made you lie across a pillow. I think they got it out of Hemingway. Then the Welshman – the stoker –

SHEILA. He wasn't a stoker. He was a policeman.

BRI. Oh, yes. He was shocked because you used bad words in a posh accent. But when it came to getting off your frock, he was so ravenous he tore it.

SHEILA. I wish I'd never told you anything. You said we should be *honest*. You told me all about yours first.

BRI (*nods*). All three. That took an hour. Then for the next few weeks you made a short-list.

SHEILA. You *made* me.

Pause.

JOE. A-aaah!

BRI. You must have enjoyed those fellows at the time.

SHEILA. No!

BRI. One or two.

SHEILA. I've told you.

BRI. Why go on with it then?

SHEILA. Once you get to a certain stage with a man, it's hard to say no.

BRI. Most women manage it. With *me*, at any rate. *Three* out of God knows how many tens of thousands I tried . . .

SHEILA. They didn't know a good thing when they saw it. You were the only one who gave *me* any pleasure.

BRI. When you first told me that I was knocked out. I walked round for days feeling like a phallic symbol. I thought well, perhaps I didn't ring the bell very often but at least I rang it loud.

She smiles.

She'll stick with me, I went on happily, because I've got magic super-zoom with added cold-start.

SHEILA. You have, yes.

BRI. Till Freddie –

SHEILA. O ye Gods –

BRI. Of all people!

SHEILA. He's never been near me.

BRI. I think we should still be honest. Even about him.

SHEILA. He leaves me cold.

BRI. And yet you'd rather spend the evening with him than me.

SHEILA. You pushed me into this drama lark. You said I should get out –

BRI. What's his speciality? His forté. Does he keep his mac on?

SHEILA *faces him for several seconds. Then goes off and upstairs.* BRI *shrugs, turns back to the room. Sighs.* JOE *sneezes.*

Bless you.

She sneezes again, falls forward on to the tray and bumps her face.

Oops.

She begins crying, feebly. He goes to her.

Did she hurt? Did she bump her nose? (*Props her up again.*) Better? (*Looks at her closely.*) You look pale, Joe. Is it those nasty fits? Never mind. (*Fondles her hand.*) Lovely soft hands you've got. Like silk. Lady's hands. *They've* never done rough work. (*Crouching by her chair.*) Now. Mum's gone to take her part. Practise her acting. So we'll have a bit of a chinwag round the oil heater. Chew the fat, watch the jumping.

Her crying has stopped.

I expect there's jumping, there usually is. (*Gets 'Radio Times'.*) No. No jumping.

JOE *sighs heavily and wearily, an aftermath of the cry.*

There's a film about an eminent surgeon and his fight against injustice in London's East End. (*He shows her.*) I know you can't resist a doctor. (*Aside, to audience.*) When you think what they did to her! (*Back to* JOE.) But before that, Daddy get her a lovely tea. Joe and Daddy have a lovely tea then Joe have a nice hot bath? Play with her ducks? (*Returning paper to its place, he looks upwards.*) Hear that noise? That's Mummy in the bedroom. Probably taken her dress off now. Might be putting her stockings on. Even changing entirely. Every stitch. Naked, looking at herself in the glass, thinking have I kept my figure? (*Pause. Dwells on image.*) But I'm not running up those stairs three at a time and falling into the bedroom and cringing on the carpet begging her not to go. No fear! I've done all I can without total loss of dignity. I might have known once I got her started on amateur theatricals she'd turn up at every bloody practice. Terrible sense of duty, your mum.

Looks at JOE *lolling in the chair.*

What am I doing talking to you?

Comes front, talks to audience.

Might as well be talking to the wall. (*Then, like a front-cloth comic –*) No, but she is a wonderful woman, my wife. That girl upstairs. In the bedroom, off in the wings, wherever she is. No, seriously. (*Drops it, goes on as himself.*) A truly integrated person. Very rare, that is, as you know. Give you an example: she's disturbed by anything, she's not just mentally upset about it, not only miserable, no, she actually grows *ill*. Boils, backache, vomiting. Not pretence. Real sickness. She works as a whole, not in parts. Unlike me, for instance, I'm Instant Man. Get one for Christmas, endless fun. I'm made up as I go along from old lengths of string, fag-ends . . . magazine cuttings, film-clips . . . all stuck together with wodges of last week's school dinner. What I mean, she couldn't *pretend* a passion she doesn't feel. Whereas I can't

sustain a passion to the end of the sentence. I start to cry –
aaaoooow! Then I think: are you mad? Who do you think
you are, God? And things go clang and wheels fall off and
people get hurt – terrible. You must have felt like this –
catching yourself in the mirror hamming away. Or somebody
says, 'My wife's just been run over,' and you want to burst
out laughing. Well, you may say, why not – if that's the way
you feel? But other people don't like it. So I pretend. You saw
me pretend with Sheila. I try to guess which emotions appeal
to her and then I sink my teeth in. I don't let go until they're
bone-dry. Like with Joe there – (*Waves to her.*) All right, are
you? Good. I felt all doomy at first but – well – ten years! I
just go through the motions now. Sheila – how shall I put it in
a way that will prevent a sudden stampede to the exit-doors?
Sheila – embraces all living things. She really does. She's
simple, so simple she's bound to win in the end. She's a sane
enough person to be able to embrace all living creatures. She
sits there embracing all live things. I get my hug somewhere
between the budgerigar and the stick-insect. Which is the
reason for all this smutty talk. Calling attention to myself to
make sure I get more than my share. Otherwise I'd have to
settle for eyes-front-hands-on-heads and a therapeutic bash
once in a blue moon. And I'm too young to die, I tell you!

JOE. Aaah!

BRI. What's the matter, crackpot?

JOE. Aaah!

BRI. Language? You think this is language! I'll introduce you to
Scanlon. He'll let you hear some language. (*Aside.*) What a
madam! Well. Let's see what she's left for tea.

JOE. Aaaah!

*Makes revving noises and pushes her chair off to the kitchen.
Going out, he struggles with the cats.*

BRI. Get back, you flea-bitten whores! Get back! (*Shuts door
behind him.*)

Pause. At least five seconds.

SHEILA *comes on from a corner downstage of the set. She has changed into a dress and is brushing her hair.*

SHEILA. One of these days I'll hit him. Honestly. (*Brushes hair, looks at audience.*) He thinks because he throws a tantrum I'm going to stay home comforting him and miss the rehearsal and let them all down. He thinks he's only got to cry to get what he wants. I blame his mother. She gave him the kind of suffocating love that makes him think the world revolves around him but because he's too intelligent to believe it really, he gets into these paddies and depressions. And when he's in one of those, he'll do anything to draw attention to himself. That beetle on his face – you saw that. And all this stuff about Freddie. And yet it was Brian made me join these amateurs in the first place, he said I needed to get out more, have a rest from Joe. But she's no trouble. It's Brian. I don't know which is the greatest baby. Watching somebody as limited as Joe over ten years, I've begun to feel she's only one kind of cripple. Everybody's damaged in some way. There's a limit to what we can do. Brian, for instance, he goes so far – and hits the ceiling. Just can't fly any higher. Then he drops to the floor and we get self-pity again . . . despair. I'm sure, though, if he could go farther – he could be a marvellous painter. That's another reason I said I'd join the amateurs: the thought that he'd be forced to go upstairs several nights a week and actually put paint on canvas. And even if he *isn't* any good, he seems to need some work he can be proud of. Something to take his mind off his jealousy of anyone or anything I talk to . . . relatives, friends, pets . . . even pot-plants. I'm sure it's because they take up time he thinks I could be devoting to him. And Joe, most of all, poor love . . . (*She puts brush on table or chair. A thought brings her back.*) Look, you mustn't assume I feel like this in the ordinary way. And even when I *am* a bit down, I shouldn't normally talk about it to a lot of complete strangers. But all this childish temper over Freddie – this showing-off – it's more than I can stand, it makes me boil, honestly! Wouldn't you feel the same? (*Checks her appearance in imaginary full-length glass.*) That's why I'm telling you all this. A lot of total strangers. But wouldn't it make *you* boil? Honestly! A grown man jealous of poor Joe —

Breaks off as she sees BRI *coming from downstage corner.*

They look at each other in silence.

BRI. What are you telling them?

SHEILA. What?

BRI. I heard you talking.

SHEILA *picks threads from her clothes.*

I heard you mention Joe.

No answer. BRI *speaks to audience.*

Sheila's got a theory about Joe's birth. She doesn't blame the doctors. She blames herself.

SHEILA. I don't say that. I say it wasn't *entirely* the doctors.

BRI (*nodding*). It was because she choked it back.

SHEILA. It was partly that.

BRI. Because she'd slept around.

SHEILA. I think it was partly because I'd been promiscuous, yes, and my subconscious was making me shrink or withdraw from motherhood, all right!

Pause. He looks away. She goes on titivating.

BRI. That vicar told us it was the devil's doing. Why don't you believe *that*? It's about as brilliant.

SHEILA (*shrugs*). It comes down in the end to what you believe.

BRI. I'll tell you what *I* believe.

SHEILA. I *know* what you believe.

BRI (*points at audience*). They don't. (*To audience.*) I believe the doctor botched it. There was no other cause. (*To* SHEILA.)

That specialist said as much, he said it had nothing at all to do with the way you'd lived or whether there was a nut in the family . . . or what kind of fags you smoked . . .

SHEILA. He didn't say the doctor did it either.

Pause. He looks at her.

BRI. No. You've got a good point there. He didn't mention that, quite true. He didn't say, 'Yes, he's a shoddy midwife, my colleague, always was, I'll see he gets struck off the register.' Very true. Weakens my argument, that.

SHEILA. Oh, you're so *clever*!

BRI. He'd only say for certain that it was a chance in a million it could happen again.

SHEILA. Mmm. We haven't had an opportunity yet to check on that.

Both pause.

BRI. It's due to this that Joe lives at home with us.

SHEILA. She's our daughter.

BRI (*to audience*). She was on the way before we married. That feeds the furnace of guilt.

SHEILA. No need to tell them everything.

BRI. It was a white wedding.

SHEILA. For my dad's sake. He was a bell-ringer and always looked forward to the day he'd lead the peal as I left the church. You said you didn't mind.

BRI. I didn't. At the reception afterwards the ringers were the only people worth talking to. All twisted and crippled. Picture them bouncing up and down at the end of their ropes.

And he tries a guess at it.

SHEILA. We might have taken them for an omen. The baby came six months later. I'd done my exercises and read the ante-natal books – mostly the ones that made it seem as simple as having a tooth filled.

BRI. But more spiritual.

SHEILA. Oh, yes, a lot about you sitting by the bed holding my hand and looking sincere.

BRI *does it.*

BRI. Giving the lead with shallow breathing. (*Does it.*)

SHEILA (*to audience*). I don't know whether any of you are like me, but I half-expected to hear snatches of the Hallelujah Chorus.

BRI. I was sympathetic but queasy. The idea of sharing the birth seemed irrefutable *qua idea* . . . but not so gay when it came to the blood and fluid.

SHEILA. As it happened, you needn't have worried.

BRI. No. (*To audience.*) How long do *your* labours last? Two, three hours? A day? Dilettantes! (*Points at* SHEILA.) Five days!

SHEILA. Yes. From the first show on the sheets to the last heave of the forceps. Five days.

BRI. You'll all be saying, 'He should have *done* something,' but I didn't *know* at the time. You don't, do you?

SHEILA. You'd know *now*.

BRI. Oh, yeah. It was all good experience.

SHEILA (*to audience*). This doctor kept on drugging me.

BRI. You were stoned.

SHEILA. I couldn't remember the exercises.

BRI. Couldn't even tell me. Just kept crying.

SHEILA (*explaining*). I couldn't make anyone understand! I couldn't salivate or swallow so I stayed hungry . . . also I kept hoping you'd be there when I opened my eyes, but it was always the midwife or your mother.

BRI. Not always!

SHEILA. Nearly always. You were getting drunk outside.

BRI. What else could I do?

SHEILA (*to audience*). My speech faculties seemed to have gone so I couldn't tell them to stop the dope so that I could manage the birth.

For the rest of this act, they hold a dialogue with each other and the audience. No further indication is given, unless essential to the sense.

BRI. Then the GP would pop in to see me with his boyish grin . . . 'Tell the truth I've got the feeling this young shaver's none too keen to join us.' And I'd say, 'All this trouble getting out and he'll spend the rest of his life trying to get back in.' And we'd all piss ourselves at that and have another Scotch.

SHEILA. You never thought it was going on too long?

BRI. Yes, but you leave it to them, don't you? My mum taught me to believe in doctors and during the labour she set an example of quiet faith.

SHEILA. And afterwards – when Joe was ill – she said she knew all the time it was lasting too long.

BRI. She always knows afterwards.

SHEILA. The pain was shocking but the worst was not being able to speak.

BRI. By the last day I thought she was going to die. And – I've never told you this, love –

SHEILA. What?

BRI. You'll find it hard to credit this. Though not normally a religious man . . . for everyday purposes making the usual genuflections to Esso Petroleum and MGM – I don't mind admitting it, I prayed –

SHEILA. Did you really? Not another joke?

BRI. No, honestly, I went down on my knees and I prayed to God. I said, 'God, I've only just found her. The baby doesn't matter. If it's a question of a swap . . .'

SHEILA. Aaaah! (*She kisses him.*)

BRI. Then I found I was so drunk I could hardly get to my feet again.

SHEILA. But never mind, your prayer was answered.

BRI. Yes, He heard all right. (*To audience.*) I see Him as a sort of manic depressive rugby-footballer. He looked down and thought to Himself, 'I'll fix that bastard.' (*Shakes his fist at roof.*) And He did!

SHEILA. By the time the damage was done, they took me to hospital. The next I knew, they handed me this hairless yellow baby with forceps-scars all over her scalp. She was gorgeous. By the time I got her home, the scars and jaundice were gone and she was in working order. You had a cold.

BRI. That's right, yes.

SHEILA. I had to look after you. It was better than having you turn up in the ward every day moaning and sniffling.

BRI. More than a cold. 'Flu. A delayed action I think it must have been. I was quite poorly.

She smiles, then goes on to audience.

SHEILA. Soon I began to notice these funny turns. We asked our friends who'd had babies but they said it was most likely wind. So in the end we took her to our new GP.

BRI has fetched a tubular cushion from the set behind them, which is now in semi-darkness. The cushion is the size and shape of a swaddled baby. SHEILA nurses it.

BRI. Baby. (*Points to himself.*) Doctor. Nice, bone-headed.

In the sketches which follow, BRI plays the funny men and SHEILA herself. They do it as they might repeat the dialogue from a favourite film. Sometimes they improvise, surprising or corpsing each other.

BRI mimes opening a door at side of stage. SHEILA wanders off to opposite side and waits.

Bye-bye, Mrs – um – you rub that in you'll soon be as right as rain. (*Mimes closing door, returns to centre, shouts.*) Next, please!

SHEILA moves in. BRI bends over writing and putting away last patient's card. Has his back to SHEILA.

'Evening, Mister – um – feeling any better?

SHEILA. It's morning, Doctor. (*To audience.*) Not very reassuring.

BRI. 'Course it is.

SHEILA. And I've never been before.

BRI. No?

SHEILA. We're new to the district.

BRI. What seems to be the trouble?

SHEILA. I don't really know. Funny turns. Face-making.

BRI. Say 'aaah'.

SHEILA. Not me. The baby.

BRI looks at the cushion.

BRI. Nothing much wrong with this little laddie.

SHEILA. Lassie.

BRI. Lassie. Funny turns, you say. How would you describe them?

SHEILA. Frightening.

BRI. No, I meant, what form do they take?

SHEILA. Blinking with her eyes, working with her tongue, shaking her head, then going all limp.

BRI (*tickling the baby, talking to it*). Funny turns indeed at your age! Saucy beggar. We are not amused.

SHEILA. But what d'you think it is?

BRI. Wind.

SHEILA. That's what our friends said.

BRI. Always wise to get a second opinion. Have you tried Gripe Water?

SHEILA. Yes, of course.

BRI. My old mother used to swear by it. Cure anything, she used to say. Well, let's see what we can find in here.

Rummages in drawer, finds medicine, reads label.

Ah, yes, this'll put a stop to it. Came in the post this morning. The makers praise it very highly.

SHEILA. Doctor – I wish you could *see* one of these turns.

BRI. Oh, I've seen them, dear. Got three great monsters of my own.

SHEILA. I am sorry.

BRI. What?

SHEILA. All your children being – um –

BRI. No, I mean great thriving brutes. Not monsters, no. Your first, is it? First baby?

SHEILA. Yes.

BRI. Well, dear, it's like this. You're throwing an awful lot of gubbins down the old cake-hole there. It's like running in a new car. Till all the tappets and contact breakers get adjusted to the absolute thou, you take it easy, give 'em a chance. Same with these chaps. (*Tickles the cushion, looks again at medicine.*) Let's see. Three times daily after meals. How often you feeding?

SHEILA. Every four hours.

BRI. Fours into twenty-four goes six. So six times a day –

SHEILA. Look. This may be one now.

They watch the cushion for ten seconds. BRI looks at his watch.

SHEILA. No.

BRI. I've got a waiting-room full of people, dear. You try her with this and come back if there's no improvement in – say – a week. Make sure you wind her well. And don't fret. (*Leading her to exit.*) They're hardy little devils, you know. Bye-bye, Mrs – um – (*Mimes seeing her off and shuts the door.*) Three days later. (*Mimes opening door and calls.*) Next, please.

SHEILA *comes back at once with cushion.*

Hullo, Mrs – um –

SHEILA (*urgently*). Doctor –

BRI. Just a minute, I'll get your card.

SHEILA. But this child –

BRI. Sit down, please.

He seats her and looks at card.

Didn't I say come back in a week? Why so soon?

SHEILA. She's gone into a coma.

BRI. D'you try the medicine?

SHEILA. She won't take anything. She hasn't fed for two days.

BRI *looks at the cushion, listens to it, claps hands by it, finally shakes it like a piggy-bank.*

BRI (*as much as to say 'so far, so good'*). Ah-ha! Mm-hum. (*Goes humming back to the table, mimes dialling.*) Get me the Children's Hospital . . . quick! No panic, dear, just a routine inquiry. Your husband with you?

SHEILA. He's in the waiting-room. Is she –?

BRI (*into phone*). Look – I'd like you to take a shufti at a baby – uh – (*To* SHEILA.) Girl?

SHEILA. Yes.

BRI. Baby girl . . . Off her chow and failing to respond to any stimuli whatever. (*To* SHEILA *again.*) Got a car?

SHEILA. No.

BRI. Hullo? . . . No car. Any chance of an ambulance? . . . Understood.

Puts down phone, returns to SHEILA.

SHEILA. There's something seriously wrong, isn't there?

BRI. Don't start worrying, dear. Look at it this way. You know when you get a starter-motor jammed? Seems serious at the time but put it in second gear and rock the whole shoot back and forth, she's soon as right as rain.

SHEILA. We haven't got a car, I –

BRI. What I want you to do – you know the kiddies' hospital?

She nods.

You and your old man go along there – not forgetting to take the baby – you catch a bus from the end of the street. And – *nil desperandum.*

Sees her to door, as before, opens it, pushes her through. Is about to close it when he remembers something and shouts after her.

Thirty-two.

SHEILA. What?

BRI. The bus. Number thirty-two.

SHEILA. Oh.

BRI (*closing door, taking out handkerchief, wiping brow*). Streuth.

SHEILA (*turning to audience*). On the bus I said to Brian, 'I've got a feeling we shan't bring her back.' But, as you know, we did. Eventually.

BRI. Every cloud has a jet-black lining.

SHEILA. I stayed in hospital with her for a few weeks, then left her there having tests and came home to look after Brian, who'd contracted impetigo.

BRI, *in the shadows, lights a cigarette.*

It was painful not feeding so Brian knelt in front of me and tried to express it orally.

BRI. You should have seen that – like the Khamasutra.

SHEILA. In the end, a woman from the clinic drew it off with a sort of glass motor-horn.

BRI *gets a coffee-table from the set, puts the cushion on it, stands behind it.*

Few weeks later they called me to collect Joe from hospital, by which time we'd gathered that she wasn't ever going to amount to much. But I was determined to know the best we could expect. And the worst. The paediatrician was German – or Viennese, I'm not too sure.

For this sketch, BRI uses a music-hall German accent.

BRI. Vell, mattam, zis baby off yours has now been soroughly tested and ve need ze bets razzer battly so it's better you take her home. I sink I can promise she von't be any trouble. Keep her vell sedated you'll hartly know she's zere.

SHEILA. But, Doctor —

He is making for the door, turns reluctantly.

BRI. Ja?

SHEILA. Can't you tell me the results?

BRI. Results?

SHEILA. Of the tests.

BRI. Vitch ones? Zere vere so many — (*Slight laugh. Lists on fingers.*) Electro-encephalograph, scree-dimensional eggs-ray, blood urine and stool analyses, zis business vis needles in ze fontanelle —

SHEILA. Is that why her hair's been shaved off?

BRI. Vell of course —

SHEILA. She'd only just begun to grow it. And did the needles make that scar on her head?

BRI. Scar?

SHEILA (*pointing*). There.

BRI. Ach, nein. Zis vos a liddle biopsy to take a sample of her brain tissue.

SHEILA. That's a relief. (*She smiles quickly.*) I thought at first you'd bored a hole in her skull to let the devil out.

BRI *looks interested, confers with his assistant.*

BRI. Sounds gut. Did you try it? . . . Ah! (*To* SHEILA.) My colleague says ve don't do zat any more. (*Shrugs.*) Pity! Vell — if you eggscuse me.

Moves to go.

SHEILA. But — Doctor, Doctor —

BRI. Donner und blitzen!

SHEILA. What can she *do*?

BRI. Do? She can't do nozzing at all.

SHEILA. Will she ever?

BRI. Mattam, let me try and tell you vot your daughter iss like. Do you know vot I mean ven I say your daughter vos a wegetable?

SHEILA *thinks for a moment, gets it, smiles.*

SHEILA. Yes! You mean 'Your daughter was a vegetable'.

BRI. Ach himmel! Still is, still *is*, always vill be! I have trouble vis Englisch werbs.

SHEILA. But – when people say to me what kind of cripple is your child, shall I say – she's a wegetable – a *v*egetable?

BRI. You vont a vord for her? (*Shrugs.*) You can say she iss a spastic vis a damaged cerebral cortex, multiplegic, epileptic, but vis no organic malformation of ze brain.

SHEILA. That *is* a long word.

BRI (*gaily*). Which iss vy I prefer wegetable.

SHEILA. Vegetable.

BRI. Vegetable.

SHEILA. But why? If her brain's physically sound, why doesn't it work?

BRI *sighs, looks at her, thinks.*

BRI. Imagine a svitchboard. A telephone svitchboard, ja?

SHEILA. I worked as a switchboard operator once.

BRI. Das ist wunderbar! Vell. Imagine you're sitting zere now, facing ze board. So?

SHEILA. So.

BRI. Some lines tied up, some vaiting to be used – suddenly brr-brr, brr-brr –

SHEILA. Incoming call?

BRI. Exactly! You plug in.

SHEILA *mimes it, assuming a bright telephone voice.*

SHEILA. Universal Shafting.

BRI (*coming out of character*). What?

SHEILA. That was the firm I worked for.

BRI. You've never put that in before.

SHEILA (*shrugs*). I thought I would this time.

BRI. Universal Shafting? Story of your life.

She stares coldly. BRI clears his throat, resumes as dcotor.

But at zat moment anozzer incoming call – brr-brr – and you panic and plug him in to the first von and leave zem talking to each ozzer and you answer an extension and he vont the railway station but you put him on to ze cricket results and zey all start buzzing and flashing – and it's too much, you flip your lid and pull out all the lines. Kaputt! Now zere's your epileptic fit. Your Grand or Petit Mal according to ze stress, ze number of calls. All right?

Makes to go again.

SHEILA. But, Doctor, Doctor –

Looks at his watch.

BRI. Gott in himmel! I'm wery busy man, Missis –

SHEILA. I know you must be –

BRI. Yours isn't ze only piecan in ze country.

SHEILA. I know –

BRI. Zere's von born every eight hours, you know.

SHEILA. No, I didn't. Is that true?

BRI. Oh, ja, ja. Not all as bad as zees case, of course –

SHEILA. Isn't there *any*thing at all we can do?

BRI. But jawohl! You must feed her, vosh her nappies, keep her varm. Just like any ozzer mozzer.

SHEILA. But for how long?

BRI. Who can tell? Anysing can happen, you know zat. Diphtheria, pneumonia . . . vooping cough . . . Colorado beetle.

SHEILA laughs. They come out of character.

SHEILA. Oh, that's terrible. Colorado beetle.

BRI. I only just thought of that.

SHEILA. It's terrible.

BRI. So – what happened then? We brought her home.

SHEILA. And the hospital passed the can back to our local GP.

BRI. The piecan.

SHEILA. He had to supply phenobarbitone and keep us happy. He used to come once a week to explain her fits. In layman's terms.

BRI. You didn't find out much?

SHEILA. About fits, no. But I learnt a lot about what happens on a switchboard when the lines get crossed.

BRI. Or at a railway junction during fog.

SHEILA. But the time came when I asked him whose fault it was.

BRI. Which is when he suggested the vicar might call.

SHEILA. Yes. Nice vicar. Sensitive. So concerned and upset at the sight of Joe – the fits were unusually bad that day – so we left her in the cot and had our chat in another room.

She throws the cushion to BRI, who puts it on sofa.
Quite a long pause while they prepare themselves for the next scene. The mood changes slightly. BRI allows SHEILA to take

the initiative and plays the Vicar quietly, even seriously, to begin with. They go upstage and she brings him down again when they are ready.

Here we are. Do take a pew.

BRI, *as Vicar, laughs.*

Oh!

She laughs too.

BRI. She's a beautiful child.

SHEILA. Yes, isn't she?

BRI. It's tragic. Tell me – when you first – knew there was nothing to be done, how did you feel?

SHEILA. Well, of course, you find out gradually, not all at once. But there is a point when you finally accept it. And that's – (*Shakes her head.*) Oh, very nasty. You think 'why me?' I don't know about the other mothers but *I* kept saying, 'Why me, why us?' all day long. Then you get tired of that and you say, 'Why not me?'

BRI. Indeed. You learn humility. You recognise that we are surely in a vale of tears and you are no exception.

SHEILA. I recognised that I was worse. I'd been promiscuous, you see. All kinds of men. It seemed to me I was responsible for Joe, being punished.

BRI. No, no.

SHEILA. No, I don't mean that either. I held the baby back. Out of guilt.

BRI. Really, my dear, you mustn't believe this. Plenty of women who've slept around afterwards become splendid mothers. Pre-marital intercourse is no longer considered a serious obstacle to being taken into the fold.

SHEILA. No?

BRI. Haven't you read our publications lately? You should. The good old C of E is nowadays a far more swinging scene than you seem to suppose.

SHEILA. I see.

BRI. Oh, surely. Where the action is.

SHEILA. I've never committed adultery.

SHEILA. There you are! That's splendid – fabulous! Crazy! Think no more about it. Tell me, what was your husband's reaction to the child?

SHEILA. He used to say, 'Think of something worse.' And of course that's easy. Joe could have grown older and developed into a real person before it happened. Or she could have been a very *intelli*gent spastic without the use of her limbs. Which is worse, I think, than being a kind of living parsnip.

BRI. Quite. You count your blessings.

SHEILA. Yes.

BRI. And that gives you fortitude.

SHEILA. No, but it's something to do. When you're up against a – disaster of this kind – an Act of God –

   BRI *clears his throat.*

   – it's so *numbing* you feel you must make some sense of it – otherwise – you'd –

BRI. Give up hope?

SHEILA. Yes. My husband doesn't feel the need to make sense of anything. He lives with despair.

BRI (*coming out of character*). Did you tell him that?

SHEILA. Why not?

BRI. Bit saucy.

SHEILA. Well, don't you?

BRI. Can't argue now.

SHEILA (*resuming scene*). He says I shouldn't look for explanations.

BRI. He doesn't believe in God?

SHEILA. His own kind of God. A manic-depressive rugby footballer.

BRI. It's a start. Provide some basis for argument.

He smiles.

SHEILA. He doesn't like me praying.

BRI. You have been praying?

SHEILA. What else can I do? I look at that flawless little body, those glorious eyes, and I pray for some miracle to – get her started. It seems, if we only knew the key or the combination, we could get her moving. D'you think the story of the Sleeping Beauty was about a spastic?

BRI. Who can say indeed? (*He stands, moves about.*) My dear, your child's sickness doesn't please God. In fact, it completely brings Him down.

SHEILA. Why does He allow it then?

BRI. How can we know?

SHEILA. Then how can you know it doesn't please Him?

BRI. We can't know. Only guess. It may be disease and infirmity are due to the misuse of the freedom He gave us. Perhaps they exist as a stimulus to research.

SHEILA. Research?

BRI. Into infirmity and disease.

SHEILA. But if He didn't permit disease, we shouldn't need research.

BRI. But He does so we do.

She sighs, shakes her head.

My dear, the Devil is busy day and night. God does His best but we don't help Him much. Now and then some innocent bystander blunders into the cross-fire between good and evil and –

Makes gunfire noises, ricochet-sounds, falls elaborately clutching his chest. Stands again, dusts himself down, before proceeding. SHEILA *watches calmly.*

Or – if you can imagine a poisonous blight that settles on an orchard of many different varieties of tree –

SHEILA. No, please, no more parables. I've had so many from the doctor!

BRI. But how can I explain without imagery of –

SHEILA. I misled you. I don't want explanations. I've asked the people who should have been able to explain and they couldn't.

BRI. What *do* you want?

SHEILA. Magic.

BRI. I was slowly coming round to that. Once or twice, over the years, we have had in this parish children like your daughter.

SHEILA. Just as bad?

BRI. Oh, yes, I'm sure, quite as bad. Now for those poor innocents I did the Laying On Of Hands bit.

SHEILA. What is that?

BRI. A simple ceremony in your own home. A few prayers, a hymn or two, a blessing, an imposition of hands. Nothing flashy.

SHEILA. Who'd be there?

BRI. You, your husband, anyone you chose.

SHEILA. My husband?

BRI. Yes. And it sounds as though he needs instruction. His prayers would hardly help us if addressed to a manic-depressive rugby footballer.

SHEILA. No.

BRI. God might feel affronted.

SHEILA. Yes.

BRI. He's only human. No, He's not, how silly of me!

SHEILA. Perhaps you could have a word with him. Over a pint.

BRI. (*after thinking*). Ah, with your husband, yes. Not that there's anything wrong with rugby. Scrum-half myself for years. Just that I feel one shouldn't make a religion of it.

SHEILA. With the other children – did you have any luck? Did God – you know –

BRI. There was one boy – no better than Joe – made such rapid recovery after I'd done the Laying On a few times – the medicos confessed themselves bewildered. He's twelve now and this spring he was runner-up in the South West Area Tap-Dancing Championships.

SHEILA. How fantastic!

BRI *begins dancing and singing.*

BRI. Happy Feet, I've got those Happy Feet,
Give me a lowdown beat –

Dances and sings without words. Then stops.

SHEILA. D'you really think you could – work a miracle?

BRI. Not me, my dear. If a miracle happens, it's only *through* me. But remember Jairus's daughter – 'Damsel, I say unto thee, arise.' Who knows? Perhaps in a few years' time we shall see little Joe –

Dances and sings again.

Animal crackers in my soup
Lions and tigers loop the loop.

SHEILA (*standing, breaking out of sketch*). But you wouldn't do it!

She moves away. BRI *drops his Vicar imitation.*

He was a good man, kind and sincere.

BRI. He was, yes.

SHEILA. And that boy was cured.

BRI. Certainly improved. And, yes, he was the runner-up in the South West Area Tap-Dancing Championships. *But.* He never *had* been as bad as Joe.

SHEILA. I don't care –

BRI. I looked into it –

SHEILA. You shouldn't have.

BRI. I spoke to people –

SHEILA. Where's the harm? What else did we have?

BRI. Nothing.

SHEILA. Well!

BRI. I'd rather have nothing than a lot of lies.

SHEILA. You're unusual.

BRI. First he'd have done it for us, then he'd have got a few of his mates in to give the prayers more Whoosh! More Pow! And before long he'd have had us doing it in church gloated over by all those death-watch beetles like the victims of a disaster.

SHEILA. It could have worked. He might have magicked her.

BRI. I'm sure it was best to stop it then than later on – after he'd raised your hopes. Sheila –

She looks at him, smiles.

Anyway. If the vicar had got her going, she'd only have had one personality. As it is, we've given her dozens down the years.

SHEILA (*to audience*). As soon as we were admitted to the freemasonry of spastics' parents, we saw she had even less character than the other children. So we began to make them for her.

BRI. Some never really suited.

SHEILA. No. Like the concert pianist dying of TB.

BRI. Nor the girl who was tragically in love with a darkie against her parents' wishes.

SHEILA. That was based on 'Would you let your daughter marry one?'

BRI. I used to like the drunken bag who threw bottles at us if we didn't fetch her gin and pipe-tobacco.

SHEILA. But they were all too active. The facial expression wasn't right.

BRI. The one that's stuck is the coach-tour lady . . . powder-pink felt hat, white gloves, Cuban heel shoes, swagger-coat . . .

SHEILA. And seasick pills in her handbag just in case there's a lot of twisting and turning.

BRI. She hates foreigners –

SHEILA. And council-houses –

BRI. And shafting. She knows to her cost what that can lead to.

SHEILA. Loves the Queen –

BRI. And Jesus. She sees him as an eccentric English gentleman. Sort of Lawrence of Arabia.

SHEILA. Very disapproving of pleasure.

BRI. Not *all* pleasure. A nice Julie Andrews film with tea after –

SHEILA. Tea in the Odeon cafe –

BRI. Nothing nicer. Which reminds me. I'm supposed to be giving her tea. In this play we started doing.

Looks at his watch.

SHEILA. We got side-tracked.

BRI. She'll have something to say to me. She'll have me on the carpet. 'Nice thing leaving the table before you've finished eating, leaving me stuck here like Joe Egg . . .'

Goes off.

SHEILA *watches him out of sight.*

SHEILA. I join in these jokes to please him. If it helps him live with her, I can't see the harm, can you? He hasn't any faith she's ever going to improve. Where I have, you see . . . I believe, even if she *showed* improvement, Bri wouldn't notice. He's dense about faith – faith isn't believing in fairy-tales, it's being in a receptive state of mind. I'm always on the look-out for some sign . . . (*Looks off again to wings to make sure* BRI's *not coming.*) One day when she was – what? – about a twelve month old, I suppose, she was lying on the floor kicking her legs about and I was doing the flat. I'd made a little tower of four coloured bricks – plastic bricks – on a rug near her head. I got on with my dusting and when I looked again I saw she'd knocked it down. I put the four bricks up again and this time watched her. First her eyes, usually moving in all directions, must have glanced in passing at this bright tower. Then the arm that side began to show real signs of intention . . . and her fist started clenching and – spreading with the effort. The other arm – held there like that – (*Raises one bent arm to shoulder level.*) didn't move. At all. You see the importance – she was using for the first time one arm instead of both. She'd seen something, touched it and found that when she touched it whatever-it-was was changed. Fell down. Now her bent arm started twitching towards the bricks. Must have taken – I should think – ten minutes' – strenuous labour – to reach them with her fingers . . . then her

hand jerked in a spasm and she pulled down the tower. (*Reliving the episode, she puts her hands over her face to regain composure.*) I can't tell you what that was like. But you can imagine, can't you? Several times the hand very nearly touched and got jerked away by spasm . . . and she'd try again. That was the best of it – she had a will, she had a mind of her own. Soon as Bri came home, I told him. I think he said something stupid like – you know – 'That's great, put her down for piano lessons.' But when he tested her – putting piles of bricks all along the circle of her reach – both arms – and even sometimes out of reach so that she had to stretch to get there – well, of course, he saw it was true. It wasn't *much* to wait for – one arm movement completed – and even that wasn't sure. She'd fall asleep, the firelight would distract her, sometimes the effort would bring on a fit. But more often than not she'd manage . . . and a vegetable couldn't have done that. Visitors never believed it. They hadn't the patience to watch so long. And it amazed me – I remember being stunned – when I realised they thought I shouldn't deceive myself. For one thing, it wasn't deception . . . and, anyway, what else could I do? We got very absorbed in the daily games. Found her coloured balls and bells and a Kelly – those clowns that won't lie down. Then she caught some bug and was very sick – had fit after fit – the Grand Mal, not the others – what amounted to a complete relapse. When she was over it, we tried the bricks again, but she couldn't even seem to see them. That was when Bri lost interest in her. I still try, though of course I don't bother telling him. I'll tell him when something happens. It seems to me only common sense. If she did it once, she could again. I think while there's life there's hope, don't you? (*Looks to wings again.*) I wish he'd talk more seriously about her. I wonder if he ever imagines what she'd be like if her brain worked. *I* do. And Bri's mother always says, 'Wouldn't she be lovely if she was running about?' which makes Bri hoot with laughter. But I think of it too. Perhaps it's being a woman.

Lights off SHEILA. *Lights on set upstage, very strong like a continuous lightning flash.*

A roll on cymbals.

JOE *skips on, using a rope.*

JOE. Mrs D, Mrs I, Mrs FFI, Mrs C, Mrs U, Mrs LTY
Mrs D, Mrs I, Mrs FFI, Mrs C, Mrs U, Mrs LTY.

Stops skipping.

Ladies and gentlemen, there will now be an interval.
Afterwards the ordinary play, with which we began the
performance, will continue and we shall try to show you what
happens when Sheila returns home with their mutual friends,
Freddie and Pam. Thank you.

SHEILA *puts her arm round* JOE, *tells her she spoke her lines
well, and goes off with her as the lights come up.*

ACT TWO

Darkness.

SHEILA *opens hall door and looks in, light behind her.*

SHEILA. No. (*Comes in, puts on lights.*) Not in here. Must be
working. Miracles never cease.

FREDDIE *and* PAM *follow in. He is suited, school-tied, with
a hearty barking humourless laugh, same age as* BRI *but his
ample public confidence makes him seem middle-aged.*

PAM *dresses well, mispronounces her words in an upper-class
gabble and her postures and manners have been taken from
fashionable magazines. She uses this posture to hold her own
against* FREDDIE's *heartiness.*

FREDDIE. Not here?

SHEILA. Must be working in the attic.

PAM. Or gone to bed.

FREDDIE. At ten o'clock?

SHEILA. Perhaps hiding? (*She looks about the room behind
various pieces of furniture.*)

FREDDIE *and* PAM *look at each other.*

No. Working.

PAM. Gorgeous room.

SHEILA. Oh, Pam, no!

PAM. Absolutely gorgeous. Not the room so much, what you've done with it.

SHEILA. Cost absolutely nothing.

PAM. It's terribly PLU. Isn't it, darling?

SHEILA. How's that?

PAM. PLU? People Like Us. That dresser, for instance –

SHEILA. Twelve and six.

PAM. No!

SHEILA. In a country sale.

PAM. Absolutely gorgeous. I'm green, aren't you, darling?

FREDDIE. Yes, but how many coats of paint did you take off?

SHEILA. Three. Cream, brown and green.

PAM. Lord, the plebs and their lavatory colours.

SHEILA. Freddie, you don't feel I bullied you?

FREDDIE. What?

SHEILA. Into coming back here? Sit down, do.

FREDDIE. No. Why?

SHEILA. I feel I did. Carrying on like that. Crying. I've been going hot and cold ever since. Don't tell Bri, will you?

FREDDIE. What?

SHEILA. How I cried.

FREDDIE. Not if you say so.

SHEILA. Please. How d'you like your coffee?

FREDDIE. Half-and-half. It's nothing to be –

SHEILA. Pam? Half-and-half?

PAM. Black, please.

FREDDIE. Nothing to be ashamed of. Wish I knew how to give way more to *my* emotions. Must be years since my waterworks were turned on.

PAM. Hope so too.

FREDDIE. It's an enviable capacity.

PAM. Gives me the creeps, a man in tears.

FREDDIE. That's why you can give so much on the stage.

SHEILA. Was it all right tonight?

FREDDIE. All right? Was it all right? A bit more than *all right*, duckie.

SHEILA. No, truly.

FREDDIE. Truly. An electric evening.

SHEILA. It felt awful.

FREDDIE. Pam, you saw it. Was it awful?

PAM. Gorgeous, you were absolutely gorgeous.

SHEILA. It's a lovely part.

FREDDIE. You draw on deep wells of compassion.

SHEILA. You are sweet.

He kisses her hand. SHEILA, *embarrassed, smiles at* PAM *as though to include her.* PAM *smiles back.*

(SHEILA *goes off upstage and calls up the stairs.*) Bri! I'm making coffee, if you want some. (*Shuts door behind her.*)

FREDDIE *looks at cowboy paintings, as though he thought of buying one.*

Pause.

PAM *looks at him.*

FREDDIE. Clever these. (*Barks.*) Done by Brian, you know.

PAM. That was good – about bullying you.

FREDDIE. What?

PAM. I nearly fell about when she said that.

FREDDIE. 'Fraid I'm not with you.

PAM. Bully you! You were so damned keen to get in here you fell out of the car!

FREDDIE *looks back at paintings, pauses, moves away.*

FREDDIE. I fell from the car because my ankle was caught in the safety belt.

PAM *laughs. She has opened her bag and taken out a cigarette.*

Go on. Piss yourself.

PAM. Don't be coarse.

FREDDIE. That yob on the motor-bike nearly went over me.

PAM. Give me a match, will you?

FREDDIE. I thought you wanted to *help* these people.

PAM. Not me, darling.

FREDDIE. They need help. We can afford to give it. (*Lights cigarette.*) You've been smoking like a furnace all night.

PAM. And all day. I always smoke when I'm bored.

FREDDIE. If you're bored, go home. Your car's outside.

PAM. I'm bored there too. All day.

FREDDIE. Then interest yourself in someone else. Sheila, for instance. We've done a lot for Sheila, darling. We mustn't stop now.

PAM. You, not me.

FREDDIE (*explaining, to audience*). Well, I'm not the sort to sit around making sympathetic noises and doing sweet FA, so naturally as soon as I heard she'd been on the stage I saw the way to help. Got her down to join the players: friendly crowd, nice atmosphere . . . worked like a dose of salts. So well in fact, poor old Bri's gone slightly hatcha – thinks I'm getting my end away with Sheila.

PAM. Hardly surprising. He's left holding the baby.

FREDDIE. Exactly.

PAM. Literally.

FREDDIE. Yes, tragic. Which is why I'm here. (a) To tell him there's nothing in it. (b) Get them both to see sense about the poor kiddie. And (c) to give poor Brian back an interest in life.

PAM *makes a face, looks at her watch.*

PAM. It's gone ten now. What sort of thing had you got in mind?

FREDDIE. What for?

PAM. To give him back an –

FREDDIE. Ah. I thought for a starter, get him down to see his wife in the play.

PAM. Of course you're joking.

FREDDIE. No.

PAM. You told me he can't stand acting.

FREDDIE. Part of his chosen image. If he *loves* the woman – and he *claims* he does –

PAM. She's not even any *good* in it.

FREDDIE. Will you shut up! (*Looks nervously towards kitchen.*)

PAM *did not lower her voice.*

Pause.

FREDDIE *moves again, like a cross father.*

PAM. Well, is she? He'll see in a flash you're giving her charity and he's hardly the kind of man who —

FREDDIE. I think I know him a shade better than you. We were at *school* together.

PAM. Same school at the same time. I wouldn't exactly call that 'together'.

FREDDIE (*to audience*). Some truth in that. He was always in the backward classes. Spent his time in the back rows farting and so forth —

PAM. Freddie!

FREDDIE. And there was no need for it, he was brainy enough. Just got in with the wrong crowd. No, that sounds reactionary but you've only got to look at him. Half-way through his life and no degree, no future, not much past . . . coping with the arse-end of a comprehensive school and driving a fifteen-year-old Popular.

SHEILA *enters from kitchen.*

SHEILA. Ginger cat didn't come in here?

PAM. Haven't seen it.

SHEILA *makes to go.*

Want helping?

SHEILA. No, thanks.

FREDDIE *scratches his arm.* SHEILA *looks at him.* PAM *scratches her thigh.* SHEILA *goes.*

FREDDIE. Not that my position's anything to boast about. I just took over the factory where Dad left off.

PAM. Oh, not quite, darling. You've worked wonders.

FREDDIE. Only because I'm dead keen. But I'm not as bright as Brian, not nearly as talented. That's what's so galling to me as a Socialist. The waste! Since school, as a matter of fact, I saw nothing of him till six months ago. On a train to Town. I leaned over and said, '*Dum spiro spero* mean anything to you?'

PAM. Must say it doesn't to me.

FREDDIE. Our school motto. While I live I hope.

PAM. Bit squaresville, darling.

FREDDIE (*stoutly*). I *am* a bit squaresville! Anyway – (*Continues to audience.*) – he couldn't get away and we had a good old belly-ache. Told me all about his poor kiddie and how Sheila was obsessed with her and how keen he was to get her back in the swim.

PAM. Sheila.

FREDDIE (*bewildered*). Yes.

PAM. Not the weirdie.

FREDDIE. The what?

PAM. You know.

Pause.

FREDDIE. Don't call her a weirdie, darling.

PAM. I know, darling, it's absolutely horrid. But she is, though, isn't she?

Pause.

FREDDIE. Try to imagine that one of ours has turned out like that.

PAM (*shocked*). Darling! They're absolutely gorgeous, how could you?

Pause. FREDDIE *gives up, returns to audience.*

FREDDIE. I don't want to sound authoritarian or fascist but there's only one useful approach to any human problem and that's a positive one. No use saying: 'This is no way to live, in every night with a hopeless cripple.' No use at all. Same with problem teenagers. You don't say, 'Naughty boy, go stand in the corner.' You say, 'Get hold of these nails and a hammer!' Then you're in business.

Door opens and FREDDIE *turns to meet a large portrait of a cowboy, life-size, something like an old photograph. It is pushed on sideways through the slightly opened door. From behind it comes a hand holding a revolver which shoots off caps.* FREDDIE *barks with laughter.* BRI *comes from behind picture, brings it right in, closes door. He is in painting clothes.*

FREDDIE. Well, well!

BRI. Nice surprise, Fred. Hullo, Pam. Nice having company. Stuck in here every night like Joe Egg.

PAM. Like who?

BRI. Joe Egg. My grandma used to say, 'Sitting about like Joe Egg,' when she meant she had nothing to do.

FREDDIE. We've been here ages. Didn't you hear?

BRI. I was miles away.

FREDDIE. In the attic. Sheila said you –

BRI. In the saloon. Painting Wild Bill Hickock. Posed for this just before his last poker game. They got him in the back. Look at his pose. He fancied himself.

FREDDIE. Very good. It really is. Very good. Witty. (*Laughs.*) And this one – from the same series? (*Points to one on the wall.*)

BRI. Ah. That's a story picture. 'Where's the sodding bugle-call?' The beleaguered fort holding out for the cavalry that never comes. Few rounds left, Sioux closing in. Inset: cavalryman polishing his harness, smiling for the recruiting posters. (*Turns up his nose at it.*) Bit preachy.

FREDDIE. Why not? If it's a message that needs –

BRI. Rather have the pure heroic image myself. Like this one. (*Moves to the third.*) The Thalidomide Kid. Fastest gun in the West. On the slightest impulse from his rudimentary arm-stumps, the steel hands fly to the holsters, he spins on solid rubber tyres and – pschoo! (*He blazes away.*)

FREDDIE. That's a bit too sick for me.

BRI props the picture against the wall. FREDDIE moves away. BRI comes down to audience, circling.

Give me a good message any time.

BRI (*to audience*). What's he doing here? (*To Freddie.*) I meant to do Geronimo tonight but Joe had to be – um – attended to – and –

SHEILA comes in with four cups.

– by the time I'd got her to bed, it hardly seemed worth blacking up.

SHEILA. You've been painting.

BRI (*defensively*). I wore my old clothes.

SHEILA. Brian, fancy saying that! I want you to paint. That's the only reason I take these parts.

BRI. How did it go – the practice?

FREDDIE. Oh, blood, sweat and tears, you know, but it's coming.

SHEILA. Did you mention Joe?

BRI. I said I had to attend to her.

SHEILA. You mean the usual?

BRI. Got some drink, haven't we?

SHEILA. Brian!

BRI (*looking in cupboard*). What?

SHEILA. You mean the usual?

BRI. Bit more than the usual.

SHEILA. What d'you mean?

BRI. Cyprus sherry or Spanish cognac. Christ!

SHEILA (*shouts*). Brian!

He stares.

What d'you mean by more than usual?

BRI (*shouts*). We had a row. She flounced out and slammed the door.

SHEILA. No silly jokes. She's all right?

BRI. I'd rather not talk about it. Here we are – all set for a civilised conversation and you keep on about *that* poor crackpot. Spanish cognac, Fred?

FREDDIE (*embarrassed, slightly angry*). Thank you.

BRI. Sheila's parents brought it back from Torremolinos. Sure you wouldn't sooner have cider?

FREDDIE. No. Why?

BRI. I just remembered you're a Socialist. So many places you've got to boycott. Worse than entertaining an RC.

FREDDIE. I don't go in for that. Misguided. A blow against Fascism, Apartheid? Very likely! All you hurt is some poor peasant.

Drinks poured and given out.

BRI. Spanish cognac with instant coffee. High life on a teacher's pay.

Sits and drinks.

SHEILA. Brian, your shoes!

BRI. What?

SHEILA. You wore your teaching shoes and look, they're covered in paint.

BRI. Oh, God!

SHEILA. Just look at them! Freddie, what would Pam say if you got paint on your office shoes?

BRI. I'm sorry, honest, love.

SHEILA. You can't get it off!

BRI. I'll get it off.

SHEILA. Why don't you *think*? Go and change them, go on.

BRI. It's done now. And I'm not painting any more.

SHEILA. Honestly.

Pause.

As though you couldn't have changed your shoes.

Pause. They drink.

FREDDIE. How *is* teaching?

BRI. Oh, we keep them off the streets, you know. Eyes front hands on heads.

FREDDIE. You still don't like it?

BRI. It's not exactly Good-bye Mister Chips.

FREDDIE. All the same I envy you. Really. In many ways I often wish I'd been a teacher.

BRI. Instead of a rich and powerful industrialist, yes, it must be lonely.

SHEILA *laughs to remove the sting.*

FREDDIE (*barking*). Rich? Where d'you get the idea I'm rich?

PAM. We're not *rich*.

SHEILA. Comfortable?

PAM. Comfortable, yes, not rich.

FREDDIE. Nor powerful! (*Barks.*) You've been watching too much telly. No, hamstrung's nearer the mark. I'm like a last-

ditch colonial running things till the natives have got enough
know-how to take the reins.

BRI. That's right? (*Tut-tuts at the thought.*) Don't know what
the world's coming to.

FREDDIE. How are things on the home front, Bri?

BRI. Oh, much the same, you know.

FREDDIE. Stuck in like Joe Egg?

BRI. Yeah.

FREDDIE. Look – perhaps I'm rushing in where angels fear to
tread –

PAM. You always do.

FREDDIE *barks*.

FREDDIE. But – why don't you see all the doctors money can
buy and tell them you want another baby. To put it bluntly –
ask why you're not having one.

SHEILA. Oh, we've had fertility counts. That what you mean?

FREDDIE. You've done that?

BRI. Yes. She was A minus, I was B plus. Must concentrate
more.

FREDDIE. Well done. I admire your nerve. Most people
wouldn't fancy knowing for sure.

SHEILA. No. 'Specially men. Our doctor had an ex-major who
turned really nasty when they told him he was sub-fertile.
Wouldn't believe it. He kept saying, 'But I was in the
Normandy landings.'

BRI. 'I demand a recount.'

FREDDIE (*barks with laughter*). Hah! Poor fellow. How
absolutely terrifying! How about boosters?

BRI. What?

FREDDIE. Fertility boosters.

SHEILA. No.

FREDDIE. I know a gynaecologist in London, did so well by a friend of mine his wife's applied to be sterilised.

PAM. Georgina?

FREDDIE. Shall I fix an appointment?

SHEILA. I don't mind.

FREDDIE. If all else fails, I'll get the adoption machinery moving. Takes some time as a rule but I can put some ginger under the right people. Get it moved to the top of the in-tray. Always back out later if you find you've hit the spot.

SHEILA *winces*.

So – whatever happens – at least you'll have a proper working child.

SHEILA (*shrugging*). Two children instead of one.

BRI. She won't like it, Mum.

SHEILA. She likes to rule the roost, Dad.

FREDDIE. Surely, my dear, you can see you're only prepared to give up your life to little Joe because there's no one else. Once you've got a normal healthy baby looking up at you, smiling at you – does *she* smile? –

BRI. She used to. Now and then.

SHEILA. Often, often!

FREDDIE. A real baby will smile every time you look at her. And she'll cry too and keep you up every night – and crawl and walk and talk and –

SHEILA. Yes, I've seen them. Then what?

FREDDIE. Well – then – at least you'll be in a position to decide.

SHEILA. What?

FREDDIE. Whether to let Joe go into a residential school.

BRI. We've tried that too.

FREDDIE. Oh?

SHEILA. Putting her away, yes.

FREDDIE. Don't call it that.

SHEILA. What else is it?

BRI. She worried all the time, wouldn't let her stay.

FREDDIE. I'm on the board of a wonderful place. They're not prisons, you know, not these days. They're run by loving and devoted teachers – hideously underpaid, but I'm doing what I can in that direction –

SHEILA. I don't care how good the nurses are – she *knows*! She was ill in that place.

BRI. Change of diet.

SHEILA. She was pining.

FREDDIE. This isn't a hospital, it's a special school.

BRI (*seeing* PAM *look at her watch*). How's the time going, Pam?

FREDDIE. A private house. Trees all round –

PAM (*to* SHEILA). There was a fabulous article in *Nova* about it. D'you remember?

SHEILA. No.

FREDDIE. And if she improves, she can join their activities –

BRI. Activities?

FREDDIE. Painting . . . wheelchair gardening . . . speech therapy.

BRI. Better not tell *her* that, eh, Mum? She thinks she's very *nicely* spoken. One thing she *does* pride herself on.

SHEILA (*to* FREDDIE). She wouldn't go to a special school. Not even if you put some ginger under them. We've seen the place she'd go. No private house. No Palladian asylum with acres of graceful parkland.

BRI. Nor Victorian Gothic even.

SHEILA. Army surplus. Like a transit camp.

BRI. Except they're not going anywhere.

SHEILA. Freddie, thanks for trying but it's too late, honestly. I shall have to look after her till she dies.

BRI. Or until you do.

SHEILA. Yes. Whichever's first.

FREDDIE. Is that possible?

SHEILA. What?

FREDDIE. She could outlive you?

SHEILA. We know one — a man of seventy-six, just become a Boy Scout. They said they wouldn't have him any longer in the Cubs.

FREDDIE. These jokes. May I say my piece about these jokes? They've obviously helped you see it through. A useful anaesthetic. But. Isn't there a point where the jokes start using *you*?

SHEILA. I thought you were going to speak to Bri about —

FREDDIE. Please. This first. Isn't that the whole fallacy of the sick joke? It kills the pain but leaves the situation just as it was? Look — when we met again — how many? — six months? — ago — you used, I remember, a striking metaphor describing Sheila's state of mind. You said a cataract had closed her eye — like your mother's net curtains, screening off the world outside.

BRI. Did I say that?

FREDDIE. It struck me as so bloody apt.

BRI. So bloody smug.

FREDDIE. But it was true, don't you see? And now – in my opinion – it's all gone arse-over-tip. Sheila's cured and you've caught the cataract. Shoot me down if I'm all to cock. I'm only trying to strip it down to essentials. Thinking aloud.

BRI. I wonder – could you think more quietly?

FREDDIE. Am I shouting? Sorry. I tend to raise my voice when I'm helping people.

BRI. Only my head's splitting.

FREDDIE. All right. (*Sits by* BRI *and addresses him quietly, earnestly.*) When I see a young couple giving up their lives to a lost cause, it gives me the screaming habdabs. As a Socialist! The waste! I think to myself: all right, I don't care, I *am* my Brother's Keeper, I bloody well am.

BRI. That's much quieter, thanks.

Pause.

FREDDIE. Another joke. Another giggle.

PAM. Come on, Freddie, let's go –

FREDDIE. The whole issue's a giggle. I throw you a lifeline and you giggle. The whole country giggling its way to disaster.

PAM (*to* BRI). She broke down tonight.

BRI. What?

FREDDIE. Pam –

SHEILA. You said you wouldn't –

PAM. In a flood of tears. (*To* FREDDIE.) Come on –

FREDDIE (*taking over*). Because she can't cope any more with your suspicions and jealousies. So I said I'd put you straight on one or two points.

PAM. Wasting your breath, darling.

FREDDIE. (a) We're not going to bed together.

BRI (*to* SHEILA). Scab!

FREDDIE. (b) It's hardly likely because (a) She loves you, (b) I love Pam, and (c) I've got three smashing kids –

PAM. Darling, I love you too.

FREDDIE. And I'm hardly likely to throw all that away for a bit on the side – however gorgeous the bit may be – (*Smiling at* SHEILA.) – and though I'm not a practising Christian, I think I know my duty –

BRI. Yes, but Fred –

FREDDIE. And – squaresville or not – I happen to believe in duty.

PAM. Terribly sweet.

They kiss.

BRI. I hardly know how to say this now. After your masterly dismissal of jokes. But – here it is – the whole idea was just another sick fantasy. I know you've never touched her, leave alone shafted her.

PAM. He's a nut.

BRI. I wanted to bring back the magic to our marriage. Stir it up, a kind of emotional aphrodisiac.

PAM. If you ever try that with me, I'll leave you.

FREDDIE. I may be squaresville but I'm not sick.

SHEILA (*to* BRI). You're so round*about*.

BRI. You wouldn't let me near you. All day I'd been running blue movies on the back of my retina – the pair of us romping about the bed shouting with satisfaction. And what did I get? – Your hands are cold.

PAM. This is too juvenile. Let's go.

FREDDIE. That's what he *wants*.

BRI *gets more drink.*

But I want to *help* him.

Comes to audience.

Am I wasting my time, d'you think?

Offstage children's voices sing: Once in Royal David's City.

BRI. Listen to that. This time of night. How can people hear the telly?

SHEILA. Oh, she loves the carols. Let me fetch her.

PAM (*showing panic briefly*). No! We're going.

SHEILA. You've never seen her. Wouldn't you like to?

FREDDIE. I'd love to.

PAM. It's twenty past ten.

FREDDIE (*shrugs*). The *au-pair* girl will have gone to bed.

PAM. Your train in the morning.

FREDDIE. What train? Not tomorrow –

PAM. I thought it was tomorrow.

FREDDIE. No, darling. You'd like to see her, wouldn't you?

PAM. Love to. Give me a match.

FREDDIE (*barks*). You'll get lung cancer.

PAM (*irritably*). They're my lungs.

SHEILA *is going.*

BRI. Sheila – don't.

SHEILA. What?

BRI. I forgot to tell you what happened – while you were out.

Pause. She comes back.

SHEILA. What?

BRI. Shall I tell you?

SHEILA. Happened where?

BRI. Here. First – I fed Joe. (*To* FREDDIE.) She was
constipated. She hadn't been for a week so I chose a nice tin
of strained prunes. What my grandma used to call black-
coated workers.

Smiles big show-biz smile expectantly, drops it.

They have to be strained still because her teeth are – a bit
stumpy . . . after I'd got that lot down, I had a bite myself,
read the paper. But she kept having little fits and whimpering
so I plonked her in the nursery. I thought to myself, 'P'raps
the spasm's hurting,' so I tried to loosen it with exercises.

SHEILA. The constipation hurts her.

BRI (*explaining to* FREDDIE). The spasm's in the back between
the shoulders. Sheila got this method of breaking it down
from a lady wrestler she·met at an Oxfam coffee party.

SHEILA (*smile to* FREDDIE). A physiotherapist.

BRI. You take her arms and wrap them across her chest – like
so – and hold them very tight – then push her head right
forward and down till her chin's rammed in between her
collar-bones. As though you were trying to make a parcel.

Demonstrates on the cushion.

I don't know whether it's any use but I faced the fact long ago
that I enjoy it. Find myself smiling when she cries. At least it's
a reaction. But tonight she wouldn't stop even when I let her
go.

SHEILA. Those fits upset her.

BRI. So I undressed her and applied a suppository. Put a rubber
sheet underneath and doubled her up like a book . . . pressed
on her stomach to help – and at last, over half an hour I
think, she managed number twos.

SHEILA. Oh, good. That was bothering her, poor love.

BRI. No, listen a minute. It was no sooner out than she started all that gulping and lip-smacking, stretching her arms, opening and closing her blind eyes . . . the Grand Mal . . . I thought to myself, that's it, the lot! All you can do. Pain and fits. And not for the first time in ten years, I thought: Is it ever worth it?

FREDDIE. It never is.

SHEILA. Worth what?

FREDDIE. The effort.

SHEILA. We've got no choice.

FREDDIE. Of course you have.

BRI. Anyway. When the fit was over I propped her in her chair and stood behind her and put a cushion over her mouth and nose and kept them there while I counted a hundred. There was no struggle or anything. It seemed very – peaceful.

The others are watching him, motionless. Pause.

SHEILA. What? . . .

PAM. God!

BRI. When it was all over I took the cushion away and . . . I said, 'Nurse, you have seen nothing. We are in this together' . . . I looked up to see the nurse throw off her cape revealing the burly figure of Sergeant Blake, Scotland Yard.

SHEILA (*relieved*). Honestly, Brian!

BRI. You almost believed me, didn't you?

FREDDIE. No almost. I *did*.

SHEILA. I should *know* by now. She *is* all right, isn't she?

BRI. Yes.

SHEILA. I'm going to see her.

Moving out, BRI stops her.

BRI. Did you feel relieved at all, even a little bit, when you thought I'd done it?

SHEILA. Don't be silly.

BRI. Not even a teeny-weeny drop relieved to think it was all over?

SHEILA. How could I? Honestly. (*She goes off and up the stairs.*)

BRI. How about *you*?

FREDDIE. What?

BRI. Were you relieved at all?

FREDDIE. Of course not. Horrified!

BRI. Because it would be murder?

FREDDIE. You can't take life, man.

BRI. Her life – what is it?

FREDDIE. I don't care.

BRI. You've never *seen* her.

FREDDIE. I'd *like* to see her.

BRI. You shall in a minute.

PAM. Darling, it's half past –

BRI (*ignoring her*). She's not alive. What can she *do*?

FREDDIE. It doesn't matter.

BRI. Asphyxiation delayed ten years by drugs.

FREDDIE. She should be put away.

BRI. Everyone's always saying, 'Do something,' but when I make a suggestion, it's all wrong.

FREDDIE. If all you can suggest is murder, yes.

BRI. Living with Sheila, you get to welcome death. With life burgeoning in every cranny. (*Moves about, listing the wild life.*) Flora, fauna, gawping goldfish . . . budgies . . . busy Lizzie . . . cats . . . cats' fleas . . .

PAM. I *knew* I'd been itching.

BRI. Fleas from Sidney and Beatrice Webb, we're not sure which. When the tom-kitten was born, Sheila wanted to call him Dick, but I drew the line there. Standing on the front steps last thing shouting, 'Dick, Dick!' Might have got killed in the rush.

FREDDIE. There are one or two great –

BRI. She embraces all living things. (*To* PAM *hastily.*) Except Freddie. She never embraces him.

FREDDIE. I said there are one or two great moral commandments and in my view they're the only hope we've got against chaos. Love thine enemy. Thou shalt not kill.

BRI *lights a cigarette.*

D'you know how the final solution of the Jewish problem began? In the mental hospitals. It's only a step from there to Auschwitz.

BRI. That kind of thing certainly gives legalised killing a bad name, but – what about the other forms? The bomb-aimer gets decorated but anyone who lets Joe die gets ten years.

FREDDIE. The cases are different. A rational intelligence can distinguish between the different cases.

BRI. So I've noticed.

FREDDIE. Put it this way. You don't agree with killing?

BRI (*shrugs*). No.

FREDDIE. But if a madman breaks in here and tries to rape your wife, what d'you do?

BRI. Kill him.

FREDDIE. Exactly. Killing is sometimes unavoidable.

BRI. Thou shalt not kill unless it's absolutely necessary.

FREDDIE (*doubtfully*). Yes.

BRI (*to audience*). Whose side is he on?

BRI smokes. Pause. The singing has ceased.

PAM. Darling – it's half past ten.

FREDDIE (*suddenly*). You're like a blasted speaking clock. On the third stroke – peep-peep-peep.

Walks away.

PAM. Oh, charming.

Looks at both men, ignoring her and now each other. Complete separation of all three people on the stage. PAM comes to audience.

It wasn't my idea coming back here in the first place. But once Freddie's set eyes on a lame dog, you might as well talk to the moon. I keep looking at that door and thinking she's going to come through it any moment with that poor weirdie. I know it's awful but it's one of my – you know – THINGS. We're none of us perfect . . . I can't stand anything NPA. Non-Physically Attractive. Old women in bathing-suits – and skin diseases – and cripples . . . Rowton House-looking men who spit and have hair growing out of their ears . . . No good, I just can't look at them. I know Freddie's right about Hitler and of course that's horrid. Still, I can't help sympathising with Brian, can you? I don't mean the way he described. I think it should be done by the state. And so should charity. Then we might have an end to all those hideous dolls in shop-doorways with irons on their legs . . . Freddie won't hear of it, of course. But then he loves a lame dog. Every year he buys so many tickets for the spastic raffle he wins the TV set and every year he gives it to an old folks' home. He used to try taking me along on his visits but I said it wasn't me at all and he gave up. One – place – we went, there were these poor freaks with

– oh, you know – enormous heads and so on – and you just feel: oh, put them out of their misery. Well, they wouldn't have survived in nature, it's only modern medicine so modern medicine should be allowed to do away with them. A committee of doctors and do-gooders, naturally, to make sure there's no funny business and then – if I say gas-chamber that makes it sound horrid – but I do mean put to sleep. When Freddie gets all mealy-mouthed about it, I say, look, darling, if one of our kids was dying and they had a cure and you knew it had been discovered in the Nazi laboratories, would you refuse to let them use it? I certainly wouldn't. I love my own immediate family and that's the lot. Can't manage any more. I want to go home and see them again. They may not be the most hard-working, well-behaved geniuses on earth, but no one in their right mind could say they were NPA. (*Turns back.*) Freddie, I'm going. You can get a taxi and –

SHEILA *carries* JOE *in, in her nightdress and dressing-gown.*

SHEILA. Aaaah! The carols have stopped.

BRI. They've stopped, yes.

FREDDIE. This little Josephine?

SHEILA. This is Joe. Say hullo to Uncle Freddie.

FREDDIE (*shakes her hand*). Hullo, Joe, what do you know?

SHEILA. Not much, I'm afraid.

SHEILA. And Auntie Pamela.

PAM. She's got – really – a rather pretty face, hasn't she?

SHEILA. She's very PLU, when you get to know her. Aren't you, sweetheart?

BRI. I'm lovely, she says.

SHEILA. But strangely passive tonight. You didn't forget her medicine?

BRI. You'd be strangely passive, she says, if you'd been fitting and crying and doing doots.

SHEILA. But her eyes are hardly open.

BRI. Who wants to open their eyes in the middle of the night, she says. And one hour before midnight's worth two after, she says.

He embraces them both. He and SHEILA *stand rocking* JOE.

SHEILA. You missed the carol-singers, darling. What a shame.

BRI. Christmas already, she says. Seems to come round quicker every year.

SHEILA (*singing*). Away in a manger, no crib for a bed –

BRI joins her and they sing together, dancing her about the stage.

The little Lord Jesus laid down his sweet head.
The stars in the bright sky looked down where He lay,
The little Lord Jesus asleep in the hay.

The cattle are lowing –

Near the end of the second verse BRI *has to prevent her pushing away.*

BRI. Oops!

SHEILA (*seeing at once*). Down here!

They put her in a chair facing upstage.

FREDDIE. What is it?

SHEILA. A fit. I thought she was too far gone for that –

FREDDIE. Nothing we can do?

BRI (*to* JOE). One day when you're doing that the wind will change and you'll stay like it.

SHEILA. D'you think she needs the doctor?

BRI. She should be in bed. I'll take her up.

SHEILA. What good's that? She's nearly unconscious.

BRI. What good's she doing down here?

Bell rings, front door.

That's the waits. I'll say we're Muslims.

SHEILA. Give them a shilling for Joe. I love the old customs, she says.

FREDDIE. Here – (*Gives* BRI *money.*) – from Joe.

BRI takes it awkwardly and goes off.

PAM. We must be off.

FREDDIE. I'd no idea she was so – torpid. One thinks of a Mongol or an athetoid or monoplegic. But – well – she really is *so* helpless.

SHEILA. She's worse than usual, aren't you, blossom?

BRI comes back.

BRI. It's my mother.

Makes frantic and spastic gestures and faces SHEILA, who silently appeals to the ceiling. They recover as GRACE follows in.

SHEILA. Hullo. How nice to see you!

GRACE. I'm not stopping, Sheila – oh. You didn't say you had company.

BRI. Mr and Mrs Underwood. My mother.

PAM. We were just going.

FREDDIE. How d'you do?

GRACE. No, I'm not stopping. Only I've been in town and thought I'd drop in Josephine's new cardie . . .

Comes to audience and speaks. BRI has taken her coat and goes off with it to the hall. Others light cigarettes, chat, etc., during her solo. BRI comes back and joins them.

GRACE *is sixty-five, suburban, fastidious. Wears light-coloured suit with frilled decorations; gloves and shoes match handbag. Very short-sighted but refuses to wear spectacles. As well as her bag, she brings a hold-all full of shopping. Her manner is generally bright but gives way to spells of gloom when she tends to sigh a lot. In her presence, BRI is more boyish and struggles to escape her maternal allure.*

GRACE. No, well I wouldn't have dropped in, not in the ordinary way, especially when they had company, only on Tuesday Mrs Parry and I make a habit of meeting for the pictures if there's anything nice. Well, after you've been round with a duster, there's nothing much to fill in the afternoons and no one wants to sit about like a mutt and don't laugh, will you, but they reduce the prices for old-age pensioners. I don't know whether anyone sees themself as an old-age pensioner – I know I don't, but when you're trying to manage on so little, a few shillings is a consideration. Not that my husband ever thought I'd be hard up – he paid enough for his private pension and his insurance in case something happened to him first – but there, they *say* it's the middle classes that have suffered the most, don't they, from inflation?

Anyway last week Mrs Parry rang and said she couldn't see me Tuesday – that was on the Thursday – or was it Friday? – as she had to stay in for a vacuum. I said, 'But surely to goodness a vacuum can come in the morning or any other afternoon, it doesn't have to be the very day we go out.' She said, 'My dear, nowadays if you're told to expect a vacuum Tuesday there's very little you can say to stop it.' So I said, 'Well, all right, I'll do some last-minute Christmas shopping in the afternoon and meet you in the Odeon café – what – about half past four? – and we can see Julie Andrews in the evening.' Then – over the week-end I finished the cardigan I'd been knitting Josephine. Well – knitting passes the time and if you didn't have some diversion, you'd sit around like a blooming nun. No company, no one to talk to or have a cup of tea with. (*Sighs, wipes her nose and dabs the corners of her mouth.*)

I don't encourage neighbours. One thing can so easily lead to another with neighbours, you find them taking advantage.

So it *is* very lonely, hour after hour, stuck like Joe Egg with no one to talk to. Why I do so many cardigans, the poor mite dribbles. Not in the way a baby dribbles even, worse than that. It's not nice to talk about, I know, but she can't seem to regulate the flow. Her garments, after a few hours on, they're stiff with saliva. (*Dabs corners of her mouth.*) Which means a lot of washing for her mother and I've said to Sheila often enough, 'She should wear a plastic bib, it would be such a saving on wool,' but of course you can't say a lot, can you, that's being an interfering mother-in-law. I do believe if I said, 'Sheila, whatever you do, don't dress her in plastic bibs,' that poor mite would be stuck in a plastic bib morning, noon and night like a blooming nun. (*Moves back to the others.*) And when we came out of the Odeon, I thought I'll go so far on Mrs Parry's bus and drop in with my grand-daughter's cardigan and p'raps if Brian's not too busy he could run me home.

BRI. Yes, right.

GRACE. So I'm not stopping. (*Sits by* JOE.) And how's Nana's favourite girl tonight? Look what Nana's brought her. I'm fast asleep, she says.

SHEILA. She's poorly, very poorly.

GRACE. Having forty winks, she says.

BRI. She's all right.

GRACE. An hour before midnight's worth two after.

BRI. That's what they say.

GRACE. Let's see how it fits, shall we? (*While speaking, holds cardigan against* JOE.) Wouldn't she be lovely if she was running about?

FREDDIE. A beautiful child.

GRACE. First time you've seen her?

SHEILA. Why I brought her down.

GRACE. D'you think the sleeves are short, Sheila?

SHEILA. Her arms are so bent.

GRACE. You must allow for that, yes.

SHEILA. Yes.

GRACE. I fancy – a half-inch longer.

SHEILA. Would you bother?

GRACE. No bother. Got to do what little we can, haven't we?

FREDDIE. Yes, exactly.

GRACE (*still trying cardie*). You should have seen the shops this afternoon. I said to the lady in Scotch Wool and Hosiery, 'You'll be glad when Christmas is over?'

BRI. What did she say to that?

GRACE. She said, 'I certainly shall.'

BRI *shakes his head slowly in amazement.*

But apart from the rush, I said to Mrs Parry, it does look nice – the decorations and the toys and birds and toilet sets.

BRI. See Jesus?

GRACE. Pardon?

BRI. Did you see Jesus?

GRACE (*cautious, not looking at him*). Well, if I *did* I didn't notice.

BRI. On the Electricity building.

GRACE (*tut-tutting*). They'll drag religion into anything. (*Pause. Looking at cardie.*) Colour's nice, isn't it? I think that sort of thing spoils Christmas.

BRI. Jesus?

GRACE (*making herself clear*). I think it's a time for children.

Brian, d'you remember the very first year I took you to see Father Christmas?

BRI. Um –

GRACE. I shall never forget it. He took one look at him and said, 'Mummy, I don't like that funny man.'

FREDDIE *laughs politely.* BRI *might not have heard.*

But you loved the toy department. You used to say, 'Oh, Mummy, I want it all, can I have it, Mummy, all to myself?'

SHEILA *laughs uncontrollably.*

BRI. We took Joe to Father Christmas. He stank of meths and he was handing out foam-rubber pandas and goosing the little girls –

FREDDIE. Why do you say these things?

BRI. It's true!

FREDDIE. It is *not* true. They're vetted.

BRI. We've got one! It stays in any position.

FREDDIE. Not the pandas. The – other –

BRI. That was true. Soon as Joe sat on his lap, she had a fit. That stopped him.

GRACE (*she scratches, to* SHEILA). D'you know, I believe I've acquired a little visitor? Not what you expect from the Odeon.

BRI. You got it here. Off our cat. We're infested with them.

GRACE. Are you really, Sheila? Fleas is something I don't believe we've ever had. Can you remember, Brian?

BRI. An occasional wood-louse.

GRACE. Not the same as fleas. (*She moves about nervously.*)

SHEILA. It's Beatrice Webb. We keep her outside now.

GRACE. I should. I know you're very fond of animals, Sheila, but surely it's an interest you must keep in proportion.

SHEILA. It's the first time we've ever had them.

GRACE. They say there's a first time for everything, don't they? (*Sits by* JOE *again.*) Don't they, loveliest girl in all the wide wide world.

SHEILA. Look! Another fit.

GRACE *stands and moves backwards.*

GRACE. Bless her heart!

SHEILA *examines* JOE.

SHEILA. She's worse. Look at this.

BRI. She's sleeping it off. (*And to* GRACE.) They left off her medicine at the centre and now –

SHEILA. How can you say that?

BRI. What?

SHEILA. Sleeping it off.

GRACE. I should have it destroyed.

SHEILA. Another dose of medicine. (*Goes to kitchen.*)

GRACE. If it was me.

BRI. What, Mum?

GRACE. I should have whatever-you-call-her put to sleep.

BRI *looks at her, having only heard this.*

FREDDIE. The cat.

BRI. Oh.

GRACE. Fleas bring disease.

BRI *sits by* JOE *and examines her intently, looking to kitchen anxiously.*

PAM. In my daughter's primary school, they had a plague of bugs brought in by some poor council-house kiddies –

FREDDIE. How d'you *know* it was them?

PAM (*frightened of his anger*). 'Twasn't the *kiddies'* fault.

GRACE. I blame the parents.

PAM. Emma got the most hideous rash.

GRACE. Some children are more susceptible, more sensitive. Brian always had a delicate skin.

BRI. All right, Mum.

GRACE. Look at his impetigo.

SHEILA *comes from kitchen with empty bottle.*

SHEILA. I can only find this empty one. Where's it all gone?

BRI. Oh yeah! She spilt it. Joe. Knocked it over. (*Pause.*) Having a fit. I had to save her first.

SHEILA. But it's like treacle. How did it get poured out?

BRI. Well, it did.

SHEILA. It's been washed clean.

BRI. I saved enough to give her a dose, then washed it out.

Pause. She puts bottle down.

SHEILA. You must get some more.

BRI. She's had enough sedation for one night.

They all look at her.

I'm turned on, she says.

SHEILA. She's having fits.

BRI. Not bad ones.

SHEILA. They weaken her. She needs the anti-convulsant.

BRI. But what time is it Pam?

PAM. Twenty to eleven.

BRI. There you are!

GRACE. Boots is open. On the Centre.

FREDDIE. Shall I go?

BRI. No, I'll manage.

SHEILA. Here's the prescription.

GRACE. I should wrap up warm, Brian. Put a scarf on.

She speaks to Pam, with whom she senses an affinity.

He's always been a martyr to colds. I've know him come in crying with his poor little fingers all yellow and all the other boys still out running about and I've had to rub them and get him a warm drink and sit him by the fire till he was over it . . .

BRI *listens to this, then smiles at them all and goes.*

SHEILA (*holding* JOE's *hand*). What's funny daddy been up to, eh, my rose?

Pause. FREDDIE's *attention drawn.*

FREDDIE. You think he's up to something?

SHEILA. That medicine's thick. You couldn't spill much. The bottle was full, I don't know. He *told* us he'd killed her.

FREDDIE. That wasn't true, so we needn't –

GRACE. Told you what?

SHEILA. He'd killed her. Yes.

GRACE. Oh, no.

FREDDIE. It was an adolescent joke.

GRACE. His jokes, I never listen.

FREDDIE. Showing off to get attention.

GRACE. It *is* showing off.

SHEILA. Like a baby. By saying that he could take my attention off poor Joe and get it on himself again. And when that palled, he'd make up another – with himself as the killer or the corpse or – anything – as long as it's the most important part.

GRACE. I can't imagine Brian doing that without provocation.

FREDDIE. Oh, no? The other joke we've had this evening was that Sheila and I are having a love affair. And for that, I assure you, we neither of us gave him the slightest provocation.

GRACE. Perhaps not *you*. I couldn't say.

SHEILA. Hullo?

GRACE. But I shouldn't wonder if Brian thought there was something – going on –

FREDDIE. Why?

GRACE. Perhaps – knowing what he did – he was apt to be over-suspicious –

SHEILA. Knowing what he –

GRACE. Probably expected it. (*To* PAM.) I mean always. Half expected it.

SHEILA. What d'you mean?

GRACE. No. Nothing.

SHEILA. Come on.

FREDDIE. Frankly I resent the –

GRACE. I didn't mean to say that, no –

SHEILA. Why should he have expected it?

GRACE. Don't you know?

SHEILA. No.

GRACE. I think you do, Sheila. Brian knew all about your past life even before he married you.

SHEILA. Of course he did. *I* told him.

GRACE. Yes.

SHEILA. How do *you* know about it?

GRACE. He told me.

SHEILA. Ah!

FREDDIE. Lord above!

PAM. This is horrid!

FREDDIE. Have you heard the car start?

SHEILA. I'd love to have heard what you said when he told you.

PAM. I haven't, no.

GRACE. I'll tell you.

FREDDIE. I'll go and see.

GRACE. I said, 'You must make up your own mind, Brian.'

FREDDIE (*to* SHEILA). Going to help Brian. (*Exit to front door.*)

SHEILA. Bet you had a shock when he did.

GRACE. Meaning what exactly?

SHEILA. Meaning you always made his mind up for him.

GRACE (*to* PAM). *This* is nice.

SHEILA. You spoilt him.

GRACE. I must say!

SHEILA. Wrecked him.

GRACE. Thank you.

Silence. Both women momentarily spent. They move about.

SHEILA. Where's Freddie?

PAM. The car hadn't started. He's gone to help.

SHEILA. Not started –

Makes to go out but BRI *and* FREDDIE *come in.*

BRI. Can't get it started.

FREDDIE. Have you tried, I wonder? You were sitting in it doing nothing when I –

PAM. Let me go. In my car.

SHEILA. Would you?

PAM. I should have gone before. (*Aside.*) Anything to get away.

BRI. Shall I come – show you a short cut?

PAM. No need.

She is going.

FREDDIE. Got the chitty?

PAM. What?

FREDDIE (*to* BRI). Give her the prescription.

BRI finds it, gives it to her, dropping it, picking it up, etc.

SHEILA. It's yellow, looks like custard.

PAM goes.

BRI. Twenty-five quid that car cost me and after only three years look at it!

GRACE. You were never very clever with your hands. You took after your father there. (*To* FREDDIE.) Poor old thing used to spend hours on end behind the radiogram and in the end we'd have to call the proper man.

SHEILA (*suddenly, vehemently, to* BRI). Great spoilt baby! Coddled baby!

FREDDIE. Now, Sheila, there's no use –

SHEILA (*to* FREDDIE). The only way he knows to get what he wants is screaming and stamping his feet, but that's a bit grotesque at his age, so he straightaway says Poor Me, but nobody listens so he makes some jokes and everybody laughs, which is better than nothing, so he makes more and more jokes and when everyone else has gone I get the 'poor me', I have to swallow that. (*Turns on Grace.*) Because you *spoilt* him.

FREDDIE. Now, Sheila, we've had our –

GRACE. I kept the house free of fleas, I admit that. I spring-cleaned every year instead of once in five. Certainly when he was a tiny mite I used to press his ears back for fear they'd protrude. I boiled a kettle in his room for croup. Made a mustard bath for the cold and kept out the wind. I believe in an insulated house. (*To* BRI.) It's still insulated, Brian, it's still home. You're welcome, I've told you that. 'Specially since I was left alone. Not so much a home these days as a blooming nunnery. I'm stuck up there day after day like a blooming nun.

SHEILA (*to* FREDDIE). There you are. 'Poor me!'

FREDDIE. Sssh!

GRACE. What did you say?

SHEILA. Your self-pity. Just like him. Poor me!

GRACE. Wait till *you're* alone.

SHEILA. Why don't you move in with your friend?

GRACE. Mrs Parry?

SHEILA. Yes. Why not? There you sit in your perfectly insulated houses each with your own TV and stove and lawn-mower and empty garage, each complaining continually about being a blooming nun. What's stopping you?

GRACE. You want your privacy.

SHEILA. Do you? I don't. I hate it.

GRACE. Wouldn't do if we were all alike.

SHEILA (*suddenly to* FREDDIE). You see their selfishness!
    We're talking about them again, d'you notice? Here's Joe – I
    think she's seriously ill – and – what are we doing?

    Noticing JOE *again, she stops, goes down by her, looks at her
    closely.*

GRACE. Has the poor mite ever been anything *but* seriously ill?

SHEILA. We must call the doctor. She's white as chalk but her
    lips are blue. Straining the heart, you see.

BRI. I'll take her back to bed, let her sleep it off.

SHEILA. Her chest is hardly moving.

BRI. A touch of flatulence, she says.

SHEILA. No.

BRI. Heartburn.

    SHEILA *stares at him. He goes to pick up* JOE.

SHEILA. Leave her!

    BRI *leaves her.*

GRACE. She ought to be in hospital.

SHEILA. I'll go if nobody else will.

GRACE. Ought to have gone in years ago.

SHEILA. But don't let Brian touch her.

GRACE. Then the marriage would have had a chance.

    SHEILA *refuses to rise, makes to go to door.*

    You can't expect a man to take second place to a child like
    that.

FREDDIE. Now, now.

GRACE. It's not *his* fault she's spastic!

SHEILA. What was that? Not *his* fault? Whose then?

GRACE. No one's.

SHEILA. Come on.

GRACE. I didn't mean that. Not your fault either. You can't help the family you were born into. When it's congenital it's not your fault, no –

SHEILA (*to* FREDDIE). What's she talking about?

GRACE. Fits I'm talking about.

Pause.

SHEILA. What?

GRACE. Your uncle's fits.

SHEILA. Uncle's fits – which uncle?

GRACE. Which one was it, Brian?

SHEILA. You told her my uncle had fits?

BRI. Oh, Mum!

GRACE. You did.

BRI (*to* SHEILA). Your cousin Geoff.

SHEILA. Infant convulsions. What baby doesn't have infant convulsions?

GRACE. Well, none of the babies in *our* family, for a start!

SHEILA. I take that for granted, dear. (*To* BRI.) What made you mention cousin Geoff to her like that? You know she'd –

BRI (*nodding, pacifying*). She'd just been telling *me* about the epilepsy in our family.

GRACE. I beg your pardon?

BRI. And I felt I had to console her by mentioning someone on your side. You pick your time to throw it back, don't you?

GRACE. Epilepsy in our family? Where d'you get that?

BRI. From you! Uncle Neville.

GRACE. Uncle Neville! Oh! (*Laughs.*)

BRI. Yes, Uncle Neville.

GRACE. He wasn't family. He happened to marry Auntie May, that's all.

BRI. So our family's only epileptic by marriage!

GRACE (*agreeing readily*). Of course! But I will say this for May. She didn't have children. Mrs Parry said to me, 'I think if you know there's a taint in the family you should refrain from children.'

SHEILA. She'd welcome any excuse – that walking sheath.

GRACE. Please don't use language to me. Brian, you stand about like a mutt while she picks on your mother in company.

BRI. Not you, Mum – Mrs Parry.

GRACE. My best friend.

BRI. You don't expect me to defend Mrs Parry. (*Mad doctor.*) Nurse, Nurse, we've done it, I tell you! With this we can make whole continents barren. The deterrent they've all been working for – Mrs Parry! (*Mad laugh.*)

Silence.

GRACE. I thought you were serious for a moment.

BRI. Come on. I'll take you home.

GRACE (*startled*). What? Back to the nunnery.

BRI. That's right, yes.

GRACE. Thank you. That's gratitude. (*She is tearful now that he shows which side he's on.*)

FREDDIE. Thought you couldn't start the car.

BRI. No, but if I crank it –

FREDDIE. You mean you didn't crank it before –

FREDDIE *and* SHEILA *look at each other.*

GRACE. I had a tartan grip.

SHEILA. What about Joe? You leaving Freddie alone with her?

BRI. Why? You going somewhere?

SHEILA. To phone the doctor.

BRI. I'll do that when I get back. If you really want to bother him.

SHEILA. No, we'll do it now. She's unconscious.

BRI. I'll only *be* twenty minutes.

SHEILA. Half an hour, if we're *lucky*. She'll make tea.

BRI. I shan't stop for tea.

GRACE. I've got some Garibaldis, I know you –

BRI. Right, I'll ring from there. (*To* GRACE.) Can I do that?

GRACE. Have I ever said no to you?

BRI (*to* SHEILA). All right?

SHEILA. No. Do it now.

FREDDIE. *I'll* do it.

BRI. Eh?

FREDDIE. While you're taking your mother home. From a local phone-box.

SHEILA. Would you, Freddie?

FREDDIE. Sure!

BRI. You interfering bastard!

FREDDIE. I'm trying to help you –

BRI. Help? You're a pain in the arse.

GRACE (*aside*). I hate a play with language.

SHEILA. Have you got a threepenny-piece?

FREDDIE *searches in his pockets for money while they talk*.

GRACE. I might have one in my bag.

She searches too.

FREDDIE. What you're suggesting is no way out.

BRI. There's no other possible way –

FREDDIE. Once start that – we'll have anarchy.

BRI. That'd be something.

FREDDIE. Don't be childish, you must have order. 'Thou shalt not kill.'

BRI. Except when it shall come to pass that thy trade-routes shall be endangered.

GRACE. I could have sworn I had a threepenny-piece.

BRI. Then shalt thou slay as many as possible of the enemies of General Motors and ICI.

SHEILA. How about you, Freddie?

FREDDIE. Nothing but half-crowns and pennies.

SHEILA. My bag's upstairs.

FREDDIE. Suppose euthanasia was legalised and your daughter let die. Then twenty years from now a cure is found.

SHEILA. Any luck?

GRACE. Pennies and shillings. What's this – I can't see.

SHEILA. A milk check.

FREDDIE. Just imagine.

BRI. You mean her brain starts working?

SHEILA. Give me a shilling.

BRI. A six-weeks-old brain in a thirty-years-old body.

SHEILA. No, that's a halfpenny.

GRACE. This light's so dim. And these nasty creatures itching.

FREDDIE. No, some kind of grafting.

BRI. An adult brain?

FREDDIE. I don't know. Yes!

SHEILA. Brian, have you got a threepenny-piece?

BRI starts looking.

BRI. Say, the brain of a woman who died at thirty? Here's one.

SHEILA takes it.

Whose soul will she have?

SHEILA. Here, Freddie.

Gives him coin.

BRI. I think that question should go to our popular TV mini-bishop. Your Grace – hey – just a minute!

Grabs back coin. They struggle.

FREDDIE. What are we doing? I'll dial emergency. The hospital.

SHEILA. Yes, the ambulance! Say it's urgent. I'll show you the box.

GRACE. Put a coat on, though. It's bitter.

But they've gone.

And you wrap yourself up properly too, Brian, if you're running me home.

She takes from her handbag cosmetic articles and spends the next few minutes doing her face, hardly aware of what is happening behind her.

Going out of the warm on a night like this is the best way if you want to catch cold. We came out of the Odeon and it was cutting down Union Street like a knife.

BRI, *hardly listening, goes to* JOE *and listens for her heart, feels her pulse.*

I said to Mrs Parry, 'Oh, my Lord, what a night!' She said they said we were in for something of the sort possibly lasting into February. I said, 'It's a shame for the old people' and she said, 'Grace, I hate to remind you but we're the old people now.' I said, 'Well, if I've got to stand about waiting for buses in this, I shall catch my death.'

BRI *looks up.* GRACE *goes on making up.* BRI *looks at* JOE, *then towards front door. He lifts the child and throws her over one shoulder. He goes out the kitchen door with her, closing it behind him.*

I said, 'I may be old but I'm not quite ready to go yet.' So if you're running me, I should put on something warm because it's not so much the cold as the contrast.

Looks round, sees he has gone, continues to audience.

Talking to myself. No, but it's an old car with no heater and draughts from all directions and he's always been susceptible to cold.

SHEILA *comes back from front door into room.*

Well, if it's your nature, I say it's nothing to be ashamed of.

SHEILA. Where's Joe?

GRACE. Pardon?

SHEILA. Joe's gone.

GRACE. How can she have gone?

Sees she has.

SHEILA. He's taken her. Where?

GRACE. He didn't say.

During this, BRI *carries* JOE *across behind* SHEILA *from back door of house to front door.*

SHEILA (*angry*). Didn't you see him go?

GRACE. One minute I was talking to him, next I was talking to myself.

SHEILA turns and goes to bottom of stairs, calls.

SHEILA. Bri!

She runs off upstairs.

GRACE. I expect he's put her to bed, poor mite. She shouldn't be sitting up here all hours, I thought that when I came in.

Talks to audience again.

Brian's Dad used to say – when he was getting on – 'Grace, I've had my life, if only I could give her what's left to me, I would.' I believe he meant it too. Though, of course, as it turned out, there wasn't much left to him because he died the following year.

Hear SHEILA *call* BRI *upstairs, as* BRI *enters from front door.*

BRI. You ready, Mum?

GRACE. What?

BRI. Ready to go, are you?

GRACE. I'm getting ready.

BRI. Put your coat on then.

GRACE. Aren't you going to put one on?

BRI. No time. I'll try and get the engine started.

GRACE. You know what that engine's like. Get that started first.

SHEILA comes downstairs. GRACE *suddenly remembers and asks:*

What have you done with Josephine?

SHEILA. Bri!

BRI runs off to kitchen, closing door. SHEILA comes into room.

SHEILA. He's not up there. Not anywhere. He must have gone outside.

GRACE. He's just been here.

SHEILA. With Joe?

GRACE. No.

SHEILA. Where's he gone?

GRACE. Out there.

SHEILA. The garden? —

SHEILA goes out to kitchen, leaving door.

GRACE. Oh, mind the cats.

Shuts kitchen door and scratches. BRI enters at main door with GRACE's overcoat.

BRI. Ready, Mum?

GRACE. What on earth's the rush? Have you got the car running?

BRI. Let's get inside first. I can push it if it won't go.

GRACE. Mind you don't strain yourself.

BRI. Put your coat on.

GRACE. Sheila's just gone off to the garden after you.

BRI. Get a move on.

GRACE. What have you done with the baby?

BRI. Me? Nothing. Hasn't Sheila got her?

GRACE. Sheila's *looking* for her.

He has now got GRACE's coat on.

GRACE. I've got to talk to Sheila about the cardigan.

BRI. Not now, Mum.

He collects her stuff and is about to go.

Come on!

GRACE. Aren't you waiting for your friend to come? Here's Sheila now –

And BRI runs off by main door with GRACE's bag. SHEILA comes from garden through kitchen.

SHEILA. No sign of them. And it's snowing now.

GRACE. Snowing? My Lord! Brian, I should put something on –

Sees he has gone.

SHEILA. Was he here?

GRACE. Where's he gone now?

SHEILA. With Joe.

GRACE. Must have gone to the car.

SHEILA. Did he have Joe with him?

GRACE. No. He hadn't seen her. He was rushing me off my feet, but I said, 'I must ask Sheila whether she wants anything else done to Josephine's cardigan – apart from the sleeves –'

SHEILA has gone to look in the hall. Now there is an explosion in the kitchen – not very loud but loud enough to stop GRACE speaking and cause SHEILA to come back into room. It is followed by the sounds of glass or crockery falling.

My Lord –

SHEILA. There he is!

GRACE. Sounded more like the gas. D'you leave the gas on?

SHEILA *goes out to kitchen.*

Mind don't let the cats in.

SHEILA (*off*). All this glass and stick!

GRACE. What is it?

She goes off, shutting door.

FREDDIE *and* PAM *come in from front,* PAM *carrying bottle of yellow medicine.*

FREDDIE. Must be upstairs.

PAM. But why the front door open?

SHEILA *comes on from kitchen.*

FREDDIE. Ah! They're sending an ambulance.

PAM. The front door's open.

FREDDIE. I met Pam coming in.

GRACE. What a mess!

FREDDIE. What?

GRACE. Glass and sticky stuff.

SHEILA. The ginger-beer plant exploded.

GRACE. I thought it sounded more like the gas.

SHEILA. Brian must have put a screwtop on. I've told him to use a cork. It gives when the pressure builds up inside.

GRACE. Nuisance – anything like that with a life of its own.

FREDDIE. Where *is* Brian?

SHEILA. He's gone mad. He's running about outside. With Joe.

FREDDIE. Outside?

PAM. D'you know it's snowing again?

FREDDIE. We didn't see him.

PAM. The door was open.

SHEILA. Snowing –

Makes towards front door but BRI *comes in carrying* JOE.

BRI. I think it's all over.

Puts her on sofa.

FREDDIE. What's all over?

BRI. You look at her.

SHEILA *kneels by sofa, takes* JOE *in her arms, nurses and warms her, wrapping her about, rocking her.*

SHEILA. My poor blossom –

FREDDIE (*quiet, authoritative*). What happened?

BRI. I took her outside.

FREDDIE. And did what?

BRI. Nothing. Left her lying on the back seat of the car.

FREDDIE. What for?

SHEILA. – little worm, poor little worm –

BRI. Something Mum said suggested it –

GRACE. Me? I never suggested taking –

BRI. No.

GRACE. On a night like this?

BRI. But you said –

GRACE. Is it likely?

BRI. You said it was bitter cold. I was going to leave her in the garden but I couldn't –

SHEILA. Can anyone do the kiss of life?

FREDDIE. I can't.

BRI. So in the end I put her in the car. I don't know what I wanted – just to stop them saving her again. When you went to phone I thought –

FREDDIE (*to* SHEILA). Can you feel a pulse?

SHEILA. No. I can't. Oh, my poor dove. She's freezing.

FREDDIE. The shock might have done it.

GRACE. Oh, my Lord. Brian, whatever made you do a thing like that –

GRACE takes one of JOE's *hands and rubs it vigorously between hers.*

FREDDIE. Have you got a looking-glass?

GRACE. One in my handbag –

SHEILA. Come along, my bird, my little dove –

FREDDIE searches in GRACE's *bag.*

GRACE. Oh, Brian, you shouldn't, not however bad she was, poor little mite, you shouldn't deliberately do that.

FREDDIE. Here's a glass.

Wipes it, gives it to SHEILA, *who holds it by* JOE's *mouth.*

SHEILA. Sweetheart, come on, sweetheart, try for Mummy –

BRI watches in dismay. The others are grouped round the sofa.

– come on, dearest love, gonna be all right now . . .

BRI moves away, sits on his own.

GRACE. Perhaps the glass isn't cold enough. To get the condensation. A piece of fluff –

PAM. What?

GRACE. A feather will show the slightest draught.

She searches in cushions for a feather.

PAM (*to* FREDDIE). This is ghastly.

GRACE. Is this a feather?

FREDDIE. Yes.

GRACE. There. Close to her mouth. This is how we knew poor Dad had gone.

Front doorbell.

FREDDIE. Here they are. Don't say anything, anyone. I'll answer the questions. You concentrate on the child. No need for unnecessary suffering. All right? –

SHEILA. Sweet flower, come along now –

They lift her and move in a group toward the door.

GRACE (*to* PAM). Wouldn't she have been lovely if she'd been running about?

Fade lights.

BRI comes down to forestage.

BRI. Sheila and I went with her in the ambulance. Mum stayed in Pam's car waiting for news. It was all-stations go in the hospital – voluntary women rushing everywhere with soup and Bibles . . . St Bernards standing by . . .

Mimes hand-mike, assumes awe-stricken voice.

If there *is* anything heartening about such a disaster, I think it's the wonderful way this great operation of mercy has moved into action. And of course the uniquely British optimism that suddenly in moments of crisis seems to suffuse the whole nauseating atmosphere. I remember – when they first came in, the husband was jibbering and shaking like some spineless dago but nobody quite knew what to do. Then one of the impressive lesbian nurses pointed to the African orderlies and said quietly, 'Pull yourself together, man, set an example . . .'

Drops the parody.

Anyway the sawbones got to work with the oil-can and . . .
'I think there's a chance, Nurse . . . all our work may not be
wasted.'

And the upshot was – Mum's feather finally fluttered.

He looks at the set, pausing for some seconds.

Sheila could hardly stand, what with anxiety and relief, so
they gave her a bed for the night. Joe was staying in, of
course, they couldn't say how long but perhaps a week.
I went in Freddie's car when he ran my mother back to the
nunnery. She begged me to stay with her. 'I'll fill a nice hot-
water bottle,' she said. And when I stood my ground, 'How
about my electric blanket?' And I said, 'No, Mum. Cheerio,
I'll be in touch,' and she started on about lighting the Valor
stove that I loved so much because it threw patterns of light
on the bedroom ceiling. I nearly choked with longing for that,
but I gritted my teeth and said no, there was the budgie to be
fed. And she said she had my old dummy and rattle
somewhere . . . so in the end I ran . . . Freddie was a hoot.
Saying it was a lucky escape and a blessing and stuff like that.
His trouble, he's too kind-hearted, too squeamish. And he
clings to law and order. Pam now. She's got the right idea. For
the wrong reasons. Or something. Look at me, delivering
judgement. Who do you think you are – God? So – after
they'd dropped me home – off they went to their three
absolutely gorgeous kiddies – every one a company director –
and the oil-fired heating – the labour-saving evergreens . . .
the fibre-glass yacht. I was glad to see the back of him. You
can't think with that loud-hailer going on and on. Not that
there was *much* to think about. Only details.

Our marriage might have worked as well as most if Joe hadn't
happened. I was too young for it, that's true, of course. I
always will be. But Sheila might just have dragged me
screaming into manhood. 'Stead of which, I was one of the
menagerie. She loved me as much as any goldfish or
aphelandra. So now it was a question of how to tell her I was
leaving her. And when I went into it, I saw it wouldn't only be
about Joe, but also my ambitions . . . and the first time I saw

Father Christmas and – this backache's worse than yesterday
and – the pattern on the ceiling – so in the end I better just
creep away without a word . . .

*Goes into room and begins hurriedly putting various objects
into his pockets, putting on coat, etc.*

So I've shaved and washed and packed a case . . .

Gets case from hall, stands it nearby.

haven't decided where I'm going yet. Up the smoke, I suppose,
get lost among the Australians.

Looks at watch.

Ordinary way I'd be leaving now for eyes-front-hands-on-
heads . . . but never again, I tell you! Want a nice slow job
. . . game-warden . . . keeper at Regent's Park . . . better still
Kew Gardens . . . more used to vegetables.

Looks at room, his back to us, fixing it for ever.

Well.

*Noise off; BRI dodges behind wall. He looks for a way out
but SHEILA enters. She doesn't see him, he attempts to go out
and she hears him. He draws guns and fires on her.*

SHEILA. You're up. I thought you'd lie in.

BRI. I've got school.

SHEILA. You're not going?

BRI. Yes.

SHEILA. No. Go absent.

BRI. Only two more days. How are you?

But SHEILA looks towards the front door again.

SHEILA (*calling*). Thank you.

*She goes to front door. BRI looks for escape routes – other
door, window, etc., but despairs. SHEILA comes back*

wheeling JOE *in her chair.*

SHEILA. There we are, lovely. Home again.

She leaves her centre. BRI *goes to them.*

BRI. I thought they were keeping her in for a few days.

SHEILA. They wanted to but – really – what's the point? I've
  nursed her through pneumonia, 'flu, more colds than I can
  count. Why bother busy nurses?

They stand or crouch either side of JOE *as at her first
appearance.*

  Anyway, Dad, did you *see* the nurses? And the doctors?

BRI. How d'you mean, Mum?

SHEILA. Every one a fuzzy-wuzzy.

BRI. I thought it was alright *doctors* being black.

SHEILA. She didn't fancy it, Dad.

BRI. How are you, lovely?

SHEILA. Still a bit dopey but her pulse is stronger and she's
  breathing well. She's as tough as old boots, Dad. She'll get the
  Queen's Telegram yet, you see.

  BRI *smiles.* JOE *sighs and turns her head. They look at her.
  That's all.* BRI *stands. Looks at his watch.*

SHEILA. But she's certainly not well enough for school. Not this
  term. And *you're* not going either.

BRI. Yes, I must, love –

  SHEILA *moves to him.*

SHEILA. All night I've been saying to myself we'll spend a few
  days in bed together. Come on . . .

  Starts unbuttoning his coat.

  I'll ring the Head if you're frightened.

BRI. Not fair on the other staff.

He struggles and she tickles him. He giggles.

SHEILA. I thought, I'll get home before he's up and make him bacon and eggs – and fried apple rings. Did you have something hot?

BRI. Tea and toast, yes. And I've fed the zoo and tidied up.

SHEILA. And I'll take them up to him, I thought, and after that I'll climb in with him. And look what I find. So I shall have to get all those clothes off him and we'll stay all day with the snow outside . . . cold and quiet . . . and us in there up to our tricks.

She embraces him. He has left off struggling.

Last night I lay there thinking what you'd tried to do to Joe –

BRI (*quickly*). I was round the twist – you know, my Mum, Freddie –

SHEILA. No, I don't blame you, honestly. It was my fault. I've been asking too much. But listen – d'you know what I'm going to do? I'm going to look for a residential hospital where I'm sure she'll be well looked after and won't pine. And when I've found it, d'you know what? You and I will leave her there

She is facing down. He looks at her.

– for, I don't know – several weeks, even a month, every year.

BRI turns away.

Means we'll be able to go abroad. Haven't been abroad for eleven years. Second honeymoon, alright? And let's start now.

Her hands are all over him.

BRI. I'll go and ring the school.

He gets free.

SHEILA. Run all the way there and back. I can't wait long. And even though you're only going a few yards, I should wrap up warm. It's brilliant sun but treacherous underfoot.

BRI. I'll be in the car.

SHEILA. What, just to go round there?

BRI. Case it's occupied I can always try another.

SHEILA. Back in one piece then, and you will be quick? Mmm?

BRI. Right.

He stands looking at her. She is on her way to the kitchen, but feels forced to say more.

SHEILA. I shall go on up. Will you carry Joe to her room when you come up? She's such a lump.

BRI *nods. She goes into the kitchen,* BRI *picks up his case and goes. Door slams off.* SHEILA *comes back, closes door on cats, scratches arm.*

(*To fish.*) Daddy fed you? He is good.
(*To bird.*) Got some seed? What a daddy!
(*To Joe.*) Aren't we lucky?

She goes out and up the stairs. JOE *remains.*

Curtain

The National Health

The National Health

In the early nineteen-sixties, my right lung kept collapsing: a condition known to medicine as a spontaneous pneumothorax. I was three times confined in medical wards while it healed itself or was surgically treated by a weird minor operation that stuck the lung to the chest by an infusion of irritant talcum powder. My spells in various hospitals in London and Bristol filled a good few pages of my journal and finally surfaced as a television play called *The End Beds*. This was a dramatic collage of what I'd seen and heard in the public wards and was a positive advance on anything I'd done so far. Despite – or because of – this, it was turned down by every script editor in the country. I put it away in a drawer and earned a living with more palatable TV comedies.

In 1968, having wanted but lost *Joe Egg*, Ken Tynan asked me to write a new play for the National Theatre. I knew he and Olivier would prefer a large cast and the hospital play had that, so I blew the dust off it by a plot involving a Labour MP who goes into a state hospital suffering from nervous collapse. Michael Blakemore persuaded me its points were better made without this character so I did it again, this time expanding the character of Barnet the orderly and adding scenes from a hospital soap opera. I renamed it *The National Health*, a title that helped me understand what I was about.

It was superbly done by Michael and a cast that might have been waiting for just this play to come along. Rehearsals were calm and conscientious, the script hardly changed after the first reading. I'd argued against casting Jim Dale but he was perfect, single-handedly injecting life into an exhausted company. Olivier had been busy elsewhere filming *Three Sisters* and arrived in a forbidding beard to watch the second dress rehearsal. His scowl never brightened and the actors somehow felt it, all desperately auditioning for next season, mugging and stretching out their pauses so that the play lay gasping. Afterwards Sir grumbled about the length, said we should cut the whole balcony scene, and was so worried about the black actors that I feared he might be about to repeat an earlier suggestion: 'Couldn't Joanie black up?' Michael persuaded him to wait till an invited audience had watched it.

That night I went home and suggested we should take our family to some remote spot to avoid the coming disaster. I had not yet heard what I learnt later: that Lord Lyttleton hated the play and had pressed Olivier to cancel it. I myself didn't have much faith in it and wrote at the time: 'there's a hole at its centre . . . however attractive, decorative, piquant or coarse it may be in parts, it doesn't work in the way it should – with an urgency of narrative movement . . . I wasn't able to *enter* these characters. They were people seen in passing.'

But the first audience welcomed it like wine. They laughed with recognition from the opening dawn chorus to the chilling finale. Afterwards Olivier hugged me and told me how clever I was, a gesture he repeated months later when I went to pick up The Standard Best Play Award. The show stayed in the company's repertoire for two and a half years.

But for me the sweetest result came the morning of its nearly unanimous rave reviews, when my agent had a call from the BBC asking if I thought the play could possibly be adapted for television.

The first production of *The National Health* was given at the National Theatre on 16 October 1969. The cast was as follows:

Patients

REES	Gerald James
TYLER	Patrick Carter
ASH	Robert Lang
FOSTER	Bernard Gallagher
KEN	John Nightingale
FLAGG	Harry Lomax
LOACH	Charles Kay
MACKIE	Brian Oulton

Nursing staff

MATRON	Mary Griffiths
SISTER McPHEE	Maggie Riley
STAFF NURSE NORTON	Cleo Sylvestre
NURSE SWEET	Anna Carteret
NURSE LAKE	Isabelle Lucas
ORIENTAL NURSE	Helen Fleming
BARNET	Jim Dale
MICHAEL	John Flint
PRINCE	John Hamilton

Doctors

MR BOYD	Paul Curran
NEIL, his son	Robert Walker
DR BIRD	Gillian Barge
INDIAN STUDENT	Malcolm Reid
OLD WOMAN	Gabrielle Laye
CHAPLAIN	George Browne

Theatre staff, other visitors, etc
Tom Baker, Frederick Bennett, Jean Boht, Michael Edgar, Roger Forbes, Michael Harding, Norma Streader

Musicians
Jack Botterell, Laurie Morgan, Norman Wells, Rod Wilmott

Produced by Michael Blakemore
Designed by Patrick Robertson
Lighting by Robert Bryan
Music by Marc Wilkinson

At the Théâtre de la Ville, Paris as *Santé Publique* (translated by Claude Roy), also at the Théâtre National, Brussels.

At the Long Wharf Theatre, New Haven, transferring to Circle in the Square, New York.

In 1975 it was performed at the Guthrie Theatre, Minneapolis, co-directed by Michael Laugham and the author.

A film version (Columbia Pictures) in 1973 was directed by Jack Gold, featuring Jim Dale, Lynn Redgrave, Colin Blakeley, Bob Hoskins and Eleanor Bron.

The play's first production won The Standard Best Play Award.

ACT ONE

Scene One

The first arrivals find the stage lit dimly by a blue bulb hanging centre, but during the next fifteen minutes a steadily increasing dawn light reveals one end of a hospital ward.

This daylight creeps through Victorian Gothic windows high in the rear wall. Above eight feet, the walls are pea-green, below this white. Against the back wall are five beds, with a locker between each and earphones and thermometers in wall brackets. The ward is supposed to continue off to the audience's left and there is no side-wall, only masking flats. The wall on the right is the end of the ward and an open way leads to Sister's room, kitchen, lavatories and the main corridor. The wall continues diagonally downstage and here is one more bed, called Bed 6. Halfway down on the audience's left is a large black coke stove with a chimney rising from it and going out of sight into the flies. Armchairs are grouped around it.

From the apron on the stage, two flights of steps go down into the orchestra pit. Between them at the bottom is a cinema organ or piano, if the production is to use music.

The directions refer to the beds by numbers from left to right. Each one has a male patient in it, except Bed 3, which is made but empty.

CLEO NORTON, *a West Indian Staff Nurse, crosses the stage from time to time while the audience is assembling. She sometimes checks a patient, giving special attention to the man in Bed 5, who is being drip-fed and drained. From the other patients come groans, snores and incoherent utterances. Sometimes we can hear what they say.*

ASH (*Bed 1*). No . . . no . . . please don't do that . . .

Someone groans at this, then snores as before. After a long time, a shout.

REES (*Bed 4*). Take your bloody hands off me!

Several groans. Then snores, as before. A dawn chorus of city birds is heard as the light increases.

ASH sits up, looks at REES, climbs out of bed, scratches his head, looks at his wristwatch. He gets a dressing-gown from his locker, puts it on: then slippers. Sitting on his bed, he looks into a hand mirror at the condition of his tongue.

TYLER *pushes on from the left in a wheelchair. We should notice that his legs have been amputated at the knee.*

TYLER (*loud and hearty*). Morning!

ASH. Oh – good morning to you, sir.

TYLER. Lovely morning.

ASH. We'll live in hopes –

TYLER. Beautiful!

ASH. – if we die in despair . . .

TYLER *has gone on off right. We hear him continuing as ASH rummages in his locker.*

TYLER (*off*). Morning, Staff Nurse.

STAFF (*off*). Morning, Mister Tyler.

TYLER (*Off*). Lovely morning.

STAFF (*off*). Looks it.

TYLER (*off*). Beautiful!

FOSTER (*Bed 2*) *has been woken by* TYLER's *reveille. Props himself on an elbow, scratches head.* ASH *has his towel and shaving bag.*

FOSTER. Morning.

ASH. Good morning to you, friend.

FOSTER. He likes to make a row.

ASH. Who's that?

FOSTER. Whosit — just been through —

ASH. Tyler.

FOSTER. What a voice.

ASH. Wonderful spirit, though, considering —

FOSTER. Oh, yes.

ASH *stands, checking his gear.* FOSTER *glances round, sees that Bed 3 is empty,*

Where's Mister Lucas then?

ASH. Of course, you didn't hear. You get a wonderful sleep.

FOSTER. I do, yes.

ASH. Very enviable. He went in the night.

FOSTER. In that condition? Never. Transferred?

ASH (*quietly*). Passed on. First I knew was the screens going round then the resuscitation unit and the heart-machine . . . quite a pantomime but . . . n.b.g. . . . I regret to say. . . .

FOSTER. I'm blowed.

ASH. The orderly cleaned him and wheeled him off . . .

FOSTER. I suppose it was a blessing.

ASH. A happy release, yes. I must find myself a basin before the headlong rush of the Gadarene swine.

FOSTER nods and ASH goes toward right, as STAFF comes on wheeling trolley with a large metal jug and some wash bowls.

Good morning to you, Staff.

STAFF. Morning.

ASH goes off. STAFF glances at Bed 5, then turns to Bed 4.

Doctor! Wakey-wakey . . . rise and shine.

REES raises his head, looks at her sternly. She moves on towards the left.

FOSTER. Hullo, Staff.

STAFF. How's Mister Foster? Full of the joys of Spring?

FOSTER. Bearing up . . .

STAFF. That's the way . . . come on, Kenneth, stir your stumps. Don't be late your last morning. . . .

Goes off left. FOSTER and REES watch. Offstage KEN begins coughing.

FOSTER. Coughing well this morning, Kenneth.

Coughing continues and KEN comes on, carrying his towel, wearing a hospital dressing-gown. He is lighting a cigarette as he crosses. He throws down the match and goes off right.

Don't throw the match down, son. Someone's got to pick it up.

REES. He smokes too much, that boy.

FOSTER. Morning, Doctor.

REES. Killed this fellow too, the cough.

FOSTER. Mister Lucas?

REES. Smoked too much.

FOSTER. With a chest like his, yes.

REES. Sixty-five, you know, that's all he was. I'm eighty-two, but I could have knocked spots off him.

FOSTER. I hope I'll be as fit as you at eighty-two.

REES. No, he's dead. He died last night.

FOSTER (*louder*). I say if I'm as fit as you at eighty, I shan't complain.

REES. Eighty-*two*.

FOSTER. Ah!

REES *leans back.* MACKIE *wakes in Bed 6. He groans and* FOSTER *looks at him.*

Cheer up, sir, you're still alive.

MACKIE. So I see. More's the pity.

REES. But Lucas has gone. That should please you.

MACKIE. A step in the right direction.

REES *and* FOSTER *laugh.* REES *leans back again.* FOSTER *puts on his radio earphones.*)

Scene Two

Light grown warmer.

SWEET, *a plump English nurse wearing glasses, comes from the right bringing a screen on wheels. This she stands around Bed 3. She goes off and returns with another screen and closes in Bed 3 completely.*

LOACH *has come from the right. He wears a dark grey, slept-in suit and carries a raincoat on his arm. He looks lost.*

SWEET *comes forward to meet him with pyjamas and a hospital dressing-gown.*

SWEET. Good morning. You've no pyjamas?

LOACH. No.

She leads him to the bed.

SWEET. Change into these. I'll come for your clothes in a minute.

She guides him through the screens. ASH comes on, left, with an unfinished basket. FOSTER takes off earphones. SWEET comes to him. ASH finds an armchair.

How's my basket coming on, Mister Ash?

ASH. Not so dusty, Nurse.

SWEET. You're slow.

ASH. Slow but sure.

LAKE, another West Indian nurse, comes from the right wheeling a dirty-linen receptacle. She checks a list.

LAKE. Which bed are we stripping?

SWEET (*coming down*). Kenneth's. He's going out this morning.

LAKE. Which is Kenneth?

SWEET. Surely you know Kenny?

LAKE (*half-aside to* AUDIENCE). They all look the same to me.

SWEET. The old ones, I daresay, but he's only nineteen.

LAKE (*checking list*). Multiple fractures?

SWEET. Yes.

LAKE. I remember.

SWEET. Of course, you're married. Even so I should have thought you'd remember Kenny –

They go off, left.

FOSTER. Doing a spot of work on your basket?

ASH. I hope I never see another basket, to be quite frank.

An OLD WOMAN in a flowered dress and white hat comes from right and goes to MACKIE's bed.

OLD WOMAN. Good morning. I have a message for you. It's that God gave His only begotten Son that whosoever believeth in Him should not perish but have everlasting life.

MACKIE. He's welcome to it.

OLD WOMAN. Isn't it wonderful news? The best ever. There is no death.

MACKIE. I'm dying.

OLD WOMAN. Dying only to live.

MACKIE. Oh, all right.

OLD WOMAN. God bless you and get well soon.

She gives him a card. He drops it unread. She goes to Bed 5.

Good day. I have a message for you. It's that God gave His only begotten Son to save us. Us – that's you and me and everyone. So you need only believe and you'll have everlasting life. God bless you and get well soon.

No reaction from the patient. She puts a card between his fingers and turns to REES, who is asleep.

Good morning.

He wakes and turns his head to her.

I've brought you a message. Good news.

REES. From my wife, is it?

OLD WOMAN. God gave His only begotten Son to save us.

REES. I thought it was about the taxi.

OLD WOMAN. All of us – you, me –

REES. Is there any message about the taxi?

OLD WOMAN. Every one of us.

REES. You could get them to hurry it up.

He grasps her hand but she gently disengages herself and steps back.

OLD WOMAN. Bless you and get well soon.

She gives him a text and he stares at it. She goes to Bed 2. FOSTER has the earphones on.

Good morning.

FOSTER (*takes off earphones*). How d'you do?

OLD WOMAN. Have you heard the news?

FOSTER. I was just about to.

OLD WOMAN. God so loved the world that he gave His only begotten Son that whosoever believeth in Him should not perish but have everlasting life.

FOSTER. Right-i-o.

OLD WOMAN. The best news ever. There is no death.

FOSTER. I've got the greatest possible respect for other people's beliefs but if what you say is true –

OLD WOMAN. God bless you and get well soon.

FOSTER. – where does that put Mister Lucas? He was in the next bed here –

She gives him a card and goes off left. LOACH comes from screens, now wearing gown and pyjamas, carrying his clothes. He looks about uncertainly.

REES. I don't want to bother you. (*Holds out hand towards LOACH, who goes closer.*) Yes, I thought as much. You've brought my clothes. (*Grasps LOACH's clothes with both hands.*)

LOACH. Hang on –

REES. Only my wife's expecting me home to tea and I can't walk the streets in pyjamas.

LOACH. They're mine.

REES. There's a taxi waiting below but all my togs are in Sister's room, so –

They are struggling with the clothes as SWEET *comes on, left.*

– if you're passing, perhaps on the way back, you'd be so kind as to –

SWEET. Not being naughty again, are we, Doctor?

REES. This gentleman's kindly offered to fetch my clothes.

SWEET. What about some bye-byes?

REES. Earlier on a lady brought me a message from my wife about the taxi . . . but my eyes are going . . . perhaps you –

Shows her the text, which she glances at.

SWEET. Now shall we tuck in nice and cosy –

REES. Only the meter will be ticking away down there . . .

SWEET. – and get some sleepy-byes?

REES. Some what?

SWEET. D'you want a bottle?

REES. I want my clothes.

SWEET. Let's see, shall we?

Tries to put hand under bedclothes but REES *slaps it away.*

REES. Take your bloody hands off me.

SWEET. I don't call that very nice behaviour.

REES. Been eating boiled sweets again, I can smell them on your breath.

SWEET. More personal remarks?

REES. Never get your weight down that way.

SWEET. I've told you before –

REES. Try Banting's diet. (*To* FOSTER.) Banting was so fat he had to go downstairs backwards. (*Laughs at this and wipes eyes with sheet.*)

SWEET. That must have been before the Ark. Everything's changed since you were in practice all those years ago. Don't forget that. You're the patient here, not the doctor.

She has reached under the clothes and now brings out a bottle full of urine.

Telling fibs too! Now lie down like a good boy and nurse will fetch you another. And I'll take those . . . thank you.

SWEET *takes* LOACH's *clothes and goes off.* REES *leans back on the pillow, exhausted.* LOACH *sidles away towards the stove.* ASH *is still at his basket.* LOACH *warms his hands.* LAKE *has come on and takes off one of the screens.*

LOACH. Nice to see a fire.

ASH. It's not alight.

LOACH. Marvellous, isn't it?

ASH. Spot of bother with Dr Rees?

LOACH. He Welsh or something?

ASH. Welsh, yes.

LOACH. I could tell the brogue.

ASH. Eighty-two. Stroke. Left him paralysed on one side. Also his brain seems at times as sound as a bell, another time completely in the grip of some delusion about a taxi. He must know he's never going out of here alive, but he won't give in. Spunky old blighter.

SWEET *returns with a clean bottle.*

SWEET. All right now?

REES *nods, takes the bottle, puts it under.*

That's nurse's favourite boy.

She goes, taking LOACH's *other screen.*

ASH. In the corner, Mister Flagg: bladder trouble and complications. He was in theatre yesterday. I find, if they keep you in the end beds, you can prepare to meet your Maker.

LOACH. That end?

ASH. Where they can reach you easily.

LOACH. I'm only third from the end.

ASH. We all start *off* near the end. Under observation. But we slowly work our way along to the furthest window by the balcony.

LOACH. Long as we know.

ASH. That bed just happened to fall vacant this morning.

SWEET *crosses from right to left.*

Next to you on the other side Desmond Foster, coronary. Young for that, only forty. Then me, Mervyn Ash, tummy ulcer.

Offers his hand. LOACH *shakes it.*

Been here a fortnight so far. On a blotting paper diet. Tapioca, semolina, boiled fish, chicken. The merest glimpse of semolina makes me heave. Always has. Don't ask me why.

LOACH *is paying no attention. He looks frightened.* ASH *observes him closely.* LOACH *pulls himself together.*

LOACH. Who's the old boy by the door?

ASH. Mister Mackie. They've pulled him through once or twice but he's lost the will.

TYLER *comes on right in wheelchair.*

TYLER. Hullo, Doc. How's Doc this morning?

REES *looks up.*

Lovely morning, Des . . .

FOSTER. Been out?

TYLER. Over to physio. Lovely spring day.

REES *waves his hand.*

Keep smiling, Mervyn.

ASH. We do our best, friend.

TYLER *goes off.*

REES. How d'you do?

ASH. Gone now, Doctor. He's gone. (*Then to* LOACH.) Friend Tyler from up the ward. Had both legs off at the knee. Some malignant growth, I'm not too sure. But what a wonderful spirit! Always full of beans. How enviable! Me, I'm up and down like a yo-yo. And when I'm down – by George! Which accounts for the ulcer, I suppose. And this endless therapy. Electric therapy, physiotherapy, occupational therapy. Chit-chat with the trick cyclist. Marquetry and basket-making. Which, quite frankly, has the same appeal to me as semolina.

Laughs and gives LOACH *a playful nudge.* LAKE *comes from left, wheeling linen-basket.*

LAKE. New patient ready for a bath?

ASH. That's you.

LOACH. What?

LAKE. Get a towel from your locker, have a bath.

She goes off, right. LOACH *goes to his bed.*

FOSTER. They keep you busy here. They'll wake you up to give you a sleeping tablet.

LOACH. Yeah? She better watch it. No blackie pushes me around.

KEN *comes in from left, now wearing black motor-cycle gear. Across the back is some fiendish emblem. He carries his helmet and a grip with his belongings.*

KEN. I'm off then. Ta-ta, mate.

ASH. Goodbye, Kenny. Take care on that motor-bike now. My father used to say 'Better five minutes late in this world than fifty years early in the next!'

KEN. He sounds like a load of fun.

ASH. He was wonderful. I only mean, if you can't consider the pedestrians, at least think about your own skin.

KEN (*shrugs*). People don't stop screwing for fear of knob-rot. (*Goes to* MACKIE.) Cheero, Dad. Get well soon.

ASH. I'm afraid you've got a one-track mind.

KEN (*leaving* MACKIE). I ain't got a one-track mind.

ASH. Sounds like it.

KEN. Who wouldn't have a one-track mind in here?

FOSTER. Should learn to control your appetite.

KEN. I touched up that fat nurse behind the screens couple of times but she wouldn't cock her leg. (*Goes to* FLAGG.) Tarrah, Dad, you'll soon be out of here. (*Comes a few steps from him.*) He ain't got long to go.

FOSTER. You're old enough to have learnt respect.

KEN (*to* REES). Bye-bye, Doc. Get well soon, me old mate.

REES (*stirring*). You the driver?

KEN. Eh?

REES. My wife waiting down below in the taxi?

KEN. No, I'm Ken. Just off home.

REES. You a patient is it?

SWEET *has wandered on from left.*

KEN. Yes. Cheerio. Get well soon. (*Comes away.*) He's bleeding ga-ga.

SWEET. You're never walking through the streets like that?

KEN. My girl's brought the bike.

SWEET. Oh, really? Must be school holidays then.

KEN. No, she ought to be in school but she took the morning off to get me. I'll be taking her straight home. See my animals have been looked after, then get round to her. Tarrah, mate.

FOSTER. Bye and keep out of trouble. You're old enough to have consideration for other people. I've been out sometimes in my minibus, suddenly there's several of you jokers in formation coming towards me on my side of the road.

KEN *starts laughing*.

I've got the kids in the back more often than not and I daren't swerve for fear of hurting them. Can't pull up, there's a car behind.

KEN. That's quite a giggle but I've never gone into no one doing that. My last pile-up I was dodging a dog. I've never killed an animal. Never would. I'm animal-minded.

ASH. Hitler liked animals.

KEN. Who?

ASH. Hitler. *He* was opposed to blood sports.

KEN. Who's he when he's at home?

ASH. Never heard of Hitler?

FOSTER. German dictator during the last war. He –

KEN. Oh, yeah, Belsen and that. I read about it. Must have been a giggle in there.

ASH. A what?

KEN. All them naked women. I read about it.

SWEET. Goodbye, Kenneth. I expect we shall see you here again.

KEN. Not if I can help it.

SWEET. Twice so far.

KEN. No more.

SWEET. We'll keep your bed warm. If you've no objection.

KEN. All depends how.

He approaches her. She retreats but he catches her by Bed 3.

SWEET. Now then –

Pushes her back on to it and lies on top of her.

– that's enough . . . stop it!

KEN is laughing.

FOSTER. You'll get her into trouble.

ASH. You've no respect at all.

KEN. Hear that? Get you into trouble?

SWEET. Leave me alone.

ASH. That was Mister Lucas's bed.

LOACH. It's *my* bed. I ain't even laid in it yet.

KEN releases SWEET.

KEN. You got my address? It's on my card. Pop round some time, have a cup of tea. Only my gran in during the day and she's stone deaf. (*He addresses the ward in general.*) Bye-bye, all! Get well soon!

Goes down front stairs as a feeble reply is given. SWEET adjusts her uniform and smoothes LOACH's bed.

FOSTER. You all right, Nurse?

SWEET. Thank you.

ASH. That's good riddance to bad rubbish.

REES (*waving his hand*). Goodbye to you!

ASH. He's gone long ago, Doctor.

LOACH. My bed, that is, haven't even laid in it.

SWEET. Aren't you meant to be in the bath?

LOACH. Eh?

SWEET. You're supposed to be in the bath.

LOACH. I'm getting a towel, me old mate.

SWEET. Hurry up then.

She goes off.

LOACH. Nobody tells me what to do. Which way's the bath?

FOSTER *points.* LOACH *goes off right.* ASH *works on his basket.* FOSTER *stretches his arms.* MACKIE *groans with pain. Pause.*

FOSTER. What's his trouble? The new man?

ASH. He didn't say. Looks a bit poverty stricken. No pyjamas or slippers of his own. His clothes very seedy. I used to tell my boys, a decent voice and a tailor-made suit will always put you a cut above the scum.

OLD WOMAN *comes back from left.*

OLD WOMAN. Good morning, have you heard the news?

ASH. Jesus died to give us life.

OLD WOMAN. There is no death.

ASH. I know.

OLD WOMAN. It's wonderful news.

ASH. It certainly is.

She gives him a text.

OLD WOMAN. God bless you.

ASH. Amen.

She goes off, down the front stairs.

FOSTER. They ought to stop her coming round.

ASH. I don't know.

FOSTER. People don't want religion when they're not feeling up to the mark. Very nice in its proper place but you don't want it rammed down your throat, do you?

ASH. I *am* religious, as a matter of fact.

FOSTER. I've got a great respect for other people's beliefs as long as it goes no further.

ASH. I believe in reincarnation.

FOSTER. There you are then.

FOSTER puts on the earphones to avoid further conversation. ASH would go on but sees there is no point.

Scene Three

BARNET *enters, pushing a wheelchair in a wide arc across the ward, arriving downstage facing the audience. As he goes, he is talking to the patients.*

BARNET. Come along, ladies, come along. Knickers on and stand by your beds. Those that can't stand, lie to attention.

Feeble laughs and cheers from the patients. Though BARNET's patter is addressed to the audience, the patients react.

SWEET comes from right with a china feeder and gives FLAGG a drink of water.

No, it's wicked to laugh. I said to this old man in the next ward, I said, 'Dad, you better watch your step,' he said,

'Why?' I said, 'They're bringing in a case of syphilis.' He said, 'Well, it'll make a change from Lucozade.'

Laughter and applause from patients.

SWEET. I didn't hear that remark.

BARNET. Whoops, sorry, Nurse, I never saw you come on.

He ogles the audience and goes upstage with the chair.

SWEET. Is that a lovely drink, Mister Flagg?

BARNET. Come on, Doctor, hands off, give it a rest, you'll be going blind. (*He winks at* FOSTER.)

REES. Shocking sight. A man being fed like a baby, through a spout. I can drink my tea and eat my dinner.

BARNET. Course you can.

REES. Mister Barnet, be a good fellow —

BARNET. What?

REES. — tell them to get a move on with my shoes and socks, where can I go without them?

BARNET. They've got to wait though.

REES. What for?

BARNET. Till your wife's been in.

REES. She *has* been in.

BARNET. No.

REES. Hasn't she?

BARNET. We haven't long had dinner, have we?

REES. Haven't we?

Pause. REES *thinks.*

BARNET. What d'you say to a spot of air, then? On the verandah. She might be in by then.

SWEET. There's a clever boy.

Puts feeder on locker as FLAGG *lies back.*

BARNET. And when she comes, no funny business!

REES (*smiling*). What d'you mean?

BARNET. Pulling her into bed.

REES *laughs.* FOSTER *too.*

No, well, it's not very nice. Front of all the visitors.

SWEET (*coming to help*). Don't make him laugh too much, he hasn't got a bottle.

REES. I don't want a bottle, I'm not a baby.

BARNET. You're a dirty old man.

SWEET *throws back covers.*

SWEET. Roly-poly on your bot-bot.

They swing his legs to the floor and lift him.

BARNET. Shall we dance?

SWEET. Ups-a-daisy!

BARNET. Shan't we put him in the chair?

SWEET. He needs exercise.

They begin to walk him, his arms around their necks, supporting his weight as he tries to find the use of his legs.

BARNET. Might make him a touch less lively when his wife comes in.

SWEET. There's a clever boy.

FOSTER. Go it, Doctor!

Cheers from patients.

BARNET. Which is why they invented rugby. Keep their minds off it.

SWEET. Off what?

REES manages a few steps, then they drag him a few. He is laughing.

BARNET. What we got to keep your mind off, Doctor?

REES. I used to be a scrum-half. I could run like a rabbit.

BARNET. Not only run.

Whispers in REES's ear. REES laughs, stops them walking. BARNET grins.

SWEET. Look out, he's doing it!

She points at REES's trousers.

BARNET. Jesus God!

SWEET. I'll get the chair, you hold him.

Goes for it. They are furthest away from the bed.

BARNET. Why didn't you have a bottle when she asked you?

REES makes frightened sounds, begins to struggle.

Don't be a soppy old madam now. You'll fall.

But the struggle grows more desperate. ASH comes to help.

ASH. Now, Doctor –

REES swings his arm and catches ASH across the head. ASH falls to the ground with a cry. SWEET brings the chair and BARNET drops REES into it.

SWEET. Naughty boy! Are you all right?

ASH. He caught me across the ear.

SWEET (*helping him up*). Have a rest.

BARNET. I'll get her a fresh pair of knickers.

Goes off, right. ASH goes to an armchair. SWEET wheels REES back to his bed.

SWEET. Whatever am I going to do with this great big naughty boy?

FOSTER. You all right, Mister Ash?

ASH. Yes, yes. Took my breath away for a second.

MACKIE. Why are you keeping him alive? Like a baby?

SWEET (*packing* REES *into bed*). Now, now –

MACKIE. You know he'll never walk again –

SWEET. Mister Mackie, save it for a more suitable occasion.

MACKIE. We know, his wife knows –

BARNET *returns, gives pyjamas to* REES. FOSTER *begins singing Gaumont-British theme.*

But no, you keep the farce going –

He gives up, coughing.

SWEET. Tuck up nice and warm and think of something nice.

BARNET (*to* AUDIENCE). Why don't you *all* think of something nice?

SWEET *finally goes off right.*

Scene Four

Lights dim upstage.

Music begins and patients look up expectantly from their positions. All those who are well enough watch the ensuing scene. Bright lights on a downstage area as a divan and screen rise into view. CLEO NORTON *lies on the divan wearing a shortie nightdress.* BARNET *has crossed down left and reads aloud from a paperback novel.*

BARNET. Her bedside alarm gave raucous tongue and Staff Nurse Cleo Norton awoke mid-afternoon suddenly, bewilderingly, and some moments passed before she could realise she was in her room at the nurses' residential hostel.

STAFF *wakes in the bed and mimes to the narrative.*

Her tousled hair and the rumpled sheets were evidence enough of a fitful sleep. If evidence she needed! She flounced over in bed, flung back the sheets petulantly and swung her lithe coffee-coloured legs round till her feet touched the pretty coconut mat she brought from Jamaica all those years ago. Stretching langorously, she reached for her housecoat and wrapped it demurely around her trim figure.

She goes to a window and draws back curtains.

Outside, the same breeze was still sending newly-laundered white clouds scudding across the blue, like members of a *corps de ballet* obeying the behest of some unseen choreographer. Suddenly nauseated, she flung herself on the bed.

STAFF. What's the matter with you anyway, Cleo Norton?

BARNET. – she demanded of herself, half angrily. But the mad ecstatic leap of her heart had already told her.

STAFF. Neil!

BARNET. In the submarine strangeness of the night ward, young Doctor Neil Boyd's fingers had fleetingly touched hers. And his usually stern features had crumpled into a yearning smile. Their eyes had met and ricocheted away.

STAFF. This won't do.

BARNET. – she chastised herself ruefully.

Roughly she makes the bed, etc.

STAFF. Here you are, a woman of twenty-six, behaving like some love-sick teenager with a television idol.

BARNET. – she opined diagnostically.

STAFF. And yet –

BARNET. And yet –

STAFF *shrugs and goes off behind the screen. Music swells. In the ward,* TYLER *comes from left to right in his chair.*

TYLER. Charwallah ready?

ASH. Sssh!

TYLER *goes off right.*

SWEET *and* LAKE *come up the front steps wearing outdoor cloaks over their uniforms.*

SWEET. I keep saying ruefully to myself: this climb should get my weight down, but it doesn't! Ssssh! Cleo may be still in the Land of Nod. No, she's up. Sit down, Beth.

LAKE *sits on bed.*

I'll put on a kettle when she comes in. I feel so honoured you finally managed to come to tea. You're certainly hard to get, Beth Lake –

LAKE. Being a nurse and a married woman isn't any rest cure, believe me, Joyce Sweet.

SWEET. Just give me the chance.

LAKE. Don't be in a hurry, Joyce. You're young yet.

BARNET. Beth flashed her large, gleaming widely-spaced teeth.

SWEET. Guess I'm just the marrying kind, Beth. Listen, Beth.

LAKE. What is it, Joyce?

SWEET. Your husband drives a bus full of white passengers and you look after a ward full of white patients – Don't you ever get hopping mad, Beth?

LAKE. Mad? No, Joyce. Why?

SWEET. When you think of the way some white people treat coloured people, I wonder you're not tempted to turn off their saline solutions or something . . .

LAKE. Oh, no, those people shouldn't be hated. They should be pitied. And understood.

SWEET. And when you think that the Health Service would pack up tomorrow if you all went back where you came from. Crikey! I'm surprised you bother to stay, Beth, honestly!

STAFF *comes in, now wearing her uniform, or some of it.*

BARNET. Cleo Norton breezed back into the room, her pert figure now trimly encased in the crisp uniform. She grinned a sunny welcome.

STAFF. Hullo, Joyce, hullo, Beth.

BOTH. Hullo, Cleo.

STAFF. How was duty?

SWEET. Methinks you don't have to be mad to work here but it helps.

STAFF. Why, what on earth happened?

LAKE. A couple of appendicectomies, no progress for the spontaneous pneumothorax . . .

SWEET. Matron decided to come inspecting just as the Registrar was doing a lumbar puncture . . .

STAFF (*laughing*). Situation normal.

SWEET. And the inguinal hernia needed morphine and Sister said I could do it –

LAKE. Oh, yes, and I didn't tell you, when I went to her room soon after we'd admitted the diabetic, I found Sister with young Doctor Boyd and they were holding hands.

BARNET. Cleo Norton flushed and her hand flew to her mouth.

STAFF *steps back, her hand flying to her face.*

SWEET. Ooops!

LAKE. What on earth's the matter? What have I said?

BARNET. Cleo stared speechless at Beth Lake, SRN, and then – wordlessly – fled the room.

STAFF *bursts into tears and goes off.*

SWEET. That's torn it!

LAKE. But – what on earth – ?

BARNET. – queried Beth Lake, crinkling her endearing button of a nose.

SWEET. Not your fault, Beth. You weren't to know Cleo's sweet on young Doctor Boyd.

BARNET. It was Nurse Lake's turn to flush.

LAKE. Mrs Clever Boots –

BARNET. – she murmured at last –

LAKE. Mrs Open-your-mouth-and-put-your-big-foot-in-it.

SWEET. Never mind. You could have been wrong in what you saw.

LAKE. They *were* holding hands.

SWEET. Was there a sheepish grin on his lean, craggy features?

LAKE (*thinks, shakes her head*). A puzzled frown.

SWEET. Then there's hope yet.

LAKE. But listen, Joyce, isn't old Mister Boyd, the young doctor's bluff father, bitterly opposed to mixed marriages?

SWEET. Crikey, yes! He's a terrible diehard.

LAKE. But what a surgeon!

SWEET. And just a tick, Beth! Doesn't Sister McPhee hail from North of the Border?

LAKE. And wait a minute, Joyce, isn't Doctor Neil unusually respectful to his father?

SWEET. And hang on, Beth, isn't Mister Boyd an eligible widower?

LAKE. I wonder –

SWEET. You mean – ?

BARNET. They stared at each other wordlessly.

Music swells as front lights fade on this.

LAKE *and* SWEET *step out of the room and go up into the ward.* SWEET *goes off left and* LAKE *goes to* MACKIE's *bed.*

Scene Five

Warm light.

LOACH *comes from right. The patients all have thermometers in their mouths.* LAKE *gets* MACKIE's *chart.*

LAKE. Have you had your bowels open?

MACKIE. My dear woman –

ASH. You've been a long time with the doctors, friend.

LOACH *turns to him suspiciously but says nothing.*

I hope they've got you sorted out now.

LOACH. Suppose you haven't got such a thing as a cigarette?

ASH *looks at his watch.*

ASH. You're in luck, it's smoking time from two to five.

LAKE *take* MACKIE's *pulse and reads his temperature.*

She writes the result on his chart and afterwards goes to FLAGG.

LOACH. Ta. Half these doctors, they turn round and tell you not to smoke but half of them smoke more than what you or I do. Ta.

ASH. I hope they gave you some dinner.

LOACH. Yes. (*He smokes with a cupped hand, as though hiding the cigarette from view. He now edges towards the stove.*)

ASH. I had my usual boiled fish and semolina. Which frankly has about as much appeal to me as basket-making.

LOACH. What d'you mean by that? Basket-making?

ASH. Occupational therapy. I take it with a pinch of salt. However, it's helped to pass the time. I was horribly depressed when I came in here. Largely because I abhor my work. Clerical. I'm a clerk, if you please. Mechanical, futile, dreary to the nth degree. I say to my fellow-inmates in our prison-without-bars: this is mechanical drudgery. And when they tell me it's a living, I come back quick as a flash: man shall not live by bread alone.

LAKE *notes* FLAGG's *temperature and goes to* REES.

I see in the daily rag now where they've got a computer thingummyjig can perform a clerk's entire lifework in ten minutes. Highly gratifying. I've known better things, there's the jolly old rub.

Handling the young is my vocation. My first year at teachers' college was a benediction. I felt: I have come home, this is where I belong. Amongst people of my own kidney.

LAKE. Have you had your bowels open?

REES. What?

LAKE. Have you had your bowels open?

REES. Yes.

ASH. I've always been able to handle boys. Why did I leave it? You may well ask. A matter of preferment. Nepotism. Muggins here didn't give the secret handshake, never got tiddly in the right golf-club. I didn't have the bishop's ear. You scratch my back, I'll scratch yours. I wasn't smarmy enough by half.

LAKE *brings* LOACH's *thermometer*.

LAKE (*to* LOACH). Under your tongue. And that patient, not so much talking, while I take your temperature.

ASH. Hunkey dorey, Nurse.

Puts thermometer in mouth. LAKE *goes to* REES, *reads his temperature and notes it on his chart. Then she goes to* FOSTER.

ASH *moves to his locker and rummages.* LOACH *takes out thermometer and drags on his cigarette.*

FOSTER (*reading*). Ninety-eight point two, Nurse.

LAKE *takes it from him, reads it and notes on his chart.* SWEET *removes* FLAGG's *drip, takes it off right.*

LAKE. Ninety-eight point two.

ASH *returns with books and a photograph.*

ASH. I never lost my interest in boys. Not even through ten years of pen-pushing. That's Gordon. (*Shows* LOACH *the photograph.*)

LAKE. Have you had your bowels open?

FOSTER. Twice.

ASH. He's my own boy.

LOACH. Got no clothes on, has he? Not by the look of it.

ASH. Swimming trunks.

LOACH. Flesh coloured.

ASH. That was taken at this private boarding school I put him to. Super duper place in its own grounds, down in Kent.

SWEET *comes back. Tidying, moving to the stove.*

You've met my boy, Nurse?

SWEET. Very nicely spoken boy.

ASH. They take trouble with elocution. Good speech is half the battle, *carte blanche* to the inner circle.

LOACH. Inner circle?

ASH. Where the good jobs are, where decisions are made. Once you can break into that, you never look back. My trouble was

I never broke into the inner circle. (*Looks at photo.*) He doesn't live with me any more. Old enough to take care of himself. I'm expecting him in for a visit one of these days but it's a long way to come. . . . I accept that. . . . If you're interested in reading matter, these might while away an hour or two. School magazines.

LOACH. Not much of a reader, know what I mean?

ASH. Time drags, in here.

LOACH. They can't keep you in here. If you don't want to stay. I shall turn round and tell them, if they start that with me.

SWEET. Better now?

ASH. Easy, friend, hold your horses. Nobody said they can.

LOACH. Once they've found out . . .

ASH. They'll fix you up, don't worry.

LOACH. Once they find out who I am. Once they can tell me that, I'll be out of here like a . . . what d'you call it . . . ?

ASH. Who you are?

LOACH. Once the police get on to that.

ASH. Who you *are*?

LOACH. Not that I want the police sticking their noses into my business. I didn't *ask* them, know what I mean?

SWEET *eases* MACKIE.

MACKIE. Oh, hell! This is hell.

LOACH. But soon as they put me straight on that, I'm off. They try to get me to take the cure, they got another think coming . . .

LAKE (*coming to them*). Too much talking, this patient.

ASH. Naughty boy, hold out your hand.

LAKE. Put that in your mouth.

LOACH *throws his dog-end into the stove and puts the thermometer in his mouth. LAKE gets ASH's chart.*

ASH. Nurse, are you going to move me along into Kenneth's place? One nearer the balcony?

SWEET. Time you had a rest, new patient.

LAKE (*to* ASH). Do you *want* to move along?

LOACH. Where's that, me old mate?

SWEET. Into bed, come on.

ASH (*to* LAKE). I'm on the mend, I deserve a move. One nearer the balcony is one nearer the outside world. Not that the outside world is anything to write home about.

SWEET. Still talking, Mister Ash?

ASH. *My* outside world, at any rate.

SWEET. Sit by your bed, stop talking and give the thermometer a chance.

LOACH *has gone to his bed. ASH now goes to his. SWEET tidies the armchairs.*

ASH. No peace for the wicked.

SWEET. Stop talking, I said.

LAKE. Have your bowels been opened?

ASH *holds up one finger. She writes it on his chart. ASH sits by his bed, LOACH gets into his.*

LAKE *writes down ASH's and LOACH's temperatures. In due course, the nurses go off left.*

Scene Six

Music.

BOYD *comes on as the lights come up downstage. He is smoking or cleaning a pipe. Perhaps wearing a pullover. NEIL comes to him, wearing a suit.*

NEIL. You wanted to see me, Father?

BOYD. Och, there you are, Neil. Come in, come in.

BOYD's *Scots accent is heavier in this scene.*

NEIL. If it's about the informality of my ward-rounds, you can save your breath to cool your porridge. I believe I am the patients' servant, not the other way round. I'm not going to have a lot of ceremony –

BOYD. Now, now, dinna fash yesel. It's noo that. We agree to differ on the question of how to treat our fellows.

NEIL. Aye. You, the firm believer, seem to regard the weak and inform as inferiors. I, the sceptic, behave to them as to my equals.

BOYD. Happily, the Almighty, in His infinite wisdom, has not denied us the use of our common sense. We have as our practice the world as it is, not as it might be. Which has a bearing on the matter in hand. Urmph! In Paradise, it would not be frowned on for white folk and black to mingle.

NEIL. Now just a tick –

BOYD. However, as you know, we are not in Paradise. We are in North London. You are a house physician in a large teaching hospital and Nurse Norton is a junior member of the staff. The poor wee girl can only be hurt by all this. Sister McPhee can only be hurt by it.

NEIL. Sister McPhee – ?

BOYD. I know ye'll come back to her in the end –

NEIL. Come back to her – ?

BOYD. But you're noo in any position to play fast and loose –

NEIL. Fast and loose?

BOYD. And wee Mary McPhee used to take you to school with your wee satchel on your shoulder –

NEIL. Satchel on my shoulder?

BOYD. She was your chielhood sweetheart.

Pause.

NEIL. Aye, Father, she was my chielhood sweetheart. But I'm no a chiel the noo. I'm a man. I've told Mary how I feel about Cleo – I want to marry her –

BOYD. Urmph? You trying to prove something, son?

NEIL. Prove something?

BOYD. A gesture, is it?

NEIL. Gesture?

BOYD. You can't hurt me. I'm here to fight. But you can hurt your mother.

NEIL. Mother's dead.

BOYD. Aye, she's dead. And almost her last wish was that you two should marry, that Mary should be one of the family. And now ye say ye're taking a wee coloured girl to wife and . . . Mary is to be left on the shelf. At thirty. Have you thought of that, son? While you're so busy with your noble sentiments? Have you given a wee thought to puir bonnie Mary at the age of thirty? Have ye?

Music.

Scene Seven

The opening blue light.

All the patients sleeping or trying to.

A steady groundbass of snores.

After a while, ASH stirs.

ASH. That boy – I warn you . . .

Incoherent speech follows.

Silence again.

After some time, one of the sleepers farts very violently, then groans with relief.

Silence.

After another pause, REES *sits up.*

REES (*shouts*). I haven't got a change of clothing here!

Resentful groans.

Not even a clean pair of socks. They can't expect the taxi man to wait there till the cows come home . . . could at least send him a cup of tea.

FOSTER. Give us a rest, Doc.

ASH. There's a good chap.

REES. Who pays for the bloody tea, I'd like to know?

FOSTER *laughs.*

FOSTER. He's on about tea.

REES. Take him a cup, you damned old Scrooge. It's like gnat's piss anyway.

FOSTER. No taxi drivers this time of night.

STAFF *comes on from right.*

STAFF. Doctor, you've let me down again.

REES. You let me have my clothes, I'll show you the taxi.

STAFF (*settling him*). I'll make you a nice hot drink, will you promise faithfully to let us get a bit of shut-eye?

REES. Poisoned drinks! No, thank you very much. Nor your sleeping drugs and formaldehydes and paraldehydes –

FOSTER (*laughing*). Knows all about it.

REES. Trying to kill me off.

MACKIE. No such luck.

STAFF. Now be a good boy.

MACKIE. They're compelled by law to keep us going.

STAFF. Not tonight, Mister Mackie.

REES (*struggling*). What I want is sound legal advice! I want to know what my chances are if it comes to litigation!

TYLER (*off left*). Nurse, look here, quick!

Sounds of coughing and choking.

STAFF. Now, lie down, while I tuck you in . . .

VOICE. Nurse —

STAFF. Coming!

She goes quickly off left.

REES. Is there a legal gentleman here?

MACKIE. There's no taxi, you crackpot. Die with dignity, for Christ's sake.

FOSTER. Try to help the nurse while you're —

REES. Help! They're trying to kill me off.

FOSTER. No, listen, while we're in here, we must do as we're told —

REES. Never done that all my life —

FOSTER. I dare say, but even so —

REES. And I've had a good life.

FOSTER. Plenty more to come too.

TYLER (*off left*). Not if you don't belt up, there won't be.

FOSTER (*quietly*). Night, night, Doctor.

REES (*angrily*). Who was that?

FOSTER. Never mind.

Both settle.

Silence.

At last the fart and the groan of relief are heard again.

MACKIE. Born in pig-sties, some of these people.

STAFF NURSE crosses from left to right and off. FLAGG, Bed 5, climbs out and stands, leaning on the bed for support. He wears only a pyjama jacket and has a bandaged pelvis. He begins moving along, step by step.

REES. Get back, you, Mister —

REES throws back covers and stands. FLAGG is at the bed's end. REES takes a step towards him, cries out and falls. Lies there cursing. FOSTER climbs out and goes to REES. Various bed lights are going on.

FOSTER. Mister Ash!

ASH wakes, sees, gets out.

ASH. Now, now, Mister Flagg, where d'you think you're off to? Half-past twelve, there's nowhere open.

Tries to persuade FLAGG back to bed. FOSTER struggles with REES.

FOSTER. You all right, Doctor?

REES. How's the *old* fellow?

ASH gets FLAGG back to bed, pulls up the bars to enclose him.

FOSTER. He's fine.

ASH (*turning to REES*). Whoops-a-daisy!

And they lift him into bed.

You shouldn't be doing this.

FOSTER. I'm all right.

REES. I was afraid he'd start to tear his bandage off . . . he ripped the skin he'd know all about it.

ASH. That's a good chap.

REES. If he'd opened the scar . . .

FOSTER. You all right now, Doc?

REES (*to* ASH). You one of the nursing staff? No.

ASH. No. Ash. Tummy ulcer.

REES. Nothing to worry about. You'll soon be out. Unlike poor old Flagg there and – you, sir, what's your name?

FOSTER. Foster.

REES. Yes. They won't be with us long, I'm afraid.

ASH. Baloney, Doctor, so much baloney. Back to bed, Desmond, I can manage.

FOSTER *returns to bed.*

REES. Flagg's had chronic urethritis. Makes your dicky sore. And this gentleman – where's he gone – ?

ASH. Snuggle down, now, leave it to the doctors.

REES. I *am* a doctor.

ASH. I know, yes.

REES *begins sobbing.*

REES. See the way I fell down? I didn't think . . . went to walk and . . . in my youth I ran like a rabbit . . . I was Area High Jump Champion. (*Cries again.*)

ASH. There, there . . .

STAFF *returns, crossing quickly from right to left with a tray and hypodermic.*

STAFF. All right?

ASH. Thank you, Staff . . .

REES. I beg your pardon. We're a highly emotional people. Ask anyone.

MACKIE. Sentimental and sloppy, if you ask me.

ASH. We *didn't* ask you, Mister Mackie.

REES. Much obliged to you.

ASH. Sleep well. (*Settles him and prepares to go.*)

REES. Could I trouble you? A bottle?

ASH. A bottle.

REES. I want to wee-wee.

ASH. I'll get you one.

> *Goes off right. Lights go out. Everyone settles. STAFF returns from left. ASH, returning, meets her.*

STAFF. Where have you been, Mister Ash?

ASH. Getting this for the Doctor.

STAFF. Thank you. Go back to bed now.

> ASH *goes to his bed.* STAFF *goes to* REES *with the bottle.*

FOSTER. This new fellow wasn't exactly helpful.

ASH. Heavy sleeper possibly.

FOSTER. His eyes were open, I saw them.

ASH. Oh, well . . .

FOSTER. He's awake now. He's laying there awake. Walking patient too. Didn't move a muscle. I hope he's listening to what I say.

STAFF. Sssh!

> *She puts the bottle into REES's bed. She turns to check FLAGG, then comes round to REES's bed, tucking him in.*

LOACH (*quietly*). Tell you what, me old mate –

STAFF. Are you talking to me?

LOACH. – I'm feeling a bit dry. And chilly. You could let me have a drink.

STAFF. All right. Which would you like – ?

LOACH. Brandy –

STAFF. Ovaltine or Horlicks?

REES sits up, staring ahead.

LOACH. Can't seem to stomach it. Lays too heavy on the stomach sort of thing, you get my meaning? Drop of brandy.

REES sits back quickly.

STAFF. No. You go to sleep.

LOACH. I got the shakes a bit, see . . .

STAFF. Have a sleeping draught.

Pause. She bends over REES and examines him.

LOACH. Can't keep me in here –

STAFF. Sssh!

FOSTER. Belt up.

She leans further over REES.

Drums and music.

Downstage BARNET comes on in a travelling spot, pushing a trolley covered with a white cloth.

Front-cloth business with the spot, losing and finding it.

BARNET (*to* SPOTMAN). You'll get your cards tomorrow. (*Then to* AUDIENCE.) No, but seriously. Sometimes the first call you get when you come on duty is: bring your trolley. I like to see my apparatus laid out like a tea-service, every instrument in its place. With a nice white cloth. It really brings me on to see that . . . you know? (*Gooses himself.*) Here! (*Slaps his own hand.*) Lady there knows what I mean. No, but look – (*Whips off cloth, shows articles as he names.*) Wash bowl, sponges, nail brush and file. Safety razor, scissors, tweezers. Cotton-wool, carbolic soap. Shroud.

Covers it again. STAFF *has gone off.*

Covered with a sheet, 'case one of the other patients catching a butcher's thinks it's all for him. So anyway I get the call. Ward such-and-such, bed so-and-so. Screens already up, of course.

NURSES *have been putting screens round* REES's *bed.*

First you strip the patient down, then you wash him spotless with carbolic. Cut the nails -- they can scag the shroud. Shave the face and trim the head. Comb what's left. Well, relatives don't want to find themselves mourning a scruff. Now the cotton-wool. Can anyone tell me what I do with that? (*Reacts to same* WOMAN *in audience.*) You're right, madam, absolutely right. Been making that answer all your life and for the first time it's accurate, not just vulgar. Yes. We have to close the apertures, the points that might evacuate bodily fluids. Miss one out, they'll raise Cain in the mortuary. Lug-holes, cake-holes, nose-holes, any other holes, all right madam thank you very much indeed! (*More ogling the* WOMAN.) What next? Tie the how's-your-father with a reef-knot. Seriously. You reckon I'm in jest? You'll all be getting it sooner or later. Yes, missis, even you, in a manner of speaking. (*Moves and looks at screens.*) Thank you very much, miss.

An ORIENTAL NURSE *comes on, takes the trolley.* BARNET *pats her rump as she passes. She gives shocked magician's-assistant smile to* AUDIENCE, *goes off.* BARNET *has gone to other side to meet, rolling on, another vehicle, like a stretcher but with a hooped hood.*

(*Sings.*) Roll along, covered wagon, roll along. No, listen! I must say this in all seriousness. Everything within reason is done to spare you the sight of an actual cadaver. This hooped cover, the screens.

NURSES *cover the exit from* REES's *bed with screens.*

A screened passageway is put up all the way to the door, as with royalty going to the toilet. You've heard about that, haven't you? If the monarch is unusually tall, attentive observers can spot the coronet bobbing up and down all the way to the velvet convenience.

Pushes hooped trolley upstage. NURSE *catches it and takes it behind screens.*

No, I don't wish to give the wrong impression. I'm sure I speak for my colleagues throughout the business when I say that we show every conceivable respect the deceased is due. We may hate the sight of them when they're living but once they've passed on, they get the full going-over. And I don't know about you, but I find that thought consoling. Whatever kind of shit is thrown at us during our long and dusty travail, we can at least feel confident that, after our final innings, as we make our way to that great pavilion in the sky – no, come on – we shall be a credit to Britain's barbers, the National Health and – last but by no means least – our mothers. Thank you very much indeed.

Exit to music.

NURSES *have removed screens, leaving* REES's *space vacant, the bed gone.*

Blackout.

Scene Eight

Daylight. Everyone in bed.

TYLER (*offstage. Sings*). We'll find a perfect peace
 Where joys will never cease

 Crosses left to right in his chair.

 And let the rest of the world go by.

 A few PATIENTS *cheer.* TYLER *goes off.*

ASH. Keeps marvellously cheerful.

LOACH. Go on.

SWEET comes in from right with letters.

SWEET. Second post. One for you, Mister Ash.

ASH. Thank you. My son Gordon, perhaps to say he's coming in to see me.

SWEET. And the last for Mister Flagg. I don't know, nothing for me again. You'd think some nice young man would send me his love.

FOSTER. Will I do, Nurse?

SWEET. Mister Foster, really! A married man. Look, Mister Flagg, a postcard. Shall I read it to you? 'I'm covered in confusion' – and there's a funny man with no clothes on, all red because he's blushing.
'I'm covered in confusion
I'm a crazy goon
I forgot to tell you
To Get Well Soon –
Daddy-oh!'
Isn't that good? Who's it from, I wonder? Looks as though they forgot to sign it. Still. You hold it like this . . .

Leaves the card in his hand, retains one letter.

FOSTER. He coming in, then?

ASH. I didn't expect it really. They're having a barbecue at the school. He's got to be there, I accept that.

FOSTER. Yes.

LAKE comes on from left.

ASH. I shouldn't want him to miss it.

LAKE. That letter for me?

SWEET. Doctor Rees.

ASH. Nurse, I'd like to be moved into Kenneth's place.

SWEET. Mister Boyd's coming round now.

LOACH. Been coming for half an hour, me old mate.

ASH. Then afterwards.

LAKE. You ask Sister.

Loud burst of laughter and BOYD *comes on in a dark suit, escorted by* DR BIRD, SISTER McPHEE *and an* INDIAN MALE STUDENT.

BOYD. Good morning, Mister. How are your waterworks – on the mend? (*Bends ear close to* FLAGG.) No good. Can't hear you. What you in a cage for?

SISTER. Tried to get out, Mister Boyd.

BOYD. Tried to get out too soon, Mister. You might have dropped a clanger.

Laughter from the INDIAN STUDENT.

All right. How's this embroidery? (*Examines* FLAGG.) Not bad at all. Feel like getting up today? Have to carry this bottle with you, all right? Well done.

Walks downstage with his party trying to keep up. SWEET *moves in and tidies* FLAGG.

BOYD. Mister's had enlargement of the prostate, you remember, with hesitancy of micturition, haematuria and acute retention. I did a retro-pubic prostatectomy and Mister's got a self-retaining catheter in his bladder. Why, Mister?

INDIAN STUDENT *racks his brains, vainly.*

Miss Bird?

BIRD. So the nursing staff can check the amount of bleeding and obviate the danger of –

BOYD. And why do I want him on his feet so soon? Hurry up, because the post-operative problems are pneumonia and deep-vein thrombosis –

BIRD (*to* INDIAN STUDENT). – leading to pulmonary embolus –

BOYD. – and he's enough to cope with as it is. The commonest cause of urethritis we should not consider at Mister's age. What's that, anyone?

INDIAN STUDENT *racks brains. DR BIRD's head nods forward.*

Wake up, wake up –

BIRD *brought to her senses, drops papers which* SISTER *and* INDIAN STUDENT *pick up.*

A dose of clap! Then we might get stricture, retention, bladder hypertrophy, the whole caboodle. A warning to us all.

INDIAN STUDENT *laughs again.*

Not funny. Still, as I say, Mister's a bit past it. Mister Who, Sister?

SISTER. Flagg.

BOYD. Well, Mister Flagg's left that particular problem behind him.

INDIAN STUDENT. Mister Flagg's only at half-mast, eh, sir?

No laughter.

BOYD. Are you disrespectful to the patients, Mister?

INDIAN STUDENT. No, sir.

BOYD. I hope not. Any questions? (*Doesn't wait for any but goes to between Beds 3 and 4.*) Where's Doctor Whatsisname?

SISTER. Last night, sir.

Whispers. He nods, turns at once to LOACH. *Consults papers.*

BOYD. Morning. They've found out who you are then.

LOACH. Yessir. Mister Loach.

BOYD. *Mister* Loach. We'll have to watch that.

Goes downstage again. They follow.

Mister's got brewer's measles.

BIRD. I thought he had a history of alcoholism, sir.

BOYD. Exactly, Doctor. Chronic gastritis, possibly cirrhosis. Came in complaining of severe cramps and loss of memory. The memory part's being looked at by the coppers but what do you make of the cramps?

INDIAN STUDENT. Polyneuritis, sir.

BOYD. Hooray! Touch of foot-drop we might expect, paraesthesia, formication – with an emm for anyone about to laugh. Creepy crawlies.

Goes to LOACH. *They all follow but* BIRD *who stands dozing with her eyes shut.* SISTER *goes back and nudges her. They join* BOYD *at the bed.*

What's your poison, Mister?

LOACH. Brandy.

BOYD. Get cramps do you?

LOACH. Funny thing you should mention that. I do get these what-I-call cramps like, in my leg.

BOYD. Have any trouble getting your foot off the ground?

LOACH. That's funny you asking that. I've said to the wife I don't know how many times: I can't seem to get my foot off the ground –

BOYD. Subject to wind?

LOACH. Like anyone, sir. Repeating.

BOYD. Open your mouth.

LOACH. Fouling the air.

BOYD. Open your mouth, I said.

He looks in, whistles in amazement. INDIAN STUDENT
laughs.

BOYD. You come to theatre tomorrow, I'll have a look at you.

LOACH. Tell you what, sir, I'll be all right now I know where I
stand —

But BOYD *has moved away already. The others follow as
quickly as they can.*

BOYD. Persuading him to take the cure, Doctor Bird?

She is the last to get there, having nearly dozed off again.

BIRD. Yes, sir.

BOYD. The houseman wants an oesophagoscopy?

BIRD. We ought to know what his insides are like.

BOYD. An illicit still, I should think. All right, what's an
oesophagoscopy, Mister?

INDIAN STUDENT. Um — let me see now —

Thinks. Long pause. BIRD'*s papers drop from her hands.*
INDIAN STUDENT *helps her pick them up.*

BOYD. Never mind that.

INDIAN STUDENT. I had it on the tip of my tongue.

BOYD. Funny place for it. Usually down the throat.

INDIAN STUDENT. Of course.

BOYD. A tube down the oesophagus, taking care not to knock
his teeth out.

BOYD *goes to between Beds 1 and 2.* SISTER *has helped*
BIRD *pick up papers again. Now she helps her stand.*

SISTER. You all right?

BIRD. Long as I stay on my feet. I've been on duty for twenty-
nine hours.

BOYD (*to* FOSTER). You one of mine, sir?

FOSTER. No, sir.

BOYD. Right, sir. (*To* ASH.) 'Morning, Mister, had enough milk pudding?

ASH. The mere sight of semolina makes me heave, Mister Boyd. Don't ask me why.

BOYD. Lovely grub. (*Scans* ASH's *X-rays.*) How are you in yourself?

ASH. Not so dusty, sir, but then I never feel what-you-call on top of the world. My doctor wrote down all my symptoms, then he said 'By George, you're a mess on paper'.

BOYD. Worry about yourself?

ASH. I get depressed. I abhor my work.

BOYD. Find a hobby. (*Uncovers* ASH *and presses on his stomach.*) Take some interest. Brass-rubbing. (*Then brightly.*) Basket-making.

ASH cries out.

Tell you what, your tummy's not much better. I want you in theatre tomorrow, do a bit of crochet-work.

ASH. *Physically* I'm not too bad, sir.

BOYD. Take away a bit of your stomach. You'll learn to do without it.

ASH. I thought I was on the mend.

BOYD. Much the best.

Moves down, they follow.

Mister's duodenal's failed to respond to a medical regimen. So what shall we do? Come on, come on, scream and hide our faces?

BIRD. Polya gastrectomy?

BOYD. At last. Of course he's a case, you can see that. Talk a gramophone to scrap by the look of him. Next, Sister? (*Takes papers, glances at them, makes for the right, saying as he goes.*) Ah, morning, Mister. Bum any better?

And off, with SISTER *and* STUDENTS.

LOACH. You won't see me down no theatre. Soon as they bring me in my clothes, I'll be off. They can't keep me here against my will.

ASH. I thought I was on the mend.

FOSTER. He'll fix you up. You trust him.

ASH. Oh, he's a first-rate man, Mister Boyd. I'm taken aback, that's all —

LOACH. Is he a gen bloke, me old mate?

FOSTER. Harley Street.

LOACH. Go on —

FOSTER. We get the best here, don't you worry. All for the price of a stamp.

ASH. No moving towards the balcony now.

LOACH. You can discharge yourself.

FOSTER. What for?

LOACH. I always been independent.

FOSTER. You can hardly move.

LOACH. Half these doctors, they tell you not to smoke, half the time they smoke more than what you or I do. You look at Churchill.

FOSTER. Churchill wasn't a doctor.

LOACH. Never said he was.

TYLER *comes from left in chair.*

TYLER. Ready for the tea, Mister Ash?

ASH. Not today, friend. Got to rest. Major op. in the morning.

FOSTER. What's he got to do with it then?

TYLER *rolls off right.*

LOACH. Well, look at the way he smoked.

FOSTER. Yes, but he never told *you* not to smoke.

LOACH. No, but these doctors, *they* tell you not to smoke.

FOSTER. I never heard Mister Boyd tell you not to smoke.

LOACH. Just let him try, that's all, me old mate.

FOSTER. He smokes a pipe.

LOACH. Next thing he'll be telling me to jack in the spirits.

ASH. Three weeks of tapioca – down the drain.

LOACH. Not bloody Russia.

FOSTER. You two need cheering up, taking out of yourselves. Soon be TV time.

LOACH. Those blackies again, is it?

They settle to watch the play. Blue overhead light goes on for the night.

Scene Nine

Lights dim on the ward but go on downstage.

Music.

NEIL comes in with STAFF. He wears a suit and she a very revealing dress – low bodice and short skirt. Also far too expensive for a nurse. NEIL pulls up one of the armchairs from near the stove.

NEIL. Come in, sit down. We'll have a wee dram.

STAFF. Is your father at home?

NEIL. Och, no. He's in Edinburgh giving a lecture on transplant techniques.

She sits. He leans over her.

What will you have to drink?

BARNET. His breath smelled fresh like pine. Cleo Norton's heart gave a painful jerk as his steely blue eyes met hers with a twinkle.

STAFF. Vodka and lime.

NEIL *goes out of the light.*

BARNET. She inhaled the masculine fragrance of the room. So this was the holy of holies, the inner sanctum!

STAFF *stands again and walks about, looking at the room, objects, etc.*

This was where Neil and his father had lived in bachelor splendour since his mother's death all those years ago. Every tiny thing was so male – the pipes in their racks, row upon row, the reassuring smell of Alsatian, the walnut shelves full of veteran car models . . . vainly Cleo tried to still the excitement that was making her breasts rise and fall like those of some love-sick teenager with her television idol.

NEIL *comes back into the light, pushing a trolley with drinks. He gives her a glass of vodka.*

NEIL. You enjoyed the concert then?

STAFF. Wonderful.

Turns back for his own drink.

BARNET. Yes, just as she'd enjoyed the village cricket-match, the rag ball and the Son-et-Lumière. But this was the first time she'd been brought home afterwards.

NEIL. Well – cheers!

STAFF. Cheers!

They drink.

BARNET. Perhaps the first night his father'd been away! Was he *ashamed* of her then? Or ashamed of what he meant to *do* to her?

NEIL *smiles.*

STAFF. So this is where you live in bachelor splendour.

NEIL. We've a dear old soul looks after us. (*Turns, puts down his glass.*)

BARNET. She pleaded with his grey flannel back: don't be like all the others. She was discovering that to say a girl was a nurse simply meant she was what the doctor ordered!

NEIL. Sit down, Cleo.

BARNET. She had given him no reason to expect anything of that kind.

She sits, exposing a lot of leg and bosom. He drains his glass, thirstily.

NEIL. So many evenings I've wanted to bring you back here.

STAFF. Oh?

BARNET. Her eyes urgently raked his face. Then why haven't you? She implored wordlessly. Perhaps your father doesn't approve of your seducing nurses?

NEIL. Only my father –

STAFF. Yes?

NEIL. Doesn't approve.

STAFF. I see. But you do?

NEIL. I approve of you, aye. No doubt about that.

STAFF. And of bringing me home to seduce me, because I'm a nurse – and a coloured nurse at that –

BARNET. She flared.

NEIL. Steady now –

BARNET. But the flood-gates were open now.

STAFF. – easy to use and throw away on the trash heap. Well – (*Stands and moves to put glass on tray.*) I'm not trash, Doctor Boyd. Your experienced eye has let you down tonight.

NEIL. You canna be serious –

STAFF. You can't satisfy yourself with me, then go and hold hands with Sister McPhee –

NEIL. Sister McPhee?

He has held her but now lets go and winces, his hand going to his back as he groans with pain.

STAFF. What's the matter? Neil!

NEIL (*recovering*). Nothing. It's nothing. Who told you that about Sister McPhee?

STAFF. Oh, it's common gossip among the nurses, you and Sister McPhee –

NEIL. Cleo, my mother always loved Mary McPhee. Her family lived in the next cottage along the glen. Her dying wish was that Mary should become one of the family. (*Takes her in his arms.*)

BARNET. He drew her to him.

NEIL. What's more, my father believes only pain can come from trying to mix the races. He's no an evil man, you ken, but he doesna want to see you hurt. So I've been waiting –

STAFF. Neil!

NEIL. But I couldna wait any longer –

He embraces and kisses her.

STAFF. Neil –

BARNET. – She groaned, when his lips let her.

NEIL. I can't risk doing anything that would upset him. He's too valuable to society.

STAFF. And Sister McPhee – what about her?

NEIL. Mary's a friend of the family. That's all, as far as I'm concerned. But, Cleo, you and I – we're on the same wavelength –

STAFF. Honey –

BARNET. Hungrily his mouth sought hers –

STAFF. Wait. You better know. I won't be only a body to any man.

NEIL (*shocked*). No, Cleo, I'm in love with you.

STAFF. Maybe, Doctor Boyd, but you and I don't spell it the same way.

NEIL. Oh, we pronounce it a wee bit differently but we spell it the same.

STAFF. Don't try to be witty with me, Doctor. You spell it s-e-x.

NEIL. No!

STAFF. I'll never do anything dirty before marriage.

She turns her back and stands, legs apart, bosom heaving, hands on hips.

NEIL. It's not dirty. It's right and beautiful. How can I make you understand that?

From behind he kisses her neck and shoulders.

BARNET. She could smell the sweet, hot, peppermint cleanness of his breath.

NEIL. We've started something we're going to have to finish.

STAFF. Oooh . . .

BARNET. His lips trailed fire . . . a warm sweetness was
suffusing her thighs —

BOYD *has entered up the front stairs.*

BOYD. Good evening.

BARNET. They spun round.

NEIL (*turning*). Father!

*In his spin, he falls, winces, seizes his back. He suffers a
spectacular paroxysm.*

BOYD. What's wrong, son?

STAFF. Neil what is it?

NEIL (*gritting his teeth*). It's nothing . . . nothing, I tell you . . .

BARNET. They stared at each other — wordlessly.

Lights fade. Music. Black.

Scene Ten

The spot searches the stage and finally finds BARNET, *pushing
on his trolley.*

BARNET (*to* SPOTMAN). Better. (*Looks at trolley, whips off
cloth.*) A woman's work is never done. Look here – shaving
brush, some lathery soap, a mug of hot water, an old strop
and a cut-throat.

NURSES *are seen in the light spilt from the spot. They come
on and prepare* ASH *for operation, putting on a white smock,
etc.*

Not that it's going to get near many *throats* today. Quite the
reverse – all right, madam, we know you're always the first to
savvy smut. Nothing to be proud of. They'll laugh at
anything, some people. This has got to be done. Not to make
them beautiful, no, it's sanitation.

ASH *wheeled forward in bed so that he is between* BARNET *and* AUDIENCE. *As one of the* NURSES *passes* BARNET, *he gooses her with the shaving brush. She makes shocked face.*

Thank you, ladies. Now let's see – (*Lifts bedding to expose* ASH *to him.*) Lie on your right side. Now relax. I know it's difficult, you naturally tend to recoil from anything nasty – unlike some I could touch with a very short stick –

Glances at WOMAN *in* AUDIENCE. ASH *makes indistinct comments and sounds during this monologue.* BARNET *lathers brush and then* ASH's *stomach.*

Which is why I try to keep talking, take their minds off it. If it's a Jew, I might ask for the loan of a fiver and that so frightens him I get on better. Now the man who used to do this job – well, it wasn't so much a *job* to him, it was a labour of love! We used to issue tin trousers whenever he was on duty. No – hospital barber, very good at short-back-and-sides, but they took him off pre-operatives. They had to, after a patient complained he'd had his privates shaved when he was only going to have his tonsils out. (*Starts to strop the razor.*) Personally I thought it was a shame. I sympathise with the customer, yes, and Vernon never learnt to hide the pleasure it gave him. But. It's not a vocation many are drawn to and most of the healing arts are bent if you want my frank opinion. (*Begins shaving.*) Now don't flinch or you'll do yourself a mischief. I've no idea what your convictions are about this highly controversial issue. You were a teacher, that's the same country. A socially acceptable sublimation. Take this case described in a medical journal I bought one afternoon in Soho. This poor berk said to his psychiatrist, he said, Doctor, Doctor, I've got a problem; I find I only fancy thirteen-year-old boys. So the Doctor said, Well, everyone to his taste, it's tricky but not insuperable. And the patient said, yes but only thirteen-year-old boys with a wet chest cough. And, d'you know, it was enough for him to *hear* them cough. Now I'm going to ask you to hold your own, if you'd be so kind. Down out of the way, you've got the idea.

Goes to shave, reacts to AUDIENCE *with arch disapproval. Then shaves.*

Anyway, d'you know how they fixed him up? He's a voluntary health visitor to the children's ward of a large London chest hospital! Welfare work combined with harmless pleasure, the secret of a happy life. But because poor old Vernon overstepped the mark, he's probably up the West End every night exposing himself to all and sundry . . . I've no idea what your views are but I feel a useful person should not be made a scapegoat because of one misdemeanour . . . did I tickle? I sometimes think I should charge. Never mind. All over now and very comical you look, if you'll pardon my saying so.

Covers ASH *and turns him on his back. Another* ORDERLY *has come on, smoking a cigarette, reading a paper and pushing a stretcher trolley.*

Hullo there, Michael, top of the morning to ye.

MIKE *coughs in reply, continuing to smoke. They lift* ASH *from the bed on to the trolley.*

How about Minestrone in the two-thirty at Chepstow?

MIKE *coughs again, pausing to recover.* BARNET *makes long-suffering face at* AUDIENCE. *They carry* ASH *to the stairs on the left and begin the descent.* LAKE *has joined them with* ASH's *charts.* SWEET *and* SISTER *upstage have moved* FLAGG *along to replace Bed 4: put* ASH's *empty bed in Position 5. As* MIKE *and* BARNET *begin to go down,* ASH *is severely tilted and* MIKE *has another fit of coughing. They pause while he recovers.*

Look at it. The International Passport to Smoking Pleasure.

LAKE *takes the cigarette and stamps it out.*

LAKE. One day you'll drop somebody.

BARNET. Don't you say that, Nurse. He's worked for all the big construction firms, haven't you, Michael? Up the ladders.

MacAlpine . . . Wimpey . . . you know what Wimpey stands for? We Import Millions of Paddies Every Year . . .

They descend out of sight.

SWEET *and* SISTER *have been getting* FLAGG *out of bed. SWEET carries a drainage bottle attached to* FLAGG *by a tube. They walk him to the armchairs and settle him in one. SWEET stands the bottle beside him. During the scene that follows it slowly fills with urine.*

FOSTER. Good old Dad! That's the way!

SISTER. Isn't he a clever boy!

FLAGG *speaks to* SISTER *but she has to bend over him to hear.*

I don't know what the physiotherapist would say, I'm sure, but – Mister Foster, can you let him have a cigarette?

FOSTER. Certainly. Help yourself, Dad –

SWEET *gets them and gives one to* FLAGG.

SISTER. Light it for him.

SWEET *lights it, puts it in* FLAGG's *mouth. He manages to smoke it by concentrating hard.* FOSTER *and* LOACH *cheer.*

Clever's not the word.

LOACH. I could do with a smoke myself.

SWEET *returns cigarettes to* FOSTER. LOACH *touches her arm.*

I say, I could do with a smoke meself, me old mate.

SISTER. You're on your way to theatre, Mister Loach, and Nurse Sweet is not your old mate.

SWEET. Thank you, Mister Foster.

SISTER. Mister Foster, keep an eye on this sprightly lad. If there's any change in the colour of the fluid, call a nurse. Understand?

FOSTER. Sister.

SISTER. There's an ashtray. Come along, Nurse.

She and SWEET *go off left.* FOSTER *laughs.*

FOSTER. Talk about tore you off a strip.

LOACH. Right. That's her lot. I got her number. She's for it.

FOSTER *laughs again.*

FOSTER. Your face!

LOACH. They pick on a man when he's helpless. Shit-scared.

FOSTER. What you scared of?

LOACH. Theatre. I never asked to go to no theatre.

FOSTER. It's only an examination.

LOACH. *They* say. Once they get you on the table, how you going to stop them? Lady friend of mine, they give her the jab, when she woke up, d'you know what they'd bloody done to her?

FOSTER. What?

LOACH. Took a breast off.

FOSTER. She must have signed a form.

LOACH. They give you a form to sign, how d'you know what you're signing? I signed a form but they don't tell you all what's in it. All the small print. Can't read it, half the time.

FOSTER. Perhaps you should have glasses.

LOACH. They'd like to see me in glasses, some of them. And dentures.

FOSTER *laughs.*

That's all right, me old mate, you have a laugh on me. About all I got left to give you.

BARNET and MIKE have come up the other stairs with the empty stretcher. They put it on the trolley and wheel it to LOACH's bed as SWEET comes back.

BARNET. Bring out your dead! Bring out your dead!

LOACH. Here, Michael, got a drop of brandy on you, me old mate?

SWEET. That's enough of that, Mister Loach.

FOSTER laughs.

LOACH. He likes a laugh at me, old Kentish Town here.

SWEET. Ups-a-daisy.

They put him on the stretcher.

LOACH. Anything to do with operations, know what I mean, Nurse?

SWEET. You'll be getting a pre-med injection downstairs.

LOACH. What, a jab? Needle in my arm?

They put him on the stretcher and wheel him to the stairs. SWEET brings charts.

BARNET. Or your bum.

LOACH. Anything to do with needles . . .

SWEET. Try to relax now.

LOACH. Drop of ether . . . go down nicely . . .

They go out of sight, MIKE coughing.

Pause.

FLAGG smokes. FOSTER watches.

FOSTER. Alright, Dad? . . . Want any help?

MACKIE. He's barely conscious. Can't even hear you.

FOSTER. Doing well though. I never thought to see him up again. The will to live, it is. My dad's the same. Eighty-two

and game for anything. I say All right, Dad, Woburn Abbey!
Up he gets, puts his mac on, always first in the minibus. Rhine
Valley, the Riviera; Yugoslavia last year. Mother's dead so we
take care of him. He's less trouble than one of the kiddies.

SISTER *returns, takes* FLAGG's *cigarette and stubs it out.*
FLAGG *seems to be dozing. She checks the bottle.*

SISTER (*loud*). Having forty winks?

FLAGG *wakes. She goes off right.* FLAGG *settles again.*

FOSTER. During the season we go most Sundays, perhaps as far
as Beaulieu for the veteran cars or Longleat, Dad likes the
lions. Picnic in the car park or on the lawns, where there's an
eating enclosure. If it's wet, we most likely nip out to
Hampton Court, have a laugh at the maze. I'm more
interested in the history side myself. I like to get by the guide
and pick his brains. Or sometimes the owner's doing a stint –
some duke or marquis – and I think to myself: your days are
numbered, old son. All these fallow deers and statues are
going to be taken over by the state – not before time either –
and you will have to buy your ticket with the rest of us. (*He
lights a cigarette.*) I find a special interest in the servants'
quarters. I say to the wife, you'd have been here, love, a
skivvy for life, and I'd have been one of an army of gardeners
scything the lawn from dawn to dusk. But these lords are only
holding on by our permission and when they've served their
purpose, they'll be out. Not that I've anything against them
personally but we're not living in the Dark Ages with Queen
Victoria sitting in state. This is the twentieth century, d'you
agree?

MACKIE. The armies of democracy on the move.

FOSTER. Pardon?

MACKIE. Columns of minibuses . . . moving up the motor-ways
. . . from Hampton Court to Woburn Abbey . . . Woburn
Abbey to Windermere –

FOSTER. Why should they have it all to theirselves?

MACKIE. – a world of lay-bys, drive-ins, pull-ups . . .

FOSTER. Better than when my Dad was a boy, never got his nose outside the street he –

MACKIE. You a Socialist?

FOSTER. I'm a Socialist, yes, I'll be quite frank with you.

MACKIE. Not a Communist?

FOSTER. No fear. I don't agree with extremes. Let the Communists try to come in here, I'll fight to keep them out.

MACKIE. Why?

FOSTER. Well, for a start, they've done away with religion, haven't they.

MACKIE. You religious?

FOSTER. Personally no. I only ever go in church to see the stained glass – but I don't reckon you should do away with anything just because you don't believe in it. That's the meaning of freedom, live and let live.

MACKIE. The early Socialists thought . . . if we achieved this, the rest would follow.

FOSTER. Achieved what?

MACKIE. This state we're in. This ward. Where men are prevented from death by poverty or curable sickness even the least intelligent . . . least healthy or useful . . .

FOSTER. You've got to do what you can for people –

MACKIE. Can't cure loneliness – boredom – ugliness . . . but at least you can see they're lonely on clean sheets . . . ugly on tapioca pudding . . .

FOSTER. Why can't you try to look on the bright side?

MACKIE. I'm dying of a stomach cancer and the pain's only bearable with pethedine and morphine. I've asked them to let me die . . . but because of their outdated moral assumptions they have to keep me going –

FOSTER. Isn't life precious, though?

MACKIE. *Good* life. Useful life. Good *death's* precious too, when the time comes. If you can get it. My heart's stopped once already, which used to be called death . . . now they bring you back . . . I've had it written in my records: don't bring me back again.

BARNET *and* MIKE *come from below carrying* ASH. LAKE *carries his drip and drain.* MIKE *is coughing. He has to pause.*

BARNET (*to* AUDIENCE). There's a requisition in for a lift.

LAKE. Has been for years.

BARNET. We'll never get it, unless we let somebody fall.

MIKE *recovers and they climb.*

They say there's been a bit of everything on this ground – a priory, a bowling green, a jail, Methodist chapel, workhouse. The present structure's a fever wing, put up to house the cholera victims. None of your modern rubbish, mind you. Built to last. It will too!

They reach the top and take ASH *to his new bed place in the corner.* LAKE *attends to his drip.* BARNET *speaks to the ward in general.*

Old Boyd has tasted blood this morning. Like a butcher's shop down there –

FOSTER *laughs.*

SISTER (*coming on and cutting* BARNET *off*). Thank you, Mister Barnet.

BARNET. Thank you, Sister. The surgeon looked at his list of operations: this lot now and after dinner four abortions. He said to me: It's Murder Mile. All morning we save the old, all afternoon we kill the young.

He and MIKE *go off downstairs with their empty stretcher.*
SISTER *checks* FLAGG's *bottle then helps* LAKE *with* ASH.

MACKIE. This fellow's returned to go. And Flagg's gone up one. They don't even bother to move me any more –

SISTER. Sing a different song, Mister Mackie.

MACKIE. At least you've shown you don't expect me to last much longer.

FOSTER. Good job we don't all talk like that, eh, Sister?

MACKIE. In lucid moments, I like to talk. My only remaining pleasure.

FOSTER. Not much pleasure for the rest of us, eh, Sister?

SISTER (*going to* MACKIE). Come on, cheer up, use your earphones.

MACKIE. Oh, good God! (*He almost laughs but it starts a cough. A short one.*)

SISTER. Wouldn't you like a chat with the Chaplain?

MACKIE. I parted company with organised religion some years ago . . . when I saw it was being used to justify the activities of cretins . . . Jesus Christ lived in a largely unpopulated world . . . disease and natural hazards killed off multitudes every year . . . kept the balance of nature . . . if He came back today, He wouldn't say, 'Thou shalt not kill', He'd advocate mass euthanasia . . .

SISTER. We can't estimate the value of a life.

MACKIE. Time we could. Not enough kidney machines, someone's going to have to . . .

SISTER. I'm not going to stand here listening to all this childish nonsense.

MACKIE. If somebody doesn't let us die – or prevent others being born – there are going to be seventy million British by the turn of the century –

SISTER. I shall get you a sedative.

She goes off. LAKE *deals with* ASH.

MACKIE. And thirty million cars . . . this sceptr'd isle with its rivers poisoned . . . beaches fouled with oil . . . the sea choked with excrement . . . the polluted air alive with supersonic bangs . . . that what you want? The Socialist Nirvana?

FOSTER. You're a whining Winnie, I know that.

MACKIE. But – abortion – euthanasıa – birth control won't be enough . . . some government will have to have the guts to stop people coming in . . . filling the country –

FOSTER. Nurse, Nurse! The bottle.

Points at FLAGG. LAKE *goes to look and finds some blood in the urine.* SISTER *comes back.*

MACKIE. Enforced emigration too . . . fill the empty spaces in Australia, Canada . . . manpower must be directed where it's needed . . .

SISTER. Better let him have a rest.

She and LAKE *help* FLAGG *back to bed.*

MACKIE. Break the power of the unions and make people do what they're told . . . close down the luxury trades, put a stop to gambling and vice . . . send the croupiers to work in penal colonies . . . get the striptease girls back to the farms . . .

BARNET *and* MICHAEL *bring* LOACH *up the front steps, with* SWEET *attending. Take him to Bed 3.*

BARNET. Can't hear yourself think down there for the squeak of rubber gloves.

MACKIE. Because, you see, it's not only a question of the natural resources of the land . . . there's a spiritual cancer too . . .

BARNET. Dear oh dear! She sowing discontent again?

MACKIE. A nation doesn't grow great on material greed
without a sense of duty . . . Churchill knew this, he got the
best from us, inspired us with purpose . . . National Service
turned boys into men . . . the world's finest youth club –

*Slowly lights go down on the rest of the ward and only
MACKIE remains lit. In the darkness, LOACH and FLAGG
are settled and BARNET, SISTER, SWEET, MICHAEL and
LAKE go off.*

– but now the Chatterley Set are destroying our moral fibre
with liberalism . . . fornication . . . paederasty, drug-taking
condoned by the Church . . . remember the fall of the Roman
Empire, as Mister Carson of Woolwich Holdings was saying
to me . . .

*LAKE comes on with a hypodermic. She cleans his arm. He
doesn't notice her.*

Mixed marriages advocated on television . . . which God
never intended . . . proved scientifically that some races are
genetically inferior . . . no good sullying sound stock with an
alien strain . . . jazz dancing and –

LAKE injects a sedative.

– factory farming . . . but first – let the old go . . . give us the
gas chambers and we will finish the job . . .

*LAKE has gone. A hand bell tinkles. SISTER comes on ringing
it and all available NURSES and ORDERLIES bring on vases
of flowers as the light grows to a warm summer evening.*

SISTER. Ready for visitors?

*And the VISITORS come, from up the front stairs and from
the right. Most of them go through the ward and out to the
left. TWO WOMEN sit at FLAGG and FOSTER's beds.
MACKIE sleeps. ASH and LOACH read, eat fruit, etc. LAKE
comes on with a trolley of tea and begins giving cups to those
patients who can drink. SISTER looks at the effect. It satisfies
her. She nods at the AUDIENCE and goes off right. It looks
like a flower show.*

ACT TWO

Scene One

A front cloth representing the end wall of the hospital. An open doorway cut in it allows us to see the ward behind. Four armchairs facing the AUDIENCE.

ASH is in one, working on his basket, LOACH *in another, reading* Daily Mirror. MACKIE *is propped up in an invalid chair. ASH has a white creamed face.*

Long wait, then LOACH *looks up.*

LOACH. Here – Cambridge.

ASH. Why d'you call me that?

LOACH. Eh?

ASH. Cambridge.

LOACH. Anyone that reads a lot I call Cambridge.

ASH. I see.

LOACH. What's that noise?

ASH. Didn't notice.

LOACH. Like a Siamese cat.

They listen.

There!

ASH. Oh! A baby.

LOACH. Go on.

ASH. In the premature unit.

LOACH. What, came too soon?

ASH. Yes.

LOACH. Babies over there . . . cemetery behind the car park . . . I don't know.

ASH. There's your National Health, friend. Look after you from the cradle to the grave.

LOACH. Marvellous, isn't it? Ah! Sod it!

ASH. Pardon?

LOACH. Got the cramps. I thought that surgeon was going to fix me up, get rid of these sodding cramps . . . then I come round – what's he done? Took a couple of teeth out. Who asked him?

ASH. Friend, they were rotting in your head.

LOACH. My business if they were. 'Twasn't a toothache I came here with. I came in here with my memory. Police brought me in. Found me wandering.

ASH. Well, you know who you are now.

LOACH. Edward Loach.

ASH. Know who your wife is?

LOACH (takes out snapshot, looks at it). Not looking forward much to her coming in.

ASH. She's frowning in the sunlight, that's all.

LOACH. She's always frowning, me old mate, wet or fine. I like a laugh and a joke, that's only human nature, isn't it? She's a good woman, I don't mean that. Keeps a good house. But always on at me to take the cure. *They* better not start . . .

ASH. You *should*. It's your only feasible course.

LOACH. I shall turn round and tell them what to do with it. Down the country, miles from civilisation. You wouldn't knob it!

ASH. But you must rest, in any case.

LOACH. Rest? Couple of mates of mine went in for it. They told me what a rest it is, thanks very much.

Rubs his leg, wincing.

Course, I *used* to drink for pleasure. I'm going back a few years now. Lately it's more like you might say medicine. Used to get *drunk* too. Used to be drunk days on end. I don't reckon there's nearly so much pleasure taken nowadays in getting drunk. Not like there was.

FLAGG *arrives, walking with two tridents, attended by* NURSE LAKE. *He no longer has a drain bottle.*

ASH. Here we are then –

LOACH. Hullo, Dad.

LAKE. What d'you think of him?

ASH. Like a two-year-old.

LAKE. Soon be bringing round the tea.

ASH. We'll take it round together. I had to drop that job for a few days.

FLAGG *is put into a chair.* LAKE *goes.*

LOACH. I was laughing then. I'm talking about Shanghai. Beach-combing I was in the International Settlement. You ever been Shanghai way?

ASH *shakes his head.*

China way? Hong Kong. Kowloon Ferry. Only cost you a ten-cent piece in the days I'm talking about. Ship Street? With all the girls hanging in cages? So you could pick them out before you went in for your jig-jig.

ASH. Poor creatures.

LOACH (*shrugs*). All they're used to, isn't it? They haven't been civilised. Some are all right. The Gurkhas, now you're talking. Good little fighters. Always give you a salute and call you sahib. Knew their place. Tikh-hai, Johnny. Give them a couple of chips, your slave for life. Salaam, sahib. I was a sort of batman to the engineers. Slept out on the beaches, never knew a day's pain.

FLAGG has been struggling to take a letter from his pocket. He holds it towards them.

FLAGG. I heard from my brother this morning.

ASH. *Did* you, sir? Well done, well done!

They tend to shout at him as if he were foreign.

FLAGG. Tells me he's just had a letter . . . posted 1943 . . .

ASH. *Go* on.

FLAGG. 1943 . . . now . . . to post a letter then cost . . . twopence halfpenny – right?

ASH. Right.

FLAGG. So the Post Office want him . . . to make up the difference . . .

ASH. Up to fourpence? A penny halfpenny.

FLAGG. Penny halfpenny . . . but they reckon it was underpaid by the sender . . . so they're asking for double . . .

ASH. Threepence?

FLAGG. For a letter sent in 1943!

ASH. And delayed by the Post Office?

LOACH. Bloody marvellous, isn't it?

FLAGG. Course . . . he's going to fight it.

Leans back, exhausted.

LOACH. Only right.

They watch as FLAGG *nods off.* ASH *fiddles desperately with his basket.*

I was a sort of batman to the engineers. Where I learnt my trade of catering. Africa this was. You ever been Africa way?

ASH. Never that far afield.

LOACH. I know Africa like the back of my hand. Stopped at a place half-way to Khartoum. Tents is all it was. Miles from sanitation. Nothing to drink but minerals and half the time they blew up before they was opened. And class distinction! Wouldn't look at you, the British civvies. I turned round to one of them, I said, look, me old mate, we're not wogs. I said, it's not for *me* MacAlpine's building the sodding pipeline. Educated people treating us no better than blacks.

ASH. We're all brothers beneath the skin, friend.

LOACH. That's what *I* said. I said, we're all British and the British ought to stand together against the wogs. Perhaps if we had, we might still have the Empire, right? But it's like I say, these doctors just the same. They turn round and tell you to jack in smoking, half the time they're smoking more than what you or I do.

LOACH *lights cigarette.*

My smoke's the only friend I got. It is. I used to have some good old mates. If they was alive to see me now, in this condition, they'd drop dead. A man needs a mucker, I don't care what you say.

ASH. That's true. I certainly –

FLAGG. What day is it?

LOACH. What d'you say, Dad?

FLAGG. What day is it? Is it wrestling?

LOACH. Coronation Street today. Isn't it, me old mate?

ASH. I believe so.

LOACH (*loud,* to FLAGG). Coronation Street. Seen the paper?

Gives him Daily Mirror. FLAGG *nods and reads.* LOACH *smokes.* MACKIE *groans in his sleep. They look at him.* ASH *suddenly loses control and throws his unfinished basket off the stage, down between the flights of stairs.*

ASH. Perishing basket! It's a losing battle. Physio-therapy. Physio-fiddlesticks!

LOACH. Easy.

ASH. How is basket-making supposed to help the frustrations of a lifetime? (*Sits again.*) When I was forced to give up teaching, I had a mental breakdown. They made that an excuse for getting rid of me, but it was they who'd caused it. In fact, I'd have to lay my perforated ulcer directly at their doorstep.

LOACH. Go on.

ASH. If you pushed me.

LOACH. Where was this?

ASH. In Bristol.

LOACH. What?

ASH. My home town.

LOACH. Chew Stoke?

ASH. You know it then?

LOACH. Chew Magna?

ASH. Just outside.

LOACH. I could have played tennis in Chew Magna.

ASH tries unsuccessfully to construe this.

ASH. I suppose what got me through was the thought of my adopted boy. My wife couldn't have children. We're separated now, it never went too swimmingly. I was awarded custody.

LOACH. Was it to do with her underneaths?

ASH. I'm sorry?

LOACH. To do with her womb, was it?

ASH. Yes.

LOACH. Womb trouble.

ASH. That sort of thing, yes.

LOACH. Mine's the same.

ASH. Still. The time seems to have come when he's ready to go on his own way. Looks as though I shall be left on my lonesome. Which is when I shall be glad of the belief in reincarnation I drew from my study of Comparative Religion. The belief that we can store up character in life after life until we attain perfection.

LOACH *feels called on to speak but finds nothing.*

Childish weakness, I dare say, but there, I take after mother, she was the timid one. Father was like a lion, with all the faults of the lion too. Proud, unapproachable, mean-tempered. I revered him. I had to find a source of strength to replace him when he passed on. A steadfast faith. (*Puts his hand on* LOACH's *knee.*) People like us need a crutch to help us.

LOACH. I never been a church-goer.

ASH. That makes no odds. People with dependent natures, we have to draw our strength from where we can. Help each other.

LOACH. Man needs a mucker.

ASH *nods.* FOSTER *arrives, with* LAKE *assisting.*

ASH. Hallo, Desmond. What you doing running about?

LOACH. Running about now.

LAKE. There you are.

LOACH. Old Kentish.

FOSTER *sits in remaining chair.* LAKE *looks at* FLAGG.

LAKE. This patient all right?

FLAGG (*opening eyes*). Dinner already?

LAKE. No, not yet. You all right?

FLAGG *nods.*

All right, that patient?

She looks at MACKIE, *who stirs and nods.*

FOSTER. Thank you, Nurse.

LAKE *goes.*

You noticed that Nurse never knows anyone's name?

LOACH. Marvellous isn't it?

FOSTER. What?

LOACH. Typical.

FOSTER. They reckon she's the best in the ward.

FOSTER *watches* LOACH *closely.*

LOACH. That's obvious, isn't it? You can see that.

ASH *has moved to edge of stage. Shouts down.*

ASH. Friend, I wonder can I trouble you to throw up the basket?

It is thrown from below. He catches it.

Ta very muchly.

FOSTER. How's your tummy, Mervyn?

ASH. Not too bad, what remains of it.

FOSTER. Kept your breakfast down?

ASH. Boiled egg, yes. My aim now is to work my way back to the semolina.

FOSTER. And the eczema?

ASH. Oh, under control, yes.

FLAGG. Look at this, Alice. This young hussy showing all she's got.

LOACH (*nervous*). Who's Alice?

FOSTER. His wife. (*To* FLAGG.) All right, Dad.

FLAGG *looks at him, then goes on.*

FLAGG. Seen this young tart here, showing all she's got?

FOSTER. Not bad at all.

FLAGG. Sixteen, it says . . . I'd give her sixteen, if she was one of mine . . . never seen Alice undressed all the years we've been together . . . our young days, no decent couple . . . would have had connection before marriage . . .

FOSTER. Time Marches On.

FLAGG. You what?

FOSTER (*shouting*). I say, Time Marches On.

FLAGG. Yes.

Closes eyes and rests. LAKE *returns with bottles.*

LAKE. Who wants a bottle?

LOACH. Depends what's in it, eh, me old mate?

LAKE *reaches under* FLAGG's *blanket and puts a bottle there, replacing a full one.*

Drop of three-star go down very nice.

ASH. Sssh.

LAKE. This patient want a bottle?

MACKIE *looks at her, shakes his head. She goes.*

MACKIE. I drift off and nearly sleep and one of these happy days I shan't come back.

ASH. Now, now . . .

MACKIE. But someone's always calling me back for a cup of tea or . . . a bottle . . . an overdose of the right drug is what I want.

LOACH. Whining Winnie's off.

MACKIE. Well, what are *you* hanging on for? You've been saying you've nothing to live for but your cup of tea . . .

FOSTER. We want a lecture, we'll ask for one.

ASH. Try to count your blessings.

MACKIE. You count them. I'm too busy coping with the pain . . . they wouldn't kill a pig like this . . .

ASH. Human life and a pig's life –

MACKIE. I've no regard for life itself, only the quality of life . . . should be clinics where you could get your death as you get a library book –

FOSTER. Tell us the same old story.

MACKIE. The Eskimos let their old die in peace.

FOSTER. The Eskimos haven't got a health service.

MACKIE. Learn a lot from primitive people . . . or old civilisations . . . I was an engineer in India . . . Burma . . .

LOACH. I was a sort of batman to the engineers.

MACKIE. Some remote station, under canvas . . . the bullfrogs barking in the dark . . . I'd walk by the water . . . hear somebody drumming . . . singing . . . I was a father to those people and I learnt from them as you learn from children . . . a world thrown away by a nation bent on suicide . . .

FOSTER. Hullo!

MACKIE. . . . too many rats will tear each other to pieces . . .
and on the roads or in the air . . .

*FOSTER has begun the Gaumont British theme song again.
The others join in, LOACH tone-deaf.*

The urge to self-destruction is given official sanction . . . kill
yourselves and leave the country to the mental defectives . . .
the senile . . .

*He is beaten by the singing, and has to leave off but his effort
to raise his voice has brought on a spasm of acute pain. For a
few moments the others sing on but his groans become cries.*

ASH. Nurse! Call the Nurse!

FOSTER. Nurse!

LOACH. Nurse! Come on, me old mate.

SISTER comes from the ward.

SISTER. What is it, Mr Mackie? Want a lie down?

SISTER begins to wheel him off.

Don't want to cry now. Frighten the other patients . . .

She wheels him off.

FLAGG. What's the matter with him?

LOACH. Nothing, Dad. You read the paper.

ASH. Poor fellow.

FOSTER. I've no patience.

ASH. Oh, Desmond.

FOSTER. All right for him going out to India, lording it. But I'm
not sorry the Labour Government gave it back to its rightful
owners. We're better off without all that.

ASH. Oh, yes, but I meant Mr Mackie's suffered more –

FOSTER. No, we could all look on the dark side. I could have let this dicky ticker get me down but soon as I grasped I'd have to curtail my summer plans I said to the wife: No Costa Brava for us, love, not this year. So we shall manage with day trips. Some of our nicest holidays were during my shifts at country junctions – I'm a signalman. Park the bus and the boys and I pitch the tent in the nearest field, Grandpa get the Volcano going, soon have a decent cup of tea. Mother give our youngest the breast . . . I join the boys in a game of cricket between trains. What could be nicer?

ASH. You're a lucky man.

FOSTER. I know it too. Five lovely kiddies. My eldest girl, she's six, she looked at me, you know the way they do, very threatening, I thought hullo, what have I done now? She said to me, Daddy, you're the only one who hasn't waggled my loose tooth.

They all laugh.

ASH. Mackie's case is different.

FOSTER. Granted.

LOACH. What's he got, Cambridge?

ASH (*almost a whisper*). Cancer.

LOACH. Get out.

ASH. Oh, yes.

LOACH. That what the smell is?

FOSTER. But you look at Mr Tyler. (*To* LOACH.) Diabetic in the wheel-chair. Nine times in here in the last two years and every time an amputation. First his toes, then his feet, then his legs –

LOACH. All right, me old mate.

ASH. Wonderful spirit!

FOSTER. There you are. Life and soul. And always busy with something useful.

ASH (*nodding*). Last few days he's been learning Mah Jong.

FOSTER. Always a joke. They say you can hardly get out of bed, when you get back in he's put a bedpan in it.

LOACH. Got to keep smiling.

ASH. But highly intelligent people can be more sensitive.

FOSTER. They've got no right to be.

ASH. Take my brother. Brains of the family, a chartered accountant, he got hold of some poppycock about there only being so much energy and we mustn't squander it. Started sleeping all day and staying awake at night, drawing off terrestrial dynamism. Finished up in a mental home, writing notes to nurses rather than speak – please let me have a bottle – rather than waste his store of energy. Raving bonkers. I worshipped him.

FLAGG. Brought some rhubarb, Alice.

They all look at him.

LOACH. All right, Dad?

FLAGG. I like a bit of stewed rhubarb, plenty of sugar. Fresh from my allotment.

LOACH. Very nice.

Silence again. FLAGG *looks at his paper.* ASH *fiddles with his basket.*

Those premature babies . . . don't half make some bloody ugly noises.

ASH. Can you blame them?

LAKE and BARNET come on, bustling.

BARNET. Come on, ladies, bustle, bustle!

LOACH. What is it now then?

BARNET. Matron's rounds.

FLAGG (*brought to his feet by* LAKE). What's up?

LAKE. Got to see Matron.

LOACH. Marvellous, isn't it?

FLAGG (*going off*). Visiting, is it? Visiting time?

LAKE. Matron.

BARNET (*to* ASH). Come on, Pagliacci.

LOACH (*laughing*). Pagliacci!

BARNET (*to* AUDIENCE). Something to pass the time.

The patients hobble towards their beds as the cloth goes up to show the ward. BARNET *clears their chairs.*

Scene Two

Bright light.

The five beds are as they were: FOSTER, LOACH, FLAGG, ASH *and* MACKIE. *As* BARNET *moves across with the chairs,* SWEET *comes from left.* MACKIE *groans.*

SWEET. All right, Mister Mackie, Doctor's on the way. Try not to make a fuss while Matron's here.

BARNET. He ought to be moved out.

SWEET. Wait till Doctor's seen him.

BARNET. Right . . .

LAKE *leaves* FLAGG *and goes off right with* SWEET. BARNET *leaves chairs at stove and turns as* MATRON *comes from right, with* SISTER, LAKE *and* SWEET *attending. She is regal, smiling, but wastes no time.* BARNET *goes off left.*

MATRON (*to* MACKIE). Good morning, how are you today?

Groan of agony from MACKIE.

Keep smiling. You'll soon be out of here.

Moves to ASH.

MATRON. Good morning, how are you today?

ASH. Morning, Matron, not so dusty, thank you –

MATRON. That's the style –

ASH. When you consider half my tummy's been –

MATRON. Keep it up.

ASH. – taken away.

MACKIE *groans. Everyone looks at him, except* MATRON.

MATRON. Good morning. How are you getting along?

FLAGG. Eh?

MATRON. Are they treating you well?

FLAGG. Not too bad.

MATRON. That's right.

FLAGG. Though I'd like to go to a toilet – you know –

MATRON. Sister –

FLAGG. – toilet with a decent chain.

MATRON. Get this patient a bedpan.

SISTER. Nurse Lake –

LAKE. Sister?

SISTER. Get Mr Flagg a bedpan.

LAKE. Nurse Sweet –

MATRON. Good morning, how are you?

LAKE. Get Mr Flagg a bedpan.

LOACH. Well, miss, I get these cramps –

MATRON (*looking at her watch*). Good.

LOACH. In my leg.

SWEET. Mister Barnet –

MATRON. Soon be out of here.

LOACH. I don't want the cure.

BARNET (*coming on left*). Hallo?

SWEET. Bedpan for Mr Flagg.

BARNET. Right. Morning, Matron.

MATRON. Good morning, how are you getting on?

FOSTER (*without removing earphones*). Lovely, Matron, everything's lovely –

BARNET *has gone off right.*

MATRON. That's what we like to hear, isn't it, Sister? Get well soon. We need the beds.

Goes off, left, with SISTER *and* LAKE. SWEET *breaks off, as* BARNET *re-enters, right, with a bedpan for* FLAGG.

BARNET. You couldn't have waited, could you?

FLAGG. What's this?

BARNET. Get the screens.

He and SWEET *go off, right.*

FLAGG. What's he brought me this for?

ASH. You said you wanted to go to the toilet.

FLAGG. No.

ASH. I heard you.

FLAGG. She said, 'Are you all right', and I said, 'All right but I'd like a toilet with a decent chain . . . like I got at home . . .'

BARNET *and* SWEET *return with screens, erect them around* FLAGG'*s bed.*

ASH. Mister Flagg doesn't want a bedpan. He only said he was looking forward to a toilet with a decent chain.

BARNET. Do us a favour, Mary Pickford. Matron says 'Do this', it's the Royal Command.

They go behind the screens and we hear them.

FLAGG. I don't want no bedpan –

SWEET. Come along, Mister Flagg –

BARNET. Knickers down – and –

SWEET. Ups-a-daisy! There.

DR BIRD *comes from right, checking papers, looking about, as dazed as before.*

BIRD. Mister Mackie?

FOSTER (*taking off earphones*). By the door, Doctor.

BIRD *goes to* MACKIE, *checks his chart. He groans. She glances at him and goes on with the chart.* SWEET *and* BARNET *come from* FLAGG'*s screens. Look up the ward to see where* MATRON *is.*

SWEET. Where's Her Majesty?

BARNET. On the balcony.

BIRD. How d'you feel?

SWEET *now notices* BIRD.

SWEET. Ah, Doctor.

BIRD. Nurse, this patient should have the screens round.

SWEET. Right. (*To* BARNET.) Get more screens for Doctor.

BARNET. They're all being used – up there, look!

MACKIE *cries out.*

BIRD. Nurse!

SWEET. Yes, coming.

BARNET shrugs, rolls one of FLAGG's screens away and puts it upstage of BIRD, so that we can now see FLAGG unnaturally high on his bedpan, as well as BIRD with MACKIE.

LAKE (*off*). Mister Barnet!

BARNET. Coming!

Goes off left. BIRD begins an examination of MACKIE, refers to his chart, listens to his chest. Her head remains there. SWEET meanwhile has shuffled the chairs about near the stove, keeping a nervous eye on MATRON's progress.

SWEET. Shall I take you off, Mister Flagg?

FLAGG. I never wanted to come on here . . . but now you better leave me.

SWEET. Oh.

Goes to MACKIE's screen and peers round the edge. Sees the DOCTOR's head on his chest. She nudges her awake.

Doctor!

BIRD (*waking*). – we'll aspirate a pleural effusion –

The movement has hurt MACKIE, who cries out. BIRD stands.

Oh, yes. Thank you, Nurse.

Leads SWEET from screens to centre stage.

He should be in the terminal ward. Ask Sister to arrange it. I'll be with the almoner if you want me –

Finishes in an irrepressible yawn. SWEET nods and goes to move the screen back to cover FLAGG. BIRD wanders towards the left.

FOSTER. Whoa, Doctor! Other way if you're going out.

BIRD turns yawning. She makes for the right, dropping papers all the way. SWEET picks them up and sticks them back under her arm as she goes off. BARNET comes from left.

BARNET. She's coming down the other side.

SWEET returns to meet him.

SWEET. Mister Mackie to the terminal ward.

Together they wheel MACKIE's bed into the centre, then back through the exit right.

Go for a nice long ride now, Mister Mackie?

BARNET. Chuff-chuff-chuff-chuff whooooooweee!

And off, as MATRON comes from left with SISTER and LAKE.

MATRON (*looking at her watch*). Those chairs are anyhow, Sister, put them straight.

SISTER. Nurse Lake –

SWEET comes back and begins rolling MACKIE's locker off, right.

LAKE. Sister?

SISTER. Those chairs are anyhow.

LAKE. Nurse Sweet –

SISTER. Put them straight.

BARNET, returning, takes the locker off and SWEET joins the MATRON's party in time.

LAKE. Those chairs are anyhow.

SWEET. Mister Barnet –

LAKE. Put them straight.

BARNET returns.

SWEET. Those chairs are anyhow. Put them straight.

BARNET shuffles the chairs about. MATRON comes downstage, speaks to AUDIENCE.

MATRON. We're removing the beds as they fall vacant because, I'm glad to be able to tell you, the whole ward block is in for a very extensive face-lift. Which I am sure you will agree is long overdue. The walls will be in washable avocado pear, the curtains and counterpanes in Cotswold Stone. High level louvres on the windows. King's Fund Beds with Slimline mattresses.

She turns to survey the ward and to imagine this transformation. SISTER, LAKE, SWEET and BARNET do the same. Appreciable pause. FLAGG farts and groans. No one acknowledges it. MATRON turns back, smiling.

Into the jet-age with one big jump. (*She crosses to right, notices MACKIE's bedspace.*) Another one gone there, Sister?

SISTER. Um – it looks like it.

MATRON. Good, good. Keep them moving.

Goes off, right, with NURSES and BARNET. FLAGG does it again.

LOACH. Dear, oh Lord!

ASH (*amused*). Musical evening.

FOSTER takes off his earphones.

FOSTER. Her Majesty gone?

LOACH. She's gone, yes.

ASH. Desmond, I've just this minute noticed something.

FOSTER. What's that, Mervyn?

ASH. I'm in the end bed.

They look. They see that this is true. They find nothing to say. BARNET comes on downstage with trolley. Spot finds him.

BARNET. Running spot man? You wouldn't know a running spot if you had them all over you. At the end, Mister Mackie's heart stopped three times and three times they brought him back. They were fetching the artificial respirator when it stopped again and some daring soul decided to call it a day. (*Peers in at the end of the cover. Pauses, speaks more quietly, not facing the* AUDIENCE.) I'm sure I speak for all those who knew him in life when I say that he will be remembered as an evil-tempered, physically repulsive old man. The distended lips, the purple ears, those malevolent eyes glaring up at you from the engorged face. But – now the pump's been allowed to pack up, the flesh has receded, that puffiness gone, an altogether younger face has appeared. You can see how – once – someone might even have fancied him. (*Looks at* AUDIENCE, *then pushes trolley off other side.*)

Scene Three

Music.

> *Lights change to a brilliantly lit downstage area. The setting cool and white with fixed wash bowls and gadgets dispensing toilet requisites.*

> BOYD *comes up front steps in light, white clothing – cap, boots, trousers, short-sleeved shirt. He takes own pulse rate. Goes down on his hands and does a few press-ups. Holds up one hand to check its steadiness.* SISTER McPHEE *comes into the area, wearing white theatre gown.*

SISTER. Mister Boyd.

BOYD. Ah, Sister – they're ready?

SISTER. Ready and waiting, sir.

BOYD (*he begins to wash his hands*). And – Neil? –

SISTER. There's been no change.

BOYD. And – the donor? –

SISTER. Staff Nurse Norton is ready.

BOYD stops washing his hands.

BOYD. Aye, she's ready. Ready to give a kidney to save my son's life.

SISTER. Aye. Because she loves him. Because her life wouldna be worth living without him.

He goes on washing. She looks at him.

I know how she feels.

BOYD stops again, looks at her. With his elbow he operates a nail-brush dispenser, taking the brush with his other hand and using it to continue washing.

BOYD. Mary – I wish I knew what to say to comfort ye. I tried – God knows I tried – to make him leave the girl.

SISTER. No!

BOYD. Aye, the girl who's about to risk her life that he may live.

SISTER. No.

BOYD. Aye. And whose fault is it his disease is so advanced? Mine.

SISTER. No.

BOYD. Aye!

SISTER. You mustn't ever think that, even for a moment.

BOYD. Why not? It's the truth, woman. I told him I wouldna speak to him again, until he'd broken it off with Staff Nurse Norton.

SISTER. No!

BOYD. Aye!

*He finishes washing, throws brush into pedal-bin which
SISTER opens with her foot and closes with a clang. He holds
out hands for towel. She takes one from the sterilising unit
with forceps and puts it into his hands. He dries hands.*

Why else d'you think he didna speak to me of the pain he
must have been suffering? And the worst of it was I never let
on to mesel what my real motives were. I thought the odour
of sanctity was in my nostrils and all the time it was the
stench of racial prejudice.

SISTER. No.

BOYD. Oh, aye. I was a pig-headed old fool. I ken well.

*Drops towel into receptacle. He takes folded gown and flicks
it open, easing into it, touching it as little as possible with his
hands.*

And, Mary, I told mesel I was doing it for you. I promised
Flora on her death-bed that you should be Neil's wife . . . and
I did my best to see that you were.

SISTER. But Neil doesna love me.

BOYD. I've told him he wants his head examined. If you loved
me as you love him –

SISTER. But I –

BOYD. And if I were thirty years younger – I'd not stand
havering here like some timorous sawney –

SISTER. But I don't love Neil. I never have.

BOYD. Urmph? Have a care what you say, woman.

*They move towards each other from opposite sides of the
room. As they are about to meet –*

SISTER. Age has nothing to do with love.

*He turns his back to her and she ties the laces behind his
gown. They play the next dialogue in that position.*

BOYD. D'you know what you're saying, woman?

SISTER. Oh, aye. I've had thirty years to learn the truth of it. To be near you yet far from you. I never dared to hope . . .

BOYD. D'you know what kind of man you'd be getting? An old fool who thought he could play God?

SISTER. No!

BOYD. Aye! Who thought he could tell people whom they should love. Who thought he knew the score but who wasna so canny as a wee bairn.

He turns to her and their eyes meet.

SISTER. No.

BOYD. Aye! And who couldna see what was before his verra nose. (*Holds out his hands towards her.*) Mary –

She presses a button which squirts a jet of powder upwards into his hands. He rubs them together as she moves further away. Then he follows her.

SISTER. Who was the only man with the skill to save his son's life!

BOYD. No!

SISTER. Aye!

They stop face to face with a machine between them. She presses a switch with her foot. A packet of rubber gloves pops up from the machine like bread from a toaster.

Staff Nurse Norton could give Neil her heart well enough but without your help she couldna give him her kidney.

He takes and flicks open the packet of gloves, then puts them on. He presses his palms together in an attitude of supplication and keeps them so for the rest of the scene.

BOYD. Great surgeons are two a penny . . . but a good woman . . . can you ever forgive me, Mary?

SISTER. Oh, dearest –

He closes his eyes and raises his face towards her. At the touch of another switch a theatre mask springs up.

She takes it and puts it over his mouth. LAKE has come on and ties the laces behind his head. He opens his eyes and looks at SISTER.

Good luck – sir.

He nods, turns and goes towards the darkness, his hands pressed together, as though to prayer. SISTER and LAKE follow.

Music swells.

Scene Four

Lights brighten the ward.

SWEET *comes from right briskly.*

SWEET. Walking patients up now. Rise and shine.

Goes off left. ASH, LOACH and FLAGG climb out of bed and come down to the stove and its chairs. FLAGG has a paper, LOACH a cigarette. FOSTER remains in bed, his eyes closed.

LOACH. Get up, lay down, drink this, swallow that . . . marvellous, isn't it?

ASH (*smiling*). The well-nigh inexplicable rituals of our confinement, friend.

LOACH. And what have they done? Time slipping away, all they can think to do is bang me knees with little hammers and come round half a dozen times a day for a sample of my blood. It's not *their* time, is it? It's mine. And time's money, I don't care what you say.

ASH. I wish mine was.

LOACH. Any more doctors come round me for blood, I shall

turn round and ask them straight what they're doing with the bleeding stuff?

ASH. They're students, practising.

LOACH. I shall say: what you doing with it, drinking it, are you?

ASH. Perhaps they're testing the alcohol content.

LOACH. Chance'd be a fine thing. I was gonna get Joyce to bring me in a drop when she come, just to soothe the cramps sort of style. But now she've gone off like that, shouting the odds, I don't reckon on seeing her back . . .

ASH. Why don't you take the cure, Ted?

LOACH. Middle of visiting too . . . no consideration – keeps a clean house, you follow my meaning, but nervous. Over-sensitive.

ASH. Forgive my saying so, she seemed to like showing off.

LOACH. Not the first time she's left home. Mind you, we haven't *got* a home, she's down the Centre. We had a very decent little room in this condemned terrace, soaking wet but independent, you follow me. But now she says the Council's pulling it down. I saw the rent tribunal, they say you've paid your rent, you stay where you are. Still, time I get out of here, it might be a flyover. How can I stay where I am when it's gone? If I hadn't lost my memory, I'd still be in possession. Nine points of the law. Fellow in our place, they said we'll put you in the Centre and like a fool he went. Now what he *should* have done, he should have let his wife and kids go in the Centre but *he* should have stood still. In possession. Get a place much quicker if they got to turn you out. So they *say*. There again, you never know. One says one thing, one another. (*Winces with cramp.*)

ASH. We're in a very similar boat.

LOACH. You got your adopted boy.

ASH. Got him? Where? Where is he? Has he come to visit me?

SWEET *returns from left.*

SWEET. Come on, Mister Foster, put those earphones away. Time to stretch your legs.

Goes off right. FOSTER *takes no notice.*

ASH. No. My boy doesn't want me now.

LOACH. You haven't got my craving. My cramps.

ASH. I've a nervous temperament, my mother's legacy. Only half a stomach . . . nervous eczema.

LOACH. Good job –

ASH. Ha!

LOACH. Education.

ASH. Well –

LOACH. Always been my handicap, no education. Take those school magazines you give me to read. I couldn't keep up the interest, see. Where you could.

ASH. Education's wonderful, that's true.

LOACH. Educated people always got the whip hand.

ASH. You remind me to count my blessings, friend. Though, of course, many so-called educated people are no better than you or I when it comes to being a Good Samaritan.

LOACH. Oh, definitely. Those sahibs down Khartoum way treating us no better than blacks.

ASH. I'm grateful to you, Ted, for pointing out the glint of sunshine in an otherwise impenetrably murky sky. That's the beauty of having a friend to talk to.

LOACH. Man needs a mucker –

ASH. My name's Mervyn.

LOACH. – don't care what you say.

ASH puts his hand on LOACH's *knee.*

ASH. Thank you, Ted.

From the right now enters a WEST INDIAN CLERGYMAN *in the most gorgeous vestments the Anglican Church allows for administering the Last Unction. The* PATIENTS *look up at him. After his impressive sweeping entrance, he falters and consults a card. He then goes to* ASH's *bed and checks his chart.*

Can I help you, Chaplain?

CHAPLAIN. Ah. I'm looking for Mister Mackie.

ASH. I'm afraid you're out of luck.

CHAPLAIN. What ward is this?

ASH. Sir Stafford Cripps.

CHAPLAIN. Yes. I've got Mister Mackie down for the end bed.

LOACH. He's dead.

CHAPLAIN. Ah.

ASH. Passed on the night before last. In the terminal ward.

CHAPLAIN. Oh, dear, somebody slipped up on their paperwork. Too many cooks spoil the broth. (*Writes on the card he brought and puts it away.*) Get my breath back a moment.

ASH. Too much red tape in your department too, Chaplain?

CHAPLAIN *sits between* LOACH *and* FLAGG.

CHAPLAIN. I'm afraid we've a very severe attack of Parkinson's Law.

ASH. Same everywhere.

LOACH. Mate of mine had that.

CHAPLAIN. Pardon?

LOACH. Nasty.

CHAPLAIN. Parkinson's *Law*.

LOACH. Shaking and falling about.

CHAPLAIN. Seen the papers this morning?

ASH. Oh, yes.

CHAPLAIN. Pretty shocking news.

ASH. It is.

CHAPLAIN. England are going to have to pull their socks up to make a hundred between them. Bad generalship. Same old story. They used to say the British Army in Fourteen Eighteen were lions led by lambs and it's the same story at Lords. Haven't I seen you at Communion?

ASH. Yes, Chaplain. Ash the name.

CHAPLAIN. Ah, yes. Sorry I haven't popped in sooner but, as I say, no rest for the wicked. I was giving the last unction to a patient in Sherpa Tensing ward and thought, while I was in this neck of the woods, I'd . . . kill two birds with one stone. I mean, by having a natter with Mr Mackie. Was he C of E?

LOACH. The way he talked, he had no time for religion.

CHAPLAIN. Ah, well, they always put C of E for that. Saves a lot of paperwork. No, I was afraid it was going to be some mistake I'd have to spend the rest of the day putting right. We're snowed under with paperwork.

Pulls up the hem of his cassock and gets packet of cigarettes from jacket pocket. Offers them.

D'you use these fellows?

ASH. I won't now, thank you.

LOACH. Don't mind. Thanks, Johnny.

FLAGG. I'll have one.

CHAPLAIN *looks for lighter in pocket, then gets attaché case and opens it on his knees.*

CHAPLAIN. You know, the great juggernaut of bureaucracy grinds to a halt. Only yesterday I was called to the intensive care unit to give Communion to a Palestinian Arab.

Laughs. From the case he takes a candlestick with candles, a spotless linen altar-cloth, a bottle of wine, a cup and paten and a prayer book. He sets them in turn on the floor.

A Moslem, needless to say. Still he was a very decent sort. The Holy Land used to be my stamping-ground in Forty-Four Forty-Five . . . so he put me in the picture on my old haunts. . . .

Finds lighter and uses it. They smoke. They help him put the articles back into his case. They smoke again.

No, it's the same old story, I'm afraid. A lot of first-rate players don't make a team without the leadership.

The OLD WOMAN *in the flowered dress has entered. She goes to* FOSTER.

LOACH. Same old story, isn't it?

CHAPLAIN (*enthusiastically*). That's it exactly.

OLD WOMAN. Good morning, I have a message for you. God so —

FOSTER, *still with earphones, does not wake. She is very slightly disconcerted to be talking to herself, but she puts a text between* FOSTER's *fingers as his hand lies over the counterpane. The men downstage have been embarrassed by her arrival, largely on the* CHAPLAIN's *behalf. She now comes to them.*

God so loved the world that He gave His only begotten Son that whosoever believeth in Him should not perish but have everlasting life. (*She notices the* CHAPLAIN's *vestments. She smiles uncertainly and goes off left.*)

CHAPLAIN. *And* it looks like being an all-Australian Wimbledon again.

LOACH. Marvellous, isn't it? We used to lick the world at one time.

FLAGG. See in the paper where they're trying to bring back capital punishment.

CHAPLAIN. Ah?

FLAGG. Bring back hanging . . . some member of Parliament . . . they come round in my street . . . petition. . . .

CHAPLAIN. Yes.

FLAGG. List of signatures . . . wanted me to sign to bring back hanging . . . I said: No fear . . .

CHAPLAIN. Did you?

FLAGG. No fear, I said . . .

CHAPLAIN. Well done!

FLAGG. I said: Hanging's too good for them. They ought to be slowly tortured to death . . . any ruffian that has a go at a little girl or police constable . . . ought to be taken limb from limb, I said . . .

CHAPLAIN. I don't know that I could altogether agree with that. (*Smiles at them all.*) Not altogether.

ASH. Nor I. I don't believe in cruelty.

CHAPLAIN. Quite.

ASH. They should be strung up. It's quick and merciful.

CHAPLAIN. So many different sides to every question. (*Stubs out cigarette.*) Well, I must love you and leave you. At least a dozen bods in this ward marked C of E Most of them turn out to be Greek Orthodox, I daresay. (*Looks at card again.*) Mister Mackie, yes. Mister Ash – wasn't it?

ASH. Yes, Chaplain.

CHAPLAIN. And you're Mister –

LOACH. Loach.

FLAGG. Flagg.

CHAPLAIN (*ticking names*). Wonderful. Now. Mister Foster –

ASH. Having forty winks.

CHAPLAIN. Better have a word.

ASH. Let me bring you a chair. You're not allowed to sit on the bed.

CHAPLAIN and ASH go to FOSTER's bed, ASH bringing an upright folding chair.

CHAPLAIN. Oh, yes, we don't want to break the rules. These nurses put the fear of *God* into me.

Laughs and sits, as ASH goes to his own locker and gets his basket.

Come along, squire, wakey, wakey.

Shakes FOSTER to wake him. He falls sideways, his head lolling over, the phones still on. CHAPLAIN pushes back chair, stands.

Mister Foster – (*He has to support the falling body.*) Nurse! Sister! I'm afraid this patient doesn't seem too well . . .

The PATIENTS stand and move as SWEET comes on from right. She looks at FOSTER briefly, feels his pulse. She looks at the CHAPLAIN, then tries to go off the way she came. LOACH is in the way.

SWEET. You patients, back into bed, please! Out of the way.

Scene Five

The PATIENTS go back to the beds. SWEET goes off right very quickly. CHAPLAIN looks again at FOSTER, then at his list, then goes off left to his next patient.

SWEET (*amplifier*). Stafford Cripps here. I've got a cardiac arrest B for Bertie. Thank you.

Meanwhile LAKE *and* BARNET *bring on screens to part-conceal* FOSTER.

BARNET (*to* PATIENTS, *as he adjusts screens*). Why don't you listen to the wireless? Much nicer.

ASH. Not working, Mister Barnet.

BARNET. Watch the telly then!

SWEET comes back with tray of apparatus and goes behind screens. We see the nurses pull back bedding and SWEET attempts mouth-to-mouth ventilation.

Light fades on this and a large acting area, coming in from above, lights the down right section. Lift comes up with two operating tables on it, attended by white-garbed figures. The PATIENTS are covered but their feet are bare: a black pair and a white.

Music; Romeo and Juliet Overture.

The ATTENDANTS wheel the tables to directly beneath the acting area. Behind the tables, a wall is flown in, white-tiled but having on it twin anaesthetic machines, X-rays, Oscillographs. Other ATTENDANTS wheel on instrument trolleys, wash-bowls, etc. The operating staff are masked and wear white boots.

BOYD comes up front steps, sideways, still in his attitude of prayer, followed by SISTER McPHEE, as before.

Their movements are ritualistic but played too much to the gods.

BOYD approaches CLEO's table, looks at ANAESTHETIST, who nods decisively. BOYD turns to McPHEE, holds out hand for first instrument. The other members of the team close in and hide the operation from view at the very moment when it promises to be interesting. Music stops.

Our attention is drawn to FOSTER's bed by one of the screens being pushed over on to LOACH.

LOACH. Here!

BARNET comes out and pulls it straight as INDIAN STUDENT hurries on from right pushing Cardiac Arrest Trolley, with Oxygen cylinders.

BARNET. Where've you been – up The Khyber Pass?

INDIAN STUDENT. I was in the canteen.

BARNET allows him behind screens. We hear the following dialogue, or some of it, very quiet and natural.

SWEET. I've tried mouth-to-mouth ventilation.

INDIAN STUDENT. No joy? We better do some external cardiac compression.

LAKE. On the floor, don't you think? The bed's too soft.

They lift FOSTER off the bed and lay him on the floor downstage of the bed, BARNET trying to hide all this from the other PATIENTS with screens. The PATIENTS try to concentrate on the Kidney Transplant.

DR BIRD comes up front steps, wearing ordinary clothes with a raincoat, which she is taking off. She gives it to BARNET as she goes to help with FOSTER.

INDIAN STUDENT. We've tried mouth-to-mouth –

BIRD. Give him oxygen.

LAKE turns to trolley and searches.

BIRD. I was just off home for an hour's sleep.

LAKE. Sorry.

She walks swiftly off to the right as BIRD crouches over FOSTER and presses his chest. BARNET closes it off with screen and comes to us.

BARNET. Typical balls up. No spanner for the oxygen cylinder. Always the same – people don't put things back where they found them. Talk about a Band of Hope Concert.

MICHAEL *comes from right pushing Defibrillator on trolley.*

That's the Resuscitation Unit.

Another man follows and LAKE *now returns with the spanner.*

With the aid of cardiac massage and electric shock, they've got a very creditable record of bringing them back from over the Great Divide.

They both go behind the screens and close off our view. Music and the lights come up on transplant. SISTER *turns from her position beside* BOYD *and checks her instruments. As the light favours her face,* BARNET *moves across downstage, bringing a hand-mike from the wings and stands near her.*

In the terrible loneliness of the operating theatre, so many times she had stood beside him, this grizzled man with the strangely tender eyes, whose love she had never dared to crave.

She turns back to hand BOYD *an instrument.*

So often she had tried to anticipate his every movement, deftly slipping the instruments between his gloved fingers. But this was no common-or-garden kidney transplant. A glint of panic deckle-edged the usually inscrutable features of the man who was trying to save the life of the boy who had carried her satchel all those years ago.

BOYD *stands up decisively, the kidney is lifted in a sterile bag and* BOYD *steps clear of the scrum. The scrum moves across to* NEIL's *table.* BOYD *comes to* MARY *and washes his hands of blood. She mops his brow.*

Above the mask, her eyes met those of the man who, in a rare moment of candour, had freely admitted that he was not God.

He nods formally and moves back to the other table. Mary stands behind him.

A cavorting lancet of pity stabbed her behind the sternum. She wanted to tell him: never mind, never mind. . . .

Lights and music out.

At FOSTER's *bed, the same clumsy movements and the same attempts to conceal them. They have got* FOSTER *back on to his bed.* BARNET *goes across downstage.*

All going well as can be expected but not so nice for the other patients. Which is where the telly is a great step forward. Keep their minds off what's going on next door. One of the problems here is not knowing how long he'd been away. Or where.

Screens open to allow MICHAEL *to come out with Defibrillator.* BARNET *goes on, to himself.*

Excuse me, sir, I understand you've just come back from that undiscovered country from whose bourn no traveller returns? – That's correct, yes. Now, as this is going to be an increasingly common experience in the years to come, I wonder if you'd say a few words about The Afterlife? And keep it short, we're running late.

BIRD *and* INDIAN *have come out and go off right.* SWEET *has wheeled off cardiac arrest trolley.* FOSTER *has been got back into bed again. There is a noticeable lack of urgency about these movements.* BARNET *stares at them and glances at the audience, awkwardly smiling. From the left, on his level, the* OLD LADY *returns from her tour of the ward.*

OLD WOMAN. Good morning, I have a message for you. God gave His only begotten Son that whosoever believeth in Him should not perish but have everlasting life.

MICHAEL *has returned pushing the hooded trolley. The* OLD WOMAN *gives* BARNET *a text and he goes up to assist in getting the trolley through the screens to* FOSTER. *The* OLD WOMAN *goes off down left, crossing the transplant area.*

Music and lights on OP.

BOYD *raises his head to the* ANAESTHETIST, *who gives thumbs-up. The scrum parts to allow* BOYD *to emerge. Music triumphant. He goes to instruments trolley and removes gloves.* McPHEE *takes and throws them on to tray. He removes his mask. The* ATTENDANTS *are wheeling away the* PATIENT *and the rear wall is flown. Before the instruments trolley is wheeled off,* SISTER *takes* BOYD's *pipe from under a white cloth and puts it into his mouth. Together they circle and he partners her in a pirouette. They dance off as the music ends.*

Lights off on OP.

FOSTER's *screens part and are removed by* LAKE *and* SWEET. MICHAEL *and* BARNET *begin pushing the hooded trolley off to the left. The* CHAPLAIN *has come on and has to pause while they pass.*

BARNET. Missed the boat again, Chaplain.

CHAPLAIN *wanders forward, taking out his list and scanning the names.* LAKE *and* SWEET *return and wheel* FOSTER's *bed off to right.*

LAKE (*as she passes*). Foster. C of E.

CHAPLAIN. Ah!

Crosses off FOSTER's *name and follows his bed out.* ASH, FLAGG *and* LOACH *watch silently as* SWEET *returns and removes* FOSTER's *locker and earphones.*

Scene Six

Strong daylight.

A large Negro ORDERLY *wheels on a trolley with a game set on it.* ASH, LOACH *and* FLAGG *have climbed out of bed and are putting their gowns and slippers on.*

ORDERLY. All right, here?

LOACH. Tikh-hai, Johnny.

ORDERLY goes off, left. LOACH, ASH and FLAGG draw up chairs and settle round the game.

He's new.

ASH. He's a prince, they tell me. The son of a chief.

LOACH. Where's he from then? Africa way?

ASH. More than likely. If I remember correctly, it was friend Flagg's throw.

FLAGG throws dice.

LOACH. Every time anyone comes in, I'm shit-scared they're going to want me for the cure. I'm all booked in. I've heard of this place and all. Down in Kent, a mile's walk from a Green Line bus.

FLAGG. Piccadilly with two houses.

ASH. That's your own.

FLAGG. Right . . .

LOACH throws dice. FLAGG looks about.

Another scorcher.

ASH. Makes you glad to be alive, this weather.

FLAGG. We could use the rain.

ASH. *You* could perhaps.

FLAGG. Soil must be parched.

LOACH. Bleeding Chance.

Takes and reads a card.

FLAGG. Son-in-law's looking after my allotment . . . well as he can . . . never had the feeling for it . . .

LOACH. Pay School Fees of a hundred and fifty pounds. Marvellous, isn't it?

ASH. You get two hundred for passing Go, so here's a fifty.

   ASH *throws a dice.*

   Have you always had green fingers, Mister Flagg?

FLAGG. Come from the country in the first place.

ASH. Did you?

FLAGG. Hertfordshire. Before my family settled in Islington.

LOACH. Never had much time for the country.

FLAGG. Then, of course, my job . . .

ASH. Free parking. What *is* your job?

FLAGG. Trees in streets . . .

ASH. Your throw.

FLAGG. Parks department . . . for the council . . .

LOACH. *I* been with the Parks department.

   FLAGG *in the act of throwing, looks at* LOACH *sceptically, then throws.*

LOACH. In my trade of catering. Well, I looked after the chalet while the rangers were out on patrol picking up the soiled French letters.

FLAGG. What for?

   FLAGG *has taken a card.*

LOACH. My job, wasn't it? Custodian of the chalet. Making the breakfast.

FLAGG (*gives card to* ASH *to read*). No, why'd they pick up the French letters?

ASH. Annuity Matures. Collect one hundred pounds.

LOACH. This was in Hyde Park I'm talking about. The tarts used to do their business in the spinneys . . . overnight this was . . . and leave this muck laying about.

ASH. Your throw, Ted.

LOACH (*throwing*). We tried putting barbed wire round but the ponces must have had cutters. Next day the rangers'd find this way cut through and all the used French letters again. What's this – Bow Street.

ASH. Mine. With four houses. Seven hundred and fifty pounds.

LOACH. Where'm I going to get my hands on seven hundred and fifty pounds?

ASH. You'll have to mortgage, Ted.

LOACH. I'm bloody mortgaged already, aren't I? Look at that – Mayfair and Park Lane, mortgaged. Even mortgaged the stations. I'm jacking it in. (*Moves from table.*)

The Negro ORDERLY crosses left to right carrying a bedpan covered with a cloth. LOACH looks up at him, frightened.

I thought he'd come for me.

ASH (*approaching him*). Don't throw in the sponge, Ted. You can owe it to me.

LOACH. I don't want to play the bleeding game. It's a kid's game.

ASH. You can't sit day after day waiting and worrying. You must fill in the time.

LOACH. I'm all shot to pieces. How can I settle me mind to anything? Bottle of Hennessy and I'd be laughing . . .

ASH. Now come on. You promised me. What did you promise? That you'd summon up your courage and face the cure. Then, once you're better – and it won't take long, you're half-way there already – then you'll come and lodge at my place and I shall help you to keep the pledge. And I can. I'm strong when it comes to helping others. (*Pause.*) All right, Ted?

LOACH nods. ASH sets his chair straight and LOACH sits in it.

My throw. Forget the rent. The important thing is to keep the game going. Regent Street. My own.

FLAGG *throws.*

FLAGG. But say what you like, there's nothing finer than a fresh English tomato . . . plenty of salt . . . fresh pulled lettuce . . . crisp white heart . . .

ASH. Two hundred pounds for passing Go. To him that hath it shall be given.

BARNET *has come on, pushing bottle trolley.*

BARNET. This ward's a dead-and-alive hole. Time something happened.

LOACH. Jesus God, I thought you'd come for me. For the cure.

ASH. Don't tell me it's got *you* down, Mister Barnet.

BARNET. Long as trade's brisk I don't mind . . . but this – ? Beds disappearing . . . gives you the creeps.

LOACH. I see you got a new wog helper.

BARNET. Prince Monolulu? Yes.

LOACH. Worming their way in. Another bleeding Chance, look at that.

BARNET. When he's carried the bedpans for a couple of weeks, he's going back to Timbuktu and run this brand new hospital they're building.

LOACH. Get out of jail free.

ASH. I told you things were looking up. You stick with me, Ted, we'll be all right.

BARNET. You could have done with that before.

LOACH. I keep it, don't I?

BARNET. Couldn't you, me old mate? Done with it before?

LOACH (*to* ASH). Your go.

BARNET. D'you get many pouffes in prison?

LOACH. Who told you anything about me being in prison?

BARNET. You did.

LOACH. In confidence.

BARNET. Funny place to put a pouffe, though, when you think of it.

FLAGG. Best place for them.

BARNET. D'you think so, Dad? I find that interesting, that point of view.

FLAGG. Give them the cat.

BARNET. Hear that, Ted? The cat. They might enjoy it, though, a few of them.

ASH. Bang on Go. That's lucky for me.

BARNET. You've got to be so careful you don't give people pleasure.

LOACH. Some of the types I saw in there, I thought to myself this is a waste of the ratepayers' money.

FLAGG *throws and moves.*

BARNET I think they can be useful members of society, long as they sublimate their libidos. Look at male nurses.

FLAGG. You're a male nurse.

BARNET. I'm an orderly, thank you. No connection with the firm next door, Fairies Anonymous. Ballet dancers. Scout masters. Teachers. There you are. Teachers! We had a master when I was a kid, name of Nash, we called him Nance. Everyone knew but him.

ASH. I bet he did know.

BARNET. What?

ASH. His nickname. You always do. The boys think you don't but you do.

BARNET. Did you know yours?

ASH. Cinders.

BARNET. Short for Cinderella, was it?

Winks at LOACH, *who does not see, busy throwing the dice.*

ASH. No. (*Laughs.*) A play on words. My name Ash, you see. Cinders – Ash.

BARNET. I'm with you now, yes. Clever, eh, Ted?

Nudges LOACH, *who is throwing.*

LOACH. I'm trying to throw these dice.

BARNET. What I really meant with this fellow Nash, this teacher, was everyone knew but him that he was as queer as a plasticine starting-handle.

BARNET *goes aside.*

Ted!

LOACH. Hello?

BARNET *signals and* LOACH *goes to him.* BARNET *shows him a quarter bottle of spirits.*

BARNET. Drop of Gordon's? Set you up again.

LOACH *looks nervously towards* ASH.

LOACH. I've been off it some time now.

ASH. Old Kent Road, friend. And two hundred for passing Go.

BARNET. D'you want it or don't you?

LOACH. I'm trying to pack it in, aren't I?

ASH. I told you, Ted, we pool our resources we'll be in Easy Street.

BARNET (*putting gin away*). Please yourself.

LOACH *goes back to game.* BARNET *comes downstage, speaks to* AUDIENCE.

You can't help some people. I'll think I'll sort the linen, have a smoke . . .

SISTER *comes on from left with* NURSES.

SISTER. Mister Barnet –

BARNET. Ah, Sister?

SISTER. Accident case coming up.

BARNET. Right away, Sister.

Goes off down front stairs.

LOACH. I thought it was for me.

SISTER. Games away now, gentlemen. Mister Flagg, you're due in physio.

The patients pack the game away. MICHAEL *and the* PRINCE *bring a stretcher up the stairs.*

BARNET. Hey. It's young Kenny. Remember him?

They take it across and off left. NURSES *follow. The patients look at the bandaged figure being wheeled by. Flurry of* NURSES *coming and going. Cardiac arrest trolley wheeled across again as* FLAGG *makes his way off right.* BARNET *comes back from left.*

ASH. By George, no! (*To* LOACH.) You didn't know young Kenneth. Motor bike mad.

LOACH *wheels game trolley off to the right.* ASH *gets back into bed.* DOCTORS *and* NURSES *continue crossing as lights go down.*

Scene Seven

BARNET *comes down and into spot.*

BARNET. I could bite my tongue off. Wishing for excitement.
Still, that's life, isn't it, madam? That's human nature. We're
all of us poised on a knife-edge between the urge for security
and a craving for excitement. But you haven't come here to
listen to philosophical speculation, you want the facts.

Young Kenneth swerved to avoid a dog, a coach driver
swerved to avoid *him*, and went head-on into another coach,
killing or maiming sixty passengers. But when I add that one
was a party of mongols and the other an old-age pensioners'
outing, you'll surely agree that one can sometimes discern A
Grand Design. The Grim Reaper certainly seems on occasion
to have his head screwed on. (*Glances at the screens.*)
Casualty's jammed solid, which is why they've brought him
here so prompt.

Goes towards left and his covered wagon is rolled to him.

SWEET comes on from right.

SWEET. Where are you going with that?

BARNET. Standing by for Kenneth.

SWEET. It won't be needed.

BARNET. Have they pulled him through?

SWEET. It looks like it.

BARNET. He must have nine lives.

DOCTORS *return from KEN's bedspace with their machines.*

SWEET *smiles and goes towards left.*

Go on, run!

SWEET *turns, comes back.*

SWEET. I beg your pardon?

BARNET. You're all of a flutter. Say you're not.

SWEET. Why should I be?

BARNET. After some of those noises used to come from the screens –

SWEET (*delighted*). I beg your pardon –?

BARNET. – when you were giving him a bed-bath.

SWEET. I didn't hear that remark.

Goes to help other NURSES.

BARNET. Now say there's nothing bent about the healing arts.

Turns to push his covered wagon off left.

Scene Eight

ASH *alone on stage, in bed. Only* FLAGG's *and* LOACH's *remain of others.* ASH *gets out of bed, puts on slippers and gown as strong daylight comes on. He gets his basket from his locker. He looks at the photographs of his son and closes them and puts them out of sight. Brings his basket down to an armchair. It is a strangely shaped basket.* ASH *views it miserably and begins work. From the left, downstage of the armchairs,* KEN *crawls on all fours. His head is still bandaged and he wears gown and slippers. He hides from* ASH *then raises both fists and points his index fingers. He imitates gunfire.*

ASH. Now, Kenny, old son, what are you up to, eh?

KEN *is now an idiot. His efforts at speech are incoherent but the others are used to his condition and talk over the noise.*

Come and sit by Uncle Mervyn . . . see what he's doing with his funny old basket. I bet you've never seen a basket that shape. No more have I.

KEN *laughs at it. He puts it on his head.*

You could use it for that, I suppose, yes.

Laughs and takes it back. KEN *goes on to stove and begins pretending to shovel coke into the grate.*

That's right. You like doing that, don't you? Not too much, though, it's warm today.

FLAGG *comes from the left, now completely recovered and dressed in outdoor clothes.*

FLAGG. Putting a drop more coal in, Kenny? That's the style then.

ASH. Made your adieus, Mister Flagg?

FLAGG. What's that?

ASH. Said good-bye?

FLAGG. Yes. All this time waiting for the ambulance, I could have been home now, made a cup of tea, if they'd let me walk.

ASH. But after you've been in here some time, the outside world can seem like the headlong rush of the Gadarene swine, they tell me. That's enough, Kenny.

KEN *stops shovelling, turns to listen, sitting on the floor.*

Besides, you're not as young as you were.

FLAGG. No. (*Yawns, moves about*). I don't *feel* old.

ASH. That's the style. You're as young as you feel.

FLAGG. Don't feel any older in myself.

ASH. But your body's old.

FLAGG. I was thinking this morning . . . Cesar Romero . . . now *he* used to be very young.

ASH. There we are. Tempus fugit.

KEN *has got an upright chair and straddles it, moving it along and making motor-cycle sounds and actions.* SWEET *comes on right with a simple wooden construction toy.*

SWEET. Dear me, what a noisy boy you are! And scraping that

chair across the floor when it's just been polished, what'll Sister say? Look what Nurse has brought. You like these, don't you?

He goes down on the floor and begins fitting the pieces together.

There's a clever boy!

FLAGG. Any sign of the ambulance, miss?

SWEET. Wherever's the fire, Mister Flagg? You can't wait to get away from us.

FLAGG. Not that. Only I could have been home . . . had a cup of tea with the old woman . . .

SWEET. All in good time.

FLAGG. Used a toilet with a decent chain . . .

SWEET. How's my basket?

ASH. Nearly done. It's a rather unusual shape.

SWEET looks at it and laughs.

SWEET. It looks like one of those old-fashioned corsets.

Goes off, left. ASH looks after her without smiling. He puts the basket aside.

ASH. How are you getting on, young Kenny? Uncle Mervyn give a hand? How here's a funny piece. Where d'you think that perisher goes, eh?

BARNET comes from right with ORDERLY.

BARNET. That one and that one, out. All right, Princess?

They clear Bed 3. BARNET drifts away and the ORDERLY gets on with it.

I suppose young Ken arouses your old interest in boys?

ASH. Once a teacher, always a teacher, eh, Kenny?

BARNET. He's going to need some teaching and all, wher*ever* they put him.

ASH. And since society sees fit to condemn me to a life of clerical drudgery, I shall do whatever I can to help him.

LOACH drifts on from the side, dressed for the outside world.

BARNET. This your basket, Cinders?

ASH. I hope you're not about to criticise that basket. I've had about all I can stand in that direction. The perishing thing's been like a reproach every day of my confinement, staring me in the face saying: 'Well, Clever Dick?'

LOACH. Same with me, me old mate, never any use with my hands . . .

ASH. But I *had* a use. I had gifts. Small gifts, which I offered humbly to the world and only asked that I be let use them. Why should I spend my life doing the very things I'm least suited for?

BARNET. Very good. Better than the telly.

The ORDERLY *has cleared the beds.* BARNET *rejoins him.*

Well done, sir. Let's go and sort the linen. Ted!

LOACH goes to him. BARNET *gives him a small bottle.*

Don't let anyone see it, all right?

LOACH. What do I owe you?

BARNET. With the money for the gee-gees, say two quid and we'll call it square.

LOACH. How's it come to two quid?

BARNET. I've got my overheads to cover.

Takes notes from LOACH *and goes off, right.* LOACH *swigs.* KEN *crawls to him, pretends to shoot him, grabs his legs.*

LOACH. That's right, Kenny, me old mate. You shoot me dead.

I'd appreciate that. The prospect I got. Great barn of a place, miles from fucking civilisation.

ASH. Don't use words like that. In front of the boy.

LOACH. He ain't a boy. He's a grown man.

ASH. What do you know about it?

LOACH *moves again, towards* FLAGG.

LOACH. We got the same ambulance, eh, Dad?

FLAGG. When it comes.

LOACH. Marvellous, isn't it? Nationalisation.

FLAGG. I could have been home in ten minutes. On the bus.

LOACH. Where's that?

FLAGG. Islington.

LOACH. Very nice.

FLAGG. Used to be beautiful there. Before the Agricultural Hall was sold to the corporation.

LOACH. There you are.

FLAGG. Used to have Market Garden Week there . . . Dairy Week . . .

LOACH *winces, rubs leg.*

LOACH. Jesus God Al-bleeding-mighty. Humorous really, when you think of me out India way. Or Africa. Malaya . . . my own bearer . . . fifty wogs under me . . . I was a sahib.

TYLER *goes across, carried by the black* ORDERLY. *He seems dwarfish and helpless.*

TYLER. How are you, Kenny, smiling through?

And they all make cheering noises as he exits.

ASH. Wonderful spirit.

LAKE *has come on too.*

LAKE. Ready, these patients? Ambulance for you now. Mister –
eh – (*Looks at her list.*) Flagg and Mister Loach. That you?

FLAGG. That's right, miss.

LOACH. Here it is then. No going back now.

FLAGG. I had a bag.

LAKE. Here.

FLAGG. Cheerio, then, all.

Shakes hands with ASH, *while* LOACH *goes to the left.*

LOACH (*shouts off*). Cheerio, me old mates.

A feeble cheer off.

ASH. Don't let me see you in here again.

FLAGG. No fear.

KEN hugs FLAGG's *legs.*

ASH. All right, Kenny.

FLAGG goes to the stairs with LAKE. *She helps him descend
out of sight.* LOACH *shakes with* ASH.

LOACH. Cheerio, Cambridge. If you feel like dropping in
sometime, I say, there's a Green Line bus not far off.

ASH. I'll see what I can do, yes. And good luck.

LOACH. And you're going to ask your landlady about the
room?

ASH. Well, I think it's probably gone, as a matter of fact, but –

LOACH. You can ask.

ASH. Yes.

KEN hugs his legs.

LOACH. Bye-bye, Kenny. Well. Now. Where's old Blackie
gone?

Goes off down the stairs after LAKE. KEN goes on with his toy. ASH looks at the ward, only his bed remains. He goes back to KEN and sits on the floor.

ASH. D'you know, son, we speak the most beautiful language in the world? That's our heritage. The tongue that Shakespeare spake. Yet most of the people you meet can utter nothing better than a stream of filth. I'm not sorry to see him go. I mean, I did my best, but he clung like a limpet. Mind you, I think one should be able to mix without actually lowering standards. Like the time I took my slum boys camping.

KEN laughs, ASH ruffles his hair.

Yes, I did. What's more, I tried an experiment. Paired them off with college boys. Nicely spoken lads, you know. And the ragamuffins visibly *rose*, they actually raised themselves. But – this is the crux of the matter, son – the college lads were totally unscathed. And that's the secret of the governing class. The secret of the Royal Family.

KEN has finished the puzzle.

Clever boy, there's a clever boy.

KEN laughs, breaks it up.

And when I was a teacher I was privileged to know many of the Royal Family personally. No side at all. Regal bearing, yes, but not the snobbery of the newly rich. Simple dignity. Which is what is missing from so much of life today. Grace. Style. We're all the same, we need something fine to which to aspire. We want to rise, not sink in the bog.

KEN makes signs that he wants ASH to help him again. Together they begin to assemble the toy.

My hat, the old Queen! She'd come inspecting. We'd spit-and-polish everywhere. Gym, library, canteen, even the toilets. Know what she'd ask to see? The brush cupboards.

Laughs at the recollection. KEN laughs at his laughter.

ASH. There isn't nearly enough of that sort of spirit about these days.

They go on working.

Scene Nine

Music, lights and a pantomime transformation. Stained glass in the Gothic windows, church bells and a wedding march.

A carpeted staircase comes down centre and two bridal pairs appear – BOYD *and* SISTER McPHEE, NEIL *and* STAFF NURSE NORTON, *the grooms in kilts, the brides in white.*

The PATIENTS, *quick and dead, appear with the nursing staff from both sides, throwing confetti, streamers, rice, and waving Union Jacks.*

The CHAPLAIN *comes up the front steps, now a bishop, mitred and golden. An acolyte bears his train.*

MATRON *calls for cheers, which are given by the whole company to the bridal group as they shake hands with the* CHAPLAIN. *The acolyte turns and we see that he's* BARNET *in black-face.*

A nigger minstrel band marches on playing 'The Georgia Cakewalk' and BARNET *joins them with a tambourine. Everyone dances but soon* BARNET *stops them and brings down each group in turn to take their bows. First the bridal quartet.*

BARNET. A double wedding ends our pantomime –
Four hearts transplanted in the nick of time.
Our nursing girls – yes, madam, you're so right! –
Under the doctor each will spend the night.

Next he presents the nursing staff, headed by MATRON.

The ship of state sails on, a bit becalmed,
Though matron on the bridge is not alarmed.

Until the sails swell out above the boom
She trusts her coolies in the engine room.

And finally the PATIENTS.

As for the rest, there's not a lot to say:
They're born, they die and then get wheeled away –

He thinks again, pats KENNY *on the head.*

The lucky ones. Don't ask me what it means.
See you again one day behind the screens.

*A silent tableau, everyone frozen in their attitudes, staring
front.*

Curtain

Forget-me-not Lane

Forget-me-not Lane

With the royalties from Albert Finney's short Broadway run in *Joe Egg*, we bought a semi-detached Victorian house beside Blackheath. A short walk across the common and through the ancient park took us to the new Greenwich Theatre. When Ewan Hooper, the founder and director, invited me to join the board and contribute a play to his 1971 season, I jumped at the chance both to have a real say in how my local theatre was run and to come up with an example of the sort of play they ought to be doing.

Though the theme was gloomy and pessimistic – however much we try not to, we'll end up like our parents – the play kept smiling through. Nothing in it was exactly new, but it worked better in performance than anything of mine before or since. It is still my favourite, the most personal and the least devious, though it's had only moderate success since that first magical run at Greenwich. As soon as it moved to the Apollo, I could see that no other stage would suit it as well as the one it was written for.

I have since worked at Greenwich on three other shows: as playwright on an adaptation of *Harding's Luck* by E. Nesbit, another local author; and as director on revivals of *Joe Egg* and in 1990 *Forget-me-not Lane*. The last was for me an almost entirely happy experience. Every day, going to rehearse in glum church halls in Borough and Pimlico, I wondered when the bolt from the blue would come to spoil my fun – when the first actor would go sick, the theatre burn down, a war start; surely I shouldn't be allowed to resuscitate the happy experience of nearly twenty years before? Through a bout of flu, I watched my youth being acted out again. At home every night I tried not to sound too euphoric. When actors worried about their scenes, I fobbed them off, never doubting that in a week or so they'd all be too busy controlling the gales of laughter from packed houses – even, as before, at matinees. Swaying feverishly, I believe I even told them so.

Even the oddly subdued previews couldn't shake my confidence. Previews were always tricky, the lighting wasn't quite right yet, the timing was a little off, it would be all right on the night. And, when that too was played to a stunned silence, well, press nights were always tricky. It was not until the reviews that I faced the truth: twenty years later this family was no longer funny but pathetic. There wouldn't be those laughs again.

There weren't. Some weeks later, Michael Frayn went to see it and wrote to me: 'A very strange experience. It was like a dream where everything's familiar but it's all been pervaded by some kind of eerie otherness that one can't quite identify. One of the oddest evenings I've ever spent in the theatre . . . Why didn't people laugh?' And, after some intelligent attempts to find a reason, he gave up and finished: 'The more one works in the theatre the harder it is to understand why things work when they do and why they don't when they don't.'

I've since identified some idiotic mistakes in my production but none so serious as to account for the audience's silence; that only comes if the passage of twenty years is added to the scales. When the play was first staged, the 1960s weren't long gone, a time when The New was all the rage, when 'contemporary' was a buzz-word and nostalgia had not yet been institutionalised into theme parks and Prince Charles Revival housing. A forty-year-old man recalling his youth as bitter to live through but sweet to remember – this was still a novelty, and audiences with younger memories shuddered at the shock of the old. Its timing was exactly right but perhaps never will be again. Its delicate clockwork has been thrown; what was then merely the past tense is now the pluperfect. In the nineties when we look back we're hoping for a friendly lie, cloth-caps or croquet-lawns, blitz bonhomie and big bands and never a hint of irony.

Forget-me-not Lane was first performed on 1 April 1971, at the Greenwich Theatre.

The same production with same cast opened at the Apollo Theatre on 28 April, produced by Memorial Enterprises.

FRANK	Anton Rodgers
CHARLES	Michael Bates
YOUNG FRANK	Ian Gelder
AMY	Joan Hickson
IVOR	Malcolm McFee
MR MAGIC	Eddie Molloy
MISS NINETEEN-FORTY	Stephanie Lawrence
URSULA	Priscilla Morgan
YOUNG URSULA	Sandra Payne

Directed by Michael Blakemore
Designed by Roger Butlin

In a translation by Claude Roy, it was presented as *Ne M'oubliez pas* at the Théâtre de la Renaissance in Paris in June 1972 with Daniel Gélin as Frank and Guy Tréjan as Charles.

In America, Arvin Brown directed it at the Long Wharf, New Haven, Connecticut and later at the Mark Taper Forum, Los Angeles, California. This was later transmitted by WNET TV.

In 1975, a BBC TV production by Alan Bridges featured Albert Finney as Frank, Bill Fraser as Charles and Gemma Jones as Ursula.

The London critics in *Variety* voted it Best British Play of the season.

In March 1990 it was revived at the Greenwich Theatre in a production directed by the author.

ACT ONE

*A semicircular screen contains perhaps six, perhaps eight doors.
Closed, they are hardly noticeable. They open inwards on to the
acting area, and only two have knobs or handles. With front
lights on, the impression is of a plain wall enclosing a space. On
the forestage this space breaks into a number of levels. A four
seater sofa centre. The screen need not be more than ten feet
high and the theatre wall can be seen beyond. One of the doors
is open at the beginning and in the opening is a tape recorder on
a cabinet. We are to assume that it is from here the music comes.*

*Before the action starts, there is a record recital for about
twenty minutes. Throughout this, FRANK comes on and goes
off several times. He is forty. First, he brings on a cheap
suitcase, open and half-full. He leaves it and goes. On his next
appearances, he brings on personal articles and puts them in
the case. He pays more attention to the music than the case
and often stops to mime to the records, which he knows by
heart. At the end of one, he bows to an imaginary audience.*

FRANK (*softly*). Thank you very much. Thank you. (*Sometimes
he looks into the case and rejects an article.*) No, no . . . (*And
after returning several times, he says:*) What exactly are you
doing, man? (*And takes the case off with him. Returning in
time to listen to a good deal of the last record, he mimes
Bechet's soprano sax. He takes a cheque-book, cigarettes and
money from drawers under the player and puts them into his
pocket, brings out a handkerchief, holds it up and looks at it,
shrugs, returns it to his pocket. He turns off the tape and*

closes the door.) Why don't you leave off packing now? (*He keeps moving.*) Not as though you show any improvement as a packer. The same feeble indecision – same refusal to believe the weather might change – shivering through a frost in light-weight suit and pack-a-mac. (*Now he addresses the audience directly.*) And when you consider how large packing has loomed in my family. Both my families. The one I was issued with and the one I escaped to. (*He takes his cigarettes out and lights one. He coughs.*) Christ. (*He recovers.*) When my wife is packing, our bedroom looks as though we've had the burglars in. Before our first second honeymoon, I said, 'Wellington boots *and* tennis rackets?' And she said, 'If you're going to stand there carping, you can do the packing yourself!' 'All right,' I said, 'then let me.' 'You can't,' she said, 'you're a hopeless packer.' My parents went over the same ground more times than I care to remember. Setting out from Bristol to Minehead at last in the Wolseley, my mother would say, 'I hope you packed my laxatives.' And Dad, 'If your laxatives were listed, they were packed. The old man's not exactly a novice at packing suitcases.' Not exactly, no. And yet – in thirty-five years commercial travelling, he never once got ready on time. Every Monday morning he'd start at dawn with the best intentions but hours later he'd still be ransacking the house for indelible pencils, spectacle cases, samples of cake decorations such as nodding robins on sugar logs – or silver horseshoes for wedding-cakes with real bells that tinkled . . .

Bow windows are projected on the screen with checks of paper strips. CHARLES *comes on, aged fifty. He wears a bowler hat, raincoat, grey spats, blue suit underneath, and carries a small leather case.*

CHARLES. Frank!

FRANK (*remembering*). Hallo?

Pause. CHARLES *takes no notice but looks off stage.*

CHARLES (*louder*). Frank!

YOUNG FRANK (*off*). Hallo?

CHARLES. Hallo who?

YOUNG FRANK (*off*). Hallo, Dad.

CHARLES. Come in here.

FRANK. Trying to get him off was like some primitive attempt at man-powered flight. The great flapping steel wings, the sudden loss of energy . . .

YOUNG FRANK *comes on, aged fourteen now, and wearing shirt and trousers, carrying a newspaper.*

YOUNG FRANK. What?

CHARLES. What? What's 'what'?

YOUNG FRANK *shrugs, reads.*

And straighten your shoulders when I'm talking to you, stand up straight.

YOUNG FRANK (*groans*). I'm trying to finish breakfast.

CHARLES. At ten o'clock! Most people have been out, done a day's work by now. Your mother pampers you, gives in to you, she's not got the least idea . . .

YOUNG FRANK. I'm on holiday. What's the matter with having breakfast . . .

CHARLES. Wossermarrer? What's wossermarrer?

YOUNG FRANK *groans, goes on reading.* CHARLES *grabs the lobe of his son's ear and peers into it.*

Have you washed the wax from your ears?

YOUNG FRANK *groans, moves away.*

FRANK. He was like an upset beetle.

CHARLES (*moving about*). I was up this morning at quarter to seven. All this time trying to get away from this house but nobody ever puts anything back where they found it. You been smoking my cigarettes?

YOUNG FRANK. No.

FRANK. But a chill of fear.

CHARLES. No who?

YOUNG FRANK. No, Dad.

CHARLES. Well, it's beyond my comprehension. I've never let smoke, strong drink or vile language pass my lips since I signed the pledge at fourteen. Your mother only has the odd cork-tipped.

CHARLES stands not looking at YOUNG FRANK but seems to be expecting a confession. He has the air of a prosecutor with an irrefutable case.

YOUNG FRANK. I haven't touched them. Honestly!

Pause. YOUNG FRANK *looks at* CHARLES. CHARLES *looks at him.*

CHARLES (*in a softer tone*). If you tell me honestly, boy, I believe you.

FRANK. Oh, yes. That sudden Band-of-Hope piety. (YOUNG FRANK *looks at his paper.*) Even if I was telling the truth, I'd blush with shame.

CHARLES. And look at me when I'm talking, you great pudden.

YOUNG FRANK *groans.* AMY *enters from a different door, wearing spring clothes with apron and turban. She is forty.*

AMY. Here. (*She gives* CHARLES *two packets of cigarettes.*)

CHARLES. Where were they?

AMY. Pocket of the winter suit you've just left off.

FRANK. She was trying to turn him over and point him in the right direction.

CHARLES (*hopelessly*). Could have sworn I looked in there.

YOUNG FRANK. Told you.

CHARLES. I believed you, Son. I know you're a truthful boy.

FRANK. Still can't tell a lie, even today.

CHARLES. Now that smokes are in short supply, branch managers appreciate a packet on the firm.

AMY. I should think they did . . .

CHARLES. Mister Steel, the manager of Yeovil branch . . .

AMY. With queues at every shop.

CHARLES (*after pausing*). Friend Steel of . . .

AMY. And they say it's going to get worse.

CHARLES *looks at her.*

CHARLES. Friend Steel of . . .

AMY. I said, I don't see how it *can* get worse.

CHARLES (*quick and loud*). Friend Steel of Yeovil branch chain-smokes from morn till night and coughs his heart up and turns a lurid purple. I said to him, 'Friend, if I speak quite frankly, you're a noodle, coating your lungs with nicotine instead of God's good air.'

YOUNG FRANK. Then you passed him another packet?

CHARLES. You've got it boy, and licked my indelible pencil and said, 'Now, friend, how you off for custard powder?' A very good line. 'Another gross of tins?'

FRANK. Early lessons in commercial duplicity.

AMY. If you don't get a move on, Friend Steel will be gone to dinner.

CHARLES. Lunch, Amy.

AMY. Lunch, then. (*He takes off his bowler hat, kisses her, puts it on.*)

CHARLES. See you Friday afternoon.

AMY. Be careful. Got your gas-mask?

CHARLES. In the car.

AMY. And your torch in case there's a power cut?

CHARLES (*looks at a list*). Yes. (*To* YOUNG FRANK.) During the air-raids, do as your mother tells you.

YOUNG FRANK (*reading his paper*). Okay.

CHARLES. Okay? What's okay?

AMY. Don't go on at him.

CHARLES. You spoil him, Amy, you side with him. How long since you had your hair cut? Buzfuz? I'm talking to you.

YOUNG FRANK. Fortnight.

AMY. It does want cutting badly, Frank.

CHARLES. No, Amy, it doesn't want cutting badly, it badly wants cutting. But we want it cut well, not badly. (*He moves about, staring over the audience.*)

FRANK. Of course he was trying to find a reason not to go.

CHARLES. Just look at the car! Standing there since eight this morning. The only car in the avenue, it looks like showing off. I detest showing off almost as much as I detest foul language or dirty fingernails.

AMY. Now's your chance to move it.

CHARLES. They can't wait to get rid of the old man. Good-bye, Frank.

YOUNG FRANK. 'Bye.

CHARLES. Good-bye who?

YOUNG FRANK *groans*.

AMY. Come on.

CHARLES *is driven to the door by* AMY, *then turns*.

CHARLES. I think I'll go down the avenue, save turning the car round, along Appian Terrace and up Tuscan Vale to the main road . . .

AMY. I should.

AMY pushes CHARLES off. YOUNG FRANK follows their progress into the wings, down stage and across the front. FRANK watches with him.

YOUNG FRANK. Go, go, go.

FRANK. Into the lobby where sunlight through Edwardian stained-glass colours the morning's loaf and milk-bottles –

YOUNG FRANK. Don't let him talk any more, Mum –

FRANK. – where open umbrellas stand drying out on rainy days –

YOUNG FRANK. Shut the gate behind him, one last wave . . .

FRANK. – and the only car in the avenue won't be seen again until Friday afternoon.

YOUNG FRANK. Another five days of freedom!

The first quarter of a tinkling Westminster chime is heard. AMY enters, carrying a loaf and bottles of milk.

AMY. Quarter past ten on washing day. Before I know where I am it's going to be dinner-time and I shan't know where I am. (*She puts down the bread and milk, takes a cigarette and matches from her apron.*)

YOUNG FRANK. Well, anyway old Hitler's gone.

AMY. You shouldn't talk like that about your father. (*She goes to the window and looks into the street.*)

YOUNG FRANK. He's *worse* than Hitler. Bet you anything Hitler wouldn't stop me using his wind-up gramophone if he already had a great big radiogram! (*He sees her.*) What you looking after him for?

AMY. Make sure he's gone.

YOUNG FRANK. He knows you smoke.

AMY. He doesn't like it. (*She comes down and lights up.*)

YOUNG FRANK. He doesn't like anything. Smoking, drinking, being with your friends and wearing the kind of clothes you like.

AMY. He's got his funny ways.

YOUNG FRANK. He's a cruel tyrant. (*He pronounces it 'tirrant'.*)

AMY. Cruel what?

YOUNG FRANK. Tyrant! This is a tyranny. He tries to crush the spirit of freedom.

FRANK. I can't have said that. Tirrant?

AMY. He's done his best for you, Frank. Put you through a good school . . .

YOUNG FRANK (*incredulous*). Good school?

FRANK. With a Latin song and motto.

YOUNG FRANK (*to* FRANK). But no girls.

AMY. Saved up all that money in cerstificates that you can draw when you're twenty-one.

YOUNG FRANK (*correcting*). Certificates.

AMY. Yes. Cerstificates.

YOUNG FRANK. I don't want money. I want liberty. I think everyone should be allowed to do as they like all the time.

AMY. Don't talk silly.

YOUNG FRANK. I think everybody should be happy and go out in the fields and have picnics and – you know – take all their clothes off even, if they want to –

AMY. That *would* be nice, I must say.

YOUNG FRANK. – and sing and dance and just be friends and no-one would have too much to eat while other people haven't got enough –

FRANK. Oh, no! (*Embarrassed, he hides his face with his hand.*)

YOUNG FRANK. – and people would stop hating each other.

FRANK. It sounds like a Pop Festival.

AMY. Have you finished your breakfast?

YOUNG FRANK. And all the people who don't agree with freedom will be put in special places to be educated. And if they still don't want to be free, they'll be put on desert islands. People like Goering and Mussolini and Dad.

AMY. I see, as the blind man said. (*Suddenly worried.*) If everyone's just enjoying themselves, who's going to clear up all the mess?

YOUNG FRANK. Mess?

AMY. After the picnics.

YOUNG FRANK. Machines. Some huge great vacuum cleaner. Machines will do all the work.

AMY. That'll be nice. Meantime I'd better get the copper going. Or before I know where I am, it'll be dinner-time and I shan't know where I am. (*She starts to leave.*)

YOUNG FRANK *reads his paper.*

FRANK. I know!

The air-raid siren sounds the alert.

AMY. Oh, not those devils again! (*She goes to the window to look out.*)

YOUNG FRANK. Mum! You say I shouldn't call him Hitler but think how he stopped you singing.

AMY (*turning back*). I had a lovely singing voice. Mister Dunn the adjudicator said I was a natural mezzo with perfect pitch and a wide range and all I needed was experience.

FRANK. The self-pity!

YOUNG FRANK. But he was jealous. He wouldn't let you follow your career because it would have meant you singing for other people, not just him.

Gunfire. They take no notice.

AMY. He is a miserable devil in some ways. I sometimes wish I'd never bumped into him at that dance. He was acting the goat and like a fool I laughed. Well, before I knew it we were out there doing the fox-trot and the whole floor stopped to watch us. He was like a gazelle with his patent pumps and his hair smarmed down.

AMY blows her nose with her handkerchief, then makes for the door. YOUNG FRANK returns to his paper.

Did you wet the bed last night?

YOUNG FRANK. Yep.

FRANK. As usual.

AMY. Do try not to.

YOUNG FRANK. I *do.*

Loud gunfire.

AMY. Poor Mother, all alone! She hates the gunfire. Twice in my lifetime those German devils have started a war with us. When my brothers came home from the trenches, Mother made them take off their uniforms in the yard, they were so infested with lice.

YOUNG FRANK. She ought to come and live here.

AMY. She and Dad are at each other's throats, she says she'd rather be independent.

FRANK. He couldn't stand the sight of Grandma drinking stout.

The front door slams.

AMY. What's that? (*She looks out of the window.*) Oh, no, the car's outside.

CHARLES *enters, as before, but carrying one shoe in front of him, at arm's length.*

YOUNG FRANK. What are you back for?

CHARLES. For what are you back?

AMY. I thought we'd got rid of you.

CHARLES. The usual sunny welcome. Mister Dick was filling Leonora with petrol when the sirens went. I said, 'There's not the slightest use rushing off to Yeovil now. Friend Steel makes straight for the convenience the moment a raid begins and for some time afterwards he's quite unable to bring his mind to bear on cake decorations and desiccated coconut.'

AMY. What you holding out your shoe for?

CHARLES and YOUNG FRANK. For what are you holding out your shoe?

CHARLES. Hold your tongue, Buzfuz. I'm talking to Woodbine Winnie here. 'In fact,' I added, 'I think there's very little point in leaving now till after lunch.'

YOUNG FRANK *and* AMY *groan. Gunfire.*

AMY. The larder's empty.

CHARLES. And Mister Dick said, 'They won't cheer to see you back.' I said, 'I don't care tuppence.'

AMY. But what's the shoe for?

CHARLES. Crossing the pavement from the car, I'm dashed if I didn't inadvertently step where a dog had used the convenience!

AMY. Fancy bringing it in the dining-room!

CHARLES. I'm on my way to wipe it clean with a copy of

Reynolds News. But it's beyond my comprehension – after I'd put up a notice: Dogs not to foul the public footway.

YOUNG FRANK. Lot of dogs round here can't read.

CHARLES. Don't try to score me off, Sonny Jim. You're not half bright enough! (*He moves towards the other door*.) And you can help me open the garage doors, we'll put the car away, it might get struck by shrapnel out there.

CHARLES *goes*. AMY *picks up the bread and milk*.

AMY. Don't make a mess in my clean scullery.

AMY *goes*.

YOUNG FRANK (*appealing to the ceiling*). Oh, God, please help us to be free of him. Please make a bomb fall on him, God.

YOUNG FRANK *goes off another way with the newspaper. The bow windows fade*.

FRANK. How could I possibly understand them at fourteen? Their complicated middle-age game of regret and recrimination? My own experience was confined to chasing high-school girls through the city museum at lunchtime. Oh, those stuffed kangaroos! Those tableaux of British wildlife! That scent of gravy! I took a party of students last week and I'm glad to say it's resisted all attempts at modernisation. The hippopotamus still yawns beside the fire buckets. (*He screws his eyes tight shut and claps his hands*.) Stick to the point, man! The point was that I couldn't understand the sophisticated war my parents were conducting – either the issues or the strategy. But I *was* in the line of fire. So instead of understanding I took sides. Dad was a monster, Mum was a martyr. What does my own boy make of it when at thirteen he watches Ursula and me growling and roaring at each other? Yes, that's one of the reasons I left her. Having seen my parents like cat-and-dog year after year, I wanted to save my son that spectacle. (*He ponders, shrugs, and does a Churchill imitation*.) We shall fight on the landing-grounds, we shall fight in the living-rooms, we shall fight in the only car in the avenue. Everyone was exhorted to take sides at the time and Dad became my personal Hitler. (*He glances at the door* CHARLES *came from, and goes on quietly.*) No wonder I wet the bed three times a week at fourteen. Poor man. Thirty years too late I can see what he must have been suffering, separated from his beloved wife five days a week, packed off gladly Monday mornings to share commercial hotels with heavy drinking, dirty-joke telling travellers. And on Fridays welcomed back as warmly as Messerschmitt.

YOUNG FRANK *comes on, opens the door to the gramophone and puts on a record – scratched 1941 'Woodchoppers Ball' by Joe Loss, or Woody Herman. He wears a suit and polished shoes. He conducts the band, miming the tenor sax.*

Especially by me and my close friend Ivor.

IVOR *comes on from the same door that* FRANK *used, arriving just in time to mime the clarinet solo.* YOUNG FRANK *signals him in and keeps the band quieter so he can be heard.* IVOR *is fourteen as well and also wears a suit.*

FRANK (*after listening for a while*). This was just before we moved from swing to jazz.

CHARLES *enters from another door, behind the boys. He is dressed as before but carries a case in one hand, a bunch of flowers in the other. He puts down the case, frowns at the oblivious boys and takes off the record.*

YOUNG FRANK *and* IVOR *see* CHARLES *and groan.*

CHARLES. I can hear that blessed racket on the far side of the street.

YOUNG FRANK. You home again?

CHARLES. The usual sunny welcome.

YOUNG FRANK *makes a face at* IVOR. IVOR *facially imitates* CHARLES. CHARLES *looks closely at the record-player.*

And still using steel needles, tearing your records to shreds. Why don't you take a bone one?

YOUNG FRANK. Cause they sound terrible. You can hardly . . .

CHARLES. Hullo, Ivor, are you quite well?

IVOR. Hullo.

CHARLES. Hullo, who?

IVOR. Hullo, Mister Bisley, I suppose.

CHARLES. And stand up straight when you speak to me. Stooping over like that, how can you expect to fill your lungs with God's good air?

IVOR (*giggles*). Good old God.

CHARLES. What d'you say? Taking the Lord's name in vain?

A piano is played off – Sinding's 'Rustle of Spring'.

Listen to that – your mother playing. Always been one of my greatest pleasures, Frank, hearing your mother play.

YOUNG FRANK. As a matter of fact . . .

CHARLES. Hold your tongue, boy, give yourself a chance to hear some decent music for a change. I shall go to her, throw open the door, and drop on one knee before her, saying, 'You, my dear, are playing "Rustle of Spring" and I've brought you a spring bouquet.' What do you think she'll say to that, boy? 'You home again?'

YOUNG FRANK. No, she'll probably say, 'That's not me playing, it's my pupil.' She's giving a lesson.

There is a mistake in the music, which has otherwise been adequate. Pause. The pianist begins again from a few bars back.

CHARLES (*without conviction*). Fancy playing records when your mother's teaching! (*He puts the flowers on the table.*)

IVOR *moves to* YOUNG FRANK *and whispers.*

YOUNG FRANK. Going up the back room.

CHARLES. Why are you both in your best?

IVOR. We're entertaining tonight.

YOUNG FRANK. An anti-aircraft station.

FRANK. Or fighter base or military hospital or isolated wireless unit.

CHARLES. Your mother, too?

YOUNG FRANK. We're all in the same concert party, you know that.

CHARLES *glares, betrayed, towards the piano music.*

CHARLES. And I've been away since Monday! She promised she wouldn't go entertaining Friday night.

YOUNG FRANK. We've all got to pull our weight.

FRANK (*to* YOUNG FRANK). Show a bit of understanding.

IVOR. If the troops want us, we've got to go.

CHARLES. What makes you think they want you? (*He imitates a sergeant.*) 'Fifty volunteers to watch some crackpots do a concert, the others will peel the spuds.' That's how it's done.

YOUNG FRANK. How d'you know? You've never been in the army. Dodged both wars.

CHARLES. I was medically unfit in the first due to the deafness caused by my father clouting me across the ear.

YOUNG FRANK. Any case, our show's much better than you and your corny old recitations.

CHARLES (*quietly*). Not so much of the jolly old buck. You don't know about what you're talking. Haven't you ever read my notices? Ivor, you?

IVOR. Yeah.

CHARLES. 'If laughing ensures growing fat, each one of the audience must bulk considerably as a result of Charles Bisley's sketches of London low-life.' 'One cannot too highly praise Mr Bisley's characterisation of Ikey Cohen.'

IVOR. Well, anyway, I reckon we all ought to do our bit.

YOUNG FRANK. Remember what old Winnie said, 'I have nothing to offer but blood, toil, tears and sweat.'

CHARLES. Acting the goat in a concert party is not exactly what Mister Churchill strove to convey by those beautiful words.

They groan. IVOR *imitates* CHARLES *facially.*

It's a pity you don't put some of your blood, toil, tears and sweat into your school work. Pass your exams and get a job in the Civil Service.

FRANK. Which is what I did in the end. Some years later.

CHARLES. Have you done your prep for tomorrow?

YOUNG FRANK. I can do it in the break.

CHARLES. You sprawl about in your best clothes, listening to rubbish and tell me you can do your prep in the break?

YOUNG FRANK. It's only revision and I'm nearly top in French, anyway.

CHARLES. *Nearly* top's not good enough. One day, when the war's over and France is liberated, you may go as your mother and I did and how glad I was to know a little of the language. No-one could claim your mother had the gift of tongues and like a piecan she said to a lady in the hotel, 'Can you tell us the way to Marshal Joffre street?' I said, 'Amy, for goodness' sake, stand aside, let the old man. *Ou est le Rue de Marshal Joffre, s'il vous plaît, Madame?*' She said as quick as a flash, '*A le droit, Monsieur, à le droit.*'

They wince at his accent.

IVOR. Lucky she was a Cockney, too.

YOUNG FRANK *laughs.*

CHARLES. You give me cheek in my house, you won't come here again, Sonny Jim.

FRANK. The strongest threat he could use. Ivor was my life.

YOUNG FRANK. I've only got to revise the subjunctive of irregular verbs from *devoir* to *ouvrir* and I know them already, Dad. Honestly.

CHARLES (*quietly*). You tell me honestly, boy, I believe you.

YOUNG FRANK *looks at the floor. The 'Rustle of Spring' has passed by and the pupil is playing scales. CHARLES looks towards the sound then back again.*

Right, Ivor, in this bag are one or two presents from branch managers.

FRANK. The few he hadn't estranged by his Puritanism.

CHARLES. A pound of bacon from Wiltshire, a Battenburg cake from Cardiff and a tin of salmon from Glastonbury.

IVOR. Black market.

CHARLES. Not at all. I'm in the distributive trades and fragments are bound to fall off here and there in the process of conveying the goods from hither to yon.

IVOR. Okay.

CHARLES. I haven't noticed your father averse to the odd hand-out.

FRANK. All the same it was wicked at a time when most people welcomed rationing as a first step towards some degree of fair shares.

CHARLES. Come here, Son.

FRANK. A step not even the ruling class could postpone any longer.

CHARLES *gives* IVOR *the case.*

CHARLES. Take it to the scullery and as you pass through the music-room . . .

YOUNG FRANK. The music-room?

CHARLES. Hold your tongue! As you pass through, look unconcerned, don't draw the pupil's attention to the suitcase in any way.

IVOR. She's only eleven.

CHARLES. If you paid more attention to what's going on in the world, you'd know children have been betraying their own parents in Germany.

FRANK. We had this pantomime every Friday because he was really excited by the thought of wickedness.

CHARLES. And take those flowers . . .

FRANK. Afraid of every kind of pleasure he had put behind him when he rose from the Edwardian poor.

CHARLES. Fill with water the vawse, vayse or vahse you will find on the window-sill and place them therein. Who said that, the old man? I'll give him a kick in the pants. (*He kicks himself and laughs.*)

IVOR. Okay.

IVOR *takes the case and flowers and goes.*

CHARLES. Got one or two more cases you can help bring in from the car, Frank. The longer I leave it standing there, the more it looks like showing off.

YOUNG FRANK *goes and* CHARLES *follows. Bow windows fade and piano practice finishes.*

FRANK. Having stowed the plunder, my mother and Ivor and I would catch the bus to meet the cars that took us into the country where we did Our Bit. Sometimes we'd have to shout through gunfire and – once I remember at a fighter station, the audience were gradually called into the air one by one and those that stayed shouted, 'Carry on!' Perhaps Dad was right and it was a choice between watching us and cookhouse fatigues. But we never believed it . . .

A Union Jack unfurls at the back. A concert party piano plays an elaborate introduction. AMY *enters in a velvet evening gown with a pearl necklace.*

AMY (*singing*). There'll always be an England
　　While there's a country lane,
　　Wherever there's a cottage small
　　Beside a field of grain.

A middle-aged man enters in the costume and make-up of a Chinese magician. While AMY *continues, he shows a number of separate silk squares: red, white and blue.* YOUNG FRANK *comes on with a Chinese kimono and shows an empty cylinder,* MR MAGIC *puts the squares into the cylinder.*

　　There'll always be an England
　　Where there's a crowded street,
　　Wherever there's a chimney tall,
　　A million marching feet.

IVOR, *as before, comes on and opens a door behind which is a large sketch-pad. He begins drawing while* MR MAGIC *and* YOUNG FRANK *continue packing squares into the cylinder.*

　　Red, white and blue –
　　What does it mean to you?
　　Surely you're proud,
　　Shout it aloud,
　　Britons, Awake!

A YOUNG BLONDE *enters, wearing Union Jack satin briefs, with roller-skates on and begins tap-dancing.*

　　The Empire, too,
　　We can depend on you.
　　Freedom remains.
　　These are the chains
　　Nothing can break

FULL CHORUS: There'll always be an England

> YOUNG FRANK *holds the cylinder and* MR MAGIC *takes from it the first square, now a Union Jack. He walks across the stage and pulls out a long tape strung with flags.*

And England shall be free –

> *They point to* IVOR's *drawing, which is now seen to be a caricature of Churchill.*

If England means as much to you –

> *They form a line down stage and the* DANCER *finishes by doing the splits, her hands held by* YOUNG FRANK *and* IVOR.

As England means to me.

> *Coda and arpeggios from the pianist. All except* FRANK *wave, bow, then go, shutting the door. The flags disappear.*

FRANK. We never gave a thought to the old man at home, listening to Beethoven, sharpening his bone needles, imagining our wickedness. My only thought was for the peroxide blonde.

> MISS NINETEEN-FORTY *enters without roller-skates.*

At eighteen, only four years older, she was already a different generation. Soldiers roared at her satin drawers, her legs browned with liquid make-up. I roared, too, but silently, inside my head. Please God let her sit alongside me in the car home. Not that I ever *did* anything – but I could smell the powder, feel the warmth, the beat of her heart, the rise and fall of her breasts . . . (*He shuts his eyes to expel the thought.*) One night she sat on my hand –

> MISS NINETEEN-FORTY *sits on* FRANK's *right hand.*

– I couldn't think how to tell her. An hour, the journey took, and when we dropped her, my fingers were paralysed. Nobody noticed. Nobody ever noticed us much. It was a time for grown-up people. And as we approached the city, the sky was orange, searchlight beams were trying to find the bombers, a balloon burned over the house, the ack-ack pounded away – and my hand was crushed beneath a dancer's thighs.

MISS NINETEEN-FORTY *rises and goes.*

Next day I was expected to be fourteen again and decline irregular verbs – from *devoir* to *ouvrir* . . . (*He moves excitedly.*) But at lunch-time down to the City Museum. British Wildlife had been hit by incendiaries but we chased the high school girls through Transport Down The Ages and struggled with them behind the horse-drawn fire-engines.

URSULA *comes on, aged thirty-eight, attractive and well-dressed.*

(*To her.*) You were about thirteen.

URSULA. Thinking about me again. You said you wouldn't. You should be packing while I'm at the evening class. Not dreaming.

FRANK. I find those years exciting to remember.

URSULA. I expect the peroxide blonde does, too.

FRANK. She must be among those middle-aged women who flock the local palais on Glenn Miller night. But at least she'll have some memories worth having. Whereas mine! God!

URSULA. Whose fault's that?

FRANK. Mine, I know.

URSULA. I tried hard enough. From the first moment I saw you.

FRANK. You didn't make it very obvious.

URSULA. You were too busy being scathing and sophisticated to notice.

FRANK. Pride.

URSULA. Yes. But a deep disapproval of pleasure, too. An urge to spoil people's fun.

FRANK. Only because I was afraid.

URSULA. You still are. Still spend most of your spare time dwelling on your lost opportunities. Remembering the war.

They are standing at some distance from each other.

FRANK. Well, the war was the last time, it seems to me, that pleasure and duty coincided. When they weren't chasing U-boats and incendiary bombs, the men and women of that time seemed to be chasing each other.

URSULA. Especially after the Yanks arrived.

FRANK. Yes, skidding about the semis in their sexy jeeps with tight-arsed trousers and Hollywood names. And the good-time girls used to . . .

URSULA. Good-time girls! (*She laughs.*)

FRANK. They used to sit in rows on our front wall waiting for their lovers to pour from the evacuated orphanage. My grandma called them brazen hussies. To me, they were at least as exotic as the camel that came by once with a circus and started nibbling our privet.

URSULA. I was arrested for loitering once.

FRANK. Did you really pick up Yanks?

URSULA. No. Mum lost her temper and told the policeman I was only fourteen and still at school, but that meant nothing.

FRANK. Most of the tarts weren't that much older.

URSULA. The nearest thing I got was spending so much time with Denise Carter.

FRANK. Denise Carter!

URSULA. I suppose she must have been flat-chested and putty-coloured, but by the time she'd got on her painted face with the huge crimson lips and plucked and pencilled her eyebrows and Vaselined her lashes – curled her hair with sugar and water – pushed her breasts up into the padded brassiére – and climbed into a low-necked magenta sweater in brushed angora, she seemed to me like a film-star. And when you consider some of the oddities we tried to look like them . . .

FRANK (*nodding*). She probably did, yes. (*He smiles appreciatively.*)

URSULA. While the Americans were here, she promoted herself through the ranks from Private to Major.

FRANK. Hands across the sea.

URSULA. Yes.

FRANK (*imitating Churchill*). Give us the tools and we will finish the job.

She laughs.

While you were being initiated in the ways of women, Ivor and I were playing puberty games in the back room.

URSULA. That back room!

IVOR *enters, opening a screen of pin-up pictures up to nineteen-forty-three.*

FRANK. You didn't come there till you were fourteen.

URSULA. Will there ever be a sexier room?

FRANK. One afternoon, if you'd been five minutes earlier, you'd have caught us at our games.

IVOR, *now sixteen and in sports clothes, takes a cigarette from a tin and lights up.*

URSULA. What games?

FRANK. I suppose there's no harm telling you now.

IVOR *leans by the door.*

URSULA. What harm could there be?

FRANK. Losing face.

URSULA. What does it matter now?

IVOR *and* YOUNG FRANK *laugh.*

FRANK. All right.

> YOUNG FRANK *follows* IVOR *on. Now sixteen years, he wears mother's headscarf, skirt, blouse, padded brassiére; also lipstick, pencilled eyebrows, rouged cheeks, etc. He carries his own clothes in a case and puts them on the sofa.*

URSULA. Oh, no!

FRANK. Yes.

URSULA. It's Denise Carter to the life.

YOUNG FRANK. Give us a cigarette.

> IVOR *offers his tin.* YOUNG FRANK *lights up.*

URSULA (*laughing*). Why didn't you ever tell me?

> FRANK *shrugs, watching her watch* YOUNG FRANK.

And now you stand here wishing you had. Wondering what I'd have said.

FRANK. Yes.

IVOR. That was terrific, man!

YOUNG FRANK. What about the Yank sentry? (*He takes off his make-up.*) What did you do when he whistled after me?

IVOR. Nothing.

YOUNG FRANK. I felt all funny. Bit scared.

URSULA (*sympathetically*). Aaah! (*She goes to Frank and kisses him, maternally.*)

IVOR. Hey, be great if your mum wears these clothes next time she goes past the orphanage and that Yank whistles at her thinking it's you again!

YOUNG FRANK. They whistle at Amy anyway.

IVOR. My old man said, 'Those Yanks go for anything in skirts between eight and eighty.'

YOUNG FRANK. Old Philip would say that, wallowing about and dreaming of terrific sexual orgies. (*Hard 'g'.*) The English are all jealous 'cause the Yanks get all the girls – but I'd go with a Yank if I was a girl.

URSULA. Does that mean, if Ivor hadn't been with you, you'd have spoken to the sentry?

FRANK. I'd never even have gone outside alone. Now I think of it, people must have known I was a boy. They *must* have.

IVOR. Hey, man, you know when you toss off –

YOUNG FRANK. Yeah.

IVOR. – d'you pretend you're a man or a woman?

YOUNG FRANK. I keep changing about. Sometimes I'm a slave girl like Hedy Lamarr and my master whips me a lot and I cringe and beg for mercy. Then I come in and the brave bloke . . .

IVOR. Alan Ladd?

YOUNG FRANK. Yeah – keep changing round.

IVOR. I pretend I'm the bloke all the time.

They smoke for a while. IVOR *coughs.* YOUNG FRANK *begins changing into his own clothes.*

YOUNG FRANK. Hey, you know Jacobs in Four A.

IVOR. Terrific swot, yeah.

YOUNG FRANK. I saw his tool when we changed for gym. You seen it?

IVOR. No.

YOUNG FRANK. It's different to everyone else's.

IVOR. More like a knob.

YOUNG FRANK. Yeah.

IVOR. I've seen some like that.

FRANK. We knew so little about the Jews.

URSULA. They were in the Bible and Shakespeare.

FRANK. But that was nothing to do with Jacobs of Four A.

URSULA. And my uncle sometimes made a veiled remark about band-leaders.

FRANK. When you think what was happening a few hundred miles away!

URSULA. And our history lessons were still about Clive and Wolfe and Arkwright's Spinning Jenny.

YOUNG FRANK. Another thing about old Jacobs – he never does Divinity.

IVOR. Wish I didn't. Divinity's a dead loss.

YOUNG FRANK. Know what old Muller told me?

IVOR. What?

YOUNG FRANK. If a bod and a woman are shagging and she gets frightened by a mouse or something, her minge can tighten up and the bod can't get it out.

IVOR. Togger White told me that. He said they come from the hospital and throw buckets of water over them and –

YOUNG FRANK. Cri-kee!

IVOR. – if that doesn't loosen it, they have to put them on a stretcher and carry them out to the ambulance.

YOUNG FRANK. With all the neighbours looking!

IVOR. And sometimes they have to operate.

YOUNG FRANK. Cut if off?

IVOR. He didn't say. He said it used to happen a lot during the Blitz. A bomb used to frighten the woman and . . . (*He makes a strangled face and sounds.*)

YOUNG FRANK. Terrific agony, man.

IVOR. Terrific embarrassment. Would you like to have been a woman?

YOUNG FRANK. No.

IVOR. Wish you had been. Be wizard to be terrific friends with a woman.

YOUNG FRANK. Wouldn't have minded having tits.

By this time YOUNG FRANK *has changed into his boy's shoes, trousers, etc., but still wears the bra. He pushes out his chest.* IVOR *touches the padded bra.*

FRANK. That's enough!

The doorbell rings, IVOR *and* YOUNG FRANK *jump up.*

IVOR. Your mum?

YOUNG FRANK. She's at the aircraft factory. And Hitler's in Newton Abbot till Friday. You go and see.

YOUNG FRANK *fans away smoke, then puts on a record of Chicago jazz.* IVOR *goes.*

URSULA. I always passed your house on the way home and when I saw Ivor's bike outside I knew you must be in. Of course it was safe if there were two of you.

FRANK. You'd have been even safer alone. I used to kiss you sometimes in front of Ivor just to prove myself.

URSULA. But I didn't know that. I thought you were experienced.

FRANK. The lost opportunities!

YOUNG FRANK, *his change finished, puts his mother's clothes away in the case.* IVOR *enters with* YOUNG URSULA, *fourteen, wearing school uniform and carrying a satchel.* YOUNG FRANK *is jazzing. He sees* YOUNG URSULA *and groans.*

YOUNG URSULA. Terrific pong.

YOUNG FRANK. We been smoking.

YOUNG URSULA. Pong of lipstick.

Pause.

IVOR. Been making up. We're going to do a Marx Brothers sketch at the end-of-term show.

YOUNG URSULA (*approaching* YOUNG FRANK). Still got some on your face. Smells nice. Sexy.

She touches his face, smells her hand. IVOR *and* YOUNG FRANK *groan.* IVOR *lies on the sofa.* YOUNG URSULA *goes to look at the pin-ups.*

This Harry James?

The boys croak and groan with laughter.

YOUNG FRANK. No. Mantovani.

YOUNG URSULA. No, it's not. Is it?

YOUNG FRANK. No. It's Eddie Condon.

URSULA. You weren't the easiest boys to make advances to.

YOUNG FRANK. How's life among the common folk?

IVOR. The salt of the earth?

YOUNG URSULA. How d'you know what it's like where I live? You never come.

YOUNG FRANK. Don't want to.

FRANK. I was too frightened. Alone with you on your home ground! You might have found out how little I knew.

YOUNG FRANK. Some of the common folk might breathe on me and give me a disease.

IVOR. They're the sort of people when they go to the pictures think it's all acted on the roof of the cinema and reflected down on to the screen by mirrors.

YOUNG URSULA. They don't!

IVOR. I argued with one of them.

YOUNG URSULA. What did he say?

IVOR. Hit me in the belly-button.

YOUNG FRANK. That's how they finish every discussion, the plebs.

IVOR. I shouted 'Brawn versus Brain', but he was half-way back to his slum by then.

IVOR *and* YOUNG FRANK *laugh and jeer.*

YOUNG URSULA. Got any maths homework?

YOUNG FRANK. Got some simultaneous equations for Thursday.

YOUNG URSULA. Easy. Do yours if you do my composition. This week it's 'My Ideal Birthday Party'.

The record finishes. YOUNG FRANK *takes off the arm. Shuts the door.*

Shall I tell you what I'd like and you can say it in wizard English?

IVOR. Hellish boring.

YOUNG URSULA *sits on* YOUNG FRANK's *lap.*

YOUNG URSULA (*ignoring him*). I should like all the best-looking boys to come to it and each of them to have a girl except you. And we should play sardines and I'd be hiding in the Anderson shelter and you'd find me straight away.

FRANK (*admiring*). You were so *rude*!

YOUNG URSULA. And all the others would give up looking and I'd be your prisoner.

YOUNG FRANK. Better not put that.

YOUNG URSULA. Why not?

YOUNG FRANK. Get kicked out.

YOUNG URSULA *smiles and takes his hand.*

YOUNG URSULA. How you getting on with School Certificate?

YOUNG FRANK. Okay in French, English and History.

IVOR. That'll be enough to get you into the Civil Service. Make your old man happy.

YOUNG URSULA. Mummy says I've got to matriculate as a present for Daddy when he comes home.

IVOR. We're not bothering.

YOUNG URSULA. You're no good at school, anyway. Only art.

IVOR. What good's School Certificate to a Film Director?

FRANK (*scornfully*). Film Director!

IVOR. Frank and I are going into films.

FRANK. Ten years later I had to slog away for A levels in the evenings. As a first step to getting my external degree.

YOUNG URSULA. Frank's father thinks you bring him down.

YOUNG FRANK. We know that. 'You want to drop that crackpot Ivor, boy . . .'

IVOR (*imitating*). 'He's beyond my comprehension.'

YOUNG FRANK. Show her your drawing of your parents, Ive.

IVOR *takes a drawing from his pocket and shows* YOUNG URSULA.

IVOR. My parents and Fran's at one of their hellish boring bridge parties. There's your mum puffing a Craven A and your dad with a great load of black market sweets for my mum. My mum's false teeth have got stuck on a toffee. And there's my old man pretending to read the rules of bridge but really it's a picture of a wore.

Pause. YOUNG URSULA *looks at the picture.*

YOUNG URSULA. A what?

IVOR. A wore. That pin-up girl in bra and panties.

YOUNG URSULA. Whore, isn't it, Fran?

YOUNG FRANK (*thinking*). Dunno.

IVOR. *Wore* it is.

YOUNG FRANK. No, hang on. I remember the blackmailed
wreck reading it aloud . . .

YOUNG URSULA. Who's the blackmailed wreck?

YOUNG FRANK. Our English master. Now I think of it, you
must be right, Urse.
'Thou rascal beadle, hold thy bloody hand,
Why dost thou lash that whore? Strip thine own back . . .'

YOUNG URSULA. *King Lear* – terrific!

YOUNG FRANK. 'Thou hotly lusts to use her in that sport . . .'

YOUNG URSULA. Kind. 'That kind for which thou whipst
her.'

YOUNG FRANK. Yeah.

Pause. IVOR *moves away, folding up his picture.*

IVOR. I might do a whole great series of these.

YOUNG URSULA. Hey, half past four! I've got to get my
mother's tea by the time she's home from the factory. (*She
prepares to go.*)

URSULA. Making bombers and getting a decent wage for the
first time.

FRANK. And your father was in North Africa.

URSULA. Yes. The government had found him a job at last.
After keeping him out of work for most of the thirties.

YOUNG URSULA. You'll do my composition?

YOUNG FRANK. I'll give you my algebra downstairs.

FRANK. Whatever did he think he was defending? The right to be on the dole?

URSULA. Oh, the poor are always more patriotic in every country. Only the rich are international. Our rich had made friends with Hitler before and they'd have done it again if we'd lost. But the poor would have been in labour camps.

FRANK. They didn't *know* that at the time. Not till we saw the newsreels of Buchenwald. During the war all we had was Churchill's word for it.

URSULA. Surely he didn't say much about that. A lot about Going Forward Together.

FRANK. That's funny, too, from a man who knew so little about us he'd never even travelled on a bus. (*To the audience.*) *Never once!*

URSULA. 'We shall fight on the fields,' he said, and a lot of people who'd hardly *seen* a field suddenly felt they were the yeomen of England. Can you imagine him in my mother's lounge?

FRANK (*imitating Churchill*). As I look around me at this humble hearth – the chair of uncut moquette – the wireless shaped like an Aztec temple – the Polyfoto of the absent father in uniform . . . the years fall away. I see another Agincourt, another Waterloo.

URSULA. We all thought he was lovely, though.

FRANK. I remember hating him when he came to inspect our officer material in the Training Corps at school and the rest of us had to stand and cheer and I didn't get home in time to hear the Radio Rhythm Club. And as for understanding what he represented . . .

URSULA. Nobody in our circles understood anything. That was left to the Brains Trust.

FRANK. None the less there were pleasures, never to be equalled! Listening to jazz. Imitating our elders. Oh Christ, those years we lost before the flesh of your thighs collapsed and the whites of my eyes turned red! No wonder you've lost interest *now!*

URSULA *folds her arms impatiently as she sees an old argument coming.*

No wonder it's 'I don't mind as long as we have the light out' or 'Quick then before I drop off . . .'

URSULA. I sometimes want it just as much as you.

FRANK. Too much too young, that's your trouble.

URSULA. Too little too late. Why dwell on it?

FRANK. Because I can't help it. Still emotionally in that back room, my mind a collage of pin-ups, craving the promiscuity you had and I missed.

URSULA. I wasn't promiscuous in fact –

FRANK. Come on –

URSULA. – not for long, anyway –

FRANK. – ah!

URSULA (*to the audience*). Only long enough to discover I don't like being treated as just a body.

FRANK *approaches behind and embraces her. She wearily removes his arms.*

FRANK. And I'm always afraid women are only after my mind. Wish someone would treat me as a body.

URSULA. You can do what you like. But with three dependent kids, no man's going to bother with me. I'll *have* to make do with memories. (*She goes towards the door.*)

FRANK. Easy for you –

URSULA *goes, closing the door.*

(*Shouting after her.*) – with memories stretching back to the Year One! (*To the audience.*) Memories of meadows – sand-dunes – innumerable divans – the upper decks of buses – once, even she told me, a wing of the Bodleian Library. (*He moves distractedly.*) But mine! Please!

The CHINESE ILLUSIONIST *from the concert party enters without make-up but wearing a cheap silk Chinese kimono. He is smoking a cigarette.*

MR MAGIC. I think it's so important to wear the proper clothes for anything, don't you, Frank? Even in our early lessons, before we go to the Baths, it's best to get the feel.

YOUNG FRANK *comes in in swimming trunks, with a vest.*

And so few boys do what you tell them, d'you know that?

MR MAGIC *makes the cigarette disappear, then reappear.* YOUNG FRANK *stares.*

I've had boys working for me. Some of my assistants. Neither use nor ornament, really. I'm not saying I'm not fond of them, they're sweet boys at heart, but you're all the same, aren't you, full of mischief. (*He takes a cigarette from* FRANK's *ear.*)

YOUNG FRANK. That's terrific, that. I'm just learning but it's hellish hard.

MR MAGIC. You stay and work with me, Frank, I'll teach you all the tricks you've ever seen. And quite a few you haven't. (*He throws the cigarette in the air and it disappears.*)

FRANK. A sad old queen.

MR MAGIC. You lack technique, that's all.

FRANK. Well, old? I suppose he was a bit older than I am now.

MR MAGIC. Next time you're in London, you mention my name to any of the impresarios in Cambridge Circus. They'll say, 'There's no finer artiste in the business than Li Chang.'

FRANK. Alias, Mr Magic, alias Walter Chambers –

MR MAGIC. Never anything cheap and nasty –

FRANK. – described as a magician, of no fixed abode –

MR MAGIC. – never anything artistically degrading, like some you see, with their half-naked tarty girls, their great chests bulging out.

FRANK. – sentenced to six months . . .

MR MAGIC. Nothing to turn your stomach. (*He sits.*) We'll have to think of a name for you. Wun Hung Down. How's that?

YOUNG FRANK *looks cold.*

Uncle's only joking. What about this breast stroke?

FRANK. No.

MR MAGIC. Come and sit here.

MR MAGIC *holds out his hand towards him.* YOUNG FRANK *approaches and* MR MAGIC *sits him on his knee. He looks awkward.*

Can you swim at all?

FRANK. No.

MR MAGIC. Float?

YOUNG FRANK *shakes his head.*

Let's start with floating. Your mother knows where you are, I suppose.

YOUNG FRANK. She knows we're rehearsing, yes. She's gone to my gran's this evening.

MR MAGIC. Now imagine yourself on the surface of the water. Completely relaxed.

FRANK (*moving quickly, dismissing them*). No more!

YOUNG FRANK *looks at him, then jumps from* MR MAGIC's *lap and runs off by the door he came from.*

MR MAGIC (*calling after him*). Frank! Whatever's the matter? What a strange boy you are! Honestly!

FRANK (*shutting his eyes as though to dismiss the thought*). Get off, get out!

MR MAGIC (*to him*). Don't you shout at me. You can't push people out as easily as that!

FRANK. Can't I! (*He moves swiftly towards* MR MAGIC.)

MR MAGIC *goes, leaving the door open.* FRANK *slams the door and holds it shut.* MR MAGIC *opens another door nearby.*

MR MAGIC. All your life you'll be wincing at the memory.

FRANK *leaves the door, runs to shut him out again. The sound of footsteps continues behind the wall and* FRANK *follows the sound until it stops on the opposite side of the stage. He waits for the door to open. It does not. He opens it wide. Nobody there.* MR MAGIC *opens the door by which he first went out.*

I'm part of your mental landscape for ever, duckie, whether you like it or . . .

FRANK *runs to the door and slams* MR MAGIC *out.* MR MAGIC *laughs behind the door.*

FRANK (*to the audience*). I ran home in the summer evening, frightened and mystified. I thought only boys did that and then only until they could find a girl. But why men? And old heavy-breathing men with brown teeth. Some of the girls I passed had great chests bulging out which far from turned my stomach. Ursula was waiting with the rest of our crowd in the local park but first I had to collect some cigarettes I'd stolen from Dad and hidden up my bedroom chimney. But I was not to be let off so easily, there was more bewildering unpleasantness to come. He appeared in a cloud of steam from the bathroom as I climbed the stairs and insisted I take over his water. 'I've used rather more than the regulation five inches, boy, and we should help the war effort any way we can.' The bathroom was exhausted, the walls sweating, the soap melting in the high humidity. And while I lay in this warm soup, he pottered about from room to room, gradually dressing.

CHARLES *comes on, wearing an open shirt without collar and trousers, but with bare feet. Around his neck is a towel and he is reading a book. He carries one slipper and one shoe. He speaks to* YOUNG FRANK *off.*

CHARLES. Cleanliness is next to godliness. I shall always remember my mother saying that.

FRANK. As soon as possible, I rubbed down and pulled on my trousers.

CHARLES. And we had no bathroom in those days, boy, only a hip-bath before the fire and a clothes-horse round with towels hung over it. I recall one night my brother saying to Sister Emma, 'Don't come in when one of us boys is in the bath, Sis. You never know what we may be a-doing-of.' (*He laughs at the thought, consults the book and rolls up his left trouser-leg, sitting on a chair to do so. He hears a movement off, and goes to look.*) You out? Bring the *Reynolds News* from the attic stairway, will you, Son?

FRANK. Later on Ivor taught me swimming in the public baths with an inflatable belt.

CHARLES *opens a door to reveal shelves full of patent medicines and toilet preparations in jars, bottles, tubes and tins.*

Ten years of samples. Friar's Balsam, Cascara, Vapour Rub, Golden Eye Ointment. It was among his boasts that he never recommended any line he hadn't personally tested.

CHARLES *takes down a bottle, a wad of cotton wool and nail-scissors.* YOUNG FRANK *comes on, wearing trousers, shirt and tie, no shoes or socks. He carries a newspaper.*

CHARLES (*taking the paper*). It's Brother Edwin about whom I'm talking. Used to frighten the life out of Sister Emma. (*He places the medicines and other articles on a raised surface and spreads the paper on the floor by his seat.)*

YOUNG FRANK *continues tying his tie.*

D'you know his term for the convenience, Frank?

YOUNG FRANK. The Gold Mine.

CHARLES. He used to call it The Gold Mine. (*He laughs.*)

YOUNG FRANK *looks at his eccentric clothes, shrugs and starts to go as* CHARLES *turns to him.*

Buzfuz!

YOUNG FRANK. What?

CHARLES. What's 'what'?

YOUNG FRANK. What is it?

CHARLES. 'What is it, *Dad?*'

YOUNG FRANK. I'm just off out.

CHARLES. Where are you going, Son?

YOUNG FRANK. Meeting Ivor in the park.

CHARLES. And what's that round your neck?

YOUNG FRANK. A dragon tie. Ivor painted it. The dragon's luminous.

CHARLES. What a way to dress!

YOUNG FRANK. What about *you!* What's your trouser rolled up for?

CHARLES. For what is your trouser rolled up? (*He pauses. He realises this is not quite right yet.*)

YOUNG FRANK (*smiles*). Up for what is your trouser rolled?

CHARLES. Don't talk big, you make yourself look small.

YOUNG FRANK. Why one slipper and one shoe?

CHARLES. If I'm doing it, Son, you can bet there's a jolly
proper reason. I wouldn't walk through the streets like it, any
more than I'd wear a luminous dragon tie and chase young
Ursula and her friends in and out of the air-raid shelters.

YOUNG FRANK. Who said we do?

CHARLES. Mister Lewthwaite lives beside the park overlooking
the static water tank. He can see you from his bedroom
window.

YOUNG FRANK. I'll bet he's up there every night with b-b-
b-binoculars.

CHARLES. I hear you making fun of anyone's afflictions, you'll
feel the back of my hand.

YOUNG FRANK. *You* do it!

CHARLES. Don't answer back.

YOUNG FRANK. You're always doing it. You always call him
tah-tah-Tiny Lewthwaite.

CHARLES. Mister Lewthwaite's an influential man these days.
Chief Buyer in Fancy Goods. And what's more, a Master
Mason. He's sponsoring me for admission to his lodge. And
that's why I'm dressed like this, you great coon. (*He
approaches* YOUNG FRANK *and seizes his ear.*) How long
since you cleaned your ears out?

YOUNG FRANK *groans.* CHARLES *peers in.*

By Jove! (*Takes a handkerchief from his pocket, folds and
twists it into a flexible spike.*)

YOUNG FRANK *finishes his tie and makes to go.*

Stand still when I tell you. (*He holds* FRANK's *head, plunges
the spike into one ear.*)

YOUNG FRANK. Ow!

CHARLES. Don't jerk away.

YOUNG FRANK. You'll break my eardrum. Uv'you got a matchstick in that hankie?

CHARLES. Don't be absurd.

YOUNG FRANK. You had last time. Nearly deafened me for life.

CHARLES. I wonder you're not deaf already. Enough wax here to furnish Madame Tussauds.

YOUNG FRANK (*breaking away*). Hey, shurrup!

CHARLES. Shurrup? What's shurrup? If I'd spoken like that to my father, I'd have felt the back of his hand.

YOUNG FRANK (*moving away*). You're not going to hold him up as an example, are you? A drunkard.

CHARLES *sits down, cutting his toenails into the newspaper.*

CHARLES. Yes, and when he was drunk, he couldn't move very fast, he couldn't see to hit us. We boys got pretty nimble dodging his fists. He used to shout: 'Come here, you little b-u-double-g-a-r!'

YOUNG FRANK. *E*-r.

CHARLES. Pardon?

YOUNG FRANK. B-u-double-g-*e*-r.

CHARLES. How d'you know?

YOUNG FRANK. I've seen it written on walls.

FRANK. In conveniences.

CHARLES. You shouldn't *read* it! You must develop the habit of turning away from smut in any size, shape or form. D'you think as a grocery traveller I haven't had to wrestle with temptation on the road? D'you think my colleagues in commercial hotels don't hang about the lounge-bars swapping smut? They sometimes say, 'Come along, Charles, be social, have a lemonade shandy with us,' and I look into the bar and smell the booze and see the landlord drawing ale and d'you know what always comes to me, Son?

YOUNG FRANK. The words of . . .

CHARLES. The words of Shakespeare, 'How like a fawning publican he looks!' (*He continues cutting his toenails into the paper.*)

YOUNG FRANK *waits.*

(*Standing.*) Get a bottle of wintergreen, I'll rub some into your legs.

YOUNG FRANK. I don't want that terrific pongy stuff wherever I go.

CHARLES. I'll empty these clippings out of the window. Do the garden good. (*He shakes the newspaper over the audience, folds it and puts it on the seat.*) And women, too, on the road. Normally decent but after a few gins, they make their loins available. These are bad times, Frank, you've been going round entertaining, you've met girls whose conduct isn't quite what it should be, I dare say. (*He fetches a bandage from the cupboard and begins binding his ankle.*)

FRANK. Had he heard about my hand beneath the dancer's thighs? Say something!

YOUNG FRANK. Why d'you put that bandage round your leg?

CHARLES. You surely know already. My varicose veins?

YOUNG FRANK (*innocently*). No.

CHARLES. During the First World War, as I was due for military service. Months in hospital, a hundred stitches. That – together with the deafness caused by that clout across the ear – saved me from the trenches, so I'm not sorry. If the war's still on when you're eighteen, you may get out with bed-wetting.

YOUNG FRANK. I'd rather go to war than wet the bed.

CHARLES. That shows a very decent spirit. But use your savvy, there are always plenty of piecans prepared to fight.

YOUNG FRANK. Your veins must be all right now. Why d'you still wear the bandage?

CHARLES. Nobody's ever told me to stop. Besides, it keeps my ankles cosy.

YOUNG FRANK *grins*.

FRANK (*praying*). Ursula, please wait for me, I'm coming as soon as I can get away.

CHARLES. Well, while you're so busy reading smut on the walls of conveniences, perhaps you could spare a glance for the Ministry of Health's announcement about g-o-n-o-r-h, no, double r-h-e-a, no . . .

YOUNG FRANK. Double-r-h-o-e-a.

FRANK. I could spell anything.

CHARLES. Your mother and I have never interfered, only tried to set an example of clean living. You follow me?

YOUNG FRANK. Okay. Going to see Ivor now.

CHARLES. Wait a jiffy. Before you go out fondling young Ursula, you can help . . .

YOUNG FRANK. I'm seeing Ivor!

CHARLES. Don't tell me fibs, Son. I called at Ivor's on the way home with a pound of bacon for his father. They're all going to his aunt's for the evening. Now tell me honestly, Son, where are you going?

YOUNG FRANK. The park.

CHARLES. To fondle young Ursula?

YOUNG FRANK. No.

FRANK. If her mother got to hear of it, she'd keep her in.

YOUNG FRANK. Honestly.

CHARLES. You tell me honestly, boy, I believe you. (*He stands and faces him.*)

YOUNG FRANK *looks at his feet.*

Do your finger-nails need cutting?

YOUNG FRANK. No. (*He turns to go.*)

CHARLES. Your toenails?

YOUNG FRANK. No. (*He turns to go again.*)

CHARLES. What's the hurry? Here, take this book. I'm trying to learn the ceremonial. (*He gives him the book.*)

YOUNG FRANK. What for?

CHARLES. My initiation. Once all the applications have gone through and no-one rules me out, I get the call, vou see.

YOUNG FRANK (*reading the book*). It says you've got to surrender all your money.

CHARLES. I've left it on the chest of drawers, all five and eightpence-half-penny. It's so that when in future I meet a Mason needing help, I call to mind the day I was received, poor and penniless.

YOUNG FRANK. You get the money back afterwards?

CHARLES. Well, what d'you think, you great pudden?

YOUNG FRANK. It's all a fake then.

CHARLES. The entire movement of Freemasonry a fake? You're going to set yourself up in opposition to all the great men who've believed in it, are you?

YOUNG FRANK. What great men? Tiny Lewthwaite?

CHARLES. Mozart, Sir Christopher Wren, George Washington, Frederick the Great, Garibaldi, our present King, Percy Tombs.

YOUNG FRANK. Who?

CHARLES. Mister Tombs, Grocery Manager for the whole South-West division. He's the Worshipful Master of the Lodge.

YOUNG FRANK. You're supposed to be blindfold.

CHARLES. Hoodwinked, yes. (*He has his handkerchief ready, and blindfolds himself.*)

YOUNG FRANK. And wear a noose round your neck.

CHARLES. You haven't a handy length of rope?

YOUNG FRANK. No.

CHARLES. We'll take it as read. Now. The Tyler escorts me to the threshold and the Inner Guard, his dagger to my bare breast, leads me before the Worshipful Master. He asks certain ritual questions, the answers to which I mean to commit to memory.

FRANK. But his memory was as cluttered as mine is now.

CHARLES. With my gift of the gab, I should find no difficulty responding in a loud clear voice like a sergeant-major. Then – with my right foot formed in a square – I kneel before the Worshipful Master.

YOUNG FRANK. Percy Tombs.

CHARLES (*kneeling*). Mister Tombs. And swear not to reveal – um – what is it, Sonny Jim?

YOUNG FRANK. Write, indite, carve, mark, engrave or otherwise delineate . . .

CHARLES *repeats these words quietly after him.*

CHARLES. The secret of Masonry, yes. These are the bits I must get off pat.

YOUNG FRANK. On pain of having your throat cut across, your tongue torn out by the root and buried in the sand of the sea at low water mark – or a cable's length from the shore. Can't wait to tell old Ivor this.

CHARLES (*sitting back on his heels*). You what? You dare, boy!

YOUNG FRANK. To think of old Tiny Lewthwaite doing this terrific Bela Lugosi act . . .

CHARLES. Not so much of the jolly old buck! The disrespect.

YOUNG FRANK. Well, it's so hellish corny.

CHARLES. It's dashed easy for you to sneer, boy, you're not away from home Monday to Friday wondering how to fill the time in draughty commercial hotels. You're not standing around in God-forsaken grocery departments awaiting the pleasure of foul-mouthed branch managers, swallowing their insults, laughing at their smut. D'you think I like that?

YOUNG FRANK. Dunno.

CHARLES. Dunno? What's dunno? No's the answer. Any more than Mister Lewthwaite liked it. And how did he get a job at HQ? When did he move from traveller to buyer? Six months after joining the Masonic Lodge.

YOUNG FRANK. Okay, I'm going out . . .

CHARLES (*taking* YOUNG FRANK's *arm*). Listen till I've finished. How else am I to get promotion, bring myself to the attention of the powers-to-be?

FRANK. I felt he was leading somewhere. But where?

CHARLES. Mister Tombs is one of those powers, boy. A very big cheese in the grocery trade. And a Worshipful Master.

YOUNG FRANK. Be getting dark soon . . .

CHARLES (*suddenly seizing his hands*). Where you off to, eh?

YOUNG FRANK. The park, I told you.

YOUNG FRANK *moves slightly, pulling* CHARLES *so that he has to move on his knees.* CHARLES *strengthens his grip on* YOUNG FRANK.

CHARLES. Going to your mother, Son?

YOUNG FRANK. Eh?

CHARLES. Have you said you'd meet your mother?

YOUNG FRANK. No. She's at Gran's place.

CHARLES. That's where she *says* she is. But you know more than I do, you're here all week. She *says* she's spending all this time at her mother's but – do you think she is, Son?

YOUNG FRANK. Why not?

CHARLES. You know.

FRANK. I didn't *know*. It was the first I'd heard of it.

   YOUNG FRANK *tries to go.*

CHARLES. Frank, don't go to her!

YOUNG FRANK. I'm not.

CHARLES. You're not seeing Ivor, you're not seeing Ursula, then where *are* you going if not to her? Listen, Son, if your mother left me, would you go with her? Please, Frank, if she goes – she might ask you to choose between us, you see what I mean, boy – well, look, stay with me, there's a good boy. Remember all I've done for you.

   FRANK *turns away, wincing at the memory.*

YOUNG FRANK (*frightened*). Going to the park . . .

CHARLES. Given you an education, put you by a nest-egg –

   YOUNG FRANK *stands, looking away.*

   – there's more in my will, if I don't change my mind.

FRANK (*wincing*). I'm not sure he said that.

CHARLES. Frank!

FRANK. But he might have, which is all that matters.

CHARLES. I've had to be strict, coming home as I do at week-ends – and sometimes perhaps I seemed too strict – it's all very well for your mother to spoil you – I don't seem able to talk to you.

   YOUNG FRANK *stands for a long time.*

Don't be late.

YOUNG FRANK. No.

   YOUNG FRANK *goes quickly.* CHARLES *unrolls his trouser leg, still kneeling.*

FRANK. More than anything, I've inherited his sexual nature. Inasmuch as I understand it. A lack of mastery. Dependence.

CHARLES *blows his nose in his handkerchief, wipes his face.*

(*He turns to look at* CHARLES. *To him.*) I didn't mention it to her. Never mentioned those two encounters to anyone. Not even Ivor.

CHARLES *does not seem to hear. He stands, puts away the slipper and shoe.*

That should give you some satisfaction.

CHARLES *shuts the door.* FRANK *turns to the audience.*

Conveniently deaf. But it's true.

CHARLES *goes off, taking the newspaper.*

I was so keen to find Ursula that I at once forgot those manifestations of the male menopause. Didn't remember them again till years later. The church clock showed half past eight as I free-wheeled past the water-tank and glimpsed our crowd lounging by the shelters. For twenty minutes we jeered at each other and groaned with derision at the girls' stupidity. Now and then there was a chase in and out of the shelters and Ursula could always find me inside by my quietly glowing dragon. Then a sudden sound, a shouting of orders, some cheers and the beautiful silver barrage balloon lurched up behind the bandstand. It had broken moorings and was now carried away over the rooftops – and giggling Waafs in battledress pursued it through the streets to mark where it fell. More than enough to make you forget your family – that great shining whale racing on the evening breeze! (*He shuts his eyes, pulls himself back to the present, looks about, then at his wrist-watch.*) Time to go for a bite. (*He goes to the door, opens it, pauses in the opening. Then goes on to the audience as an actor.*) If you'd like a drink, there are several bars you can go to.

Another door opens and YOUNG FRANK *appears.*

YOUNG FRANK (*imitating* CHARLES). What's 'you can go to', you great coon?

IVOR appears at another door.

IVOR (*also imitating* CHARLES). To which you can go, boy . . .

YOUNG FRANK. ⎫
IVOR. ⎬ To which you can go.

CHARLES appears at another door.

CHARLES. Don't talk so big, you make yourself look small.

AMY appears at another door.

AMY. Oh, do stop going on at the boy.

MR MAGIC appears at another door.

MR MAGIC. Boy! That was a long time ago and through a gauze!

FRANK. Can't you lot leave me alone for ten minutes!

They all slam the doors together.

ACT TWO

During the interval there is another record recital:
  'The Day War Broke Out' by Robb Wilton
  'Don't Get Around Much Any More' by Duke Ellington
  'Room 504' by Hutch
  'Milkman, keep those bottles quiet' by the Andrews Sisters
  'High Society' by Bing Crosby

*Towards the end of the records, FRANK comes in finishing a
newspaper of fish and chips. He stands listening to the music,
then eats the last chip, screws up the paper and discards it in
the bin below the record-player. He wipes his hands on his
handkerchief. He alerts the source of the speakers from
records to tapes, sets one playing, and steps back. The tape
continues with a recording of FRANK, URSULA and the
younger children singing 'A Song of Sixpence'. FRANK leaves
it playing, goes off, and returns at the end with a glass of
milk. He stares again at the recorder. After the songs, FRANK
and URSULA tell the children how well they sang.*

FRANK (*on tape*). Now shall we listen to that?

*Recording ends. FRANK switches the tape off, closes the
door, and comes down, drinking.*

FRANK. Is the family inevitable? Even our religion is based on a
family – and with *two* fathers. I always identify with Joseph,
the best-known victim of *droit de seigneur* – sawing away out
the back while angels are streaming in and out of the bedroom
window. When we're kids we don't really question the adult

world, just blunder about in a jungle of meaningless rules. But at twelve or so, confused by erections and periods, armed with the pure logic of puberty, we start fighting in earnest. Which scares our parents and sets up conflict. French verbs and wanker's doom. Then at last – escape, freedom! – lovely to start with but eventually we need a regular cuddle at night and there's no other way but a family of our own choice. One without rules. Paradise. But before we know it, most of our time's spent dabbing snot, healing greedy screams with ice-lollies – saying do this, don't do that – law-and-order becomes first a necessity, then, if you're not very careful, attractive for its own sake. Our wives, who were sex-pots a minute ago, are nagging shrews from a seaside postcard. Our girl Jenny, at three, already took profound pleasure in organisation, bullying her dolls, lining them up, smacking her teddies and being motherly. When Matthew was born, of course, and began to grow, she set him down amongst the teddies and nagged him, for all the world as though they were married. I used to watch him dreaming through it all and in the end he'd crawl away and she'd come howling that he'd spoilt the game. Our lives are an extrapolation of infancy – termagant girls and dreamy boys. Then of course, infants are imitating adults. So how do you break the circle? (*He pauses and moves away.*)

URSULA *comes in quietly and stands listening.*

How d'you escape the tender trap, the family car-trips, children's telly, Wellington boots – fish-fingers . . .

URSULA. If you loved your children, you'd accept all that.

He turns to her.

FRANK. I love them.

URSULA. Not enough.

FRANK. What is 'enough'? There were times when I thought them the whole reason for living.

URSULA. On the Kibbutzim, they tried to break up families. Most of them have voted to have the children back.

FRANK. The women. I wonder what the men had to say. And the children for that matter. It'll take a couple of generations to form a proper opinion.

URSULA. And the opinion will be the same: the family's inevitable.

FRANK. Then God help us.

URSULA. And while working out this crappy theory did you ever consider me? My life afterwards? A woman of – (*She pauses.*) – past her best . . .

FRANK (*to the audience*). Thirty-eight . . .

URSULA (*glancing at the audience, then smiling icily at* FRANK). Thank you. With three children.

FRANK. Of course and it kept me with you for years. But you're tough, Ursula, you're a survivor. Other people tend to say, 'Wait till Ursula comes, she'll know what to do.' I knew you could manage without me far more easily than I . . .

URSULA. And do you think I *want* to be like that?

FRANK. You *are* like that.

URSULA. Because I have to be. With four people depending on me.

FRANK. That's my point. Without the family, you wouldn't. You and I could chase each other from room to room. But you spend more time buying potted geraniums than making love to me.

URSULA. Are we back to this? Who mentioned this? I'm talking about my life and what I should like to be.

FRANK. Well?

URSULA. I'd like to do what you do. Sit about all day with a lot of students and set the world to rights.

FRANK. Before we had kids you were so exciting.

URSULA. You're jealous of them.

FRANK. I think I had cause.

URSULA. It's your age. You remember it as better than it was.

FRANK. I remember. (*He opens the pin-up door.*)

YOUNG FRANK *comes on wearing nineteen-forty-five utility casuals, with* YOUNG URSULA *in school uniform, carrying a satchel.*

YOUNG FRANK. How d'you get off hockey?

YOUNG URSULA. Forged an excuse-note.

URSULA. I was a clever counterfeiter. I used to forge everyone's notes.

YOUNG URSULA *drops her satchel and takes off her raincoat.*

FRANK. Excited, breathless, gratified, but wishing I'd never asked you.

YOUNG FRANK *yawns.*

URSULA. Scared as a rabbit with a snake, wondering when you'd start.

YOUNG URSULA. Your mum's out?

YOUNG FRANK. Pictures. And Dad's in Worcester. (*She sits.*)

YOUNG URSULA. Your holiday's nearly over.

YOUNG FRANK (*nodding*). Go next week.

YOUNG URSULA. You frightened?

YOUNG FRANK. Glad to be getting away from this dump. With Ivor gone and everything . . .

FRANK. He'd been called up a few months before.

YOUNG URSULA. Have you heard from him again?

YOUNG FRANK. Nearly finished square-bashing. Sent some traffic drawings of the plebs. He says quite a few of them can't even read the comics. Blokes of eighteen and twenty can't even read!

YOUNG URSULA. Hellish dim.

He stands by her, yawns again. She stretches her legs out in front of her, looks at them. Then she takes his hand.

Hullo, Handsome.

YOUNG FRANK. Oh, Christ!

YOUNG URSULA. What d'you want me to say?

YOUNG FRANK. Hullo, Skinny.

YOUNG URSULA. You're not skinny, you're slim.

FRANK (*like someone watching a prizefight*). Get on with it, man!

YOUNG URSULA (*kissing his hand*). I like thin boys.

YOUNG FRANK. Then why've you been going round with that brawny crowd from near the Baths?

YOUNG URSULA. They were hellish boring.

URSULA. Because you seemed to prefer Ivor. But when he went I came running back.

YOUNG URSULA. All they talked about was getting in the air and shooting down Germans and Japs. They never saw it as a film like you and Ivor.

YOUNG FRANK. 'I can't stand any more, I tell you, let me go.'

FRANK. 'Pull yourself together, for Pete's sake, Jerry's watching.'

YOUNG URSULA. I like boys who make me laugh.

She stands, puts her arms round him, and kisses him on the mouth. He embraces her.

URSULA. I deserved a good hiding.

FRANK. You were marvellous, but look at me!

URSULA. When Dad was released, he took me in hand.

YOUNG URSULA *pulls out* YOUNG FRANK's *shirt. He yawns.*

YOUNG URSULA. You tired?

He shrugs.

Let's lie down. Shall we? (*She sits again.*) I'm hot. Aren't you? Hellish hot today.

He goes on his knees and takes off her shoes.

URSULA. This isn't nice at all.

FRANK. It's improving.

YOUNG FRANK *kisses* YOUNG URSULA's *knee, then sits by her.*

YOUNG URSULA. You're terrifically attractive, Frank.

FRANK. Tell her! Tell her she's attractive! Tell her about your dreams!

YOUNG FRANK *plays with* YOUNG URSULA's *school tie. She waits. She unties it. He opens a shirt button. She opens one of his.*

YOUNG URSULA. Quite a few hairs since last I looked.

YOUNG FRANK. Four.

FRANK. Mostly grey now.

YOUNG URSULA. I cried the other night in bed because I thought you might not come back.

YOUNG FRANK. Why not?

YOUNG URSULA. Might get killed.

YOUNG FRANK. The war's nearly over.

YOUNG URSULA. Not in the Far East.

FRANK. The Bomb was coming.

YOUNG FRANK. That's mostly the Yanks. They won't send me.

URSULA. But they did.

YOUNG URSULA. Shall I wait for you? While you're away.

YOUNG FRANK. If you like.

FRANK. What eloquence!

YOUNG URSULA. I'm fagged out. Shall we lie down?

She lies down and he leans over her.

URSULA. Why d'you have to dwell on this?

FRANK. You were wonderful.

YOUNG FRANK *kisses her, then takes something from her cheek with his finger.*

YOUNG URSULA. What is it?

FRANK. A piece of amalgam.

YOUNG URSULA. Silver stuff.

YOUNG FRANK. I had a tooth filled this morning.

FRANK. Remember that?

URSULA. Yes. I kept it in my souvenir box till you came home.

CHARLES *comes in, wearing a suit and carrying a case. He shuts the door behind him.*

YOUNG FRANK (*jumping up*). That's the front door.

YOUNG URSULA *gets up.*

YOUNG URSULA. Are you sure?

YOUNG FRANK. Mum must have come home early.

CHARLES (*calling*). Anyone home?

　　YOUNG FRANK *and* URSULA *start dressing rapidly.*

YOUNG FRANK. Hullo?

FRANK. I knew I had to answer.

URSULA. Why?

FRANK. If he'd thought I was out, he'd have gone to my room to read my diary.

URSULA. Would he, really?

FRANK. Yes. And found us –

CHARLES. You up there, boy?

YOUNG FRANK (*dressing*). Coming down.

URSULA. Why?

FRANK. To see what I'd written about him.

URSULA. How d'you know he read it?

　　CHARLES *puts his case on the sofa and opens it, pushing through the papers to find a paper bag. From this he takes a half-pound of butter and a packet of tea.*

FRANK. He couldn't resist correcting what I'd put.

URSULA. 'Preposition at end of sentence'?

CHARLES (*shouting*). Come on, noodle!

FRANK. Yes, or once, I remember, I had written: 'In a vase on the mantelpiece there is a Remembrance Poppy. Is the old man keeping it till next November to save a shilling?'

　　YOUNG FRANK *and* YOUNG URSULA *go out by the same door.* CHARLES *unpacks half a pound of cheese and some biscuits. The pin-up screens close.*

And he added in the margin, 'Do not tell untruths or show ingratitude to a father who has shown you every generosity.'

YOUNG FRANK *and* YOUNG URSULA *enter by the same door as* CHARLES.

YOUNG FRANK. Thought you were in Worcester.

CHARLES. The usual sunny welcome home. Hullo, young woman, are you quite well?

YOUNG URSULA. Hullo, Mister Bisley.

CHARLES. What are you a-doing of upstairs with Sonny Jim? My brother Edwin used to frighten the life out of Sister Emma, you know. He used to say, 'Don't come in when the old man is in the bath, Sis. You never know what he might be a-doing-of.'

YOUNG FRANK. I been helping her with her schoolwork.

CHARLES. Judging by the showing you made in your exams, she'd be better off without your help.

YOUNG FRANK *groans.*

You warm, Ursula? You look warm, your face is flushed. So's yours, boy. Open the window if you're warm. It was sweltering in Tewkesbury.

YOUNG FRANK. Why d'you come back then?

CHARLES. I'd completed all my calls in double-quick time and here I am, in person, the one and only, Charles the First and Foremost. And you can give me a hand unloading one or two samples from the car.

YOUNG FRANK (*taking a paper bag from the case*). Some samples of fresh eggs here.

CHARLES. Leave them alone. They're a gift. Would your mother like a couple of eggs, Ursula? Naturally. Mister Lewthwaite of Fancy Goods, a real coon if ever there was one, said to me, 'There's massive supplies on the way from America.' I looked up at the ceiling, then at the window, then I looked him in the eye and I said, 'Oh?' very slowly, you know, boy, that frightens the life out of them.

YOUNG FRANK. Makes them curl up laughing.

CHARLES. I said, 'Then am I to assume that you are privy to Mister Attlee's innermost thoughts? Or have you received a p.c. from Mister Truman this a.m.? Good morning', and I walked off and left him gasping.

YOUNG FRANK. Left him thinking you were hellish corny.

CHARLES. Not so much of the jolly old buck, thank you, from a boy who can't even do up his shirt on the right buttons.

CHARLES *begins unbuttoning* YOUNG FRANK's *shirt at the neck.*

YOUNG FRANK (*embarrassed*). I can do it.

CHARLES (*continuing to do it*). Hold your tongue.

YOUNG FRANK *suffers it.*

URSULA. Touching you again, you see. He always struck me as a very tactile person, always trying to touch you and Mother, but you both avoided him.

CHARLES (*to* YOUNG URSULA). Your buttons all right, young woman?

YOUNG URSULA *giggles.*

URSULA. I've always been ashamed of the way we must have appeared to him that day. And me only sixteen!

FRANK. I'll bet his puritan imagination ran riot.

CHARLES. You shouldn't go up to that back room amongst those photographs of uncovered girls. Might give you the wrong ideas, eh, boy? Might start uncovering herself. And if Buzfuz here starts making free with you, send him packing. Take a leaf from my mother's book. If the old man came sniffing round her in his cups, she'd say, 'Hands off, private property!' I've heard her.

YOUNG FRANK. No wonder he drank.

CHARLES. Your hair badly wants cutting.

CHARLES *touches* YOUNG FRANK'*s hair. He backs away.*

URSULA. Touching again.

CHARLES. All curly in your neck. However. Look at that car standing out there. The only car in the avenue, it looks like showing off. Take these things to the kitchen, boy, pending your mother's return from the flicks. And both of you come and help unload.

YOUNG FRANK *takes the packages,* CHARLES *closes the suitcase and holds it.*

D'you know this great coon has requested, nay demanded that the back room shall remain unaltered till he comes home from the army? Just fancy, His Majesty's Government, in their wisdom, have decided he's A1, in the pink and fit to defend our far-flung empire. Especially now he's stopped wetting the bed.

CHARLES *laughs and goes off, followed by* YOUNG URSULA, *shyly.* YOUNG FRANK *goes by the other door.*

FRANK (*shouting at the door by which* CHARLES *left*). Insensitive, pre-Freudian clown!

The door opens and CHARLES *looks in.*

CHARLES. Don't raise your voice at me, Son.

FRANK *slams the door on him.*

URSULA. Did he keep the room as it was?

FRANK. Yes.

URSULA. I didn't go there again for years and the pin-up girls had gone by then.

FRANK. You were busy elsewhere.

URSULA. At school and then at college. My dad came home, with all the other men who'd voted Churchill out. He got a well-paid factory job and my brother and I went to college. Life was certainly better for us than before the war. I studied dressmaking.

FRANK. Funny name for it.

URSULA. What else would you call it?

FRANK. Dress removing?

URSULA (*understanding, and deciding*). Right. (*She goes to the door.*)

FRANK. No, love, wait . . .

But URSULA *goes, shutting the door.*

Ivor and I never met again till I was released. What my mother would have called a blessing in disguise. We vowed to write to each other every week and more or less kept the promise, but it was like a stale marriage. The crazy gags and caricatures of our adolescence weren't an adequate response to what I was seeing now: the end of British India, the cruelty of Calcutta, Ghandi's death. I knew that sooner or later I should have to tell him it was finished but sufficient unto the day, as my mother would have said.

AMY *enters from a door, aged forty-seven, dressed for nineteen-forty-eight.*

AMY. You got home about – what? – half past two. Dad was in Cardiff so I'd had a spot of dinner on my own, after finishing the spring cleaning in the morning, because I wanted it looking nice. So I thought, 'I'll just sit down for ten minutes with a cork-tipped,' when this knock came and there you were. (*To the audience.*) Very sun-tanned but thin as a rake, I thought to myself, I'll soon fatten him up. You'd had dinner on the train, so I said, 'How about some tea?' and you said, 'Coffee,' you said you'd acquired the taste, and luckily there was just enough essence in the bottle.

FRANK. Before I'd drunk it, Ivor came on a second-hand motor-bike and I had to struggle to remember our mutual vocabulary.

The pin-up screens open. The bow window fades. IVOR *comes on, a twenty-one-year-old civilian.* YOUNG FRANK *follows, tropical tan and uniform of RASC private.*

YOUNG FRANK. It's so small.

IVOR. The houses look terrific small. I found that when I came home.

YOUNG FRANK. But otherwise unchanged.

IVOR. *You've* changed. You've got a posh voice.

AMY. How scruffy he looked.

> IVOR *and* YOUNG FRANK *are embarrassed.* YOUNG FRANK *studies the collage.*

> He still looks scruffy.

> AMY *goes.*

IVOR. Like a record? One of the old ones. (*He opens the door revealing the player.*)

YOUNG FRANK. The acoustic gramophone!

IVOR. Acoustic? Bloody hell. Used to be 'wind-up'.

YOUNG FRANK (*with a shrug*). 'Acoustic' is the proper word.

IVOR. Bloody hell. 'Maple Leaf Rag' – or Beiderbeck's 'Royal Garden'?

YOUNG FRANK. Tell the truth, Ivor, I find the insistent syncopation and predictable harmonies of jazz pretty boring these days.

IVOR (*in imitation posh*). Oh, well, jolly good, what?

YOUNG FRANK. I've been listening a lot to Debussy and Ravel.

IVOR. Well, they were interested in jazz.

YOUNG FRANK. They transformed and elevated it.

FRANK. Poor prig.

> IVOR *shuts the door to the gramophone.*

YOUNG FRANK. What's it like here?

IVOR. England? Bloody awful. Over in Germany you could get all the booze and fags you wanted, dead cheap. When I went first, you could get a Leica for a couple of bars of soap. Get a fraulein for a pound of coffee. And later on I had this bint, her parents were killed at Dresden. Couldn't half shag.

FRANK. The old familiar fear. Was I the only twenty-one-year-old virgin left?

IVOR. Worse than during the war here. Nothing in the shops, queues everywhere. Nobody cares that you've been doing your bit.

AMY comes in, wearing a hat and coat.

AMY. Frank, I must just run up to Montpelier's the bakers. Mrs Stock says they've got some cream horns in. You still like cream horns?

YOUNG FRANK. Expect so. Can't remember.

AMY. If I hurry, there might be one or two left. What a business, queueing still! Ivor says there's plenty of everything in Germany. Well, it makes you wonder who won the war. (*She pauses.*) I blame the Labour Government.

YOUNG FRANK. Where I've spent the last three years, they aren't very upset about the shortage of cream horns.

AMY. Well, I don't suppose the Indians eat many cream horns. Even if they can get them. Mostly rice, isn't it? (*She pauses, and looks to* IVOR *for help.*) I mean, they're not used to decent standards.

YOUNG FRANK. That's true, yes. I've sat in a Calcutta restaurant spending most of my pay on a tasty meal, with the faces of boys pressed against the window. Then the waiter sent them off and I saw them shoo the kitehawks from the dustbins and rummage through for anything the birds had left.

AMY. You must be glad to be home.

IVOR. Not our fault, though, is it?

AMY. Not our concern. We didn't send you out there, did we?
And you didn't want to go. I said to Mrs Bentley, well, it's
silly, taking boys away from nice homes and sticking them
down among a lot of natives.

FRANK. Thank Christ they did!

AMY. Exposing them to nasty diseases.

YOUNG FRANK. But – it *is* our concern. Your nice cup of tea
comes from India, Mum. And your cotton dresses. The petrol
for Dad's car and the tyres it runs on from the Middle East
and Malaya. Most of the food he sells is grown in countries
where people are starving: coffee, chocolate, cinnamon,
pineapple, coconut, sugar, pepper – we rely on Asia and
Africa for all that just as the posh people in London rely on
Crewe for their Rolls-Royces.

IVOR. Hey, you sound like one of those blokes used to spout
politics on the Downs.

AMY. Oh, them. Mother always pushed us children past. 'Never
mind them,' she used to say, 'we don't want our houses burnt
down.'

YOUNG FRANK. What did she mean by that?

IVOR. That's what politics leads to, isn't it?

AMY. I think there was a man saying he'd send people to burn
our houses if we didn't vote for him.

YOUNG FRANK *laughs.*

IVOR (*after a pause*). Politics are boring. Only thing is have a
good time, like I did in Germany. Wine, women and song.

YOUNG FRANK *goes up to look his last at the pin-up
collage. It fades as he watches.* AMY *listens to* IVOR.

Get a guitar – decent woman – one or two mates you can
have a drink with – a bit of money coming in but not too
much – old car – paint some luminous dragons on it –

YOUNG FRANK *looks at* IVOR *and goes off.*

— few Sidney Bechet records . . . (*He takes out and lights a cigarette.*

FRANK. Ivor tried to warm the embers for a few days but I went off to London to stay with one of my new service friends, discussing E. M. Forster and personal relationships. Listening to Debussy.

IVOR *goes off, smoking. The others watch him go.*

AMY (*coming down*). He's never grown up, Ivor. Even now he's got six children, I call him Peter Pan.

FRANK. I wonder which of us retarded the other. He held back my understanding and I tried to spoil his good nature.

AMY. He was very good when Mother died, I've always had a soft spot for him because of that. Staying with her right to the end — banging the wardrobe to show there were no monkeys in it — telling her again and again there wouldn't be any more bombs. (*She takes her handkerchief from her sleeve and blows her nose.*) Whenever some ordinary plane went over, she used to say, 'Not those devils again?'

FRANK. I was watching a French film.

AMY. What?

FRANK. When she died.

AMY. Oh, you'd done a hard day's teaching, hadn't you, and in any case you were serious about films. What was it you wanted to be, when you were young?

FRANK. A director.

AMY. There you are. (*To the audience, as she goes.*) He's always ready to blame himself . . .

AMY *goes.*

FRANK (*moving and thinking*). Who'd have thought I'd make a good teacher? But my newly-developed sense of duty prevailed and I began to think of myself as useful. Then at a party I met

Ursula again, the same brazen hussy she'd always been but now twenty-three. She could spend days on end in bed, smiling to show the pleasure she took. (*He recovers from the dream.*) She never organised a thing in those days. But, of course, what women hide is not their dark inner sexual core but their urge to make arrangements. Still – laughing always comes to crying, as my mother would say, and all this joy led to a hasty scene at the registry office during which our great coon of an elder son gave Ursula such a kick in the stomach that one point she said 'ow'. And is that fifteen years ago? Nearly. The calendar pages fall away at silent film speed – the forties are my golden age, ten years of austerity. I know they were drab but austerity sounds so morally superior to affluence, with its suggestion of sewage and greed and waste. What there was then was shared – people gave you lifts in their cars – and Ursula's father voted Labour in the hope this might continue. Well, these days he's got an enormous Vauxhall, a motor-mower, a Japanese cine-camera and holidays in the Black Forest, so . . . (*He shrugs.*) Whereas mine declined in fortune, retiring on a pension the size of which showed that other people had profited by his thrift. An enormous confidence-trick. (*He moves up stage.*)

The bay-windows projection comes on: the living-room at home. It now lacks the strips of adhesive brown paper.

My parents couldn't afford repairs and Corinthian Villa began looking the worse for wear. The radio with the lightning-flash motif only crackled now, despite the old man's desperate struggles with its insides. The cube-shaped Staffordshire teapots had lost their lids. The only car in the avenue had passed to me and finally gone for scrap. Whenever Ursula and I took the children to tea on Sunday, the house felt insufficient to contain my memories . . . (*He opens a door and pours himself a drink.*)

CHARLES *enters by another door, aged sixty-five, wearing cardigan, shirt, flannels and slippers.*

CHARLES. Where are you, Buzfuz?

They meet.

Look at this boy. Just the job. (*He holds out a pair of woollen underpants.*)

FRANK. Just the job for what?

CHARLES. I said to Mister Champness, the great manager of men's outfitting. 'These would be the very ticket for my son, whom you will remember as a mere boy but who has since become a huge ninny of nearly thirty, for ever complaining of the cold.' I said, 'Put me aside a dozen pairs.'

FRANK. Are you still buying wholesale?

CHARLES. Cheaper by the dozen, boy.

FRANK. Only if you *want* a dozen.

CHARLES (*sharply*). D'you want them or not?

FRANK. Yes, thanks. If they're not too big.

CHARLES. Nothing worse than pants too small. Notice the gusset, boy. (*He handles it.*) No restriction on your scrotum. Ample room for your parts. Easy access. (*He sticks a forefinger through the fly.*)

FRANK (*taking the pants*). Right. Thanks very much.

CHARLES (*moves about, sniffing*). Smells like a four-ale bar in here.

FRANK. Mum told me to help myself to a drink.

CHARLES. Where *is* Old Mother Hubbard?

FRANK. Helping Ursula put Jenny to bed. I did Bill.

CHARLES. He's a fine boy, they're both fine children.

FRANK *pours a drink.*

If you'd seen the sights I saw as a youngster, you'd put strong liquor behind you. My old man – he was a master butcher – I've seen him so drunk he brought the cleaver down on his

own hand. Standing there, his blood mingling with the blood
of the lamb, swaying about shouting, 'Bee-you-double gee-
aye-arr the arr-you-double dee-wye thing! – and he wrapped a
rag soaked in methylated spirits around his hand and finished
hacking the joint – and when he lit a fag, boy, his fist was
alight, enveloped in a bright blue flame. And he stood there
laughing. Laughing boy! I hear anyone pine for the Good
Olde Days, I say, 'For goodness' sake hold your tongue, you
can't possibly know about what you're talking!' That
frightens them to death, boy . . .

FRANK (*nodding*). Never put a preposition at . . .

CHARLES. That gets them groggy. Then I proceed to lay them
low with eloquent denunciation. Have you heard my epistle to
the Old Codgers on this question?

FRANK. Yes.

CHARLES. You've missed a treat. (*He sits, takes out and opens
a wallet, taking from it a fat wad of newspaper cuttings, many
yellowed with age. He lays them out carefully, sorting and
separating.*) And – as I happen to have a copy to hand . . .

FRANK *looks at his watch, drinks again. From a door comes
MISS NINETEEN-FORTY, now dressed as a Hollywood
slave girl, TONDELAYO, all bangles, briefs and long hair.
She implores FRANK to help her. MR MAGIC follows, now
a slave-trader with a whip. He threatens the girl but FRANK
with one kick sends him flying backwards through the door.*

Yes. This was the letter which riled me, written by some
piecan from Ipswich. 'Your article, the Dear Departed, stirred
in us many happy memories of the days of yesteryear. In times
like these, when the very air we breathe is full of germs and
atoms . . .

*The SLAVE GIRL embraces FRANK's legs beseechingly. He
stands with his whisky looking down as she begins drawing
herself up his body, caressing him, circling him.*

'When young layabouts wait at every corner, is it any wonder old-age pensioners fear to walk abroad? But we cherish fond thoughts of times when children honoured their old folk, when a fair day's work earned a fair day's pay . . .' – you listening, crackpot?

FRANK *is about to remove the* SLAVE GIRL'*s scanty clothing but now he turns to* CHARLES *and she runs off.*

FRANK. Yes.

CHARLES. 'Cherish fond thoughts of sunny days when a farthing would buy untold dolly mixture.' Which provoked from the Codgers the reply: 'Not arf, Alfred. We reckon the likes of you and your missus can teach the rest of us a thing or two when it comes to the March of Time. Makes you wonder if we aren't all barmy!' (*He puts aside this cutting and takes a piece of notepaper, much folded and worn.*) And here is my reply. 'Oldster of Ipswich can hardly know about what he's talking. My memories are of a different ilk and may be summarised as the Three D's: dirt, drunkenness and disease. The twin stars of our tiny firmament were Big Jim, the fawning publican, and Ikey Stein the pawnbroker.

AMY *and* URSULA *enter.* AMY *is now fifty-five or so, neat and particular, in a twin-set and skirt, smoking a cigarette.* URSULA *as at present, though she may dress differently.*

On the streets women of ill-fame plied their unholy trade . . .'

AMY. Oh, not this again! The Good Olde Days! (*She laughs and goes to the drinks.*)

CHARLES. Hold your tongue, Woodbine Winnie!

FRANK (*to* URSULA). She gone down all right?

URSULA. She's playing with her plastic baa-lambs.

CHARLES. 'Sitting here now before a cosy fire listening to the Eroica symphony of Beethoven, I am indeed . . . '

AMY. You like sherry, don't you, Ursula?

URSULA. Yes.

CHARLES. 'I am indeed . . .'

FRANK. I'll get it.

CHARLES. 'I am indeed . . .!'

AMY. I'll have a vodka.

CHARLES. 'I am indeed . . .'

AMY. Vodka and orange.

FRANK. All right.

CHARLES. Talking to myself here.

AMY. Nobody asked you to.

Pause. CHARLES waits long-sufferingly.

CHARLES. 'I am indeed happy to have heard the last of the Good Olde Days.'

AMY. I wish we had. (She sits.)

URSULA sits beside her.

CHARLES. 'Yours Charles Bisley, Corinthian Villa, etcetera.' Absolutely beyond my comprehension why they never printed it.

FRANK (pouring drinks). Bit too avant-garde perhaps.

CHARLES packs up his cuttings.

CHARLES. Too what?

FRANK. I only mean it's a column for the simple-minded by the simple-minded. The most subversive they can get is oh, for the days when the poor knew their place and there was more sunshine. A pink map and a closed mind and believing what Lord Northcliffe's papers told you – and sitting there throughout the thirties being thankful you've got the only car in the avenue.

AMY. Look out, Frank, you'll . . .

FRANK *pours too much orange into the vodka and spills it.*

URSULA. Too late!

AMY. All over my clean carpet, oh dear.

URSULA. I'll get a cloth.

URSULA *goes.*

FRANK (*putting the orange on the cabinet*). But God bless the Prince of Wales and shall we take the boy to Weymouth?

AMY. If you'd stop talking for a second, Frank, you'd see that sticky orange is all over the carpet I've just shampooed.

CHARLES. Give him enough rope he'll hang himself.

FRANK. I'm trying to talk to you.

CHARLES. Talk? You talk? I will content myself with repeating to you what I said to Mister Lewthwaite of Fancy Goods.

URSULA *returns with a floorcloth.*

AMY. Thanks, Ursula, I'll do it. (*She rubs the floor.*)

CHARLES. You remember him, Buzfuz? Little squirt of a fellow about so high, pronounced stammer. I kept trying to get a word in edgewise but he was bah-bah-bahing away, I said, 'Mister Lewthwaite, I haven't got all day to stand here listening to your speech impediment.' And I added, 'Leave the talking to those with a gift of the gab. And – at the risk of blowing my own trumpet – for, after all . . . (*Mock clerical.*) Verily, verily, I say unto you, blessed is he that bloweth his own trumpet, lest it be not blown at all.'

URSULA *laughs and* CHARLES *plays up to her.* FRANK *swallows a drink and opens a door. The scantily clad* SLAVE GIRL *is there, bound by her wrists, struggling to free herself. As she sees* FRANK *she cowers back in terror.*

You should have seen his face, Ursula. I said, 'When it comes to talking none is more able' – notice, Buzfuz, none *is* more able, not none *are* –

FRANK *comes back, shutting the door, impatiently listening to* CHARLES.

– 'none is more able than the weird, wise and wonderful Colossus, Charles the First and Foremost.' I said, 'Good day to you, friend,' and left him gasping, boy, thinking to himself . . .

AMY. Good riddance to bad rubbish . . .

CHARLES. 'Good riddance to b . . .' – what d'you mean, good riddance? Hold your tongue, Capstan Connie. No, I left him thinking, 'That man is a veritable marvel. How was he born so wonderful?'

AMY. Why was he born at all?

CHARLES. 'Why was he born . . .' (*He breaks off again.*)

URSULA *laughs.* FRANK *stares with a stone face.* CHARLES *looks at him. Having finished the carpet,* AMY *sits again and drinks.*

Never one to outstay my welcome, Ursula, I shall leave you to your own devices for a moment while I use the convenience.

CHARLES *goes.*

AMY. I believe he's worse the older he gets.

URSULA. No, he's lovely.

FRANK. All very well for you to come and find him amusing *now*, now he's becoming a comedian.

FRANK *gives* URSULA *her sherry. The women sit drinking.*

CHARLES *reappears at the same door.*

CHARLES. Talking about the old man the moment his back's turned? (*He comes in.*) No, I meant to say apropos of the Good Olde Days –

AMY. You set my teeth on edge about the Good Olde Days.

CHARLES. – think of your own enviable position, the advantages you had. Look at your lovely house, central heating – not that I like it, dries your mouth, I find, but very nice if you're used to it. No central heating here, that's because I gave up so much to give you a good education.

FRANK. Good education!

CHARLES. Fed and clothed you, gave you everything a boy could want, threw my money about –

AMY. – like a Jew with no arms –

CHARLES. Like a Jew with no arms. Who said that? Goldflake Gertie again? I'll give you a kick in the pants.

AMY. Why don't you go on up to the toilet?

CHARLES. And look at you, with a university degree, a wonderful job, teaching grown-up people, imparting your knowledge. Superannuation scheme.

FRANK *howls with derision.*

Nothing to laugh at. I made sure of my pension.

AMY. Lot of good it's done us, too. Navvies earn more than us these days.

FRANK. Don't you think they should?

CHARLES. You should be grateful, boy.

URSULA. He is.

CHARLES. Just as I'm proud, Ursula. Proud to have helped my son up the ladder a few steps. If I've done that and it's appreciated, my life will not have been in vain. (*He takes out his handkerchief.*)

URSULA *looks at* FRANK *as though demanding that he express some thanks. He doesn't.*

Oh, I've made mistakes in my time, I admit it. In a life as full as the Old Man's, it would have been a miracle not to have made the odd mistake. Perhaps some I shall regret until the day I pass away.

Pause. URSULA *looks at* CHARLES. AMY *drinks.*

(*Suddenly.*) This shirt was a mistake! (*He pulls out his shirt-tail.*) I like a shirt I can wrap round my buttocks and keep me warm. I said to Mister Champness, Big Cheese in the Men's Wear Department, 'Next time give me a shirt big enough for Lockhart's.'

URSULA. Lockhart's?

AMY. What's he on about now?

URSULA. Private parts.

CHARLES. What?

URSULA. Rhyming slang!

CHARLES. No! Big enough for Lockhart's elephants. They were the great music-hall turn when I was a nipper. Nothing to do with private parts, young woman. What d'you think of her, Amy? Got a one-track mind, I should think.

AMY. Your endless chatter makes my head sing, I know that.

CHARLES. No wonder she's got two nippers already. I shouldn't let young crackpot make so free with you in the jolly old double-bed.

AMY. Very nice. Could we change the subject?

CHARLES. Not having another, are you?

URSULA. Not yet.

CHARLES. I only thought when I saw you this afternoon, by Jove, Ursula's breasts look larger than ever.

AMY. Take no notice, dear, I don't.

CHARLES. She never takes a scrap of notice of me, Old Mother Hubbard. Do you?

CHARLES *goes down on one knee by* AMY *and tries to kiss her. She recoils.*

AMY. Not a scrap. Why don't you go to the toilet?

CHARLES. No chance of a spot of the slap-and-tickle these days.

URSULA *moves to* FRANK. *They stand watching.*

URSULA. See what I mean about touching?

FRANK. I know all about that.

URSULA. Kiss him, you block of ice! More bothered with your shampooed carpet than your man.

CHARLES *stands.*

CHARLES. I sometimes think of the chances I missed, the girls I turned away. Vicky Edmunds, for instance, lived in Leytonstone. I wonder what Vicky's doing now.

AMY. Drawing the old age pension, I should think.

CHARLES. Drawing the old age . . . ? (*He goes to a door and turns.*) I shall boil a kettle to fill my hot-water bottle. Once in bed, I shall place it scalding between my thighs.

AMY. I don't think Ursula's interested in what you do in bed.

CHARLES. Nobody is these days. Which accounts for the water-bottle. A last resort, eh, Ursula?

URSULA *stops* CHARLES *on his way out and kisses him.* FRANK *turns away.* CHARLES *goes.*

AMY. D'you think he's gone for good? Are we going to enjoy a conversation for a change?

URSULA *looks at* FRANK *but he is turned away. She goes to stand near* AMY.

No, what I was saying upstairs was we could have the children for a day or two so you and Frank could go away.

URSULA. Do you think it's possible?

AMY. Frank could do with a break, he looks so drawn.

URSULA. Would Mister Bisley mind?

AMY. Him? No. He'll take Bill to the park, give him something to occupy his mind, instead of hanging about the house and getting in my way. He's under my feet the whole day long otherwise.

A door opens near FRANK *and* MR MAGIC *throws the* SLAVE GIRL *to the ground at* FRANK's *feet.* MR MAGIC *now seems to be a eunuch and threatens the* SLAVE GIRL *with a whip. He bows to* FRANK. FRANK *raises her from the ground and stands her before him. There is no pause in* AMY's *speech.*

Tell the truth, he hasn't known what to do since retirement.

URSULA. I thought he enjoyed it.

AMY. After his fashion, yes, pottering about, getting in my way.

URSULA. He's got so many interests. Music, rugby, cricket . . .

AMY. When he was on the road, at least he was out from under my feet from Monday to Friday.

FRANK reaches out and tears the brassière off the SLAVE GIRL. *She flinches and turns her head away.* FRANK *stares at her.*

But now he won't go anywhere, he sits listening to his blessed records. I give him something to do now and then, nothing difficult. Well, he's like a baby half the time, he knocked a pot of plastic emulsion down the stairs last May. And only yesterday he vacuumed an enormous leaf off the rubber plant in the greenhouse.

FRANK gestures to MR MAGIC, *who turns the* SLAVE GIRL *so that she submits to* FRANK, *raising one leg. He takes her ankle in his hands and begins to remove her bangles.*

And sometimes I think if I don't get out of the house, I shall go stark, staring mad.

URSULA. Perhaps after all those years travelling, he wants to settle down.

AMY. Settle down? Fossilise! I feel like a fossil in a glass case.

*AMY seems on the edge of an emotional outburst but
URSULA stares at her unsympathetically so AMY blows her
nose in her handkerchief and turns to FRANK.*

Frank!

FRANK goes on taking off the SLAVE GIRL's bangles.

Look at him, dreaming again. Always got his head in the
clouds. Frank!

FRANK. Hullo? (*He turns from the SLAVE GIRL.*)

*The SLAVE GIRL and MR MAGIC go out through the
nearest door. FRANK moves to AMY and URSULA.*

AMY. I was telling Ursula, Dad vacuumed a leaf off the rubber
plant yesterday.

FRANK (*absently*). Oh, dear.

AMY. Yes. I found him trying to put it back with a tube of
Evostick. You do look drawn, don't you think so, Ursula?
Working too hard at college? Reading too much? I think you
can overdo reading.

*FRANK leans over URSULA and kisses her. She recoils.
CHARLES reappears wearing one slipper, one shoe, one
trouser rolled, blindfold, length of rope about neck and
carrying a flat box of long playing records.*

CHARLES. He's back and to prove it he's here!

AMY. Thought that was too good to last.

CHARLES. Well, what d'you think? Do I look the part?

URSULA. Depends what the part is. If it's Camille, for instance,
no, you don't.

CHARLES. What does it look like?

AMY. Looks as though you've escaped from Doctor Fox's.

CHARLES. Old Mother Hubbard's not far off. This, believe it
or not, is the crackpot way a Mason has to dress for
admission to a lodge. Almost beyond one's comprehension
that all those creepers and crawlers are prepared to make
themselves look small for the sake of advancement. High on
my list of dislikes: creepers, what-I-call Masonic types. Those
who climb by licking aye-ar-ess-ee-ess. Little Lofty
Lewthwaite sucking up to Mister Tombs. Some years ago I
learned the oaths of allegiance with the sole purpose of baiting
my colleagues in the Lodge. Friend Lewthwaite said to me,
'Freemasonry is Bah-bah-Betty Martin.' Now among his
disabilities is a pronounced cast in one eye and whenever he's
getting flummoxed, this eye starts swivelling round, you
know, as though he's looking for an avenue of escape. My
Number One Anathema: Creepers. Have you heard my list of
dislikes?

FRANK. ⎫
⎬ Yes.
AMY.   ⎭

CHARLES. I was asking your good lady here.

URSULA (*laughing*). I don't know.

FRANK (*to* URSULA). We had it last time we came here!

CHARLES (*to* URSULA). You've missed a treat. (CHARLES
begins listing on his fingers.) Creepers. Filth in all forms: filthy
fingernails, filthy talk, dog's soil on the footpath. I put up a
sign on the tree outside:
'Dog-owners:
Let it not be said unto your shame
That all was beauty here until you came.'

AMY. And I took it down again.

CHARLES. And cork-tipped Katey took it down again.

AMY. Don't want the neighbours reading that.

CHARLES. Where was I, Ursula?

AMY. Think we've escaped from Dr Fox's.

URSULA. Filth in all its forms.

FRANK *moves away.*

CHARLES (*listing again*). Bartok. Unmelodious, I always say. Central heating. Dries the mouth. Booze. Masonic types.

CHARLES *moves after* FRANK *and confers with him quietly, showing the flat box.*

AMY. Mister Lewthwaite sponsored Charles for his lodge but nothing came of it. They none of them liked him.

FRANK *looks at the contents of the box – long-playing records.* CHARLES *opens the door to reveal the forties gramophone. He moves away, with a leaflet, leaving* FRANK *to put on a record.*

CHARLES. And then, of course, my list of likes.

AMY. Likes and dislikes, good old days, you'll have us all in Dr Fox's.

CHARLES (*listing again*). Cleanliness of thought and body. Giving people a fair chance in life. The ideals of the Co-operative Movement. A roaring fire. (*He considers.*) On reflection, I'm not sure I wouldn't put a roaring fire *before* the ideals of the Co-operative Movement. (*Music begins: Grieg's 'Hall of the Mountain King'.* CHARLES *begins dancing and conducting.*)

URSULA. Oh, good. I was about to ask for music.

AMY. Bang-bang-bang-bang.

CHARLES. You're a music-lover, Ursula?

URSULA. There was never any in our house, only Vera Lynn, but I'm . . .

CHARLES. I never creep and crawl. I won't. (*He reads from the leaflet, conducting the record.*) 'Hearthstone Concert Hall. Sixty-five complete selections of light classical music by thirty-eight immortal composers. These are the tunes to set toes tapping, heads nodding, fingers drumming . . .' – or in Mister Lewthwaite's case, eyes swivelling, eh, boy?

URSULA *laughs.*

'For Father, the hard-pressed business man, a musical education without tears. For Mother, almost twelve hours of companionship to keep the blues at bay. To help you waltz through the dish-washing.'

AMY. I don't think. Bang-bang-bang-bang, all day long.

URSULA. I thought you liked music.

AMY. In its proper place.

URSULA *appeals to* FRANK, *who comes down to join them.*

CHARLES. And listen to this, Old Mother Hubbard, listen, here's the bit you'll like: 'At Almost Half the Price in the Shops. Music your family will bless you for.' (*He tut-tuts disapprovingly.*) Music for which your family will . . .

AMY. Just a minute.

CHARLES. 'Costs absolutely nothing.'

AMY. Is this something you've brought?

AMY *goes to* CHARLES, *who moves away.*

This music? Is it one of these records? Is it?

CHARLES (*laughing*). No, wait a minute, Amy. 'Costs nothing to receive this astounding bargain . . .'

AMY. Oh, yes, I'll bet. But something to keep it.

CHARLES. No, wait a minute. Come and help me, boy.

AMY *chases him about as he holds the leaflet out of her reach.*

(*Reading.*) 'Handel's Largo, one of the all-time greats!'

AMY *runs at him again, but he dodges her and moves away with the leaflet, laughing.*

Butterfingers, butterfingers. You'll have to move more smartly than that to get the better of the old man.

AMY *bursts into tears. Everyone is astonished and upset.*

FRANK. Give it to her.

FRANK *takes the leaflet from* CHARLES *and gives it to* AMY, *who reads it, sobbing aloud.* FRANK *comes down.*

(*To the audience.*) I'm trying to remember exactly how sad it was. But in retrospect it seems funny.

AMY. Fifteen pounds! It costs fifteen pounds. Then you can send it back.

CHARLES (*subdued*). I can't do that, Amy.

AMY. You've had it on approval, you can say you don't like it.

CHARLES. I've sent the cheque off.

AMY. I don't believe it.

CHARLES. Wonderful bargain. Twenty-five pounds . . .

AMY. He does it to spite me. (*She cries even more.*)

CHARLES *has not managed the moment as he planned and does not know what to do.* FRANK *takes off the record.* URSULA *stands near* CHARLES. AMY *recovers and speaks to the audience.*

Only last week I asked for the money for a new spring outfit and he said we couldn't run to it. As though he hasn't got enough blasted records banging away all day and night.

FRANK. Why don't you take some interest in his music? Isn't that one of your common interests?

CHARLES. Hold your tongue, Sonny Jim.

FRANK. Sonny Jim? I'm nearly forty. A middle-aged man with three whopping kids.

URSULA. No, at this time you were nearly thirty and Matthew hadn't been born.

FRANK. Oh, Christ!

CHARLES. Don't take the Lord's name in vain.

FRANK. The Lord's name? You haven't been inside a church since my christening. The nearest you've come to godliness is cleanliness.

AMY. You've no idea what I have to go through with him, week in, week out.

FRANK. But you're to blame as well.

AMY (*frightened*). Me? To blame?

FRANK. You make no effort to understand him.

AMY. I don't expect much. No car, we never go on holiday, the house is falling about our ears. I'm only saying I expect a certain standard. Don't you think at our age you deserve a certain standard? Ursula? Don't you?

URSULA. I've never taken any standard for granted. It has to be worked for. Marriage has to be worked *at*. Understanding has to be achieved by hard work.

FRANK. Let it go.

URSULA. No, why should we allow them to use us as shock-absorbers? Every time they postpone their fights until we visit them. It's easy to blame your father but she's worse.

CHARLES. Now don't you raise your voice against Mrs Bisley.

FRANK (*to* URSULA). There!

AMY. He's getting round me now. Like when he buys another lot of junk. Twelve straw boaters he brought home last week.

CHARLES. A dozen for half a sovereign, Amy. That's less than a shilling each.

AMY. Oh, wonderful, if you happen to know twelve people who want straw boaters.

CHARLES. Say young crackpot here wants to do a Nigger Minstrel turn at his college show . . .

FRANK (*to the audience*). But with his late-Victorian, Edwardian background – 'Appy 'Ampstead, Derby Day,

drunk for two-pence and women were either old maids or
always pregnant –

AMY. Our family wasn't like that, thank you . . .

FRANK (*continuing*). – his way out was to resist the
indulgences that gave pleasure to the poor – the harmless
sedatives that, taken in small doses, might have made branch
managers and other travellers welcome him instead of turning
away.

CHARLES (*to the audience*). Nobody ever turned away from
the old man . . .

FRANK. I went with you. I saw them dodging out through the
back doors. You were an embarrassment, you were dreaded.
(*To* AMY.) I'm trying to make the point that his nature
demanded some addiction, some indulgence. And his
occupation showed the way: bargains, something for nothing.

CHARLES. We're getting a lecture, now, Amy.

FRANK. I suppose this is *my* occupational hazard. Lecturing.

CHARLES. We're not your students.

URSULA. It might not hurt you to listen, though.

CHARLES. Oh, d'you hear that, fag-end Fanny? We can profit
from piecan's education here.

AMY. If you call me that once again, I shall scream. An
occasional cigarette's not much to ask. In our family we were
poor but happy. Mother was widowed twice but she brought
us up, my brother and I. She slaved in a factory.

CHARLES (*conciliatory*). She was a dear old soul.

AMY. She enjoyed a drink, a laugh and a song. When I told her
we were marrying, she said, 'Considering you could have had
your pick, you chose a miserable devil.'

URSULA. Why did you marry him then?

AMY. I didn't know any better. I was only a girl.

CHARLES. Twenty-eight.

AMY. What about you? Middle-aged *you* were.

CHARLES. Yes.

AMY. And set in your ways, like a fossil.

CHARLES. And I was her Last Chance, Ursula. Last Chance
Charlie, eh, boy? Saved her bacon.

AMY. I had plenty of chances, then and later on. I only didn't
take them for the boy's sake.

FRANK. That's enough, Mum.

AMY. He knows very well.

CHARLES *goes and packs up his box of records, hiding from
this revelation.*

Because, after a time, it's not just what you want to do, is it?
No, after a time, only the children count. You have to sacrifice
your own desires. And though Frank used to say sometimes,
while he was away, 'Let's go off somewhere . . .'

FRANK. No.

AMY. Oh, yes – (*To the audience.*) – but I wanted him to finish
his schooling and how could I have been sure with anyone
else . . . ? A lot of those Americans, we didn't know what
they were at home. I could have been stuck in some shack like
a blooming nun.

FRANK. Will you shut up!

AMY. Of course I could have been in Hollywood.

CHARLES *goes off, taking the records, without turning
back.*

AMY. You did say that, Frank.

FRANK. I didn't understand him then.

AMY. Oh, I don't *understand* him even now.

FRANK. Well. Perhaps Ursula's helped me.

AMY (*to the audience*). Easy for her. So late in the day.

> AMY *goes.*

FRANK. We only seem to understand people when there's no longer any need. When that phase of our life is over.

URSULA. We carried the sleeping children down to the car and made subdued farewells at the gate.

FRANK. Dad told me for the billionth time how to point the car in the right direction. 'I should go down the avenue, along Appian Terrace and up Tuscan Vale to the main road . . .'

URSULA. As soon as we got home, I felt sorry for them both.

FRANK. And excited.

URSULA. What?

FRANK. We were excited. After we'd put the kids to bed, you went for a *bath* and I came in and had you, all warm and slippery, my belly slapping on the surface of the water.

> URSULA *makes for the door and goes out as soon as he starts on this subject. He runs to the slammed door, opens it and shouts after her.*

– I made you groan, deep down in your throat! Your tongue was everywhere! Like before we were married. Control yourself, man. Have you finished packing? (*He looks into the case, dreams again.*) After retirement, the old man gave up packing. Hardly ever left Corinthian Villa. So, to save Mum from fossilising we took her to a film from time to time. Or she would baby-sit if we were invited out. I'd drive over to fetch her and, while she put her coat on, Dad would give me one of his comic turns. (*Imitating* CHARLES.) You've heard my list of likes, boy?

AMY (*coming on*). Have I kept you waiting, Frank? (*She puts on her gloves.*)

FRANK (*as* CHARLES). Have you got everything? Mintoes? Spectacles?

AMY. Yes.

FRANK (*as* CHARLES). Laxatives.

AMY. We're only going to the theatre.

FRANK (*as himself*). He led us out to the pavement, laughing and excited, picked up a passing child and stood him on our front wall. Then turned on the child's father and told him to take his hands from his pockets and stand up straight.

AMY. Wasn't that awful? A man of thirty-five.

FRANK (*as* CHARLES). Which way you going, Frank? Down the avenue, perhaps, along Appian Terrace and up Tuscan Vale to . . .

AMY. D'you think Frank doesn't know the way by this time?

FRANK (*as himself*). I shot the car away from the kerb as he belatedly signalled that the way was clear. In the nearside wing-mirror, I saw him picking rubbish from the gutter.

AMY. That was one of his funny ways – picking rubbish from the gutter.

FRANK. When I brought you home afterwards, the *Eine Kleine Nachtmusik* was being played so loud we couldn't make him hear the doorbell.

AMY. I didn't want to get my key out but in the end I had to.

FRANK. He was lying dead on the kitchen floor, his milk boiling over.

AMY. He must have gone very suddenly. The best way.

FRANK. Oh yes.

AMY. Funny thing, a few days earlier he'd asked for a drop of Scotch, where before he wouldn't even eat a trifle if he detected sherry.

FRANK. I always seem to be in cinemas or theatres while my relatives are dying.

AMY. Not your fault, though, is it?

FRANK. D'you realise, while he was lying there with the milk and Mozart, we were in the same theatre where one night during the war – d'you remember, Mum?

AMY. What?

Music. The lights change.

MR MAGIC comes on as a comedian, wearing a mock-elegant outfit and removes his gloves in parody of a toff. MISS NINETEEN-FORTY comes on as a showgirl and takes them for him. He also removes his hat and overcoat and she takes these, grinning, swinging her hips. As she goes off, passing him, he pinches her and she gives a shocked squeak and smile. He looks after her, then turns to the audience.

MR MAGIC. No use you looking. That's under the counter, that is. But I'll tell you this for nothing: she's got a beautiful little chihuahua. She has. Very fond of it, too. She showed her friend and her friend said, 'Yes, lovely, but those little short hairs aren't right. You want to get rid of those.' So she went to the chemist, she said, 'I want something to get rid of little short hairs.' He gave her some ointment, he said, 'Rub it on your legs twice a day.' See? She said, 'It's not for me legs.' He said, 'No?' She said, 'No, it's for me little chihuahua.' He said, 'In that case don't ride your bike for a fortnight.' No – listen . . . ! A little monologue: There was an old cow from Huddersfield –

From the auditorium comes a single slow handclap. MR MAGIC pauses.

CHARLES (*from the audience*). Get off!

AMY. Yes, I remember this.

CHARLES. Women and children present. If you can't do better than that, get off! (*He continues the slow clap.*)

MR MAGIC. Now don't you knock your pipe at me, Grandpa. You don't know how lucky you are. This is all continental stuff I'm giving you.

CHARLES. No more filth! Get off home!

FRANK. I sat there, hot under the collar of my utility shirt.

MR MAGIC. I tell you what. We'll put it to the vote.

CHARLES. Get off! No more smut.

CHARLES *has come down the aisle and is standing by the stage, still giving the handclap. From other parts of the audience come boos and cries of 'Shut up' and 'Throw him out'.*

(*To the audience.*) Don't talk so big, you make yourself look small.

MR MAGIC. No, give him a chance . . .

CHARLES (*coming on to the stage*). Anyone who has to resort to the private parts of women to get a laugh . . .

Cries of 'Shame'.

AMY. Come on home, Charles. Everyone's looking.

CHARLES. Many of us have our wives and children with us here tonight.

FRANK. Yet I was proud of him.

MR MAGIC. Now, listen, Dad, I only mentioned a chihuahua.

CHARLES. Cleanliness is next to godliness.

MR MAGIC. All right, mate, I've nearly finished anyway. (*To the audience*). I'll come back in the second half after he's gone.

MR MAGIC *goes off, to cheers.* CHARLES *remains with* FRANK *and* AMY.

CHARLES. Jokes about conveniences and bee-you-double-gee-ee-are-why.

Loud boos. CHARLES *turns in their direction and bows, slowly, with dignity.*

I bowed slowly, boy, you remember?

FRANK. Shall I ever forget?

CHARLES. Frightened the life out of them.

AMY. You don't care how much you embarrassed me, I could hear people saying, 'He's escaped from Doctor Fox's.'

CHARLES. For a moment I toyed with the idea of giving an excerpt from my most successful recitation 'Jeremiah in the Turkish bath'. (*He takes up a posture and recites in a cockney dialect.*) 'And now, Jerry, if you'll lie on the table here, I'll just finish you awf.'

FRANK. All right, Dad, thanks . . .

CHARLES (*after an extravagant horrified reaction*). 'Finish me awf?'

FRANK. Yes, fine, that's enough now.

FRANK *and* AMY *try to usher* CHARLES *towards a door. He escapes and returns down stage.*

CHARLES. 'I'm darned near finished awf already.'

FRANK. Come on, you've had your turn.

FRANK *and* CHARLES *argue in whispers.*

AMY (*to the audience*). The band struck up and the dancing girls came on and he ran down the aisle peering at them through his opera glasses, cheering.

CHARLES (*to* AMY). Nothing smutty about the female form. Only lewd innuendo.

FRANK. Right. Thank you.

AMY (*persuading him through the door again*). Soon after that I got him into the foyer and on to the bus. (*She shuts the door on* CHARLES.)

FRANK (*to the audience*). Well, the day of the funeral . . .

The door reopens and CHARLES *appears.*

CHARLES (*continuing his recitation*). 'I've been pushed and pummelled, pummelled and pushed. I'm black and blue.'

The audience cheers.

FRANK. Will you let me tell the rest of the story!

CHARLES. You tell a story, boy? You couldn't make a pudden crawl!

FRANK. And you're dead! So go!

CHARLES *looks at* FRANK, *then at the audience. He bows slowly three times to mounting derision, then goes, leaving the door open.* FRANK *runs to the door, slams it, waits, then returns down stage.*

The day of the funeral a heat-wave started. So, where once had stood the only car in the avenue, there was now barely room to squeeze his hearse in.

AMY. Mister Lewthwaite turned up at the crematorium. And Mister Champness of men's outfitting who had supplied your father with long underpants at wholesale prices.

FRANK. 'Man that is born of woman hath but a short time to live and is full of misery. He cometh up and is cut down like a flower,' said the priest and pressed a button and the coffin slid into the wall. I half expected him to slide out again for the last word but no, this *was* his final exit.

AMY. He was a good man, a good husband. He never kept me short. He had his funny ways – who hasn't? I blame his mother – all in black with her hair strained back and her lips a thin white line. Real Victorian. No wonder his father drank. In our family we were poor but happy. Mother enjoyed a drink, a laugh and a song. (*Exit.*)

FRANK *looks at his list, brings some outer clothes to pack in the case.*

FRANK. His death made me feel the likelihood, the certainty of my own. I was the oldest man in the family now. The greater part of my life was behind me and the rest didn't look too hot. Somewhere between the black-out and the marriage-bed I missed young love, ecstasy, surrender. I suddenly saw my own son claiming the benefits of the new state I'd helped bring about – the new freedom – and it was so unfair!

Rock music blares out. FRANK *puts hands on ears as* YOUNG FRANK *comes on, now late teens, dressed modern casual, carrying loud boogie box. After him comes* MISS NINETEEN-FORTY, *modern too, wartime nostalgia style, 1940+. They embrace and kiss, not seeing* FRANK, *who turns down their music.*

FRANK. Hullo, Bill.

YOUNG FRANK. Oh, you here again?

FRANK. Usual sunny welcome. Who's your friend?

YOUNG FRANK. Sammy.

FRANK. And was that you on that scooter, making such a filthy row all up the street?

YOUNG FRANK. Yeah, Sammy's Yamaha.

FRANK. Well, I'm sure I speak for the whole street when I say it was tremendously impressive.

YOUNG FRANK *and* MISS NINETEEN-FORTY *begin dancing in a copulative way. During his speeches, they get on the sofa, undressing each other.*

I'm sure even those of our neighbours who had managed to get to sleep before you arrived were tremendously impressed when you woke them up. Motor bikes. Electronic groups. Jet flights to Kathmandu. Your rejection of capitalism is a piece of cant until you reject the muck it produces. And rejection's not enough. You've got to know what kind of world you want instead. I've a far more defined view of that than you have. You haven't heard my manifesto?

YOUNG FRANK. If I were king –

FRANK (*listing on his fingers, as* CHARLES *did*). If I were king – or president or whatever – first: ban all heavy transport using residential streets to convey another load of sea-dredged aggregates. Next: ban motor bikes to anyone under forty and over fifty.

About now, BILL *and* SAMMY *tire of the noise and go off, taking the radio. He doesn't notice, goes on lecturing. Soon after this* URSULA *comes on by another door.*

Go for strictly limited aims, you see. Legislate against luxury. We did very well without luxury during the war, very well without petrol and prawn cocktails and all the grotesque inequality of the present day.

URSULA *is 38, wearing an outdoor coat, etc., carrying a large bag and portfolio with patterns, samples of material, etc. Kicks door shut behind her.*

URSULA. Hello.

FRANK. Hello. How did it go, darling?

URSULA. Great – can't think why I enjoy it so much. Even if the money wasn't so useful, I'd still go on taking these evening classes. I like schools when all the children have gone home.

FRANK *follows her back and stands listening, nodding.*

All the chairs up on their desks. I like the fact that these people of all ages and shapes and colours come along in their spare time to learn dress-making – have a chat – no-one's pushing you to get you past exams – it's real teaching – how have you been? The kids slept soundly?

FRANK. Yes.

URSULA (*seeing the suitcase open*). You have finished our packing?

FRANK. Um – well, I was just . . .

URSULA. I told you all that had to go in. Our sweaters, your jeans, your woollen socks to go inside your boots. And you put the four pairs of wellies in the car?

FRANK. Ah – now . . .

URSULA. I stood here and told you every single thing that had to go in! I asked you if you wanted me to make a list but you said no, you could remember. What were you doing – dreaming again? Haven't you put the boots in then?

FRANK. Well, not yet. I was just . . .

URSULA. And what about the sick bags? The polythene bags in case Jenny's car-sick? She always is. D'you want it all over the safety-belts like last time?

FRANK. No.

URSULA. You haven't done that! I don't believe it. What *have* you done? Gone into another bloody dream? Oh, God, honestly! Been playing that old wartime tape again. We're supposed to be getting off before dawn to miss the traffic and have as long in the country as possible! Now we shall have to do all this bloody packing in the dark and . . .

FRANK. No, I'll do it now.

URSULA. You won't. I'm dropping on my feet and if you potter about now you'll only wake me up again when you come blundering into bed. We'll do it in the morning. And even as I say that I know I mean: *I'll* do it in the morning because nothing wakes you until the last possible moment.

FRANK. D'you know what this trip started as?

URSULA. What?

FRANK. A second honeymoon. Our parents were supposed to be having the children and you and I . . .

URSULA. Well, they couldn't, as it turned out, could they? So that was the end of . . . (*She looks round uneasily, sensing something.*) What's the smell? The casserole! Have you only

just had it then? The oven switched itself off at nine, I told
you that, I told you to take it out soon after that before it got
dried up or cooled off. Was it all right?

FRANK. Christ – d'you know, love, it must have slipped my . . .
I'll have it now . . .

URSULA. You mean you haven't eaten it? Haven't eaten at all?

FRANK. Would you believe it, I had some fish and chips from
round the corner?

URSULA. It took me half an hour to prepare that casserole. I
haven't stopped all day. I nearly fell asleep in class tonight –
oh . . . (*She groans and shakes her head, then thinks again.*)
Fish and chips? Did you go and buy them?

FRANK. Yes.

URSULA. Left the children alone in the house?

FRANK. It was only ten minutes.

URSULA. When are you going to think of someone but
yourself? When are you going to consider something but your
own precious comfort? The answer's never, isn't it? You never
have and you never will. So not only did I manage all the
housework and all the preparations for going away but most
of the packing, too, and bathed the children and got their
meal and washed that up and made you a casserole and took
my class and what were you doing all that time?

FRANK (*quietly*). I was trying to . . .

URSULA. Standing about doing nothing!

URSULA *grabs her bags and goes out by another door,*
slamming it behind her. FRANK *holds his head, then goes to*
the case and looks in it confusedly.

FRANK. Can I stand much more of this? (*He moves away,*
assessing the value of two pairs of socks.) Oh, yes. Much
more.

Music: 'You stepped out of a dream' (Tony Martin). YOUNG
URSULA *comes on from another door. She is wearing a
school hat, blue raincoat, white socks and shoes, but nothing
else.* FRANK *turns to her. She stands down stage of him,
unbuttons her raincoat and opens it so that he can see her
body. He stands where he is, devouring her with his eyes. She
moves slowly towards him and embraces him. He caresses her
beneath the coat. A door opens and* URSULA *looks in. Music
pause.*

URSULA. Don't bother with that at this time of night. I want to
get to sleep.

URSULA *goes, slamming the door. Music resumes. With a last
kiss,* YOUNG URSULA *steps back, wraps her coat around
her and goes off the way she came, making one final obscene
gesture at the door.* FRANK *packs the socks again, closes the
case, and goes after* URSULA *turning out the lights.*

After their bows the actors line up and sing:

> Rainy days don't worry me,
> There's a rainbow that I can see
> And it's waiting for me
> Down Forget-me-not Lane.
>
> Fortune never comes that way,
> I'll keep singing a song each day,
> Keeping troubles away
> From Forget-me-not Lane.
>
> It's just a heaven they've made
> And if you're a stranger there
> You'll find a table well-laid
> And you're welcome to a chair.
>
> There's no highbrow etiquette,
> Just plain people and once you've met,
> They will never forget
> Down Forget-me-not Lane.

They go by various doors, all at once.

Hearts and Flowers

Hearts and Flowers

In November 1969, I was struggling to begin a new play that would finally appear on the stage as *Forget-me-not Lane*. At the start, I had a good deal of trouble and, says Diary, in looking through my old journals for clues, I came upon the long account of my father's funeral:

> It seemed almost complete as it stood and I pitched in at once, after the usual miserable hours thinking up names for the people. Why shouldn't they be called 'Peter', 'Dick', 'Vi', 'Thelma', etc? Because we're only the starting-points, of course, and false names allow the characters to grow away in directions the real people didn't.

This play, *Hearts and Flowers*, is a good example. Bob lives in Bristol and teaches in a secondary school. His elder brother Tony left home years ago and is a well-known television journalist and presenter. Bob suspects and derides Tony's facile sentiments, his ability to turn on the tears like tapwater. But he's envious at the same time – of Tony's success, the glamorous life that enables him to do a programme on air pollution then 'fly off to New York in a trail of diesel and supersonic bangs'. As the play goes on, we learn of his deeper reasons for resenting his brother – that Bob's wife Jean married him after being jilted by Tony and harbours an unsatisfied longing for the elder man.

At the time I wrote it, my brother was still a teacher in Bristol and I was a playwright in London. There is a superficial resemblance between Tony/Bob and Peter/Geoffrey, and relatives and friends may have thought that I was debunking my own pretensions as

Tony and claiming that my brother envied me as Bob. The truth is that, at the time of my father's death, I too lived in Bristol and had only recently been teaching in the same school as Geoffrey. Tony and Bob are two aspects of myself. Like everyone I know – including my brother – I am a divided character, hoping for an exciting and passionate life but equally enjoying the claims of work and duty. The play is based on that tension and the father's funeral is the setting which brings it briefly to the surface.

Some years later, the British Film Institute wanted to include the play in a season of TV plays at the NFT. They were told that the tape had been wiped. It had been a fine production by Christopher Morahan with well-judged performances from a cast headed by Anthony Hopkins, was well reviewed and had been watched by an audience of eleven million. An almost certain candidate for obliteration. It seemed that only the script remained but finally a black-and-white copy turned up that had been pirated from the first transmission. Even in this state, it 'watches' better than my other TV plays and it's included here as the most readable of twenty or so scripts for that medium.

Hearts and Flowers was first performed for BBC TV, 1970 and repeated a year later.

BOB	Anthony Hopkins
JEAN	Priscilla Morgan
MARIE	Constance Chapman
TONY	Donald Churchill
WILL	Leon Cortez
LIONEL	Eric Francis
ERIC	Clifford Parrish
PHYLLIS	Betty Bascombe
VERA	Freda Bamford
UNA	Sheila Keith
MR FOWLER	Martin Wyldeck
MRS FOWLER	Grace Arnold
WITTS	Jeffrey Segal
LINDA	Maryann Turner
VICAR	Bill Horsley
WOMAN AT STATION	April Wilding
MR BRITTAIN	Roy Hepworth

Directed by Christopher Morahan

1. Interior. Bob and Jean's Bedroom. Night.

Double bed lit by table lamp. BOB's head on one pillow, reading newspaper. He is thirty-two. He is wearing pyjama jacket. Sound of door opening and closing. He goes on reading but soon looks up and continues looking off-screen. Music: 'Salut d'Amour' by Elgar. Slowly.

Opening Captions

He is still watching as JEAN joins him in bed, wearing a demure nightgown. Settles her head on the pillow and smiles at him briefly, but is overcome by a yawn. Under the bedclothes, he reaches out to touch her. She smiles again briefly, and moves her feet against his. She closes her eyes. Then moves her feet again and opens her eyes.

JEAN. No pyjama trousers.

BOB. No.

JEAN. You hot?

BOB. Sweltering.

JEAN. I'm not. Sitting on Bill's bed waiting for him to use the pot, my feet are like ice. (*Turns away from him and closes eyes.*)

He looks at back of her head, puts away paper. He kisses the back of her neck.

JEAN. Mmmm. (*Turns head, slightly smiling, eyes closed.*)

He kisses her lips gently. She yawns.

JEAN. Oh, dear . . .

He props himself on one elbow and looks at her. She yawns again.

Oh, dear . . .

BOB. Terrific.

JEAN (*opening eyes*). What?

BOB. I kissed you and you yawned.

JEAN. Did I? Sorry, love, only I'm dead. Bill's been a monkey, tramping chocolate mousse right through the Spanish rope mat . . . and making monster noises during Susan's science programme . . . (*Tails off into yawn.*) Oh, dear . . . it's her school holiday in case you've forgotten.

BOB. It's not only during school holidays.

Pause. Her eyes have closed again.

I don't much like admitting something's gone wrong with our sex-life . . . but what else d'you suggest? What about the way you undress? In that dark corner. And you put on your nightdress before you take your skirt off. And you won't let me *help* you either. All day you walk about with attractive clothes on but when we come up here you won't . . .

JEAN. It's no good, I find it very embarrassing having someone take my clothes off.

BOB. You used to like it.

JEAN. No.

BOB. You *did*.

JEAN. I used to *pretend* to.

Pause. He is sitting up, wide awake. Her eyes keep closing.

BOB. You used to be more – social – about it all. With a lot more smiling and chasing about and – unusual rooms. During the day. Why is it always in the dark nowadays? D'you hate the sight of me?

JEAN. All that was before children.

BOB. But what about when my mother has them for the day? Or when Dad takes them to the zoo? How do we spend those valuable hours? In bed? (*Shakes his head.*) Shopping.

JEAN (*angry*). D'you think I *like* shopping?

BOB. I think *all* women like shopping.

JEAN. The house doesn't run itself. I'm busy morning till night and at bedtime tired to death and can't stand bright lights shining in my eyes.

BOB (*gently, caressing her*). But, love, d'you think the busy-ness is to fill the time I might otherwise try to occupy taking your clothes off?

JEAN (*eyes open, angry*). How often do I deny you?

BOB. It's not a question –

JEAN. How often do I refuse when you come telling me how much you –

BOB. It's not a question of how often –

JEAN. Isn't it?

BOB (*louder*). – but of what it's *like*. Whether you seem to be suffering some nasty necessity that crops up every so often.

JEAN. Think yourself lucky.

BOB (*imitation*). 'My husband's very good, he only troubles me twice a week.'

JEAN. You talk as though you're some pathetic lurker in a mac, forced to pick up tarts in doorways. It's a joke – really!

BOB (*as though he finds the description fits*). Well – (*Makes a little face.*)

She turns away and makes to sleep.

(*He speaks softly.*) Do understand, love, I'm not complaining, I'm apologising . . . for not knowing how to keep our marriage fresh, surprising. Because I'm – not widely experienced. So perhaps I *should* pick up tarts in doorways.

Pause.

JEAN (*seems not to have listened, then*). D'you *want* to?

BOB. I don't *want* to. I think perhaps I *ought* to.

JEAN. What d'you expect to learn?

BOB. I don't know. They're doing it all day.

JEAN. How d'you know your sessions with the tart won't be enough? All you want?

Pause.

BOB. Would that worry you?

She turns again, eyes open, decisively.

JEAN. *I* don't want you going with tarts. I'm happy with my sex-life as it is. I don't happen to like electric lights in my eyes last thing and you *have* put on weight a bit this year –

BOB (*while she continues*). Then let's try a different –

JEAN. I'm sorry if you want me to dress as a nurse or a nun, I'm afraid I couldn't keep a straight face.

BOB. When we first married, we didn't need any frills, we excited each other so much.

JEAN. We only had ourselves to think of. (*Yawns.*) Oh, dear.

BOB (*noting this*). Before the boredom set in.

JEAN. I'm not bored, I'm dead! (*Yawns again.*) Oh, dear. D'you know, when I sing Bill a lullaby, it's me that falls asleep. And what if I'm pregnant? What if it's about to start all over again? You do remember, don't you, I'm going to the doctor tomorrow for the test results? You know I'm late?

BOB. You lost the pills, yes.

JEAN. Forgot them, then couldn't find them. Three days. It's sure to be all right.

BOB. Well, if you are, the damage is done. If you're not, we must continue to place our faith in the drug manufacturers. Still, as you wish.

Turns out bedside lamp. As it goes, she yawns. Pause.

JEAN (*cockney*). Hallo, dearie.

BOB. What?

JEAN. Want a nice time?

BOB. What's this?

JEAN. I'm the tart in the doorway.

BOB. You wouldn't know where to start.

JEAN. Think so?

Sounds of movement. Giggles, a little scream. Telephone bell rings. Movements stop.

BOB. Who the hell – ?

Bell rings.

This time of night?

He answers it and with other hand puts on light. JEAN flinches, hides under sheets.

Hallo? . . . Mum!

JEAN *makes long-suffering face.*

Yes, we are, as a matter of fact . . . it's all right . . . (*Manner changes.*) Oh . . . where is he? . . . right, I'll be over as soon as I can . . . you've called the doctor?

JEAN *looks at him.*

Good. Nothing else, no. Shan't be long . . . 'Bye . . . (*He puts down telephone, swings legs round.*) Dad's collapsed.

He goes. JEAN *left alone, stares at him, off-camera.*

JEAN. Where was she phoning from?

BOB. A neighbour's.

JEAN. Oh, Bob. Let me know what happens.

BOB. Yep.

JEAN *thinks, closes her eyes at her thought.*

JEAN. Poor dear.

2. Interior. Marie's Living Room. Night.

Neither large nor small, trying to be cosy, but with too many pieces of pre-war furniture; overhead light. BOB's *father lying awkwardly on floor in foreground, eyes closed. See nothing else for some time, hear the dialogue.*

MARIE. Bob –

BOB. Hallo, Mum.

MARIE. I walked right through the house without seeing him.

BOB. Where is he?

MARIE. There.

BOB *and* MARIE *have come in behind, and* BOB *now approaches his father, crouches by him. Slightly lifts him, dislodging an arm that is awkwardly twisted.*

I'd been to the whist drive with Mr and Mrs Fowler and they dropped me at the door and I asked them in for a cup of tea but they said they'd better get on home.

BOB *is trying to detect a pulse in his father's wrist.*

Well, you know the way your father tries to pull Mr Fowler's leg and I don't believe he ever really likes it. So they wouldn't come in for a cup of tea and I could hear the gramophone playing so I knocked on the window as usual but he didn't come, so I thought he's probably off in some other room.

BOB sits back, looks at her, nods, returns to father, puts his hand on father's chest to feel a beat.

Well, Linda next door dialled the number and I spoke to his wife. He was out on a call, but she expected him back any minute. That was – what? – twenty-five minutes ago.

BOB sits up again.

BOB. I suppose we shouldn't move him, or anything.

MARIE. Not till doctor's seen him, I don't think. What do you think?

BOB. No.

MARIE. He's comfortable enough.

BOB. Oh, yes.

MARIE. Perhaps a cushion under his head – what d'you think?

BOB. No.

MARIE. No.

BOB sits back on armchair.

BOB. It can't have been long before –

Doorbell rings.

MARIE. There he is.

Goes and BOB stands. Moves to a twenty-year-old radiogram. He opens the lid, turns the tone arm back to its rest, takes a long-playing record from the turntable and returns it to its sleeve and the sleeve to its rack. MARIE comes in with DOCTOR, an elderly man.

DOCTOR. Hullo, Mister – um –

BOB. Hullo, Doctor.

DOCTOR. Goodliffe.

Smiles, goes down beside father, begins examination.

You found him like this, Mrs – um –

MARIE. The funny thing was I didn't see him right away. I couldn't make him hear by knocking on the window so I thought well, he must be out the back. So I went right through to the kitchen and found the milk boiled over he must have put on for his bedtime drink. Then when I came back here, I saw him lying there . . .

MARIE weeps. BOB takes her hand and holds it with both of his, giving her a be-brave look.

DOCTOR (*looking for a pulse*). Mmm.

BOB. There was still a record playing. When did it stop?

MARIE. I don't know. I know it was playing when I came in.

BOB. It had switched itself off but the radiogram was still –

DOCTOR. Have you got a small hand-mirror?

MARIE goes to her handbag.

BOB. Well, he can't have collapsed long before. A record takes twenty minutes to play.

MARIE brings mirror to DOCTOR, who holds it by the mouth for a few seconds. He looks at the glass, then at BOB, who is now crouching beside him.

DOCTOR (*quietly*). I'm afraid he's gone.

BOB nods.

MARIE. I thought he was.

DOCTOR. He can't have known much about it. Much the best way.

MARIE. It's the way he would have wanted himself. Oh dear . . .

DOCTOR. How old was he?

MARIE. Seventy-two.

DOCTOR. Well –

MARIE. Seventy-three in August.

DOCTOR. Not a bad innings, when you look at it. (*He stands.*) Now. He hadn't been in to see me for some weeks, so there'll have to be a coroner's post-mortem.

MARIE. Oh, no.

DOCTOR. A legal formality, nothing more, when somebody passes over unexpectedly.

MARIE. He had some pains over the weekend. In his chest.

DOCTOR (*nodding*). Angina.

MARIE. And I said shall I ring the doctor, but he said no don't disturb him on a Sunday.

DOCTOR. Perhaps it's best. I might have prolonged his life for a time, but. . . .

MARIE. This is how he would have wanted to go. Sooner than drag on, a burden to everyone. (*She cries.*)

BOB. What shall I do now?

DOCTOR. I'll give you a certificate to send to the registrar. Then in the morning, I'll notify the coroner. They'll be along some time tomorrow to take him away. Meantime – have you ever made arrangements with an undertaker?

3. **Interior. Marie's Hall. Night.**

BOB *crosses and knocks on door of front room. The door is opened by* WITTS, *a neat middle-aged man in black suiting. Seeing* BOB, *he smiles, opens wider.*

BOB. My mother wanted to know if you'd like a cup of tea.

WITTS. I shan't say no, if a cup of tea's being made.

BOB. What about your – friend?

WITTS. Mister Morley won't say no, sir. And – sir? – would you step in for a moment?

BOB *goes in.*

4. Interior. Front Room. Night.

Larger than living room, with better furnishings. A coffin stands on trestles. MORLEY, the other man, is tidying up. WITTS shows BOB some articles on a table.

WITTS. The contents of the pockets, sir. His wallet. A quantity of silver and copper coin. Sundry keys on ring. A handkerchief. (*Shows him chair.*) His outer clothes. We usually leave the underwear on, though you can have it returned later, should you wish. More often than not, of course, it's soiled, so you may give us permission to destroy it.

BOB. Yes, fine. We shan't be wanting it, I'm sure . . . (*Smiles apologetically.*)

WITTS. That's all, thank you, sir. We'll take advantage of the lady's invitation as soon as we've finished up in here. (*Hands him contents of father's pockets.*)

BOB *goes.*

5. Interior. Bob and Jean's Bedroom. Night.

JEAN *in double bed, on BOB's side, using telephone.*

JEAN. Alright . . . I'll make the bed in the playroom . . . is she takıng it well? . . . I'm so sorry, Bob . . . I meant sorry for you, too . . . no, it can't be helped but even so – . . . yes, see you. (*She puts telephone down. Lies back on BOB's pillow, staring at ceiling, tears in eyes.*)

6. Interior. Living Room. Night.

MARIE, BOB *and the undertakers standing with cups of tea.*

WITTS. Beautiful cup of tea that.

MARIE. I should think you need it.

WITTS. I always say, at a time like this, that's all you can do, really and truly, drink tea.

BOB *returns his to tray.*

MARIE. Want another?

BOB. No, thanks.

MARIE. Dad never had a cup of tea at night, he always had a milky drink. He said tea kept him awake.

WITTS *nods. They drink.*

WITTS. He was a well-built man.

MARIE. He always walked like a serjeant-major, with his shoulders back.

WITTS. My words to Mister Morley: military bearing. I said he had a military bearing. Late seventies, was he?

MARIE. Seventy-two.

WITTS. Very well preserved.

MARIE. He was always athletic, you see.

WITTS. Kept him young.

MARIE. Cycling, football, rowing.

WITTS. Preserved him.

MORLEY *nods.* WITTS *finishes tea.*

This won't get the work done. Thank you, madam. And you'll be here, sir, nine o'clock or thereabouts to let in the coroner's officers?

BOB. Yes.

WITTS. Goodnight, sir.

> BOB *goes with men.* MARIE *puts cups on tray.*

7. Interior. Hall. Night.

BOB *returning from closing front door. He speaks into living room.*

BOB. You've packed your case?

MARIE. It's there.

> *She comes to door.*

BOB. Might as well get home then. Back to my place.

MARIE. I'd better wash the tea things.

BOB. I'll clear them up in the morning.

> *She comes into hall, switching off light of living-room.* MARIE *nods, takes down overcoat.*

MARIE. Is it still warm out?

BOB. Sweltering.

MARIE. But it could turn. I'll wear my coat save carrying it.

> *He helps her on with her coat.*

I can ring Tony from your place.

BOB. Yes.

MARIE. He'll want to make arrangements to come to the funeral. He and Dad were very close.

> *She begins to cry.* BOB *turns to door, opens it and waits.*

8. Interior. Bob and Jean's Bedroom. Night.

Double bed, as at start. JEAN *and* BOB, *sitting back to back on the edges of the bed.*

JEAN (*quietly*). She's not too bad.

Pause. JEAN *starts to get into bed.*

She had a little cry in the kitchen.

BOB *gets in other side.*

BOB. And another little one as we were leaving Forty-Two.

He pulls feet into bed. JEAN *looks at him. He examines toe nails.*

And a big one on the phone to Tony.

He pulls off silver of nail, pulls up sheet. Sniffs hand.

JEAN. You surely don't begrudge her a few tears.

BOB. Shame she didn't shed them sooner. They're no use to the old man now.

Pause. He stares at ceiling. JEAN *half-turns away.*

As soon as death was certified, the whitewashing started. 'He was always athletic, rowing, cycling, football.' Not for the last thirty years, to *my* knowledge. There won't be anything left of Dad by the time she and Tony have finished.

JEAN. It seems only right to me for people to cry a bit. Even crocodile tears are better than nothing.

BOB. D'you think so?

JEAN. Yes.

BOB. Why?

JEAN. He'd like to feel mourned.

BOB. He doesn't exist any more, he's out of the question. What I'd mourn would be his lack of achievement. Seventy years and nothing to show for it! He did no harm, I suppose, but no good either.

JEAN. You and Tony.

BOB. That's all. Family. His entire energy devoted to his wife and sons. I loathe family life. As an idea. Net curtains and privet hedges and the sound of slamming bedroom doors. If all the energy lost in domestic friction could be canalised, we'd solve the traffic problem in a week.

Pause. He turns to her, realising he has upset her and wanting to mollify her.

Love –

JEAN *moves from his touch irritably.*

JEAN. What if I die first, is that all you'll feel?

BOB. I shall want to die too. But it's different, we *chose* each other.

JEAN. She chose your father. Presumably. Then shouldn't she cry?

BOB (*thinks, then nods*). I only meant we don't choose our parents. We can't feel the same for them.

JEAN. I shall cry when my mother dies.

BOB. You're very close. Perhaps because your father left her. You drew together.

JEAN. Don't you expect your children to cry at your death?

BOB. Why should I want them to? I shan't be here to see it. I shouldn't enjoy it, if I could. (*He turns and embraces her from behind.*) Eh, my love?

JEAN. No. (*Pushes him off.*) All you think about.

9. Interior. Marie's Front Room. Day.

Bright morning sunlight filtered through drawn curtains. Coffin on trestles, as before. After a few moments BOB comes in wearing lightweight office clothes, with no sign of mourning. Blows air out and goes to open one of the windows a few inches at the top. BOB *turns back to room and approaches coffin. He pulls back sheet over father's face. He looks at it for some seconds, then leaves the room.*

10. Interior. Marie's Living Room. Day.

At rear of house, overlooking garden. Windows uncurtained and light coming in. BOB *enters, takes from mantelpiece the contents of father's clothes. He spreads out the handkerchief on a table and puts the wallet, money and keys into it, folding it over into a parcel. He leaves it there. Sound off from front door.* BOB *goes out.*

11. Interior. Marie's Hall. Day.

BOB *arrives at front door and finds the morning's mail on the doormat, one or two circulars, and a picture postcard.*

12. Interior. Bob and Jean's Hall. Day.

JEAN *at mirror, checking her appearance. Hear* MARIE's *voice off, speaking on telephone.*

MARIE. . . . well, Eric, if you give me a ring here at Robert's place, I can let you know for sure what time the funeral's starting . . . yes, alright, I know he'd have wanted you to be there . . .

JEAN (*speaking through doorway, hastily*). I shan't be long. You'll keep an eye on the children, they're in the garden.

MARIE. Yes, bye-bye. No, Eric, I was saying bye-bye, Jean, she's just off out.

JEAN *goes.*

13. Interior. Marie's Living Room. Day.

Mail now on table beside father's personal effects. BOB at mantelpiece, lighting a cigarette. He has a small, official-looking booklet in his hand, open at a page. He sits in an armchair and puzzles over it.

BOB. 'It is essential to inform the coroner if you want cremation rather than burial, so that he may issue his certificate-for-cremation, which is free of charge and obviates the use of forms B and C. Form F is signed by the medical referee of the crematorium on the medical evidence of forms B and C, or H, or in the case of a post-mortem, after the issue of the certificate-for-cremation.'

He closes the book and puts it in his pocket, goes to table and opens picture newspaper. There is not a lot to read, but he glances with some relief at the girlie pictures and scans the sports page. At last he returns to the girlie pictures. Doorbell. He closes paper, stubs out cigarette in ashtray on table, hesitates, wondering why he did not finish his smoke, shrugs, goes on stubbing, then makes to answer the door.

14. Exterior. Marie's House. Day.

MARIE's house from opposite side. Sixty-year-old semi with small front garden. Parked cars line both sides of street and Coroner's van has had to double-park. Two men come from the house carrying the body in its coffin, now closed. They put it into their plain van. BOB watches from the front door. A motorcyclist roars through the narrow gap between the van and the further row of cars.

15. Interior. Bob and Jean's Bedroom. Night.

Double bed, as before. JEAN awake, no book. BOB climbs in, full pyjamas.

BOB. Why didn't you go to sleep? No need to wait for me.

JEAN. I'd only wake up when you climbed in.

BOB. We could always get twin beds. Eh, love? (*Touches her.*) Separate beds?

JEAN. Mmmm.

BOB. How's Mum been?

JEAN. Busy telephoning her relations with the news. Tony's coming Thursday morning, he's got a programme Wednesday night.

BOB. I suppose London will somehow manage to survive without him for a few hours.

JEAN. So she's kept busy.

BOB. I saw the body off. Then went to the office to find a blazing row going on about who'd leaked the Ring Road Proposals to the local press. Well, I say a blazing row but it was more a puff of smoke. And I couldn't dodge this evening's Action Group because I'm the prime mover. The Civic Society bloke was there.

JEAN. She was very helpful at bath-time.

BOB. We think the Fine Arts Commission will be on our side. Getting in with some funny company.

JEAN. And looked after the kids while I was out.

BOB. Good. Gave her something to occupy her mind, too, I expect.

She looks at him as though wondering what he's doing there.

Where d'you go? Shopping?

He is winding his wrist-watch.

JEAN. No. I went to the doctor.

BOB. Doctor? What ab – Christ! Oh, love, I'm sorry, what did he say?

JEAN. He said yes. Positive. I'm pregnant. (*She smiles coldly, ironically.*)

BOB. Oh, no.

JEAN. Oh, yes.

BOB *shakes his head*.

BOB. What are we going to do?

JEAN. Apply to the milkman for our subsidised pintas. The dentist for free fillings. Start buying maternity wear again. . . .

BOB. No, I mean. . . .

JEAN. I gave Peggy my old clothes for her prison visiting or whatever it is. . . .

BOB. That's what you want, is it? I mean, the doctor thinks you'll be alright?

JEAN. I'm only thirty-three. Of course I'll be alright!

BOB. Just as Bill's about to start at the Montessori!

JEAN. I know.

BOB. All that again!

JEAN. The third child means a second family allowance.

BOB. So much for the pill.

JEAN. I missed three. I left them in that duffle bag in the back of the van.

BOB. Look – you know the money we've been saving for the car? Perhaps if you felt, you know, you couldn't face it, well perhaps we could use it for a – nursing home.

JEAN. I didn't want to be pregnant, but now that I am, I suddenly feel – coming at the same time as your father's death, I'm very excited about it. I nearly sang in the bus coming home. I think I must have a touch of the tar-brush. Why can't we let off fireworks or put on masks or dance in the streets? Cause some kind of public nuisance?

BOB. I don't feel like dancing.

JEAN. And you didn't feel like crying at your father's death. What about those women we heard in Killarney, howling all night?

BOB. Professional mourners.

JEAN. Alright. They helped the other . . . people find a voice for their grief.

BOB *considers. Pause.*

BOB. Yeah. The undertaker said: All you can do at a time like this is drink tea. And I remember thinking: couldn't we scream or curse the gods or rend our clothes . . . but no, we're a long way from that. It worries me sometimes, I don't feel a lot. I can't pretend an emotion I don't feel.

JEAN. Ever tried? Perhaps you never feel because you never try to feel.

BOB. I feel for you.

JEAN. That's greed. (*She turns away, tired of trying.*)

BOB. Tony will show us how to feel. He's an expert.

16. Exterior. Main Line Station. Booking Hall. Day.

TONY *and* WOMAN *come from platform with arriving passengers.* TONY *is 38, dressed in dark suit with black tie, carries suitcase and large brief-case. She is young, bold, impressive. They are chatting.*

BOB, *also in a suit and black tie, sees them coming, frowns.*

TONY. . . . find my childhood closes in on me as soon as I reach this station . . . Hullo, Bob . . .

BOB. Hullo.

TONY *offers his hand.* BOB *shakes it.*

TONY. D'you want a porter?

WOMAN. No. I'm being met.

She takes her case.

TONY. Bye-bye, then.

WOMAN. I shall watch you on the screen with a new interest.

TONY. Bless you.

WOMAN. Goodbye.

She goes off.

BOB. I thought you'd brought a friend.

TONY. Christ no. I made the mistake of smiling at her, then it turned out she knew me from the telly and talked my head off all the way down. Serves me right.

BOB. Smashing piece.

TONY. One of the problems of being on the box. People won't leave you alone.

BOB (*looking after* WOMAN). Must be awful.

PORTER *crosses,* BOB *collides with him.*

Sorry.

TONY. One day, on this station, I called a porter and d'you know who turned up?

BOB. Uncle Arthur.

TONY. Right. Talk about embarrassing.

BOB. He's retired now.

TONY. I stared at this dominating figure of my childhood and he stared at me and picked up my case and carried it and asked me about the family.

BOB. I don't suppose it worried him.

TONY. No.

BOB. It must have happened before.

TONY. To him, perhaps, but not to me.

17. Exterior. Station. Day.

They are now crossing road to parked cars.

TONY. How's Jean?

BOB. Fine.

TONY. The kids?

BOB. She's expecting another.

TONY. No! Terrific! I don't know. *Is* it terrific? You tell me.

BOB. Oh, yes, she'd got to the stage of drooling over other people's. It's come just at the right time.

They have reached a Minivan; BOB unlocks the driver's door.

TONY. Why didn't you let me know?

BOB. Didn't know ourselves till a couple of days ago.

TONY. Talk about: in the midst of life.

BOB. Yeah.

He gets into the van and opens the passenger door.

TONY. I can't take it in. Mum's message came when I was halfway through an in-depth interview and I'm afraid the rest was a total cock-up. (BOB *puts case into van.*) How's she taken it?

BOB (*emerging again*). What?

TONY. How's Mum taken the old man's death?

BOB. The funeral arrangements have kept her busy.

TONY. One justification for a funeral – takes your mind off it.

BOB *seated at the wheel.* TONY *gets in.*

BOB. Don't see a lot wrong with funerals. It's a way of showing you're sorry someone's gone. I hope people show they're sorry when I die.

TONY. *I'm* sorry he's gone. I don't need to show it. After that interview was over, I sat in my dressing-room and cried my bloody eyes out.

BOB (*almost laughing*). Aaah!

BOB *starts the motor and* TONY *stares at him.*

18. Interior. Marie's Front Room. Day.

Begin on a splendid bunch of cut flowers, mostly roses, and move to show the room full of similar but less impressive bouquets, sprays and wreaths. Front door bell rings.

19. Interior. Hall. Day.

JEAN *comes from kitchen, elegant in simple black dress.* MARIE *and her neighbour* LINDA *may be seen in kitchen preparing food.* JEAN *opens door.* MRS *and* MR FOWLER, *in their sixties, carrying flowers and other things.*

MRS FOWLER. Hullo, Jean.

JEAN. Good morning. I'm sorry. I know you're friends of Mrs Goodliffe but . . .

MRS FOWLER. Mr and Mrs Fowler.

MR FOWLER. We were at your wedding.

JEAN. Yes, of course!

MR FOWLER. We gave you the carpet sweeper.

JEAN. It's still going. Do come in.

They come in, laughing slightly, MARIE comes from living room at back letting out a murmur of subdued conversation from many voices.

MARIE. It is nice of you to come.

MRS FOWLER. Are we the last?

MARIE. There's the boys yet.

MR FOWLER. We'd have been sooner but I wanted to get these flowers fresh.

MRS FOWLER. He's just this moment picked them.

MARIE. Aren't they beautiful?

JEAN. Lovely.

MR FOWLER. And while I was down the garden, I thought to myself, perhaps she'd like a few sticks of rhubarb. (*Gives MARIE that, too, wrapped in newspaper.*)

MARIE. Harry loved your rhubarb.

MRS FOWLER. Well, I said, 'You can't take rhubarb to a funeral' and he said to me 'Harry liked my rhubarb' and he said 'I think Marie liked it too'.

MARIE. Oh, yes.

MR FOWLER. I said 'I know Harry liked it but I'm not sure whether Marie did, but anyway,' I said 'she might as well have it'.

MRS FOWLER. He said 'Life goes on regardless'.

MARIE. You better take that, Jean.

JEAN *takes the rhubarb to kitchen.*

Come and see the rest.

They move off to front room. Favouring them for a moment, hear them exclaiming.

MRS FOWLER. Aren't they glorious?

MR FOWLER. I was only saying 'There's one consolation, it's a beautiful time of the year for blooms.'

JEAN *in kitchen doorway,* LINDA *working beyond.*

LINDA. What's that you've got?

JEAN. Rhubarb.

LINDA. For the buffet?

JEAN. No, someone brought it.

LINDA. To the funeral?

JEAN. Yes, for Mrs Goodliffe. What can I do now?

Doorbell rings. She leaves rhubarb and crosses hall again to front door, opening it to BOB *and* TONY.

Hullo, Tone.

TONY. How are you, love?

JEAN. Fine.

They neither kiss nor shake hands.

I'm sorry about your father.

TONY. I know you are, you were fond of him.

JEAN. Your mother's in the front room.

MARIE (*emerging*). It's the boys!

TONY. Mum!

They kiss.

MARIE. You got your train alright then. (*She begins to weep, then stops. She turns to* FOWLERS, *still in front room.*) Tony and Dad were very close. They wrote each other these great long letters.

TONY. His in Victorian copperplate, mine in portable Olivetti. He never stopped complaining how ill-mannered it was to type personal correspondence.

MARIE. He had some funny ways but he was a very good father.

TONY. I know he was.

She cries again. TONY *holds her.*

MARIE. You didn't always see eye to eye. (*To* MRS FOWLER.) I think because they were too much alike. Bob never used to quarrel, he just went his own way, but Tony and he were always at each other's throats. I think the eldest boy's bound to be closer . . . and the father's bound to feel closer to him, I think, because –

TONY. Mister Fowler, how are you?

BOB *and* JEAN *have not looked at anyone during this scene.* TONY *cut it short on purpose.* BOB *takes out a list and begins checking it.* TONY's *move takes him into the front room to greet* FOWLER.

20. Interior. Front Room. Day.

MARIE. You remember Mister Fowler in confectionary?

MR FOWLER. I say, you're looking well.

MARIE. I thought he looked drawn.

TONY. Mrs Fowler –

JEAN. Drawn? With that expensive sun-tan?

MARIE. *Under* the sun-tan.

TONY. I've been doing a filmed report from Israel.

MR FOWLER. We like your films. I say to Mrs Fowler, 'Switch it on, might as well see young Tony pop his head round the screen.'

TONY. Bless you.

MRS FOWLER. I said, you sent a lovely bouquet.

TONY. Is it all right?

21. Interior. Hall. Day.

BOB, *checking list*, JEAN *with him*.

BOB. According to my figures, there are thirteen people between two cars.

   JEAN *looks at list*.

JEAN. Linda's staying here to do the food.

   BOB *crosses off* LINDA.

BOB. Even so, that leaves – say – six in the limousine, at the most, and six to squeeze into your mother's eleven hundred, which is really only big enough for four, five at a pinch.

   LIONEL *comes downstairs, winks at* BOB, *goes to look through hall windows. A kindly apologetic friend of the family.*

JEAN. There's Mister Fowler's!

BOB. Mister Fowler's Humber, completely slipped my mind. I was thinking I'd have to take a couple of aunties crouching in the back of the Minivan.

LIONEL. Panic stations, Bob. The hearse is arriving.

MR FOWLER (*also coming from the window*). The hearse seems to be arriving.

BOB. Right, thanks. Now. I'd better get Uncle Will and Cousin Eric and few of the aunties on the move –

LIONEL. No, it's driven by.

BOB. Driven by?

LIONEL. Another funeral in the street this morning, is there?

BOB. I don't know. Had I better go and shout after them?

MR FOWLER. No room to turn here, see. They're going to the roundabout, then come back pointing in the right direction.

LIONEL. Better get the troops fell in, Bob.

BOB. Right, yes. Now the way I see it is: chief mourners in the limousine – that's Mum, Uncle Will, Cousin Eric, Tony and me. Then in your mother's car –

JEAN. Stop organising.

BOB. This morning you told me to keep on my toes and make sure everyone was happy. (*Turns to door of living room.*)

22. **Interior. Living Room. Day.**

WILL, ERIC, PHYLLIS, UNA *and* VERA *waiting.* ERIC *moving about looking at various objects.*

BOB. The cars have arrived.

They all seem relieved that something is happening at last and at once stand with sounds of assent.

23. **Interior. Hall. Day.**

They fill the hall and MARIE *and* MRS FOWLER *come from the front room.*

MARIE. Oh, Mrs Fowler, d'you know my cousin Una?

MRS FOWLER. How d'you do?

UNA. Pleased to meet you.

MARIE. Vera Lambert you know already.

VERA. Hullo, Mrs Fowler.

MRS FOWLER. How are you?

VERA. Not getting any younger.

MRS FOWLER. That's true –

MARIE. Have you met my nephew – Eric?

And so on, while WILL *struggles through and climbs the stairs. When he is halfway up.*

That's Harry's brother Will on the stairs. Will!

WILL. Hullo?

MARIE. This is Mrs Fowler.

BOB. Uncle Lionel, someone, will you open the front door, please? (*Waving his list.*) Mister Fowler, could you open the door, d'you think, and let somebody out?

24. Interior. Front Room. Day.

TONY *alone, looking about.* MRS FOWLER *in doorway, trying to get out.* TONY *picks up and examines with undue interest a plaster figure of a boy and girl beneath a parasol.* JEAN *comes in.*

JEAN. I left my coat in here.

TONY. Yes. (*He helps her on with it. Quietly.*) How are you, Jean?

JEAN. Oh, fine.

TONY. Happy?

JEAN. Yes.

TONY. Good for you. Bob tells me you're –

PHYLLIS (*coming in*). Had to say hullo to my favourite teevee star.

TONY. You sending me up, Mrs Long? How are you?

JEAN. Where's your coat, Mother?

PHYLLIS. In the hall, dear, but I can't get to it.

25. Exterior. Marie's House. Day.

*Two great black limousines tower above the family cars on
either side. One is a hearse. Beside that, BOB's Minivan. Behind
the other funeral car, an 1100 and a Humber. The usual other
parked cars. The undertakers, WITTS and MORLEY, approach
the front door, as it is opened by MR FOWLER. WITTS stands
aside.*

26. Interior. Front Room. Day.

UNA *and* VERA *have come in.*

PHYLLIS. I was saying that's a bouquet and a half you sent,
   Tony.

VERA. At my husband's death, we had no flowers. He had it in
   his will. You can.

UNA. I think a funeral's nothing without blooms.

VERA. They make such a nasty mess on the carpet.

JEAN. Ours is a terribly skimpy bunch, considering what we
   paid.

UNA. Still, there you are, you don't much like to complain, at a
   time like this.

PHYLLIS. That's what they rely on to make their exorbitant
   profits.

VERA. I never believe in bringing live things into the house. You
   never know.

WITTS (*pushing in*). Thank you, ladies. Perhaps you'll pass on
   out to the cars.

   *The older women go. WITTS collects some bunches and
   wreaths and follows. TONY has broken off a rose from his
   bunch. Now he offers it to JEAN.*

JEAN. Thank you.

He adjusts it on her dress, using a brooch to fasten it. She smiles and follows the others.

27. Exterior. Marie's House. Day.

They all move through the front garden to the street. WITTS *organises them into the limousine, the Humber and the 1100.*

MR FOWLER (*on pavement*). See the police put 'No Waiting' signs on the road here?

BOB. I suppose the undertakers fix that.

MR FOWLER. No, it was me. I rang the station last night. I said 'We can't have the hearse double parking, infra dig.'

28. Exterior. Front Door. Day.

MARIE *is on the path and* LINDA, *her neighbour, is inside.*

MARIE. I should pop the sausage rolls in the oven about half-past-eleven, Linda.

LINDA. Right you are.

MARIE. Just for a warm through.

LINDA. Yes.

MARIE (*doubtfully*). You'll be all right now?

LINDA. You go on.

MARIE. You know where everything is?

LINDA. I can find it. You better go.

MARIE. All right.

LINDA. And – have a good –

*Breaks off and smiles awkwardly. MARIE goes up path to
limousine. LINDA waves and closes door.*

29. Exterior. Marie's House. Street. Day.

*The hearse moves out to occupy the centre of the road, between
the two rows of parked cars. The second limousine is about to
follow the hearse when a small yellow sports car suddenly
accelerates with a roar and pulls up sharply behind the slowly
moving hearse. The second limousine leads the other two cars in
the procession to a position behind the sports car. The sports car
is driven by a swinger in dark glasses and the passenger is a
blonde optional extra, also hidden behind enormous black
glasses. The DRIVER realises his position too late and crawls
along behind the hearse. PHYLLIS's car is next.*

30. Interior. Phyllis's Car. Day.

UNA *in front passenger seat*, PHYLLIS *driving*, LIONEL *and*
JEAN *behind.*

UNA. If I hadn't seen that with my own eyes, I shouldn't have
    believed it.

PHYLLIS. Oh, it's absolutely typical.

LIONEL. Time and tide wait for no man.

PHYLLIS. Not these days they don't. (*Lights a cigarette from
    the lighter on the dashboard.*)

UNA. No respect.

PHYLLIS. It's a rat race. They wait for no-one. Kids today.

31. Exterior. Funeral Procession. Day.

*Close on DRIVER and PASSENGER of sports car: middle aged
beneath their misleading gear. Slowly the procession continues.*

32. Interior. Limousine. Day.

BOB *and* TONY *on one seat behind the* DRIVER. MARIE *near them. On another seat,* UNCLE WILL *and* COUSIN ERIC.

WILL. Funny thing, I never cared that much for funerals, but recent years I seem to go all the time.

33. Exterior. Funeral Procession. Day.

The procession reaches the main road. The hearse waits, then moves forward, turning left. The sports car roars away to the right. The limousine follows the hearse.

34. Interior. Limousine. Day.

WILL (*laughs*). There he goes! Now perhaps we can get a bit of a move on.

MARIE. We may not have much money, but we do see life.

35. Interior. Phyllis's Car. Day.

UNA. The hearses never go slow these days. Not like they used to.

PHYLLIS. They'd hold up the traffic.

UNA. Mind you, with burial it's different. But cremation, they can't wait to get you out the way. When I buried my Jack out Fairview, the attendants walked the street, one to each pavement, silk toppers and crêpe bands, as much as to say; look here.

PHYLLIS *coughs over her cigarette. In the back seat,* LIONEL *winks at* JEAN.

36. Interior. Limousine. Day.

WILL. A funeral was a big thing then, I'm talking about the turn of the century. Only time our street saw carriages.

TONY. Well, things haven't changed that much. You don't get many Rollses in your street, do you, Mum?

MARIE. Only funerals and weddings.

TONY. There hasn't been that much of a social revolution.

37. Exterior. Funeral Procession. Day.

Funeral goes under some railway arches.

38. Interior. Limousine. Day.

WILL. Another thing in our street, Tony, when your Dad and I were boys, was the urine woman.

TONY. The what?

WILL. The urine woman. She used to come with a cart full of vessels collecting urine.

TONY (*curious but smiling*). What for?

WILL. The local dye-works. Apparently it was cheaper than ammonia.

Laughs. TONY *smiles, tries not to laugh.*

MARIE. Will!

WILL *takes out handkerchief to wipe his eyes, looks embarrassed, stares ahead.* TONY *and* BOB *catch each other's eyes and struggle not to laugh.*

ERIC. I once did a pen-and-ink landscape study from this very spot, d'you remember, Auntie?

MARIE. Did you, Eric? No, I can't.

ERIC. Some time ago now. Coming back after all these years, I find this quite a sentimental journey.

WILL *mops his sweating brow with the handkerchief. They all look warm.*

39. Exterior. Funeral Procession. Day.

The procession passes some houses with washing visible. A lot of West Indians about, staring at the cars.

40. Interior. Limousine. Day.

WILL. Bit slummy these houses, Marie.

ERIC. Late Regency, aren't they? That portico's typical.

MARIE. They call it The Jungle now.

41. Exterior. Funeral Procession. Day.

A thirties street. Half-timbered detached houses in a variety of pre-war styles.

42. Interior. Limousine. Day.

WILL. These are a bit smarter.

MARIE. That one there, see, Will? That's where I wanted to move when our neighbourhood started going down. I can't tell you the Sunday afternoons we spent standing in empty houses arguing the toss.

BOB. He couldn't bear the sight of funerals going past.

WILL. That what it was?

MARIE. That's what he said.

BOB. 'Your mother and I stood and watched them for an hour, going slowly, coming back fast'.

WILL *laughs at the imitation.*

MARIE. That was an excuse. He was happy where he was, that was his trouble.

43. **Exterior. Funeral Procession. Day.**

Traffic lights. The cars wait for green: the DRIVER *of the limousine glances at his watch.*

44. **Interior. Limousine. Day.**

Close-up BOB *as he notices.*

BOB (*Voice-over*). An important factor of the successful funeral is timing the arrival of the cortege at the place of interment or cremation. Many cemeteries and crematoria penalise latecomers by increasing or doubling their charges.

45. **Exterior. Cemetery. Day.**

Solemnly the hearse and limousine turn into the cemetery, leaving the other cars to wait for a break in the traffic. Beyond the gates are monstrous monuments. The road follows a circular course to allow funerals to approach the chapel and on the central island formed by this curve are memorials of great seniority, mock-classic temples decorated with statuary or vast petrified boxes with iron railings round them.

46. **Interior. Limousine. Day.**

TONY. God!

47. Exterior. Crematorium. Day.

The hearse arrives at a more recent porch and the procession halts. The UNDERTAKERS *and* CHAUFFEURS *get out. A* MAN *in sports coat and trousers crosses in front of the limousine. He also wears a clerical collar and carries some vestments. He hurries into the Chapel.* THREE MEN *in dark suits are sitting in a car which has arrived earlier.*

48. Interior. Limousine. Day.

BOB *leans forward to open the door.*

WILL. Wait till they open it.

BOB. Oh. (*He leans back and waits.*)

49. Exterior. Crematorium. Day.

Silence for some time but for birdsong and quiet traffic. The UNDERTAKERS, *joined by two others, carry the coffin into the Chapel.*

50. Interior. Limousine. Day.

ERIC. I could spend a week among these monuments without losing interest.

MARIE. That's nice and cheerful.

ERIC. They represent a broad spectrum of the visual tastes of the eighteenth and nineteenth centuries.

BOB. That one there reminds me of the Elephant House.

TONY. Superb location for a film.

BOB. I'd bulldoze the lot and make it into a children's park.

TONY. Look at the class distinction – carried to the grave.
These lavish memorials here and – up on the hill – the
ordinary stones in serried ranks. Just as they were in life.

BOB. Oh, come on –

TONY. What?

BOB. Let's be practical, at least. I'm not going to feel guilty
about what happened before I was born.

51. Exterior. Crematorium. Day.

PHYLLIS's and MR FOWLER's cars pull up behind the
limousine. LIONEL gets out of the 1100 on the driver's side and
opens PHYLLIS's door, then moves round to open UNA's.

UNA. Nobody move. Nobody move till the chief mourners
move.

LIONEL stands embarrassed, his gesture spoilt. He closes the
door and stands by it awaiting orders.

At the Austin, MR FOWLER opens his door. VERA speaks to
him urgently. He pulls door to quietly.

52. Exterior. Crematorium. Chapel Porch. Day.

Undertakers hear organ music from Chapel and now open the
door of the limousine. TONY gets out and turns to assist
MARIE. BOB follows and the UNDERTAKERS lead the mother
and two sons to the Chapel. At the 1100 LIONEL pulls open the
door again. UNA speaks. He closes it again.

53. Interior. Chapel. Day.

An USHER directs MARIE and sons into a front pew. In a
modest pulpit, of the same style and material as the other

furnishings, stands the MAN *who ran across before the car, now wearing his cassock and surplice. The coffin is on a catafalque between him and the mourners.*

VICAR. I am the resurrection and the life, saith the Lord: he that believeth in me, though he were dead, yet shall he live.

54. Exterior. Crematorium. Day.

ERIC *and* WILL *have got from the limousine and are moving after* MARIE *to the Chapel. At the 1100 we see but don't hear* UNA *say: 'Right – now'.* LIONEL *opens the door and* UNA *begins to get out.* PHYLLIS *and* JEAN *follow suit. At the Austin the* FOWLERS *get out too.*

55. Interior. Chapel. Day.

WILL *and* ERIC *are directed into second pew.* MARIE, BOB *and* TONY *are finding their place in the prayer book.*

VICAR. We brought nothing into this world and it is certain we can carry nothing out.

56. Exterior. Crematorium. Day.

Other mourners now standing by cars. PHYLLIS *and* LIONEL *are locking the doors of the 1100,* MR FOWLER *the Austin.* MR FOWLER *even locks the boot.*

57. Interior. Chapel. Day.

ERIC (*quietly*). D'you want a Prayer Book, Uncle?

VICAR. Psalm Twenty-Three.

WILL. I know the words of the Twenty-Third Psalm.

ALL (*reading*). The Lord is my Shepherd, therefore can I lack
   nothing –

WILL. I shall not want – what's this?

ALL. He shall feed me in a green pasture and lead me forth
   beside the waters of comfort.

WILL. These aren't the proper words.

ERIC. Sssh.

Hands him Prayer Book, open at Psalm. WILL *tries to read.*

ALL. He shall convert my soul.

58. Exterior. Crematorium. Day.

The women watch while MR FOWLER *locks the passenger
doors.* LIONEL *stands between; the* UNDERTAKERS *watch
them.* UNA *nods at* VERA *and they lead the women towards
the Chapel.* LIONEL *waits for* MR FOWLER. *The three* MEN
in dark suits get out of their car.

59. Interior. Chapel. Day.

As UNA *and* VERA *appear and are shown to a pew.*

ALL. But thy loving-kindness and mercy shall follow me all the
   days of my life and I will dwell in the house of the Lord
   forever.

VICAR. Amen.

ALL. Amen.

   JEAN *and* PHYLLIS *and* MRS FOWLER *follow.*

VICAR. Please sit down.

   Everyone sits.

   The lesson is from Corinthians one fifteen.

LIONEL *and* MR FOWLER *enter and sit. They are followed by the three* MEN *in dark suits.*

We shall not all sleep but we shall all be changed. In a moment, in the twinkling of an eye, at the last trump: for the trumpet shall sound and the dead shall be raised incorruptible and we shall be changed.

WILL, *moved, blows his nose violently.* BOB *and* TONY *notice that* MARIE *is weeping.*

60. Exterior. Chapel. Day.

WITTS *and* MORLEY *light cigarettes.*

WITTS. See that fellow? One of the sons? Image of the fellow on TV, what's his name? On TV.

MORLEY *shakes head.* WITTS *checks list.*

Cox, Holloway . . . Goodliffe . . . that's him. Tony Goodliffe. Told you I knew him.

61. Interior. Chapel. Day.

All are kneeling on hassocks.

VICAR. Forasmuch as it hath pleased Almighty God of his great mercy to take unto himself the soul of our dear brother here departed.

JEAN *screws her eyes tight shut to control her tears.*

We therefore commit his body to the flames.

The coffin begins to sink out of sight. WILL *stares appalled at* HARRY's *disappearance.*

In sure and certain hope of the Resurrection to eternal life through our Lord Jesus Christ, who shall change our body of low estate that it may be like unto his glorious body.

Close up: BOB.

BOB (*voice-over*). Cremation begins with the coffin going to a committal room, the body remaining in the coffin. Each coffin is individually burnt in a cremator, the ashes being removed after about ninety minutes and reduced to a fine powder.

When the coffin has sunk far enough a blue cover slides across concealing it.

62. Exterior. Chapel. Day.

WITTS and MORLEY are bringing bouquets from hearse to garden plot nearby. WITTS approaches the Chapel to listen. MORLEY glances at a folded newspaper. WITTS stubs out cigarette.

63. Interior. Chapel. Day.

With a click, organ music begins. See the discreet loudspeaker. VICAR leaves his pulpit, MOURNERS stand. Doors opened by WITTS and VICAR stands at doorway nodding politely as MARIE leads out.

VICAR. Good day.

MARIE. Good day. Thank you.

VICAR puts out his hand and shakes TONY's.

TONY. Good day.

VICAR. Like to say how much I enjoy your programmes.

TONY. Bless you.

TONY goes out. BOB follows him.

VICAR. Good day.

BOB. Goodbye.

64. Exterior. Crematorium. Day.

The THREE MEN *in dark suits stand by porch.* MARIE *draws* BOB *and* TONY *towards them.*

MARIE. This is Mister Keys of Footwear.

   TONY *and* BOB *shake hands with him.*

   And Mister Britain of – uh –

BRITAIN. Soft furnishing.

MARIE. Oh, yes.

BRITAIN. And Mister Lang, of Electrical Goods, representing our staff association. Just paying our last respects.

MARIE. Thank you.

   MORLEY *waiting with open door at limousine. They go and climb in. Once the* MOURNERS *are all in limousine, it is driven off.*

65. Interior. Limousine. Day.

MARIE *tearful.* TONY *holding her hand.*

WILL. Those weren't the proper words to the Psalm.

ERIC. That was the Prayer Book version, Uncle.

WILL. They're not the words most people know.

ERIC. No.

66. Exterior. Gates of Cemetery. Day.

Limousine turns into main road and is driven off very smartly.

67. Exterior. Crematorium. Day.

At 1100 and Austin other mourners getting into the cars, MR
FOWLER *unlocking the passenger doors.*

68. Interior. Limousine. Day.

Travelling fast.

TONY. No, I'm sorry, but I think if the church agrees to
recognise this man's death, there should at least be a decent
ritual, not a lot of tatty machinery going on and off.

BOB. Why? He never went inside but to listen to recitals or see
the stained glass.

TONY. Then play some music. Where's the organist?

BOB. The vicar only gets a pound. The whole thing only costs
about ten. What d'you expect – King's College Choir?

TONY. A man dies after seventy years of –

MARIE *is crying.* TONY *stops, takes her hand and holds it.*
They drive on.

69. Interior. Marie's Hall. Day.

JEAN *coming from kitchen with tray of teacups and saucers.*
MARIE *coming from living room, meets her, stops her.*

MARIE. Linda –

LINDA (*coming from kitchen*). What?

MARIE. Where d'you get these teaspoons?

LINDA. I couldn't find yours, so I had to run and borrow mine.

MARIE. Fancy making people think I haven't any teaspoons. In
the sideboard, Jean, you'll find a set of apostle spoons. Mister
Fowler's wedding present.

JEAN. In the sideboard –

She moves into little room as ERIC *comes from front room.*

ERIC. Auntie, I shall have to be phoning a taxi soon. To the station.

MARIE. You can phone from Linda's next door. Later on.

ERIC. Alright, after the eats.

Goes into living room as WILL *comes down the stairs.*
LINDA *has gone to kitchen and returns, with a tray of food for living room.*

WILL. I was sitting on the toilet, Marie, –

MARIE. Were you?

WILL. Thinking it's a good job Harry didn't pass away up there. You'd have had to up-end the coffin to navigate this turn in the stairs.

70. Interior. Living Room. Day.

TONY, BOB, JEAN, PHYLLIS, LIONEL, UNA, ERIC *and* LINDA, *eating and drinking:* JEAN *and* LINDA *passing the food from a table laden with plates of sausage rolls, cake, meat and cheese, biscuits, etc.*

ERIC. No sign of the Fowlers' car yet.

PHYLLIS. It was all I could do to keep up with the limousine on the way back.

UNA. And that service. Talk about short-but-sweet.

LIONEL. Mister Fowler and I'd hardly got our knees on the hassock before old Sandy McPherson started up again on the theatre organ.

PHYLLIS. These days people are having too much fun to dwell on death. And old age. Don't blame them either. Give me the chance.

UNA (*firmly*). Excuse me, but in my young days we didn't know that much about life but we respected the dead and who's to say we were the worse for it?

LINDA. Mrs Long, d'you want a Scotch egg?

PHYLLIS. I'm supposed to be on a diet.

UNA. My husband and I reserved our plot when we got married and never mentioned it again until the day he crossed over. But I know where he is and I know we shall meet again out Fairview.

PHYLLIS (*eating Scotch egg*). God forbid I should ever meet my old man again. The day I left him at the divorce court, I said 'Good riddance' and I've never felt the lack of a husband since. Nor Jean of a father, have you, Jean?

JEAN *smiles and goes out with tray as MARIE comes in with teapot.*

MARIE. Why don't one of you boys open the window? It's stifling here.

71. Interior. Hall. Day.

JEAN *leaves tray in kitchen and goes up the stairs.*

72. Interior. Rear Bedroom. Day.

Twin beds, walnut wardrobe, dressing table with stools and chest of drawers. Lloyd loom armchair. Door is open and top of stairs can be seen on landing outside. JEAN comes up and into room, sits on bed.

73. Interior. Hall. Day.

FOWLERS *and VERA being let in by MARIE.*

MARIE. Gracious me.

MRS FOWLER. All behind like the cow's tail.

MR FOWLER. Thought I'd take a short cut but the swing bridge was open.

74. Interior. Rear Bedroom. Day.

JEAN *is crying.*

75. Interior. Living Room. Day.

The company is joined by the FOWLERs *and* VERA LAMBERT. *The meal is nearly over and* PHYLLIS *is knitting.*

VERA. But this friend I was telling you of, her husband died on the beach at Portofino, in front of everyone. And you've no idea the fuss and expense she had transporting him home for burial.

PHYLLIS. Waste of money. I should want to be buried there.

UNA. I've never been abroad, I hope I never shall. But if it happened to me, I should want to be brought home to lie with Jack. Excuse me.

PHYLLIS. 'If I should die, think only this of me –'

VERA. Cremation for me. No dirt and decay.

PHYLLIS. 'That there's some corner of a foreign field that is forever England', eh, Tony? (*She winks at him.*)

TONY. I'll drink to that, Mrs Long.

PHYLLIS. You ought to do a programme – Auntie Una and I, Burial versus Burning.

TONY. Bit too controversial for me, dear. (*He stands and makes to go.*)

MARIE (*frowning*). I see you brought your knitting, Phyllis.

PHYLLIS. One of the manifestations of my neurosis.

WILL. I shouldn't mind a slice of cake now, Marie.

BOB *lights a cigarette.*

76. Interior. Rear Bedroom. Day.

JEAN *still face-down on the bed. Hears someone climbing stairs. She gets up and fetches handbag from chair, goes to sit at dressing-table and repairs her face.* TONY *appears at top of stairs, comes in.*

TONY. God, those people! The giants of our childhood. Towering uncles reeking of tobacco. Aunts and quasi-aunts all talcum powder and plump white arms. Auntie Una, grim and upright, always avid for a death. 'I shall lie with my Jack out Fairview.'

JEAN *listens, amused.* TONY *moves about.*

Cousin Eric, Osterley's Huw Wheldon. Mister Fowler, sprouting rhubarb from his fingertips. A living reproach to Dad, who killed everything he touched.

He examines the furniture. The pictures, the wallpaper, the knick-knacks.

Even nowadays when they've shrunk to nothing, I've only got to hear their voices and part of me becomes a child again. (*He has come close and looks at her in the glass.*) Been crying?

JEAN. The funeral upset me. And, after that, my mother. She said I'd never missed having a father and, of course she's got to pretend she doesn't feel the need of a man, though I know she does. Two women alone is all wrong. Which may be why I was always fond of your Dad.

TONY. I know. Well, he's gone now. And Vera Lambert's removing every trace.

JEAN. She could hardly wait to get her hands on his muddle. Tipping the dustman to cart it off. The clothes she's mostly given to Uncle Lionel.

TONY. I wish to God I had the time to go through it. I might have found some clue to the man – or some hint of my first five years, which are a total blank.

JEAN. I doubt there was anything but useless rubbish.

TONY. I might have caught a scent . . . I feel my answers are here if I could spare the time to look. My dreams take place here, still. But this will probably be the last time I see it.

She, having paused, goes on making up.

This is the room, where Bob and I grew up. That mirror, where I did my first acting. This bed where I used to lie as a virgin wondering what it was like. And where I found out. (*Turns to window. Lifts net curtain to look out.*) On a day very much like this. You were as bold as brass. 'Shall we go straight to bed?' you said and I followed you upstairs, shaking with fright. (*Goes to bed, lies on it.*) But there was nothing to be frightened of. It was so easy. You kept whimpering with pleasure.

JEAN. I can't remember.

TONY (*shaking head*). Oh, Jean –

JEAN. I remember but not the details. It's a long time ago. Sixteen years?

TONY. I don't believe you. It was unforgettable.

JEAN. I was your first, that's all. You were a late starter. You can't bear to think it was ordinary.

77. Interior. Living Room. Day.

More convivial. A lot of tobacco smoke and teacups still being passed. BOB is listening to MR FOWLER. LINDA offering cake.

MR FOWLER. Half-inch quadrant. No more, thank you.

BOB. No, thanks.

MR FOWLER. Nail and glue the half-inch quadrant, say, two, two-and-a-half inches from the back of your shelf. Five-eighths panel pins at nine, twelve inch intervals.

LINDA *moves on past* WILL.

WILL. That chocolate cake? I shouldn't mind a piece of chocolate cake.

But she doesn't hear.

No, I was saying – what was I saying?

MRS FOWLER. About hyacinths.

WILL. That's right. Every nipper would receive a pot of hyacinths to put on a family grave . . . and we'd have to troop to the cemetery and put out all these blessed pots. And later on old Gran would hire a pony and trap and drive through the graveyard . . . is that chocolate cake, Marie? . . . and woe betide any boy who'd got tempted by the four-ale bar. I'd like a piece of that cake, yes.

LINDA. A piece of this? (*Cuts him a slice.*)

WILL. Ta. (*Bites cake, makes face.*) Ginger.

ERIC *is prowling about the room, looking at gramophone records in albums.*

78. **Interior. Rear Bedroom. Day.**

TONY *is still on the bed,* JEAN *putting on perfume. He watches her.*

TONY. I want it back.

JEAN. What?

TONY. Youth.

JEAN. You can't.

TONY. I don't know. Here we are. In this room.

JEAN. You didn't like me quite enough at the time. You left me for Tina Carpenter. Two hours I waited outside the Central Library and when it began to rain, I went to the pictures. You were a few rows in front with Tina Carpenter. So I left again.

TONY. I didn't know you'd seen me.

JEAN. No, well, I never told you because by the time you were after me again, I was going with Bob. And I suppose you only came back because you'd had no joy with Tina Carpenter.

TONY. If I could start again, it would all be very different.

JEAN. No, you were too ambitious and she lived in the Paragon. She went riding on the Downs, for God's sake!

TONY. Born into the class we were, are you going to blame me for ambition? When I see those people downstairs, I'm bloody glad to have been ambitious. But it meant I took wrong turnings and in the process of escaping, somehow missed my youth.

JEAN. You can keep youth, there was too much crying in the rain and hurting each other. Whatever life's like now, at least it's painless.

She stands and moves, tries to see herself in the dressing table mirrors, straightening her dress etc; TONY goes to wardrobe. Opens the door, showing her the mirror on the inside. She smiles.

TONY. That could be boring.

JEAN. Satisfying. No time for tears.

TONY. Doesn't sound like you.

She shrugs. He moves from wardrobe and stands beside her as she uses mirror.

You're a passionate woman, like your mother. Still are. You have to steal away up here to cry.

JEAN. Having children cools your passion.

TONY. I wouldn't know. But I believe we don't change our essential natures. We stifle them, thwart them, pervert them, but our natures survive. We were passionate lovers and we still are. Or would be.

He embraces her from behind. She goes on looking into the mirror. He moves his hands down to her hips, caressing her stomach and moving upwards to her breasts. He kisses the back of her neck and she raises her head, closing her eyes. She slightly turns her head and he kisses her ear. Suddenly he stiffens, looks at the door, steps away from her.

Among other things, I remember we used to play lifts going up and down in that wardrobe.

BOB *appears in the open doorway,* JEAN *goes on titivating.* TONY *goes back to the wardrobe.* BOB *stays in doorway.*

Ah, hullo. I was just saying we used to play lifts in here and one day we tipped it over, you were only four or five. Mum and Vera Lambert were downstairs and Vera lifted the whole thing bodily and stood it up.

BOB. Mum was worried in case the glass had broken.

TONY *laughs.*

JEAN. Anyone missed me?

BOB. Uncle Will. I'm on my way for a pee.

TONY (*imitating* WILL). 'Where's young Jean? Well-developed young woman!'

JEAN. His voice is so like your father's

TONY. I know, it keeps taking me unawares. Keep thinking, what's *he* doing here?

BOB. Oh, Tone, I thought, as you're going back to London any minute, we ought to –

TONY. Not till this evening.

BOB. No, well anyway, while Mum's not around, we ought to talk about her and the old man's debts and the house. I mean, Jean and I will be *doing* it all, so we'd better be sure you approve.

TONY. I'll pay his debts.

BOB. Okay.

TONY. Goes without saying.

BOB. I'll send on the outstanding bills. Your secretary will know what it's all about, will she?

TONY. I'll tell her.

BOB. Mum wants to sell the house –

TONY. I know –

BOB. So until we find her a flat, she can stay with us.

TONY. Is that okay?

BOB. What else d'you suggest?

JEAN *has returned to dressing-table stool and is listening.*

TONY. No, I'm sure that's what she wants. Are you happy, Jean?

JEAN (*shrugs*). Least we can do.

BOB. What she doesn't take of the furniture we'll have auctioned. It won't fetch a lot.

TONY (*moving*). All these redolent chairs and tables, the landscape of our childhood. They're like the aunts and uncles, I've measured out my life against them. And now it's a quantity of nineteen-thirties junk in the corner of a sale.

BOB. It was always a quantity of thirties junk.

TONY. And dustmen cart the rest away for a small consideration. His samples of merchandise, his ludicrous letters to the local rag, his war-maps. . . .

BOB. He wasn't Tolstoy.

TONY. He was a good man who lacked our advantages. The advantages he gave us. A good man who's gone. And deserved better than a ten-quid cremation and a cut-price prayer.

Pause. JEAN raises her head to look at him. TONY finishes, moved, and turns to look out of the window.

BOB. You could do a super piece on him in your next programme.

Pause. He makes to go on to bathroom.

TONY. What's wrong with showing a bit of feeling?

JEAN. Now come on –

BOB (*shrugs*). Nothing. For you it's a good living. I just think there are more pressing matters. Nostalgia is enervating . . . in Britain almost a disease.

TONY. What are the more pressing matters?

BOB. Oh – sewage disposal, noise abatement, traffic control, clean air, population . . . all good for a belly laugh on your TV show.

TONY. You haven't been watching. Half my programme last Saturday was given over to the problems of air pollution.

BOB. Yeah, then you fly off to New York in a trail of diesel and supersonic bangs.

TONY. How d'you expect me to go? By rowing boat?

BOB. It's all too easy to do your bit on pollution, like the politicians. No-one expects any action. Like your bit on Dad's funeral. I don't hear you asking Mum to share your London flat.

TONY. She doesn't want to.

BOB. Have you asked her?

TONY. She wants to be near your children. I haven't got any, if you remember.

BOB. You could have done. You've had two wives. You were too busy feeling all over the place to see that it's hard work, marriage, like sewage disposal.

TONY laughs. JEAN smiles slightly. Both men have been partly aiming their remarks at her and we have seen her reactions.

I told you it would get a belly-laugh.

TONY. Well, honestly! Jean, is that how you see your marriage – sewage disposal?

JEAN. With young children, sewage disposal certainly plays a part.

BOB laughs and she smiles at him. By this gesture she shows that she has decided to take BOB's side, as she must.

TONY. No, I mean the new person will depend on sewage disposal – liver, kidneys, bowels – just as a new university depends on plumbing. But you don't establish a university so as to have more loos.

BOB. As an architect who works more on council flats than colleges, perhaps I'm too preoccupied with plumbing. A lot of people living decently is better than a few witty undergraduates.

JEAN. Can't you have both?

TONY. Exactly, Jean!

BOB. I don't want both. I believe in the ordinary, the prosaic. People who see themselves as special and who can't stop their brains working, gurus and pundits and so on, they create élites and make the rest of us feel excluded. And they raise our expectations of life.

TONY. But you're a special person –

BOB. Most of us would be happier with our lot if it wasn't for public spokesmen with their clouds of abstractions and nostalgia. The Free World. East of Suez. The Classless Society. The Golden Age. Our Finest Hour. Every time there's a mains water burst, the local rag comes out in a sweat about the old wartime spirit. You'd think this was Dresden or Nagasaki. But how many actually died in all the raids on this city? Twelve hundred. And every year of peace, seven thousand are killed on the roads. Four thousand died in the last London smog.

TONY. All these numbers! They're meaningless. I can't take in *one* man's death. (*Looks at his watch.*) By now he'll be a handful of ashes.

ERIC *comes into doorway from stairs.*

ERIC. Auntie says I must look in the attics and see if Uncle's left anything I might want. As a memento.

BOB. Yeah, fine, carry on.

ERIC *goes further upstairs.*

JEAN. I must go down. They'll be wondering where we are.

But MARIE *and* LIONEL *follow* ERIC.

MARIE. What are you doing up here, you boys? (*To* LIONEL.) This used to be their old bedroom.

LIONEL. Very nice.

MARIE. It's a nice room. Uncle Will's been asking for you, Jean.

JEAN. I know. I'll go and see him. (*She goes.*)

MARIE. Uncle Lionel's trying on some more of your father's shoes. We found half a dozen pairs in the kitchen cupboard. (*Takes shoes from wardrobe.*)

LIONEL. Shame to throw them out.

BOB. Absolutely.

MARIE. He took care of his boots and shoes, polishing them every day like a sergeant-major.

BOB *goes to bathroom.* LIONEL *tries on shoes.*

79. Interior. Living Room. Day.

JEAN *arriving to* WILL. *Also present:* UNA, VERA, LINDA, PHYLLIS.

WILL. Here she is! Old Harry used to call you 'The Girl with the Ample Thighs'.

VERA. Very pretty.

WILL. But I think you've lost weight lately.

JEAN. I shall soon be putting it on again.

WILL. How's that?

JEAN. I'm going to have another baby.

WILL (*roars*). Hear that, Marie?

VERA. She's busy upstairs.

WILL. D'you hear this, Vera? Young Jean pregnant again.

VERA. I should think the street's heard the way you shout. (*She goes out.*)

WILL. Your daughter, Phyllis.

PHYLLIS. Another millstone round her neck, I know . . .

WILL. How many will this be? Three.

JEAN. Yes.

WILL. I shall have to send you a manual on birth control. A word to the wise by Marie Stopes, eh? (*Laughs and wipes his eyes.*) Did brother Harry know?

JEAN. No.

WILL. He'd have been tickled.

JEAN. Yes.

WILL. Nothing made him happier than ordering nippers about.

Suddenly sad. Blows his nose with handkerchief.

80. Interior. Rear Bedroom. Day.

TONY *watching* LIONEL *try on shoes.* MARIE *brings pair of plimsolls.*

MARIE. These white daps any good to you?

LIONEL. On the beach in summer, just the job, yes.

VERA comes up stairs carrying overcoat.

VERA. I thought Lionel might like this overcoat of Harry's we found under the stairs.

LIONEL is putting on the plimsolls as VERA holds up the coat for him to look at.

MARIE. He loved herringbone.

ERIC comes down attic stairs, carrying several golf-clubs, a golf-bag and a metal ARP helmet.

Found something you want in the loft, Eric?

ERIC. Not really, Auntie, it's mostly rubbish, but I'll take these clubs as a souvenir and the warden's helmet for the children.

TONY watches them all.

VERA. Attics only collect dirty filth.

Lavatory flush off.

I used to tell Harry that.

LIONEL has the shoes on and now puts on the coat.

ERIC. Is Uncle still downstairs? The taxi's due any minute.

VERA. He was bellowing about Jean expecting another baby.

ERIC. He gets a bit excited.

MARIE. It's nothing to shout about. Poor Bob's hard-worked enough already without another mouth to feed.

ERIC. I'll look through the books in the front room, shall I?

Goes downstairs. BOB *comes from bathroom.* LIONEL *looks at his reflection in glass, now wearing overcoat and white plimsolls.*

LIONEL. Perfect.

BOB. What the cautious Englishman is wearing on the beach this summer.

MARIE. You'll need something to carry them in.

BOB. This case. (*Pulls it down from on top wardrobe.*)

MARIE. Mind the dust! Oh, my Lord!

BOB *bangs the sides of it.*

VERA. Not on the carpet.

She stoops and picks pieces of fluff from carpet as BOB *throws case on bed and opens it.*

BOB. Taking all these, Uncle?

LIONEL. Yes.

He takes off coat and MARIE *folds it.* BOB *packs shoes into case.* TONY *suddenly goes from the room and down the stairs.* BOB *smiles.* VERA *puts fluff into waste basket or out of window and claps her hands clean.* LIONEL *takes off plimsolls.*

81. Exterior. Marie's House. Day.

Taxi waiting in space between BOB's *Minivan and the* FOWLERs' *Humber.* WILL, ERIC *and* LIONEL *saying goodbye to* MARIE, BOB, TONY *and* JEAN.

WILL. You had a nice day for it, Marie. You'll come and see me soon, I hope.

MARIE. I shall have to see.

WILL. There's only me left now. I'm the last.

MARIE. That's nice and cheerful. Bye-bye, Will.

Kisses him. He gets into cab. ERIC now carries golf-bag, helmet, book and album of old records.

You sure you can manage all that, Eric?

ERIC. I took this Silver Jubilee Book as a memento.

MARIE. Thank you for coming. Love to your family.

Kisses him. He gets in. LIONEL carries suitcase.

LIONEL. Now don't forget. As soon as you're straight, come down and stay. My sister and I have got a bathing-hut for the season.

MARIE. Out of the wind.

LIONEL. Got an electric kettle in it.

MARIE. I'll have to see.

They shake hands. LIONEL goes. The taxi moves off, all waving.

JEAN. We're late for the kids.

TONY. Who's got them?

JEAN. Patsy. She can't control her own three, let alone mine.

MARIE. She's always up in the clouds.

JEAN. See you at home then.

She and BOB turn towards the minivan.

MARIE. Mr Fowler will give us a lift.

She walks back to the house. TONY shuts the front gate and follows her. See the ordinary house from his point of view.

82. Interior. Inside Minivan. Travelling Daylit Streets. Day.

BOB, JEAN *and their children,* BILL *and* SUSAN. *The children are sitting or crouching on a mattress in the back.*

ALL (*singing*). Lloyd George knows my father. Father knows
  Lloyd George. Etc. Etc.

83. Exterior. Bob's House. A Victorian Terrace. Day.

Minivan arrives. JEAN *gets out and lets out children by passenger door, while* BOB *opens rear doors and begins unloading the equipment of their day away: a pedal jeep, a large plastic lavatory seat, a rubber bouncer with horns, spare clothes in bunches, a toilet-bag, a school satchel. He half-carries, half-wheels this load to the house. On the pavement a toilet-roll falls off and rolls to the gutter.* JEAN *is looking for her key as she climbs front steps but the door is suddenly thrown open and* TONY *appears, half-hidden by door. He 'shoots' the children and they immediately return fire.* TONY *makes expert ricochet sounds and then is hit and staggers out, his face contorted in agony.* JEAN *smiles, goes into house.* BOB *comes up steps as* TONY *finally collapses, dying. Makes one last effort to shoot his killers but fails.* BOB *struggles by with gear. Children delighted.*

84. Interior. Nursery. Day.

We see only JEAN's *head against a door, in half light through drawn curtains.*

JEAN (*singing*). Where is the boy who looks after the sheep?
  He's under a haystack fast asleep.
  Will you wake him? No, not I,
  For if I do, he'll surely cry.

  Stifles a yawn.

  Night-night, Bill. Sleep well. (*Opens door and goes.*)

85. Interior. Bob and Jean's Hall. Day.

TONY, BOB, MARIE *and* JEAN.

TONY. Now promise me, when you've had enough of these two, you'll come and stay with me in Town.

MARIE. When they've had enough of *me*.

TONY. Promise now.

MARIE. I'll write to you.

TONY. Ring up, then we can fix the date.

MARIE. All that expense on a phone.

TONY. Reverse the charges.

MARIE. But then you pay.

TONY. It all comes off the income tax, love.

MARIE. Alright. But mind – until I come look after yourself, put a bit of colour back in your cheeks. Make sure you get plenty of fresh air and exercise and a cooked meal at the proper time.

TONY. Right, Mum.

MARIE (*partly to others*). Because it's all very well, as I said to Vera, to think of him meeting all these famous people but I think of the face the public don't see. At the end of his programmes, I think 'Yes, and now he's going back to a lonely flat with no-one to talk to, no-one to share his troubles.'

JEAN *sings 'Hearts and Flowers'*. BOB *laughs*. TONY *joins in the song*. MARIE *smiles*.

TONY. You're right, Mum, it's hell out there. (*Kisses her.*)

MARIE. Take care.

TONY. Bless you. Bye, Jean.

JEAN. Bye, Tone.

Offers her hand. He shakes. BOB opens front door and they go.

86. Exterior. Bob's House. Day.

BOB *and* TONY *getting into the Minivan.* MARIE *and* JEAN *wave from the front door. Van drives off.*

87. Interior. Bob and Jean's Hall. Day.

JEAN *closes door.*

MARIE. But all the same I do feel sorry for him. The second child's lucky in many ways. We like to spoil the firstborn and make him think he's Lord Muck. For six years there was only Tony to fuss over. He had everything. But look at the way it's turned out — two rotten marriages, no family. Nearly forty and nothing to show for it. Bob even got *you* in the end.

JEAN. Bob doesn't see it quite like that. He thinks I'm one of Tony's cast-offs.

88. Interior. Bob and Jean's Bedroom. Night.

Lower part of BOB *and* JEAN's *bed. On the untidy counterpane,* JEAN's *black dress has been carelessly thrown. We stay on it, hearing dialogue.*

BOB (*ecstatically*). Jean, love!

JEAN. Ssssh . . .

BOB. You bitch, I love you —

JEAN. Darling, ssssh, . . .

89. Interior. Children's Playroom. Night.

A single bed, bedside light on. MARIE sitting up, going through an envelope bulky with old snapshots. She looks aside for a moment as though she'd heard something, then turns back to the photos. See one or two: her own married life with TONY and BOB as boys, herself in twenties and thirties fashions. One stilted portrait of her husband. One as a young man in athletic costume.

90. Interior. Bob and Jean's Bedroom. Night.

BOB *and* JEAN's *bed again, lit as at beginning by table light.* BOB *and* JEAN *lying apart. He is buttoning up his pyjama jacket. Takes off wrist watch, looks at it, winds it. She is doing exactly the same.*

BOB. Would you like to read?

JEAN. Little read, I think. Settle my mind.

She turns her back to him, takes book. He takes a book too. Before turning from her, he speaks to her back.

BOB. Why was it so important to be quiet?

JEAN. Embarrassing for your mother.

BOB. Oh, hell. This is our house. I'm not giving *that* up. (*Then turns back to her, finds page in book.*)
Was it all right, Jean?

JEAN. What?

BOB. Treats. Just now.

JEAN. Smashing.

BOB. It's so hard to tell. You're so undemonstrative.

JEAN. Isn't that what you want?

BOB (*brief pause*). Hardly make a sound.

JEAN. I never have made sounds. (*Rubs her foot against his. Yawns.*) Oh dear.

BOB. As long as you enjoy yourself.

JEAN. Mmmm. Oh, dear.

Yawns again. They apparently read. But we see that he stares beyond his book and looks frightened. She stares beyond her book at the rose from TONY's *bouquet, which is in a glass of water on her bedside table. Stay on the rose. 'Salut d'Amour' by Elgar. Fade out.*

The Freeway

The Freeway

'The Great Traffic Jam is not a new theme. I first came across it in 1946 in James Hanley's strange novel, *What Farrar Saw*, which had been prompted by the thought of a return to pre-war motoring. J. G. Ballard has described the new landscape of motorways in a couple of recent novels. The cinema, which began by celebrating the car's infancy, has taken to abusing its old age in Fellini's *8½*, Godard's *Weekend* and Tati's *Traffic*. But *The Freeway* was, as far as I know, the first stage play to use the idea and, in view of its critical reception, may well be the last.

Most reviewers complained that the play wasn't horrible enough, but I don't think a jam would be all that nasty, even if it were allowed to happen. Far worse is our present reality – that almost every civilised requirement in town and country has been sacrificed to keep the traffic moving. 'Now that we can travel easily,' wrote Aldous Huxley, 'we spend all our lives travelling.' This urge for mobility has made the private car the most important single factor in advanced economies, East and West. The motor and haulage industries have pressed successive governments to adopt road-building programmes of such magnitude that nothing seems able to reverse the process. Lorries built for continental autobahns will thunder through our narrow streets and rattle along the flyovers past curtained bedroom windows, commuters' cars will pour every morning into city centres the size of villages, and about 8,000 people will be killed each year on roads bearing one vehicle every twenty-four yards.

The more I thought and read about the traffic, the more it appeared that motors themselves aren't to blame, any more than aircraft could truly be said to have bombed Dresden. The real villain of this piece is the widely held conviction that the car is liberty incarnate, the great surviving champion of the free-for-all life-style. The motorist is persuaded to see the streets as something between the jungle and the Spanish Main, alive with Jaguars, Hunters, Thunderbirds, Corsairs, Mavericks and Rovers. Facing the usual barrage of red lights, crossings, lane markings and parking meters, is it any wonder that he can't see the connection? Or feels he's been robbed? There must be a better way. There is, but not many are prepared to consider it because it means co-operation. Allowing our towns and country to be wrecked is easier than voting for a rational transport system. The alternative to freedom is not necessarily a police state. The Nazis weren't the only people to get the trains running on time.

J. K. Galbraith has said that in cities Socialism is inevitable. In large towns, people aren't expected to dig their own drains, generate their own power or put out the fire when their houses burn. The solutions to these problems have been rational and co-operative. Why is the car such a diehard? I hope *The Freeway* suggests a few answers.

Anyone thinking of doing the play should be warned that, though set in the future, it is not an Orwellian nightmare. The world outside the jam seemed to me grisly enough without bring-ing tatty violence on to the stage. The mood is spring-like, a sunny weekend. There should be a colourful English landscape beyond the cars – pastiche-Constable – with a bright blue cyclorama which only darkens at the end. 'A honeymoon bride', interviewed after an enormous traffic-jam in Florida, said: 'It was like being stranded on a desert island with a lot of happy people.'

I wrote that fifteen years ago for the Faber edition of this play. In 1991 we have a decrepit tube system, roads clogged by millions of parked cars and a government like its forerunners terrified to tamper with the 'right' of motorists to destroy cities, fields and sky. Britain is about to join a crusade to save the holy oil that America and the rest of us burn day and night in a sort of ecstasy of destruction. I wish I'd called the play *Auto Da Fe*.

The play was written for Peter Hall's National Theatre and directed by Jonathan Miller at the Old Vic. Miller writes in his book on directing: 'I find it hard now to pinpoint why it was such a failure'. My own view is that the play wasn't ready and that, much as I admire him, he was not the right director. His strength is in reappraising the classics but new plays don't need interpretation, they simply have to be got right and that's a process that, to use his sort of metaphor, begins early in the pregnancy with ante-natal care and goes on right up to delivery. Jonathan was loath to alter what I'd written, even when I wanted to. 'I'm not a script editor,' he'd say, 'we're doing your play as you wrote it.'

It is flawed in two crucial respects: its theme is mobility but its situation is static; and it partly derives from a television play of mine called *The Gorge*, of which some elements – the Lorimer family, and their picnic, for instance – never quite survived the transplant. I still believe more work on the script might have turned the trick. Dr Miller isn't a surgeon and it was left to Hall during some unhappy previews to apply the knife – too late. The first night was a tense occasion as we watched an elderly cast trying to remember where the next cut came. After that it was a quick trip to the mortuary.

The Freeway was first presented by the National Theatre at the Old Vic in October 1974. The cast was as follows:

LES	Paul Rogers
MAY	Irene Handl
WALLY	Lionel Murton
EVELYN	Joan Hickson
JAMES	Graham Crowden
NANCY	Rachel Kempson
GRANT	Pip Miller
TRACY	Doran Godwin
COX	Antony Brown
PAYNE	Sara Van Beers
NURSE	Veronica Sowerby
BARRY	Mark Dignam

Directed by Jonathan Miller

A radio version was broadcast in 1991.

CHARACTERS

LES LORIMER, 60
MAY, 60
WALLY, 60+
EVELYN, 60+
JAMES RHYNE, 55
NANCY, 75
GRANT SCALE, 25–30
TRACY, 25–30
COX, 40+
PAYNE, 20
NURSE, 18+
WATERMEN
BARRY POTTER, 50

A racing walker, stretcher-bearers, soldiers, security man, photographer, Scrubber, neighbours.

Radio voices.

Directions left and right read from actor's point of view.

A section of the approach-road to an inter-city freeway.

Downstage, between the audience and the main acting area, is a barbed-wire fence. Downstage of this a forestage.

The main area is a grass verge, sprinkled with paper and plastic containers. On either side are trees or shrubs for masking. On the right, also, a large road sign, facing the road at 45 degrees, so that we see only its plain back.

Some way upstage grass becomes road and on the road is a stationary queue of vehicles, facing right to left. Our view takes in the sides of three vehicles – or rather the whole of one in the middle and part of those on either side. Left to right: an estate car, rear only; a Motor Home, the whole; a sports car, the front. The estate car is sober and British, the sports car foreign and fibreglass. The Motor Home is large, flashy and American-styled; has a window to the cab and a door with a window on its right. The rest of the side facing us is a plain panel, relieved by vents and Red Indian motifs. On the roof are sun panels and storage units. The single door facing us leads either to the driving cab or living quarters. Curtains can close off the windows.

Upstage of the road is more verge, another barbed-wire fence, then trees and sky, hillside and village, a traditional English landscape.

The vehicles, like the clothes, are imaginative developments of present styles.

The clothes of the Lorimer family are of synthetic fabrics in futuristic styles, contrasting both with their traditional interests and attitudes and with the Rhynes's clothes, which are arrogantly dowdy. The Scales are trendy but that, of course, may not mean modern.

ACT ONE

Scene One

Morning.

> *House-lights dim and we hear the lowing of cows. This gives way soon to a chorus of motor-horns, beginning with one and rising to a climax.*

> *At this, the curtain rises and for some moments the horns continue. LES LORIMER is standing or crouching beside his Motor Home polishing the bodywork. MAY, EVELYN and WALLY are sitting inside the driving cab, smoking and eating sweets, only partly seen.*

> *If no curtain used, these four are in position while audience comes in; at first they sit waiting for traffic to move, then LES gets out to look, muttering with drivers from other cars, who come from upstage or off to look towards front of queue, left. There may be one or two horn-choruses during the half-hour before the house-lights go down. LES occupies the time more sensibly, polishing his vehicle.*

> *LES is sixty or near it, once active, but growing fat through lack of exercise, speaks with London accent. He is always fiddling with some small manual job. He now looks up from his polishing towards the front of the queue, off left. Then he straightens up and looks again, as the chorus dies away. He turns and looks off, right. Then returns to the bodywork. MAY opens window.*

MAY. Any sign of moving?

LES. Moving? The cars stretch out of sight both ways.

MAY. That many joined on behind?

LES. Coming all the time.

MAY. That case I think I'll stretch my legs.

> LES *opens door and lets down the steps. She climbs down,*
> *speaking back into the bus.*

You two want a breath of air?

> WALLY *and* EVELYN *discuss it.* MAY *is a good-looking*
> *woman of fifty-five, but like her husband, putting on weight.*
> *She wears trousers and a tunic, has binoculars slung round her*
> *neck. Speaks with Welsh accent. She stands on grass, looks*
> *through glasses first left then right.*

Seems to be solid right up to the Freeway. And look at them
joining on the end every second. Blind as bats.

LES. *We* joined on the end. You don't know till it's too late.
Then you can't back out. Ought to be a diversion.

MAY. *But those behind cried 'Forward'*
And those before cried 'Back!'

LES. Rest assured someone's trying to clear it. But blowing their
horns like that is pointless. Childish. Making that row. Upset
the animals.

MAY. Animals?

> *Searches with glasses.*

LES. Somewhere beyond that fence.

> *She turns glasses towards audience and moves forward,*
> *peering at them.*

MAY. Can't see any animals.

LES. You can hear them. Now and again. When the wind's in
this direction.

MAY. Must be in those sheds.

LES. I told you we should have got away last night, avoid the Friday morning rush but no, you had to see the Pelota Championships . . .

MAY. I can see a farm-hand! I can see his white overall!

WALLY comes out, stretching, then gingerly climbs down steps. He's sixty, lean, wearing clothes in style of lumberjack or pioneer. Speaks with Canadian accent. He breathes deeply, filling his small chest and raising his arms. Pretends to cough. MAY laughs.

Every picture tells a story.

WALLY staggers and reels about, to show he is fainting from the fresh air. LES has finished cleaning the bus and looks at him without a smile. EVELYN laughs inside and MAY on the grass. LES shakes his head and goes into bus with dusters. They pause, then laugh again.

Laugh and the world laughs with you, cry and you cry alone.

WALLY walks about and down to fence, looking around.

WALLY. This the Yorkshire National Park, Les? Don't see any elephants.

MAY. Have to make do with cows.

WALLY. Don't see any cows either.

MAY. In those sheds down there.

She gives him glasses.

WALLY. Must be a dairy complex.

They look over audience for a moment.

British Columbia, they got this flock of chickens, they bring them to all the country fairs, you know, the neighbourhood fairs, for the kids to see. The old-fashioned kind with the beaks left on.

MAY. That's nice, keeping up the old ways.

LES comes from bus with ciné-camera.

LES. Come on, Evelyn, don't you want to be in the film? Bring a touch of glamour?

Winks at MAY and WALLY. EVELYN follows, sixty-two, wearing elaborate blonde wig and safari suit. Moves sedately, ladylike manner, smile fades at unpleasantness or nature. Genteel London accent.

WALLY (*sings*). Did you ever see a dream walking?
Well, I did . . .

EVELYN. Is there a breeze? D'you think my head needs a dacron square?

MAY. Not a breath. It's a perfect day.

EVELYN at first holds her wig, then takes down hand and moves gingerly across the verge.

EVELYN. Gracious, fancy being stranded here! The last place God made.

LES. Don't come any further, Eve, by the bus is where I want you.

EVELYN poses. LES lines up shot.

That's the style. Where the others? Come on, May, let's be having you.

MAY. You didn't say you wanted me.

LES. Shouldn't have to say by now. Been taking you long enough.

MAY (*moving to join* EVELYN). Like a lamb to the slaughter. (*The women link arms.*)

LES. Shouldn't have to tell you where to stand either. Not by this time. Where's Wally?

WALLY is at the fence, smoking a cigarette.

WALLY. Me too?

LES. It's your holiday! Blimey O'Riley! You want a cinematic record! Think I'm doing this for my own amusement?

WALLY. How about me walking over and you kinda following with the camera?

LES. What for?

WALLY. That's a movie-camera you got there!

LES. Leave the photography to me, all right? The last shot I had on here was – what? D'you remember?

WALLY. I guess not.

LES. Anyone?

The women can't either.

No. Well, it's all in here!

Taps his head.

That's the difference, see? It was a slow pan across the pedestrian precinct at Green Park. Finishing with you lot feeding the ducks.

MAY. Oh, yes –

LES. And now you're saying another follow-shot the opposite way? You want to make your Canadian friends all giddy? Show them a film with nothing but shots of you on the move, they'll be getting a false impression!

Laughs. So do women.

They'll say 'Gee, Wally, didn't they give you no rest over in l'il old England?'

WALLY *joins the women.* LES *lines up again.*

Closer to Eve, you're off frame. Not too close, don't stand behind her. I've lost you altogether now.

MAY (*sings*). Stand up, stand up for Jesus,
The beggars at the back can't see!

LES. That's better. Give us a smile then. This is only a camera, not a missile-launcher. Look as though you're enjoying yourselves.

EVELYN. Chance to do some acting.

LES. Here we go!

WALLY. Roll 'em!

They smile and stand motionless while LES runs the camera.

MAY. A picture no artist could paint.

LES. It's not a talkie, thank you.

After some time, TRACY SCALE comes on from sports car, right. She is in late twenties, her real prettiness almost hidden by a trendy outfit – perhaps a Mao tunic and black cap with huge dark glasses. Something of that sort anyway. We can see that she has a good figure too.

MAY. Look out!

TRACY. Sorry.

LES (*taking down camera*). That's ruined that shot.

TRACY. Very sorry, I didn't see.

LES. Can't be helped.

TRACY. Only going to meet my husband.

EVELYN. He been up to have a look?

TRACY. That's right.

LES. To the Freeway?

TRACY. Well, I mean, how long are we expected to wait here? I've got two young children in that Kamikaze.

LES. They'll get us through as soon as possible.

MAY. Can we break away now, Les?

LES. I should, if I were you.

MAY. Stuck here like cheese at fourpence.

> MAY, WALLY *and* EVELYN *move away and* LES *stows camera as* GRANT *comes on from left, wearing expensive jungle-green or camouflage suit, boots, dark glasses. Like* TRACY, *has slight London suburban accent.*

TRACY. Well, did you get there?

GRANT. Yes.

TRACY. Do we look like moving?

GRANT. No way.

LES. What seems to be the trouble?

GRANT. Everyone tells a different story.

LES. Then it's not just an everyday super pile-up?

GRANT. They'd have cleared that by now.

LES. What I thought.

GRANT. Every lane's solid, far as you can see, both ways.

TRACY. Both ways?

GRANT. The kids all right?

TRACY. All right so far. Sholto's gone to sleep and Stephanie's modelling a rabbit.

GRANT. Might as well picnic now, save time later.

TRACY. Right. Hope we're not too late at Mother's, she gets jittery.

GRANT. Give her an interbuzz if we're held up long.

TRACY. Right!

> *She goes off to their car. He opens boot, which is bonnet, takes out picnic and goes after her.*

WALLY (*watching them*). They're going to have themselves a spot of chow.

MAY has gone left and is looking off through glasses.
EVELYN sits on step of bus. WALLY turns back to LES.

What d'you say, Les? Spot of chow? Good idea –

LES. If they threw themselves under a bus, would you follow suit?

MAY. Difference between scratching your head and pulling all the hair out.

LES. Mind out, Evelyn.

EVELYN (*on step, in his way*). Consider yourself squashed.

LES. How's that?

EVELYN. Wally was only making a suggestion. There's no call to bite his head off.

LES. Fair enough, get out the chairs and tables, cook the dinner. What if this lot suddenly clears, d'you expect me to hold up all those cars while you lot get the equipment back in the Cherokee?

EVELYN stands and moves away to WALLY, who is now at fence.

EVELYN. Let's you and I console ourselves with a menthol.

They light up cigarettes.

May! D'you care for a menthol?

MAY. If we can't eat, we may as well smoke ourselves to death.

Joins them as WALLY coughs.

LES. We could have some *elevenses*.

EVELYN. We had some elevenses at half-past nine.

WALLY. That was half-past nineses.

LES. That was coffee. We could have some tea.

EVELYN. We *could*. We haven't had tea since breakfast.

LES. Wally, come on, stir your stumps.

Goes back into bus. WALLY *moves to bus.*

WALLY. No rest for the wicked.

MAY (*sings*). *I like a nice cup of tea in the morning . . .*

She follows LES *into bus.*

JAMES RHYNE *comes from upstage of the estate car, left. He opens the boot with a key and rummages inside, producing a plaid blanket. He comes down to the grass verge and clears a few square feet of litter. He is fifty-five, attentive, extremely courteous. Bewildered by techniques of all kinds, he is at home with words and ideas, immensely appreciative of others' qualities. Speech, often hurried, indistinct; the diction of a gent. He is wearing dinner-jacket, black tie, etc. Having cleared a space, he spreads the blanket on the ground. He is followed by* NANCY, *seventy-five, a dowager with a grand manner but a bark worse than her bite. She can be put down by her son's quiet insistence on the true state of affairs. She carries an elegant container. Kicks aside more rubbish. She is wearing a rather dowdy evening dress and an unbecoming perm.*

NANCY. Were I ever asked for the most emblematic feature of modern Britain, I should point to her ill-kept verges.

JAMES. Executed by you, Mother, that could hardly fail to be an impressive gesture. However, I'm sure you're aware that the likelihood of your being asked is extremely remote. You're not exactly *vox pop*.

They sit on the blanket and during this NANCY *opens the container and takes out a thermos flask and two mugs. She pours coffee and offers a biscuit.*

NANCY. You persist in that opinion against all evidence to the contrary.

JAMES. What evidence, Mother?

LES *has come from bus, with a cylindrical device like a kettle and some newspapers.* MAY, EVELYN *and* WALLY *are watching the* RHYNES.

LES. Get weaving, Wally.

WALLY. That the paper?

LES. Yeah. You got to tear it up.

LES *returns to bus while* WALLY *sets the kettle on the verge and tears the newspaper into shreds, stuffing the pieces into the open top.* EVELYN *helps him, tearing the paper while he lights the shreds in the kettle.*

NANCY. I'm often stopped in the street, for my views on this and that. The state of the nation. The place of drugs in the modern Church. Do I think Nagasaki Knickers are too revealing? Not revealing enough?

JAMES. I'm sure they *ask* you, Mother. That's not in dispute. In a count of heads, yours would serve as well as another. I'm only making the point that you are not exactly An Average Housewife.

NANCY. I hope I'll never be seen as an average anything.

WALLY. Is the water in?

LES. Yes. You only got to boil it.

JAMES. When someone says Old Age Pensioner, your image is not the first that springs to mind.

NANCY. You, on the other hand, rather fancy yourself as The Man in the Street. A freeman of the caste system moving freely acrawse the divisive boundaries or whatever they are.

LES *brings folding table and chairs from bus and begins to erect them on the verge.*

JAMES *offers* NANCY *the biscuits and she chooses.*

JAMES. I'm not sure what you mean by a freeman of the caste system. And I'm not sure you're sure either. As long as —

NANCY. I'm very clear what I mean –

JAMES. Mother, please, will you allow me to finish? As long as you don't mean I'm a sycophantic creep of some kind, then I accept the definition, with some reservations.

MAY comes from bus with tray, on which are set melamine cups, saucers, a teapot, biscuits, sugar, milk, etc., puts tray on table and lays them out.

MAY (*to the world in general*). They also serve who only stand and wait.

EVELYN helps while WALLY struggles with kettle and LES opens chairs. NANCY glances at him.

NANCY. Everything but the kitchen sink. And I suppose *that's* in the bus. Or whatever they call it.

JAMES. The Motor Home.

NANCY. I thought you'd know.

WALLY is creating clouds of black smoke with his burning newspaper. MAY waves it away.

MAY (*sings*). There's a silver lining.
          Through the dark clouds shining –

LES. What's up, Wally? Spot of bother with the Vesuvius?

He goes to help. NANCY coughs pointedly and MAY looks at them nervously.

MAY. Sorry about the smoke.

JAMES (*half-rising*). I absolutely hadn't noticed.

He sits again. EVELYN takes teapot to kettle and WALLY pours in the water, now hot. LES moves to JAMES and NANCY, smiling and making faces towards his family.

LES. Talk about Fred Karno's Army.

JAMES (*rising again*). I beg your pardon?

LES. I say, talk about an awkward squad.

JAMES. I was about to praise your impressive *esprit de corps*. *(And quickly enlarging, explaining:)* Everyone with a job to do.

LES. I try to keep them up to scratch. No margin for error when you're halfway across Bulgaria.

JAMES. No indeed.

LES. Or up the Pyrenees.

MAY. When you see a vacant place at a lay-by, you've got to grab it.

She pours milk into each cup.

LES. But our drill's bound to be a bit rough today. We got a raw recruit. My wife's brother over from Canada. We're showing him the sights. And teaching him to boil the Vesuvius.

EVELYN comes to table with teapot and stirs. WALLY stands and puts cork into kettle.

You finished with the bonfire, Wally?

Laughs and winks at JAMES.

JAMES. Are you Northward bound?

LES. Only as far as Yorkshire National Park. See the dolphins at Fountains Abbey. We thought of nipping up to the Braemar Games after but this means our schedule's gone for a burton. And we only got food and water for a day, so I reckon we'll have to make do with Hadrian's Wall, stay overnight, then off back home tomorrow afternoon.

MAY. Oh yes, let's see the Wall. *(To JAMES.)* I've been taking Roman Britain in evening classes.

LES. Always got her nose in some historical novel.

MAY. I like anything hysterical.

She laughs and goes to help EVELYN pour tea. WALLY comes, wiping hands.

JAMES. As an experienced traveller, what's your view of the situation? Would you hazard an informed guess at the outcome?

LES. What, the jam? Couldn't say. Got to sit tight. Grin and bear it.

JAMES. That would be your general approach? Remain calm?

LES. Definitely. No use blowing horns, for instance. Childish. Making a row won't help.

JAMES. I can't tell you how heartily I agree. However, the futility of such gestures should not be advanced as a reason for preventing them. The right to make futile gestures is an inalienable part of our way of life. A thread in the intricate pattern of freedom. We must trust that wiser counsels will prevail.

MAY. Tea up! Them as wants it come and get it.

The two men have been standing centre, the others sitting and pouring, eating, etc.

LES. Lorimer's the name. Les Lorimer.

JAMES had thought the conversation over and was returning to sit by his mother. He stands again and comes to shake hands.

JAMES. How d'you do? James Rhyne. (*Pronounced 'Reen'.*)

LES. My wife May.

MAY (*reaching across LES to shake hands with JAMES*). Excuse me retching, I've just come off the boat.

JAMES. My mother.

LES (*crossing to her*). You all right on the ground, Mrs Rhyne?

NANCY. Perfectly, thank you.

LES. Only if you'd like to share our furniture, Wally can easy sit on the verge.

NANCY. Most kind of you but this is what I'm used to.

LES. Hoping to go far?

NANCY. Ross eventually. Ross and Cromarty.

JAMES. Scotland.

LES. For the skiing or what?

NANCY. The stalking.

LES (*not understanding*). Oh, yes.

NANCY. Lest you should think us unsuitably clad, I ought to explain that our first call will be at the Tithe Barn Festival. *Mary Stuart.* Donizetti. Though it seems unlikely now, that this will clear in time for the overture. If I tell the truth, the picnic's the part I most enjoy.

> LES *knows no more than before she started.* MAY *draws* JAMES *towards the table where* EVELYN *and* WALLY *are sitting.*

MAY. My colleague, Evelyn.

JAMES. How d'you do? You did say 'colleague'?

EVELYN. We're in the same dragshop. I'm on the wig counter, May's in the knitwear.

MAY. And my kid brother, Wally.

WALLY. Hi!

JAMES. Seeing plenty of changes?

WALLY. Thirty years since I was here, it's changed all right.

JAMES. And getting wonderful weather.

MAY. I told him, he must have brought the sunshine in his suitcase.

JAMES. Yes indeed! Well, if you'll excuse me –

LES (*returning to meet him*). This pantomime with the Vesuvius, that's not usual. Primitive. Wasteful. Pollutes the environment. No, we normally have hot water on tap in the Cherokee. You seen one of these jobs, have you?

JAMES. Your Motor Home? Most impressive!

LES. If we're stuck here long, I'll give you the guided tour.

JAMES. Would it be any trouble?

LES. Say the word.

JAMES. Most grateful.

MAY, EVELYN and WALLY are at table drinking tea.

LES. Got a hundred-litre storage tank with twenty thousand BTU heating and air conditioning throughout. Just at the moment, though, she's having one or two teething troubles. The recirculating toilet's leaking into the water system and the refrigerator thermostat's on the blink.

MAY. You can cut the milk with a saw.

LES. So we've had to bring water in a jerrican. Only natural the first year.

JAMES. Really?

LES. Since they rationalised inspection.

JAMES. You seem extremely well-informed.

LES. Spent most of my life in a motor works. Started on the shop-floor and finished on the staff. *Works* staff, mind you. Still a working man.

NANCY. James! Your coffee will be cold.

MAY. And your tea.

LES (*winking at* JAMES). In the dog-house.

JAMES. Absolutely.

Smiles and they return to their drinks. On the road upstage people pass back and forth, looking at their vehicles, etc., occasionally travellers go by on the grass, downstage, by the fence.

Two Autoguards enter. COX, the man, is a middle-aged servant, reassuring, avuncular. He has the slow and deliberate demeanour of a gardening expert or cricket commentator. His uniform has many features taken from the old motoring clubs: boots, breeches, Sam Browne belts, peaked caps. PAYNE, the woman, is young, scrubbed, fresh, everyone's ideal nurse. She has an outfit which uses same colour scheme as COX's but has features taken from those of air hostesses, meter maids, police-women. They enter up right.

COX (*saluting casually*). Morning all.

At first they treat only with the LORIMERS, not seeing the RHYNES.

LES. Good morning, officer.

COX. Lovely morning.

LES. Not too bad.

COX. Sort of weather makes you thankful to be in good old England. Not rotting away in some prison camp.

LES. Any news from the front?

PAYNE. Only just arrived on duty, haven't we, Sarge? They've told us nothing.

COX. We're as much in the dark as you are, friend.

PAYNE. Nobody ever tells you anything, do they, Sarge?

COX. That's enough cheek from you, young Payne. Some of these young Guardettes, they get above themselves. (*Winks at LORIMERS.*) Any more and I shall take you across my knee. I'm still big enough.

PAYNE. I'd like to see you try.

COX. Watch your step, young lass, or you'll find out.

LORIMERs *laugh at all this, as at a much-loved television series.*

PAYNE. All right, Sergeant, I'll come quietly.

COX. Cheeky young article. (*Laughs warmly.*)

PAYNE. Well this won't get the membercards checked. Can we see your card, sir?

WALLY. Oh, I don't have one. I'm Canadian.

PAYNE. Haven't you got a Canadian membercard?

WALLY. I'm not a motorist.

LES. He's my passenger.

Offers membercard, which COX *scrutinises.*

PAYNE. You ladies associate members?

MAY. I am.

EVELYN. I only go on the Freeway in their car. It's hardly worth me joining.

PAYNE (*offering brochures*). You can't have read our literature.

COX. All right, Mister Lorimer. (*Punches card with register which bleeps.*)

EVELYN. I can't really afford it, dear, since my hubby passed away.

PAYNE. But don't you think you *should* afford it? After all, you use the Freeway –

EVELYN. Only when they take me out –

PAYNE. – you're happy to take advantage of all that's been achieved so far in the motorist's struggle against victimisation –

EVELYN (*cornered*). It's a free country!

COX. Steady on there. Take it easy, young Payne, you get a bit hot under the collar. What I think my young friend's trying to say is that this is only a free country because we make it so.

PAYNE. Those who are not for us are against us.

COX. Your name will be turning up on one of those pedestrian petitions. You mark my words.

EVELYN. I've never joined anything. I never have. I've never voted. I never would.

COX. You can't be sure. *Some*body signs them. Somebody wants to clear city centres of private cars. It's not me. It's not Mister Lorimer here.

LES. I've talked till I'm blue in the face. Women can't grasp politics.

COX *moves to* RHYNES *and takes* JAMES's *card.*

PAYNE. You have a think. Consider the benefits. For only half the annual subscription you receive a free badge which makes you an Associate Freewoman and once a month a free copy of our magazine, *Free-for-all*, which includes features on fashion, showbiz and ecology, with many free offers and exciting new competitions.

COX (*handing back* JAMES's *card*). Thank you, my lord.

Everyone looks at JAMES.

JAMES. Sarnt. What information can you give us?

COX. Precious little, my lord.

JAMES. But surely something must be known about this delay.

COX. It seems to have begun with a routine pile-up but now, with more cars joining on the end all the time –

JAMES. But there appears to be no movement at all. Can't the obstruction be cleared? Correct me if I'm wrong – I understood that mobile casualty stations could be on the spot within ten minutes.

COX. That's true, my lord, up to a point.

NANCY. Up to a point, Sergeant? Sergeant – ?

COX (*saluting*). Cox, my lady.

> PAYNE *has crossed to join the* RHYNES. MAY *and*
> EVELYN *clear tea-things into bus.*

NANCY. Up to what point?

COX. Well, the truth of the matter is we're a bit understaffed at
the moment and the patrols already had one incident to cope
with on the same stretch of Freeway. A lot of metal-cutting
and some tricky amputations.

PAYNE. Can be difficult. The welders jostling the anaesthetists.
TV cameras nudging the surgeon's arm.

NANCY. D'you think we can be in Yorkshire by half past four?

PAYNE. I wouldn't bank on it, madam.

NANCY. We'd better skip the Donizetti and get straight up to
Edinburgh.

JAMES. Forgive me, Sarnt, if I appear to be teaching my
grandmother to suck eggs, but shouldn't you and your fellow
guards be preventing more cars joining on the end of the
line?

LES. They ought to be diverted on to the old motorways and
A-roads –

> EVELYN *and* MAY *have been clearing away the tea-things
> during the last dialogue.* WALLY *has fallen asleep in his seat.*
> COX *ignores* LES.

COX. Now, now, now, my lord, keep your shirt on. Over the
past few years the British motorist has weathered a good few
crises, what with our Arab friends; and the unions . . . but
one way or another he's kept on the move. Oh, there may be
some rotten apples amongst them but your average
Autoclubman is steady, independent, not easily roused but
when he is, watch out, you'll find he won't let go in a hurry –

Breaks off, takes out handkerchief and blows nose.

PAYNE (*putting her hand on his arm*). Sarge –

COX. All right, young Payne, I know. (*Then gruffly.*) We'd best be cutting along.

PAYNE (*to* EVELYN). I'll leave you this free copy of *Free-for-all*. See if it changes your mind about joining. And if you decide to, that's my number on the cover. Quote that and your application will be dealt with personally by my own computer.

EVELYN. Thanks very much.

COX. Anything you want, my lord, give us a shout . . . my lady.

They both salute.

NANCY. Good-day, Sergeant. Keep us informed.

Guards make towards right. PAYNE *goes but* COX *turns.*

COX. Morning, all. Mind how you go.

Suddenly the loud battering sound of an approaching helicopter. Everyone looks up, following its course from left to right. Other travellers, passing along the road between vehicles, pause to watch it pass. COX *goes off. The wind of the propellers blows the grass as the helicopter goes over.* WALLY *wakes suddenly, stands, realises what it is. The noise and wind die away.*

NANCY. Military, Autoclub or what?

LES. Media, TV

NANCY. Theirs would be first.

JAMES. Therein lies our safety, Mother. The broadcasting of uncensored views and information.

LES. Looks as though we'll be here for a good while yet.

NANCY. We may as well eat.

LES. Have to scrub round Fountains Abbey. That all right, Wally?

WALLY. How's that, Les?

LES. I say: scrub round the dolphinarium.

WALLY. Sure. They got dolphins over there. When you seen one dolphin you seen 'em all.

JAMES. Will you bring the basket, Mother? I'll see to the wine.

They make towards their estate car, taking their coffee-cups, etc. MAY has come from bus, with a dinky apron like EVELYN's.

LES signals to them to follow downstage. He glances at the RHYNES.

LES. D'you hear what the Sergeant called them?

MAY (*to WALLY*). You never expected to meet the gentry.

LES. That's not much of a car for a lord and lady. Flat tyre, too, by the look of it.

EVELYN. You'd think they hadn't got two pee to rub together.

WALLY. Maybe they've happened on hard times?

MAY. They dress the part anyway.

EVELYN. But if that dress was the best I could afford, I should die of shame! It might be made of furnishing fabric!

From offstage right, hear GRANT, TRACY and their two children singing 'I'm a Suitcase'.

MAY. Oh look, that couple in the next car, they're having a sing-song with their kiddies. We used to have to do that with ours on long journeys, d'you remember, Les?

RHYNES begin to return and LORIMERS break up.

EVELYN. Dinner's nearly ready. May put it on when she heard that Autoguard –

LES. Might as well have lunch, yes, why not?

MAY. That's a relief: my stomach thinks my throat's cut.

LES. All right. The more practice Wally gets, the easier it'll be on the Continent.

NANCY brings modest picnic basket and sits on rug, taking out a good deal of traditional cold fare: meats, salad, Stilton, fruit and bread, all of which they eat with their hands.

LES fetches clip-board and whistle from bus. He checks stopwatch, gives starting whistle. Women go into bus and LES hangs clip-board on bus.

LES and WALLY unscrew fittings on lower part of bodywork, unfolding hinged section, perhaps half of wall facing us. They lift this until it becomes an awning. They detach two poles clamped inside and plant them in ground.

Revealed are MAY and EVELYN at the vinyl fittings of their ideal kitchen: in upstage wall are a sink, eye-level grill and two burners with pans simmering; fridge; etc. MAY attends to steaks, hammering and trimming.

EVELYN switches on her radio, which plays a jaunty number from the Tijuana Brass, which continues as music for the sequence.

WALLY brings a rush mat from bus and LES kicks aside paper rubbish and directs WALLY to unroll mat where he's cleared, a position right of centre. MAY comes from bus with a battery-operated dustette and vacuums the mat. LES and WALLY then move table on to mat and place chairs round it.

Now the central area is clear, RHYNES picnicking one side, LORIMERS the other.

JAMES has returned, brings bottle of claret, which he stands opening. NANCY takes glasses from basket and in due course they pour and drink.

EVELYN comes from bus with laden tray. MAY takes a plastic cloth from it, with a hole in the centre. She lays this on the table, then EVELYN *puts tray on it. They lay four settings with glasses, paper napkins, pepper and salt, table mats.*

LES *has gone round the bus to the upstage side, right.*
WALLY *goes to consult the clip-board, putting on glasses to read it, taking them off afterwards. He follows* LES *as* LES *emerges on top, opens storage unit and passes things down to* WALLY, *who returns downstage with a bright canvas sunshade.* EVELYN *to bus with tray.* MAY *goes back to bus with dustette.* WALLY *opens umbrella and shows a large shade with a short pole. He holds it above him, then puts pole through central hole of table. Umbrella rests on table, covering the surface. He puts hands on hips and looks at it, on top and underneath.* EVELYN *comes from bus with plastic pedal-bin, puts it near bus.* LES *comes from upstage with a canvas bag. Passing* WALLY, *he sees umbrella, pauses, throws an extension pole on to ground, passes on.* EVELYN *helps* WALLY *take out umbrella and fix extension pole, put it back through hole in table.*

LES *throws contents of bag on to ground, down right: canvas, metal poles, pegs. He begins to sort them.* MAY *from bus with tray of bowls, tin, tin-opener, bread in packet and bread-basket,* EVELYN *goes to bus.* MAY *takes sliced bread from packet and arranges it in basket, then pours fruit salad from tin into bowls, four portions. Perhaps cream too?* WALLY *goes to look at rota and enters bus, as* EVELYN *comes out with plastic vase and polythene bag, goes to table.*

LES *is erecting a toilet-tent downstage, first piecing frame together, then sorting canvas.*

RHYNES *eat, drink, and watch with interest.* EVELYN *takes from bag plastic flowers and puts them in vase, puts bag on tray, which* MAY *now returns to bus, as* WALLY *comes out with a spiked stick.* MAY *drops empty fruit tin into pedal-bin, then goes into bus.* WALLY *begins picking up plastic and paper debris from whole area, putting it into plastic bin at intervals.* EVELYN *goes into bus and* MAY *comes out with wine bottle, cork-screw and cheeseboard. Puts all on table.*

EVELYN *reappears with folding washstand and plastic bowl to fit; erects this near door of bus.*

WALLY *leaves spike near bus and reads rota again. Bell rings once offstage and* MAY *reacts, hurrying off to bus.* WALLY *goes round it upstage and off. The whistle of a boiling kettle sounds and* EVELYN *hurries into bus.* MAY *comes from bus with hot vegetable dish, which she puts on table.* EVELYN *then comes with kettle of hot water, which she pours into the washbowl.* WALLY *comes from upstage, rear, with a chemical lavatory seat and bucket. Takes it down to tent and looks for* LES, *who indicates that he put bucket down and helps* LES *finish tent. This they do.*

Bell offstage rings twice and MAY *runs back to bus.* WALLY, *hammering in a tent peg with a mallet, hurts his finger and backs away, sucking it, shaking it, etc.*

EVELYN *comes down to him, but* LES *goes on working, ignoring him. Bell offstage rings three times and* EVELYN *has to run, meeting* MAY *coming out with second vegetable dish.* WALLY *makes to go on helping* LES, *but* LES *points upstage and* WALLY *goes.* LES *gets tent finished and goes inside with the lavatory.* MAY *finds room on table for dish and* WALLY *goes upstage of bus.*

EVELYN *reappears with a box with a red cross on it but seeing no* WALLY *returns to bus with it.*

WALLY *comes from upstage of bus with chemicals in plastic jars, goes into tent with them.*

EVELYN *comes from bus with two plates and two steaks.* LES *goes up to washbowl and washes hands.* MAY, *seeing this, runs into bus, as* EVELYN *puts out steaks on two plates and sets them on table.* MAY *comes out with handful of paper towels just in time for* LES *to wipe his hands, afterwards disposing of towel in pedal-bin.*

Bell offstage rings four times and MAY *goes to answer.*

WALLY *backs out of tent, goes to rota, checks it.* LES *takes position at table, removes cork from bottle.* EVELYN *takes off apron, goes into bus as* MAY *reappears with two more plates and steaks, which she sets on table.*

LES *pours wine in each glass.* EVELYN *comes with radio and takes seat.* MAY *removes her apron and takes it into bus,* WALLY *washes his hands and looks for towels as* MAY *comes again, showing them. He wipes his hands.* MAY *sits at table.* LES *looks at his watch, then at* WALLY, *who hurries to take his place.*

EVELYN *stops radio music.* LES *looks at watch, blows whistle. Silence.*

LES. Not too bad. I suppose we can't expect miracles. Everyone got their Liebfraumilch?

They raise their glasses.

Buon appetito!

OTHERS. Skol, cheers, bottoms up, etc. . . .

JAMES *is watching and* LES *sees him.* LES *raises his glass.* JAMES *half-rises from the ground.*

JAMES. Your very good health.

EVELYN's *radio is on the ground beside her. She switches it on at once, and to the music of the Tijuana Brass, the* LORIMER *family help themselves to vegetables.*

Lights plunge to black. Music continues as both sets of picnics are cleared.

Scene Two

During change, hear media voice on speakers.

NEWSMAN. The Autoclubs report that travellers on the Royal Freeway may experience some delay. The cause is apparently another demonstration by the Scrubbers, the anti-motor group whose avowed aim is to paralyse the Freeway. The incident began with two ordinary collisions, each involving less than thirty vehicles, but rescuers arrived to find the terrorists already occupying the wreckage. Mobile mercy teams were given access to clear the dead and wounded although the Scrubbers have remained in position, blocking the Northbound Freeway, chanting slogans and, as these pictures show, exposing their private parts to the watching newsmen.

Light gradually shows the same scene, now lit by the moon. Several other sources of light. The kitchen panel of the bus is now closed. JAMES is rummaging in the boot of his car with a gazlamp; LES is lying on the ground by the RHYNES' car, looking at the tyre by torchlight.

The furniture is as it was.

JAMES emerges with a bottle and a cigar box, crosses to table and puts them there, leaving the gazlamp there too. He is still wearing dinner jacket. Now the announcement comes from the bus.

A spokesman says the situation is not so far regarded as serious, though travellers are advised to avoid the Freeway and its linkroads. Those with unavoidable journeys might, at their own risk, try exploring the old A-roads and motorways. In this case, drivers should be armed and are advised to keep their windows firmly closed against marauding bands of lorry-drivers.

JAMES returns to his car and takes out some glasses.

JAMES. You will, of course, let me know if there's anything at all I can do to help?

LES. Not at the moment.

NEWSMAN. At Royal Albert Hall, the gold medal in the International Pelota Championship went to Duk Soo Chung of Korea for the third year running . . .

Hear the viewers groaning.

JAMES (*bending slightly to show concern*). Is it serious? Will it be a tremendous job?

LES. Only a matter of changing a wheel. Still you don't want to waste time stopping at the next oasis. I'll change it for you in the morning. Easier in daylight.

JAMES. I'm extremely obliged to you.

LES (*standing and showing him*). The bodywork's had a bash here, see, your wing's been rubbing against the wheel. We shall have to pull that out a bit. D'you remember it happening?

JAMES. Yes, indeed. A container-truck went into the back as my wife was waiting at the lights. Yes, that's right, the driver jumped out at once and started hammering on her roof with his fist and kicking the door and shouting at her in Italian.

LES. Going through his accident drill.

JAMES. Precisely.

LES. As laid down by the intercontinental haulage combines.

JAMES. Quite so.

Together they walk towards the table.

Les, this hardly seems a recompense for the sweat of your brow, but I hope you'll give me the pleasure of accepting a cigar?

LES. I won't say no, thanks very much.

JAMES. And some Armagnac?

LES *stares until* JAMES *shows the flask.*

I fear by your expression that Cognac is your drink. Foolishly I have none with me, though you may enjoy Armagnac almost as much.

LES. Kind of brandy, is it? Fair enough.

As they talk, JAMES *lights his cigar and pours them each a drink.* LES *sips.*

JAMES. Is it in any way comparable to what you're used to?

LES. Japanese, is it?

JAMES. Only French, I fear.

LES. Not bad. Not bad at all. Very nice. No, as I say, these kind of teething troubles, only natural the first year, now they've handed inspection over to the customer.

JAMES. How fascinating! Do enlarge on that point.

LES. Well, inspection used to be a time-wasting process. Then somebody with brains invented the warranty. See, what they call a warranty is only saying: you find the faults and we'll repair them free.

JAMES. The advantage to the customer being – ?

LES. To keep down costs.

JAMES. Of course.

LES. After a year the vehicle's usually over the worst. From then on it's trouble-free motoring all the way. Only snag is changing ours every year we tend to lose the benefit. Still, common sense to change every twelve month, good part-exchange, up-to-date refinements.

JAMES. I must say it's extremely reassuring to hear this policy of rapid obsolescence upheld by a man with such vast experience. I'm afraid it's had the usual mud slung at it by the lefties.

LES. I wouldn't say 'vast'.

JAMES. All your working life? One man can't do more.

LES. I'd like to show you something, James.

Goes to bus as WALLY *comes out.*

Anything on the news?

Goes in without waiting for reply.

WALLY. They reckon it's some fellows called the Scrubbers are at the back of it.

Sits at table.

JAMES. I might have known.

WALLY. Who are they?

JAMES. A group of simple-minded extremists. They have youth on their side and the sentimental appeal of push-bicycles and canal barges but so far they enjoy no broad popular support.

WALLY. They got them over in BC. Same shaven heads but a different name. They call them Greenhorns.

JAMES. Scrubber was originally a pejorative term which they – and their PR people – have shrewdly embraced. Rather as the Methodists and Quakers did, –

WALLY. And the Tories.

JAMES (*laughing*). Precisely! Now, Wally, will you give me the pleasure of accepting a brandy?

WALLY. Fine, thank you.

JAMES. And a cigar?

WALLY. Why not?

JAMES. Marvellous.

LES *comes from bus to find* WALLY *being waited on.*

LES (*puts on table a photograph album and himself sits*). There you are, James! A photographic record of my working life presented to me free, gratis and for nothing by the Ford company to mark the completion of my fortieth year.

WALLY. D'you really think he should see it, Les? That's pretty hot stuff.

LES. You'll have to pardon the smell of sour grapes coming off my brother-in-law. He was on the shop-floor too –

WALLY. Over there –

LES. Even a steward. But he couldn't stay the course. So now he's struggling along in retirement with only the old-age pension. Not even got a car.

WALLY. I *never* had a car –

LES (*over this*). As you see, James, we start with group pictures of the lads on the floor. Before the war these. Tell by the haircuts.

JAMES. You in the back row there?

LES. Just got my face in, see? Metal Stamping and Body Division, that is. And there's the lads from Enamel Booths. Wet deck there. Engine Dress. And that's outside the welding shop, on the forecourt, where we used to play soccer before they made it into a car-park. Well, nobody *had* a car in those days. What we call the dark ages.

JAMES. Ah, now you're in the front row, with a white coat.

WALLY (*sings*). The working class
Can kiss my arse
I've got the foreman's job at last.

LES (*to him*). That may be some supervisors' attitude but not mine.

WALLY. They bought you off with a white coat.

LES. I never lost my sympathy with the lads. I knew life on the line. I'd seen the struggles we had just to get control of the key.

JAMES. The key? To what?

LES. To control the speed of the line. There's a rate for the job laid down by management. So many cars an hour.

WALLY. In the last minute a guy on the high track has fitted a gas tank, a fellow on the Engine Dress is putting in his second gear-box, the second of forty gear-boxes he'll put in during the next hour, three hundred and twenty the whole shift.

That's supposed to be what an average man can do on an average shift.

LES. All agreed by negotiating committees, Walt, meeting with the management.

WALLY. What the hell is an average man? Or an average shift? Or an average time of day? Who feels the same at night as in the morning? Who feels the same after eight hours trying to keep up with the track? There's no average time, only Ford time.

LES. All the same that was a big step forward, getting those times established. Before, they could speed up the line whenever they wanted. We'd be doing thirty cars an hour, just coping, no time to spare, and suddenly we'd find we were falling behind. They'd changed the speed, we were doing thirty-five.

JAMES. Who was responsible?

LES. The production manager. Only way he could make more money was increasing output. Only way he could increase output was pushing more cars along.

WALLY. That's a growth economy, brother.

LES. They had a factory in Cologne. If we started getting too bolshie, they'd put us supervisors on what they called 'a course'. Which was to see how they did things in Cologne. But there was no Germans on the line down there – only Spanish and Turkish immigrants. Transients. They could do thirty-five an hour and if they didn't they were sent back to their mud-huts.

WALLY. Which is what they call an economic miracle.

LES. All part of the rat-race.

WALLY. Same thing before the war in Detroit. Ford hired gangsters to beat us up. I swore then I'd never take promotion. What for, Les? A white coat, a clock, a cheque-book?

LES. What about the Cherokee? I'd never have got that as a line operative.

WALLY (*to* JAMES). Still working, the track. Never stops. (*Looking at watch.*) Since I last mentioned him, the fellow on the Engine Dress has fitted three more gear-boxes.

JAMES. Absolutely fascinating!

He liberally replenishes their glasses.

LES. You never been on the shop-floor, James?

JAMES. I fear not. An appalling omission.

LES. You'd find it wonderful in many ways.

JAMES. I must arrange to go.

LES. Nothing stops the line. If a man's hurt, the supervisor's top priority is filling the job. Only after that's done, you can see if the casualty needs to go to sick bay. Right, Wally?

WALLY. Right.

LES. And I think if the lads got faith in their supervisor, they see that's the best way. One night, I remember, just as a shift was starting, a fellow drops down right by the line. . . . 'Course, all the lads crowd round but just then the buzzer goes and the line starts moving. I said 'All right, lads, get on with your work.' And being as they trusted me, see, James, they turned to it, sticking on the hub-caps while I got an operative to take the casualty's place, then called the ambulance men. D'you know, he was stone dead. Gone off the first instant, they reckoned, and been laying there ever since. So – as I said to the lads during tea-break – no purpose would have been served by disrupting the line, losing bonuses. No, that line never stopped.

WALLY. Nor did the men. That's why I quit.

NANCY *and* MAY *come from bus.*

NANCY *has changed to something tweedy.*

NANCY. It's been confirmed that the Scrubbers are the cause, James.

MAY. Dirty little animals.

NANCY. They should be thrown into gaol along with the trades-union leaders. Don't you agree, Mrs Lorimer?

JAMES. Mother, you must learn to distinguish between a gang of unwashed narcissists and a body of democratically elected delegates. Mrs Lorimer, a brandy and soda?

MAY. Gracious me! What with the Snowball earlier and all that wine over dinner, you'll have me squiffy.

JAMES. I do assure you, the claret could have only a benign effect.

WALLY. He means you're not as thunk as you drink you are.

MAY. No, thanks, really.

LES. Won't you sit down, Lady Rhyne?

NANCY. Thank you, I'm on my way to bed.

MAY. Now are you sure you'll be comfy in the car?

NANCY. I'm as tough as old nails. Hill-walking, climbing –

MAY. Only that, if you wanted to come in the Cherokee, we could easily kick out Wally.

NANCY. Most considerate, but absolutely not. Good-night. God bless you.

They wish her good-night and she goes to estate car and rummages in boot for blankets. EVELYN comes from tent.

EVELYN. Smells like Christmas out here.

LES. I'm turning in. (*To* MAY.) You left that drop of water?

MAY. In the galley sink.

LES. 'Night, all.

They say good-night and he goes into bus.

JAMES (*to* EVELYN). Evelyn, may I get you a nightcap?

EVELYN (*hand instinctively to her wig*). Pardon?

JAMES. A little brandy?

EVELYN. Gracious no! You'll give me heartburn.

> NANCY *has found blankets in boot and shut it. She has also looked at nearside wheel and now comes down.*

NANCY. James, I thought your friend said he'd replace our wheel.

JAMES. In the morning, Mother.

NANCY. Well, I hope so. *You* can't do it.

JAMES. He needs the morning light.

NANCY. We want to make an early start.

JAMES. We must hope that's possible. Good-night, everyone. Sleep well.

> *They go off together left.*

> *A child cries, not far off. An adult's voice shouts.* EVELYN *is sitting with* WALLY *at the table, preparing her face for sleep, by the light of the gazlamp.* WALLY *pauses in smoking to look towards the cry.* MAY *wanders down to the fence and stares over audience.*

MAY. By the shore of Gitche-Gumee
>By the shining big sea-water
>Stood the wigwam of Nokomis
>Daughter of the moon Nokomis –

WALLY (*joining in*). Dark behind it rose the forest,
>>Rose the black and gloomy pine-trees,
>>Rose the firs with cones upon them –

> *They stop, laughing silently.*

EVELYN. That's cheerful.

MAY. Wally and I learnt that as kids, didn't we, love?

WALLY. We used to say it over and over –

MAY. I always say it when I'm frightened.

EVELYN. Are you frightened now?

MAY. Oh, no!

WALLY. When I first went out to Canada, I used to say it over when I was all alone.

EVELYN. How could you stand it?

WALLY. What?

EVELYN. Being all alone like that?

WALLY. I wasn't alone that much. Not enough, in fact. Pretty soon like everyone else I finished in the city. But I never forgot those days. The extremes of hot and cold. Some nights maybe you've bivouacked under canvas in the Rockies. And you leave your tent-flap open, 'cause in the foothills it can stay pretty warm. But you'd be sorry! Halfway through the night there'd be this god-awful stench so bad it would wake you up. And this breathing and snuffling right there in the tent. –

EVELYN. Oh, Lord –

WALLY. You'd open your eyes and turn your head, real slow, so's not to notice and there he'd be. This durn great grizzly bear . . .

EVELYN. I should die of fright.

MAY.   This is the law of the Yukon,
            That only the strong shall thrive,
            That surely the weak shall perish –
            And only the fit survive.

LES *appears at door with wet hands and face.*

LES. Where's the flipping towel then? Eyes full of soap and water –

MAY. Wasn't it hanging on the bulkhead by the barometer?

LES. No, I felt there.

MAY. Can't you think where you last had it?

LES. I *haven't* had it.

MAY. Oh! Lie down and I'll breathe for you . . .

They go back into bus, arguing. Pause. Sounds of a party, drunken voices. Someone sings.

WALLY. Yessir, the wide open spaces, not a living soul for miles.

EVELYN. I should hate it. I like people. People are my life. When my husband Freddie was alive, he used to take me on these walks. Not a car in sight, just birds. I cried on one occasion. He said, 'Sweetheart, what on earth's the matter?' I said, 'It's all this country!' He said, 'This is beautiful.' I said, 'It may be beautiful, but I can't stand it.'

Song ends. Applause and cheers. Sounds of party breaking up.

Civilisation's good enough for me. People. The dragshop. Dancing.

WALLY. You a dancer?

EVELYN. Latin and off-beat, yes. And you?

WALLY. At one time, in a sociable way, nothing serious.

EVELYN. I was only thinking perhaps that's why you never took the plunge -- not being stuck on dancing? Sixty per cent of the married couples in this country first bumped into each other on the dance floor.

WALLY. Sounds kinda clumsy.

She looks at him. He laughs helpfully. She laughs too.

EVELYN. You're pulling me leg. But really, I'm surprised you never felt the need of a partner.

WALLY. I was a rolling stone. A maverick. Besides as a young man I was awful shy.

EVELYN. You're the image of my late hubby. Shy. Suffered with his back. And to look at him on paper you'd have said he could no more dance than fly. But I think it's the challenge, the sense of achievement, the stimulus of other young couples all mad keen to win. You'd find yourself swept along in the mounting excitement of the championships. You must come and see my dresses. They fill two rooms. Together with Freddie's.

WALLY. He wore dresses?

She looks solemn and again he smiles.

EVELYN. I like a man with a sense of humour. No, his suits and shoes. What size shoe are you?

WALLY. Nine and a half.

EVELYN. The same as Freddie!

She has finished her toilet and stows the equipment, closes the mirror. WALLY's still smoking. Sounds of the crowd have died away. A dog barks. Someone shouts it to silence. An owl hoots.

WALLY. Hear that?

EVELYN. What?

WALLY. Listen!

The hoot again.

EVELYN (*scared*). What is it?

WALLY. Only an owl.

EVELYN. I should be so frightened if you weren't here.

WALLY (*putting his hand on hers on table*). I'll take care of you.

EVELYN. Freddie and you! *He* was all for the call of the wild.

WALLY. Don't you ever get to feel romantic?

EVELYN. On occasion.

WALLY. Sure you do.

EVELYN. I sometimes sit for hours, dreaming away, my head in the clouds.

WALLY. You gonna tell me what you dream about?

EVELYN. When I'm in that mood? Oh, acquiring property. I own the house, of course, Freddie's life policy saw to that, but I'm afraid the upkeep comes expensive. So, in my position, I'm obliged to go on taking paying guests. And being a woman alone I'm always afraid they're going to take advantage. I remember one morning when my hubby was alive, I turned round to him I said, 'Darling, that new fellow in the top back – ?' He said, 'What about him?' I said, 'I believe he's got a dog in there.' He said, 'Never!' I said, 'Well, if he hasn't he's been making some very funny noises in the night.' Well, Freddie said he'd ask later and he went off to business. Now this was a day we'd organised a buffet for one of the girls in our formation team. She was like you, lived all alone, so we assumed she'd appreciate the gesture. Well, as I say, I went to the larder to see how my trifle had set. And there it was, just where I'd left it on the shelf in my best cut-glass bowl but, among the cream piping and sponge and tangerines, curled up in the middle, was a dead hamster.

WALLY. Jesus.

EVELYN. He'd gorged himself until his insides burst.

WALLY. That's awful.

EVELYN. Well, it may not sound that much compared to your grizzly bear . . . but when you think of the size of my larder and the size of the Rocky Mountains . . .

WALLY. Sure.

The SCALES gave up the animal fair some time ago but we now hear them droning through 'Lloyd George Knows My Father'.

EVELYN. Your place in Vancouver, you own the freehold?

WALLY. No, I just got a ground-floor room in a boarding-house. It ain't much but it suits me fine.

EVELYN. And you live there all alone?

WALLY. All on my lonesome, yeah. 'Cept for Bruce.

EVELYN. Bruce?

WALLY. My airedale.

EVELYN. No ties, then, no connections?

WALLY. No strings to my affections. That's right.

EVELYN (*sings*). Fancy free and free for anything fancy . . .

MAY *appears in door of bus.*

MAY. Les says we're wasting the gas.

EVELYN. He would.

MAY (*coming to turn out lamp*). He's not too bad.

WALLY. I guess it's time to hit the sack.

SCALES. Father knows Lloyd George . . . , etc.

MAY (*fondly, looking towards them*). Ah, bless their little hearts.

EVELYN. I hope they're not going to keep that up all night.

WALLY *puts out cigar and takes glasses. All go into bus, closing the door behind them.*

Pause. Distant sirens. The singing of 'Lloyd George' falters and finally ceases as GRANT *comes on cautiously from right, looks about. He signals and* TRACY *follows on.*

TRACY (*singing quietly*). Lloyd George knows my father . . . , etc.

They both continue singing but she goes into the toilet tent, zips up the front. GRANT *remains on guard, conducting his daughter offstage, signalling to her to sing up.*

GRANT. Father knows Lloyd George . . .

Scene Three

*In darkness hear cockcrow, then later morning sounds –
birdsong, gusts of radio music, children's cries, etc. borne on
breeze.*

> *Lights up: bright early sunlight. People come across on the
> verge; they look about guardedly. Others are seen moving on
> verge beyond farther line of cars. The people on the verge
> unzip the front of the toilet tent and look in. One makes to go
> in, then stops, turns and shrugs to the others, pointing to
> inside of tent.*

> *MAY comes from bus with the waste-paper spike. She looks
> at the intruders pointedly.*

MAY. Can I help you?

> *They go off, the way they came. She zips up front of tent.*

> *A RACING WALKER crosses the stage swiftly, on the
> verge, right to left, wearing track suit and running shoes.
> MAY comes down to see him off as NANCY comes from
> upstage left, with blankets. MAY picks up litter.*

Good-morning!

NANCY. Oh, good-morning!

MAY. Manage to sleep?

NANCY. Like a top. And you?

MAY. I'm used to Les's snoring, but, what with my brother and
Evelyn at it too, I was put in mind of a silver band.

> NANCY *stows blankets in boot, then locks it and comes
> down.*

NANCY. It would seem like a bar of chocolate for breakfast
unless James finds something in the village.

MAY. When these jams happen, they usually plague the life out
of you with southern fried chicken.

NANCY. There wouldn't be any left by the time they got to us, we're too far in.

MAY. Sit down at our table, do.

NANCY. Absolutely not –

MAY. And share what's left of our food.

NANCY. You've been most generous but I'm quite happy on grass. When you can find any these days. Under the litter.

MAY. Shocking mess!

NANCY. The malaise of Britain: too many people.

MAY. And more pouring in every day, every shade and persuasion.

NANCY. They should have enforced emigration years ago. Got rid of the slackers. And stopped more coming in, too.

MAY. You ought to see our local post office. All in there with their turbans sending money home to God-knows-where. I said to my husband, 'Things are looking darker every day.' I'm not having you on that grass, you'll catch your death with the dew . . . now come into the body of the kirk.

NANCY. I'm extremely obliged.

Sits at table. MAY *goes on clearing litter.*

MAY. We can pool the food that's left. Share and share alike. What there is. If we'd known this was going to be so serious, we'd have been less wasteful yesterday. We could have spread the day's food over.

NANCY. My dear, you're not to blame. Not alone. The modern world is possessed by greed. Any idea of selflessness, fair shares, working for the common weal, seems to have gone by the board.

MAY. The more they get, the more they want.

NANCY. Time will come there'll be none left. And serve them right. You and I remember, don't we?

MAY. The shortages? Yes. Les and I were married in forty-seven. I got extra coupons for my dress.

NANCY (*takes out a packet of cigarettes*). Cigarette?

MAY. Are they menthol?

NANCY. Yes.

MAY. Well, thanks.

They light up. MAY *remains standing, pauses in work.*

NANCY. I never expected to advocate a return to Socialist austerity but, largely by default, the Labour régime stumbled early upon a simple principle: you can't give everyone everything. For instance, everyone can't live in a castle. There aren't enough to go round.

MAY. And even if there were it wouldn't do. No. A few people should live in castles and the rest of us go and look at them.

NANCY. When I was a gel, only well-off people expected cars. Look what happens when you try to put the world on wheels!

She gestures at their situation.

MAY. The happiest time for Les and me was our early years. We didn't have much money but we did see life. If we went in a coach we thought it was our birthday.

NANCY (*nodding*). Simple pleasures.

MAY. I've always enjoyed simple things: working in the dragshop, a nice mystery with tea and biscuits in the interval, a day by the sea with our children. And now our grandchildren. Searching for unpolluted rockpools.

NANCY. The English coast was quite enough for most people, but now who goes there? The mentally handicapped, the senile. Every able-bodied person is off to Tunis for the afternoon.

MAY. We had good times, too, during the war. Real characters people were in those days. Phyllis Griffith, now, an absolute dragon. Died at the age of eighty, still in harness, lighting one cigarette from another. During the blitz she spent every minute in the toilet, no one else could get in, but soon as the all-clear went she was down in Swansea looking at the corpses.

NANCY. That's why you'd love the Highlands.

MAY. Oh yes!

Pause. MAY resumes work. NANCY smokes.

NANCY. Life's still peaceful there, like it used to be during the war. People there don't expect much and they don't get much and they know their place and when I say to my son, 'Why can't life be like that everywhere?' he says, 'You can't interfere with people's freedom.' But do they appreciate freedom?

MAY. No.

NANCY. What they lack is a sense of purpose, moral purpose. You give them a new Freeway, they just take it for granted. When I was a gel, we had wonderful times but we were expected to reciprocate: housing committees, prison visiting, breaking the National Strike . . .

MAY. The juniors in our dragshop, they hardly know they're born!

NANCY. You never tolerate mutinies, I'm sure?

MAY. Mutinies?

NANCY. I believe in calling a spade a spade, Mrs Lorimer – others may call them strikes, I call them mutinies.

MAY. Oh, we don't strike, no –

NANCY. And your husband in his car factory, I'm sure he's no agitator?

MAY. Well, at one time he had some funny ideas but since they put him on the staff –

The RACING WALKER returns from left to right. NANCY pauses and watches him.

NANCY. Is there any sign of the traffic moving?

He gives one bark of laughter and continues off.

MAY. I'd better wake the sleeping beauties.

NANCY. May I use your lavatory tent?

MAY. You can't at the moment. My husband was first up and he's taken the bucket. . . .

JAMES *returns from right, wearing tweedy clothes, carrying walking-stick. Other hand is clasped inside jacket. Seems upset.*

JAMES. Good-morning, May.

MAY. Good-morning.

JAMES. Good-morning, Mother. I hope you slept well?

NANCY. Don't tell me you had no luck. We've nothing for breakfast.

MAY. You can share our dry toast and milkless tea.

JAMES. I rather think we should discuss this *sotto voce*. As you may well imagine, the situation's giving rise to an acute food shortage.

NANCY. How are things at the end of the line?

JAMES. I didn't get to the end of the line. Only as far as the first village. . . . Mrs Lorimer, take these inside quickly –

GRANT *enters, as before, right. Sees* JAMES *take out two cartons of milk.*

GRANT. Good-morning. D'you get that milk in the village?

JAMES. Ahm – yes.

GRANT (*checking wallet*). I hope they accept credit cards. About a mile, isn't it?

JAMES. Nearer two.

GRANT. Four miles walk! Oh, well, the kids are starving, so –

JAMES. I fear you're too late. I had to wait in a queue of several hundred yards and was one of the last to be served.

TRACY (*coming on during this*). Last? Why?

JAMES. Their stocks were exhausted.

TRACY. Surely there'll be more deliveries?

JAMES. Hardly possible till the road's cleared.

GRANT. Can't they use the far lanes to get through?

JAMES. If you recall, the high street forms part of the one-way link-road. The village can only be approached from one direction – and that direction is now jammed solid.

Moment's pause as everyone begins to realise how serious the situation has become.

MAY (*to* GRANT). *Too late, too late, shall be the cry,
Arnold the ice-cream man's gone by.*

TRACY. How am I supposed to manage? My little boy virtually *lives* on milk.

NANCY. Won't he take the breast? Or are you too vain?

TRACY. Sholto's five and a half.

NANCY. Didn't you bring any food with you?

GRANT. There's very little room in the Kamikaze and usually we're at my wife's mother's place in a couple of hours.

MAY. You have one of these.

TRACY. Oh, no, thank you, we couldn't make you –

MAY. We've got no kiddies with us. If I had my grandchildren here, I like to think I might get a helping hand.

GRANT. How much do I owe you?

JAMES. Please don't think of it.

NANCY. Take the other inside quickly, Mrs Lorimer.

TRACY. Well, thanks very much.

GRANT. Any point trying the other way? The Freeway?

JAMES. I was told the queues there are two miles long.

TRACY. It's totally mad, don't you think so? I mean hark at those cows in the sheds down there!

GRANT. And woken up by those bloody hens at dawn and we can't get an egg for breakfast. Krishna!

They go, right. MAY *has gone into bus with milk.*

NANCY. Have they stopped people joining on the end?

JAMES. I put that question to an Autoguard who was setting up a membership booth in the village. He said no.

NANCY. Well, they must.

A helicopter passes from right to left. The battering sound and again the blowing of the grass. NANCY *and* JAMES *look up to it. It recedes.*

JAMES. The Seventeenth Gloucestershire Light Horse! My old regiment!

LES *comes from upstage, left between other vehicles. He is carrying a chemical lavatory bucket, with the lid closed. He watches helicopter go, comes on to verge and puts down bucket. Wipes brow with handkerchief.*

Good morning, Les.

LES. Morning, all.

JAMES. You should have waited. I'd have helped with that.

LES. Good job I didn't. Bad enough as it was finding a place to empty it where the families were still asleep. Couple of times they woke up while I was trying to do it. Got very nasty.

Unzips front of tent and takes out plastic bottle of chemical.

I was pouring it over the fence, of course, on to the field the other side but . . . understandable people not wanting that outside their front door. Odourless, but still unsightly.

Pours chemical into bucket.

NANCY. It wasn't nearly full last night.

LES. And d'you know what? I reckon people have been availing themselves in the hours of darkness.

JAMES. Do you really?

LES. People without facilities.

JAMES. That's intolerable.

LES. Can't blame them. Very awkward.

Puts bucket and bottle in tent, leaves flap open.

JAMES. We'll post a guard. I'll work out a duty roster.

LES. You reckon?

JAMES. Much as it goes against the grain, we can't have you emptying that bucket every five minutes.

NANCY. No indeed! There are far more pressing jobs to be done. Have you had a chance to look at our tyre yet?

LES. Not yet, no.

NANCY. That sort of thing.

She goes into tent, zips front. MAY comes from bus. JAMES has gone to open boot of his car and put in stick. He rummages. MAY brings on more rubbish to put in the pedal-bin.

MAY. *Home is the sailor, home from the sea*
And the hunter home from the hill.
D'you manage, love?

LES. Just about. Like to wash my hands.

MAY. The pitcher's empty. Evelyn's used the last for tea. *And* she had to use the gas, there's no paper left for the Vesuvius.

LES. P'raps a drop in the kettle for me.

JAMES (*coming down with shotgun*). Les, I hope you won't consider this melodramatic but we may need to make a show of arms.

LES. Go on.

JAMES. A polite request may not cut much ice with people desperate for a pee. I'm remembering the ugly scene in the village hypermarket. Can you handle a gun?

LES. I don't know. Must be thirty years since I —

JAMES. No matter. A glimpse will almost certainly suffice.

MAY. What for?

LES (*bewildered*). Keep strangers out the toilet.

MAY (*uncertain*). Oh?

JAMES. I don't travel armed in the ordinary way. So happens this weapon's been with my gunsmith.

EVELYN *comes from bus.*

EVELYN. I found a tomato juice in the cocktail cabinet. You'd like it for breakfast, I expect?

LES. Long as you don't come whining to me later on when you want a Bloody Mary.

MAY. Have to make it a Virgin Mary.

EVELYN. The vodka's gone in any case . . .

WALLY *comes from the road, up left.*

WALLY. Hi. Good-morning.

JAMES. Good-morning.

LES. Where've you been? I thought you were still in the Land of Nod.

EVELYN. Been laying breakfast all round your bunk, curtains drawn and everything.

WALLY. Got up early. Been down in the meadow yonder, picking mushrooms and blackberries.

Shows two plastic bags of fruit.

JAMES. How extremely enterprising of you!

WALLY. May be a little squashed. Had to keep them outa sight, people are getting hungry.

MAY (*taking bags*). My clever old brother!

EVELYN. We're eating inside this morning.

LES. I bet there's a good few toadstools amongst them.

WALLY. D'you sleep tight, Evelyn?

EVELYN. Not too bad, considering the quiet . . .

Goes into bus, taking bags of food.

WALLY. Got a shotgun, James?

JAMES. I judged it might be prudent to mount a guard. Over the loo.

WALLY. Yeah?

Takes gun and looks at it, working the breech, etc. NANCY has come from the tent.

A NURSE comes on, down left, the first person to appear on our side of the fence. She carries a red-cross satchel, wears traditional uniform but rubber boots on feet, looks tired, grubby, anxious, aged eighteen plus.

Everyone looks at her, then as she turns towards left, they also turn to see what follows. Two STRETCHER-BEARERS carry on a YOUNG MAN with cropped head and some face hair. He's covered mostly by blanket but some wounds can be seen. BEARERS are Indian or North African.

NANCY (*at fence*). Casualties? Through here?

NURSE (*to BEARERS*). You all right? Have a rest.

NANCY. Why are you bringing casualties through here?

MAY. Would you like some tea?

NURSE. Thanks very much.

NANCY. Good girl, May. Tea, as quick as you can.

> MAY *goes into bus as* GRANT *and* TRACY *wander on from their car. Everyone tends to move down to the fence for a good view of the casualty. The* BEARERS *put him down and stretch.*

Why aren't the casualties going by helicopter?

NURSE. They're for reporters and VIPs.

JAMES. The Freeway itself then? The service tracks?

NURSE. Accident victims only.

> *She makes the casualty more comfortable. He is unconscious.*

NANCY. Then who's this?

NURSE. A Scrubber.

> *General surprise, curiosity, some draw back.*

JAMES. They're not firing on the Scrubbers?

NURSE. All they told us was this fellow was in a group that started taking off their clothes and walking out to embrace the guards and offering posies of wayside flowers. One of the patrolmen panicked and fired three times in self-defence.

NANCY. Where are you taking him?

NURSE. Cottage hospital, the end of the linkroad.

NANCY. A National Health hospital?

TRACY. Oh, no!

GRANT. Poor bastard!

NURSE. I'm only doing what I'm told.

NANCY. He must be taught a lesson.

TRACY. All the same . . .

JAMES. Is it a sizeable demonstration?

NURSE. I believe it's over. They're helping the police with their inquiries.

NANCY. High time.

LES. How many were there?

NURSE. A dozen or so.

LES. And managed to cause a hold-up over a hundred miles long. Anyone that does that deserves no mercy.

JAMES. This will put paid once and for all to the Scrubbers' case against the Freeway. Their Puritanical performances on television, together with some fashionable indecency, have won them a measure of popular support. But I have always maintained that if the electorate heard their argument, they would see that it demands self-sacrifice. And seeing that, they would reject it.

MAY *comes from bus with cups on tray.*

MAY. We're out of sugar, I'm afraid.

NURSE. Oh, thanks.

MAY Where are you taking him?

NURSE. Hospital in the village.

MAY. Poor kid.

LES (*turning on her*). He brought all this hardship on innocent people . . . halted the Freeway . . . old-age pensioners without toilets . . . they're no better than the A-rabs.

TRACY. Pardon me, I thought their idea was to bring the community back to a sense of community. I'm not saying theirs is the right way but surely –

LES. What? Share and share alike? Lot of rubbish! Public transport? Going *where* people tell you *when* they tell you. Call that freedom?

JAMES. Ah, but, Les, you forget that, whereas you and I would defend that freedom to the last drop of blood, the Scrubbers and their followers –

NANCY. Come on, James, wholesale freedom won't wash. Not for all this lot! A little bit here and there, by all means, but we can't let people wallow in it.

MAY (*to* NURSE). So is it all over now?

NURSE. The demo? Yes.

MAY. We'll be moving then. None too soon.

NURSE. Shouldn't count on that. Come on, Abdul . . .

The BEARERS *finish their tea and give cups back to* JAMES.

JAMES. How d'you mean?

NURSE. There's a work to rule or something. Farther up the Freeway. Nice cup of tea, thanks very much.

LES. Work to rule? Who's working to rule? Who said?

NURSE. Some of the Autoguards were saying. I didn't listen, I was busy.

NANCY *has taken a note from her purse and gives it to* NURSE.

NANCY. You'll see he's well looked after, won't you? Give the least harmful treatment?

NURSE. He'll be all right.

They go.

MAY. I wonder if his mother knows where he is? Not a bad-looking boy! If only he'd come to his senses, grow his hair, get a nice job and a car . . .

JAMES. Mother, I marvel at your buying him preferential treatment.

NANCY. I deplore the Scrubbers' methods, but their message makes sense. They want a return to a hardier, simpler way of life.

JAMES. A profoundly reactionary movement –

NANCY. Whereas your blessed unions are obstructing the
Freeway just as effectively and for what? Greed. A bigger slice
of the cake.

LES. Now just a minute, ma'am. We don't know yet what's
happening on the Freeway but whatever that may be I can't
allow you to mention those perverts in the same breath as a
properly constituted trades union.

JAMES. Hear, hear.

LES. I come from a Labour family – you'll forgive me speaking
frankly, James?

JAMES. My dear Les, your loyal support for the Labour
movement only renews my faith in the *status quo*. Everything
in its proper place.

LES. My father was a Labour man and his father before him.
They spent half their lives queuing up for the charity handout,
licking the boss's BTM, you'll excuse my French? I wonder
what the Scrubbers would think of walking if they'd had to
march all the way from Jarrow to make themselves heard in
London?

MAY. Your father never marched from Jarrow. Nor your
grandpa.

LES. Who said they did?

MAY. They lived in East Ham.

LES. I know that.

MAY. They used to go up West on the Fifteen bus.

LES. I only said they were working men. And their first taste of
freedom was when my old man got a secondhand Prefect.
Middle-aged he was by then. Spent his life making cars for
other people and now he had his own. That old banger was a
magic carpet to my dad! But if you'd tried to tell him his son
would one day own a centrally heated Motor Home he'd have

told you to pull the other. I got my own grandstand for point-to-points!

LES *displays his bus to the others: this is a Credo.*

If we feel like an Elizabethan blow-out, with jousting as an optional extra, then it's up the Freeway to Castle Howard. Anyone wants a look at Africa, we poodle down through France, ninety ninety-five, no sense pushing, over the Pyrenees, take in a bull-fight. Then by ferry to Tangiers, Marrakesh, Casablanca, nothing to it. Tea in the Sultan's Palace, use a bit of film on the beggar boys, get some movie-shots of May on a camel –

MAY. Never again!

LES. – have a peek at the belly-dancers.

MAY. And the countryside can be super too, if you had the time to look.

LES. We've parked the Cherokee in some five-star car-parks, no doubt about that.

MAY. Red Square, all the old women cleaning up with their dustettes. Milan Piazza's got the best facilities. The Wailing Wall in Jerusalem wasn't much to write home about.

LES. A real let-down.

MAY. But I think my favourite for atmosphere is Mozart's house with the Viennese waltzes on the speakers.

LES. And all without leaving home – because our home's there with us!

TRACY. Oh, come on, you talk about Morocco, *I* used to be a belly-dancer. Before my husband and I were married. *And* I worked the Moroccan circuit.

GRANT. Perhaps it was you they saw.

TRACY. Perhaps. You drove out in your Motor Home and I flew from Gatwick. Don't you see that's absurd?

GRANT. Tracy would gladly have danced for you at home – in Henley-on-Thamesway.

LES. Belly-dancing was all laid on in the Sultan's Palace. All included in the one price. Tour, belly-dancing, savoury tea.

TRACY. It's not that I'm one of those ecology nuts –

GRANT. That whole Environment thing has been so commercialised!

TRACY. – but I like to think there'll be some country left when Stephanie and Sholto grow up.

GRANT. Right!

JAMES (*heatedly*). Arnold of Rugby rejoiced at the coming of the railway age, because he saw in it the end of feudalism. Perhaps he was premature. But the *car* is the most powerful democratic instrument yet conceived. More effective than good intentions, more eloquent than assemblies. You cannot tyrannise the man with a Motor Home!

NANCY. While you're so busy not tyrannising people you don't seem to have noticed that the world's become one vast garage!

JAMES. The great cultures thrive, virtually unscathed. London is London still.

NANCY. Hyde Car Park, St James's Car Park, Regent's –

JAMES. Hostages to fortune.

NANCY. Thamesway.

JAMES. As an open river the Thames had been obsolete for years.

NANCY. The Seine too, I suppose? I remember when you could walk along its banks.

JAMES. Les can drive his Cherokee into the very heart of Paris, park by the Louvre, saunter through Île Saint-Louis –

LES. Where the French fall down is in their toilets. Don't you think so, James?

JAMES (*to* NANCY). Freedom of choice is more than river banks! The people have chosen traffic jams. Freely.

LES. I say, where the French fall down is in their toilets.

JAMES. I've never seen them do that, no . . .

MAY. Oh, yes, all through France, plenty of well-kept wargraves, nice crispy leaves, but finding a decent toilet's another story.

TRACY. That's what I came to ask – if I could possibly use your tent? My legs have been crossed ever since those birds woke me up at dawn.

LES. You the people used it last night?

GRANT. Not the only ones. There was a constant to-and-fro. I was singing lullabies into the early hours so –

LES. Then I'm supposed to empty it?

TRACY. Just that being next-door neighbours –

MAY. That's all right, dear, you go on.

GRANT. Thank you. Thanks a lot.

TRACY *crosses to tent, goes in, zips up.* GRANT *waits.* EVELYN *comes from Motor Home.*

EVELYN. First sitting for breakfast. Mushrooms on toast, tomato juice –

LES. Keep your voice down, Evelyn.

She looks about nervously. MAY *collects cups left by* NURSE. *Group breaks up.*

EVELYN. I can take three of you.

MAY. My lady, you go in first.

NANCY (*moving towards door of bus*). Are you sure it's no inconvenience?

Follows EVELYN *in.* WALLY *makes to follow.*

LES. James, you first. Wally can wait.

JAMES. Quite out of the question.

LES. Then I'll wait with you.

JAMES. How kind.

LES. Leave us some, mind, Wally, I know you.

> WALLY *follows* MAY *into bus.* JAMES *and* LES *remain,*
> GRANT *going off right to his car.*

> The only hearty thing about him, his appetite.

JAMES. Les, may I say how inspiring it was to hear you defend
our cherished way of life so warmly?

LES. I never meant to argue the point with Lady Rhyne, only –

JAMES. Please! Mother's extreme views sometimes cause her to
lie down with some quite unsuitable bedfellows. Scrubbers,
trendy-wendies, breast-beaters. How did Burke put it, d'you
remember? Yes: it is a general popular error to imagine the
loudest complainers for the public to be most anxious for its
welfare.

LES. Fair enough.

JAMES. I'm happy to say the PM has never for a moment been
taken in by their pleas for the simple life. What he rather
quaintly calls The Golden Age Bit.

LES. Who's that?

JAMES. The Prime Minister.

LES. Ah.

JAMES. You've never met?

LES. He came round the works one day. Our paths crossed in
Paint, Trim and Assembly.

JAMES. What impression did you form?

LES. I didn't get all that close.

JAMES. Great shame because I'm sure that, despite your doctrinal differences, you'd find him a man after your own heart. And I shall certainly pass on to him your support for his policy of a car to every citizen.

LES. Fair enough.

JAMES. On Tuesday, in fact. He'll be at our game lodge for a few days' stalking. We're driving up to make it ready and my wife's arriving later by air. So if you find your ears burning, you'll know the name Les Lorimer is being bandied about over the port and Stilton. With your permission?

LES. That's all right.

JAMES. Much obliged.

LES. What sort of a fellow is he?

JAMES. Most agreeable.

LES. A lot of the lads on the floor reckon he's a bit lah-de-dah, you know, with his hunting, shooting and fishing.

JAMES. You may assure them that he hides an essentially forward-looking character behind a studiously antique manner. No Englishman would trust him otherwise. Look at the harm done to the government's image by that awful little shit, his cousin.

LES. Who?

JAMES. The Minister for Growth.

LES. Used to be a woman?

JAMES. That's him.

> TRACY *comes from tent and looks for* GRANT, *who comes from downstage of tent bringing children's plastic pot, which* TRACY *takes in. Suddenly a loudspeaker voice from behind the audience. Everyone onstage looks towards it.*

VOICE. Attention, please, attention, all travellers. Under its present emergency powers, the Royal Freeways and Linkroads

Authority has issued a movement order, the purpose of which is to restrict individual and collective mobility. Travellers may, by mutual agreement, enjoy the recreational facilities of those areas adjacent to their own on either side but longer journeys will be made only in emergencies, for which special passes will be required.

LES. What we going to eat if we can't go shopping?

VOICE. Voluntary services will be providing meals on wheels.

TRACY *comes out.*

LES *looks at* GRANT, *crosses to tent, zips up front.* TRACY *takes* GRANT'*s arm and leads him off, up right.*

Trespassers may be detained and questioned by armed rangers.

JAMES. This makes an armed guard imperative.

LES. People without facilities got to go somewhere.

VOICE. We hope for everyone's sake that the Wreckers' and Breakers' Union will accept the government's generous pay offer soon and help us get the Freeway moving again. Thank you.

LES. What's the unions got to do with it?

JAMES. Evidently some wage dispute's got stuck in the pipeline.

COX *has come on from the right. Speaker's voice is heard repeating the message off left for another section of linkroad.*

COX. Morning, all.

JAMES. Sergeant Cox, you can surely put us in the picture? How are the unions involved?

COX (*taking off cap, scratching head*). Lord above, I don't dabble in politics, my lord. I leave those to our friends in Whitehall.

LES. Last we heard it was the Scrubbers. What's the Wreckers got to do with it?

COX. I should like a word with Lord Rhyne, sir, if you wouldn't mind. (*Pointedly.*) In private.

LES (*taking hint, going into bus*). I'll see if breakfast's up yet.

JAMES. How very kind of you.

COX *takes from his satchel a net bag containing oranges and chocolate. At the same time, JAMES takes out wallet and a letter. Food and a banknote change hands.*

I'm extremely grateful.

COX. That's what we're here for, my lord.

JAMES. Could I put myself yet deeper in your debt by asking you to see this note's delivered?

COX. Leave it to me, sir.

JAMES. Glorious weather.

COX. Just what the gardens need.

Sound of sirens off left on Freeway. COX stows letter in satchel. LES looks out of bus.

LES. When you want it, James.

JAMES. Are you sure there's enough to spare?

LES. Fair shares for all.

JAMES goes in. COX looks at envelope.

COX. Downing Street?

Announcement continues off left.

VOICE. Attention, please, attention, all travellers. Under its present . . ., etc.

Loud outcry from offstage listeners. COX was moving across to left, about to continue along the road but the angry sound stops him.

The noise breaks out again, with some bleating and a lot of yelling. This time it continues and turns into unison singing of

'Why Are We Waiting?'. COX, *without haste or any betrayal of indecision, turns about and makes off in the direction he came, right.*

Singing rises to climax and police whistles are blown as the lights fade.

ACT TWO

Scene One

A news bulletin from House Speakers.

NEWSMAN. The Queen was at Greenwich today to welcome the Amir of Kuwindi on his first state visit to the United Kingdom. A report from our Royalty Correspondent:

WOMAN REPORTER. Many thousands of people added their modern motley to the already resplendent panoply of this right royal occasion. Not a few had spilled from office blocks lining the north embankment of Thamesway, some were tourists on a few days' safari in the capital and there was a party of Kuwindi nationals whose traditional costume contrasted gaily with the sombre Nagasaki knickers of the crowd. The Amir arrived from Essex airport, an impressive figure whose sudden bursts of uncontrollable laughter soon won the hearts of the crowd and earned him the title Merry Monarch. Her Majesty awaited him on the steps of Wren's Naval College, beside it the rigging of *Cutty Sark* dwarfing the brave outline of *Gipsy Moth*. And, behind, as the sun shone at the bidding of the state trumpets, rose the dazzling glitter of Greenwich Car Park. After exchanging greetings, the two sovereigns went walkabout among a casual throng of powerful merchant bankers. Then, almost as if by magic, it seemed, the royal motorcade was off upstream to Westminster and the Palace!

Lights up.

Late evening. Moonlight.

EVELYN's radio is on the table, beside a lighted gazlamp. The three families are standing downstage at the fence, each holding a vessel of some kind, waiting, faces turned towards right. They span the whole width, left to right: JAMES, EVELYN, LES, MAY, NANCY, GRANT, WALLY and TRACY.

The side panel is open, as at end of Act One, revealing the kitchen.

Sound FX from speakers replace voice: cannon, fanfares, ceremonial.

From the right a water-tank on wheels is pulled by two WATERMEN, uniformed West Indians. They use two half-litre bottles to measure out water, one filling from tap, the other pouring into the waiting vessels. A spotlight follows their work.

WATERMAN. Water! Get your water here!

Pours TRACY's. She expects more.

TRACY. That all?

WATERMAN. Half a litre each.

TRACY. And two children?

WATERMAN. Where? (*As she points.*) Another litre.

GRANT. How long's that supposed to last?

WATERMAN. Same time tomorrow night.

GRANT. Krishna!

WATERMEN *go on to* WALLY.

NANCY. That's impossible. I'm sure you could allow us more than that. I understand there must be rationing but –

WATERMAN. Half a litre each, lady. I don't make the rules, I'm only doing my job.

GRANT and TRACY go off, right, to car. WALLY goes up to bus with his ration, leaves it, comes down again with another jug or pan and takes a new place between EVELYN and LES.

(*Pouring hers.*) Any case you got a Motor Home. They carry a hundred litres. More.

NANCY. That's not ours. No, no.

WATERMEN move on to MAY.

MAY. No, that's ours, but it's less than a year old so it's not in working order yet.

LES. We only had a jerrican and that's all gone.

WATERMAN. Should have been more careful when you had it.

NANCY has taken out purse and MAY takes her water to bus.

NANCY. It's barely enough to wash one's hands.

WATERMAN. This is for drinking. There's people on the Freeway had none at all.

WALLY gets a second ration and goes up to pour it into the first. No one seems to notice. NANCY has found a banknote. The doling out continues.

NEWSMAN. Afterwards the Amir told reporters how surprised and dismayed he'd been to see so many empty parking spaces along the banks of Thamesway. He gave one of his roars of laughter and wondered whether Britain still deserved her position as a second-rate power if so few of her citizens could afford cars. Or petrol? He added, laughing even louder.

All have now been served. The men are going off, left. JAMES, LES, EVELYN, MAY and WALLY go to kitchen.

WATERMAN. Water! Get your water here!

NANCY. I say, look here! We'll make it worth your while . . .

They go off. She waves money and follows. In the kitchen there are furtive preparations.

NANCY returns, putting banknote back into her purse. She sits at the table.

Radio crackles and we hear the distorted voice of the NEWSMAN. NANCY turns up volume, but no use.

NEWSMAN. . . . Church leaders and TV stars have joined the government's plea to get the Freeway moving. In places of worship throughout the country . . .

Fades for good. NANCY shakes the radio then switches off.

NANCY. Too much! Really!

Others have come from bus and stand formally behind her. MAY and EVELYN carry plates, JAMES brings glasses on a tray and WALLY a glass jug.

MAY (*singing*). Happy birthday to you –

EVELYN, LES & WALLY. Happy birthday to you –

ALL. Happy birthday, dear –

JAMES (*as others falter*). – Mother! –

ALL. Happy birthday to you!

NANCY. How terribly kind. You really shouldn't have.

They put the plates on the table, on one a bar of chocolate, on the other some mandarins, broken into segments.

EVELYN. Don't thank us. Your son provided the food.

LES. Black market.

JAMES. I fear so, what little there is. But I couldn't allow your birthday to pass without some ceremony, however humble. Many happy returns, my dear.

He kisses her.

WALLY. Only got water to drink.

MAY. And none too much of that.

A glass is poured for each.

LES. That's where *my* little surprise comes in.

Shows small glass of red liquid.

The very last drop of Cherry Heering.

NANCY. For me? I simply couldn't.

MAY. No arguing now.

NANCY. Most kind.

LES. James ought to propose the toast.

JAMES. Indeed. As a political animal, I am bound to observe Robert Frost's precept that – ahm – a diplomat is a man who always remembers a woman's birthday but never her age. So – sincere congratulations, Mother, and may your future celebrations be in rather more agreeable surroundings. Many happy returns!

ALL. Lady Rhyne, many happy returns, etc.

NANCY (*touched*). Dear friends – more agreeable circumstances, yes, perhaps, but surely not more pleasant company.

JAMES. Hear, hear.

NANCY. Or more generous. I sometimes look at our countrymen today, the spoon-fed young, the factory workers living on the fat of the land, the dreadful people they put on television with their awful voices, and I wonder if all sense of obligation has quite gone with the wind. But meeting you has reminded me of the essential decency of the British, their love of the old ways. The old order changeth certainly but in such a fashion that here in England at least it never quite yields place to new. We are still in our places, all of us, despite the efforts of trade unions, TV communists –

JAMES (*firmly*). Mother, will you break the chocolate or shall I?

NANCY. Oh, yes, I will. You'd crumble or melt it.

JAMES. May has already divided the mandarins.

Watched hungrily, NANCY breaks the bar into squares. Church bells are borne on the wind.

That can't be Evensong surely, it's far too late?

NANCY. Apparently the clergy are leading urgent prayers for the mutiny to be put down.

EVELYN. Gracious! Sunday! We should be back at business tomorrow.

Hear off, right, TRACY and GRANT pacifying a child with another song.

SCALES. When we are married we'll have sausages for tea, Sausages for tea – sausages for tea – sausages for tea –

Child cries louder.

TRACY (*off*). All right, love, we won't sing that one. 'What shall we do with the drunken sailor?' –

As they sing it, MAY turns back.

MAY. Poor kiddies are hungry.

Quickly, almost furtively, they swallow their oranges and chocolate.
Women sitting at table, men standing round. A searchlight sweeps across, settles on them for a moment, they squint into it, it moves on.

Why do they keep doing that?

LES. Some of the men with young kiddies, they're ganging up, roving about, breaking the movement order, taking food by force –

EVELYN. Oh, my lord!

WALLY. Don't you worry your pretty little head. We'll take care of you.

JAMES. You're well protected, Evelyn, I assure you.

WALLY. James's got a gun.

EVELYN. I can't stand bangs.

LES. You haven't touched your Cherry Heering.

NANCY (*sipping it, smiling*). Delicious.

LES. Too sweet for me, but I know the ladies like it.

Bells again.

WALLY. I seen that church when I was down the valley . . . real olde worlde with a country churchyard . . .

JAMES. I should have joined them in prayer had it not been forbidden to climb the –

Gazlamp flickers. They all look at it while bells give way to other sounds – sirens, a speaker, a scream.

EVELYN. What's that?

WALLY. Kids playing. Hey, didn't a little bird tell me it's Evelyn's birthday this week too?

EVELYN laughs excitedly.

And how many candles will be on your cake?

JAMES. Wally, I appeal to you to remember Robert Frost.

EVELYN. I don't mind telling. Twenty-one!

MAY laughs and sings.

MAY. She's got the key of the door
Never been twenty-one before –

EVELYN. That's better. A song to cheer us up.

MAY. Music hath charms to soothe the savage breast.

EVELYN. Let's find some. We can dance as well. Who'll be my partner? Can anyone tango?

Switches on radio but no sound comes.

NANCY. The wireless is finished. Kaput.

LES (*turning it up in vain*). Shouldn't have wasted all the juice on ballroom music.

EVELYN (*hotly*). It's my portable! Dancing is my life! Are you telling me how to use my own things?

LES. Steady, steady, simmer down –

EVELYN. If you had your way it would be news, news, news, party politics. How we're falling behind the rest of Europe and must get bigger lorries to catch up and the Lord knows what! Where's the fun in that?

LES. Don't bite my head off – blimey O'Riley!

EVELYN. People want something cheerful, to take you out of yourself, so we can't hear those blessed bells, they're enough to drive you cracked.

NANCY. Pull yourself together, young woman.

MAY (*comforting*). There, there, love –

EVELYN. I don't know which is worse, the quiet or the bells and screams –

LES. If people are going to lose their sense of humour –

EVELYN. What's funny about it? Look at us all! What is there to laugh at?

Cries. Others try to pacify her.

MAY. Never mind, love – worse things happen at sea.

WALLY *suddenly sings.*

WALLY. Last night you slept in a goose-feather bed
With the sheet turned down so bravely oh,
But tonight you will sleep in a cold open field

Along with the raggle-taggle gypsies oh –

MAY. That's not very cheerful. Give us one of your army songs, Wally.

LES. Keep it clean. Mixed company.

WALLY. Give you one about the navy, one you can all join in. You join in, Evelyn?

She nods bravely. WALLY stands apart and sings.

Sons of the sea –
Bobbing up and down like this –

Each time he sings this he bounces on his feet.

Sailing every ocean –
Bobbing up and down like this –

Sings it through, replacing every other line with this phrase and bouncing to it. The others gradually join in, as he bids them. Even JAMES and NANCY find themselves bouncing the second time round until the spotlight sweeps across and finds them. They stop ridiculously as it lingers on them. The light goes on.

EVELYN. I'm not sitting down again, not now I'm on my feet. Isn't someone going to ask me to dance?

LES. Better make it the last waltz.

WALLY. Maybe I can manage that.

MAY sings a popular waltz. WALLY bows to EVELYN and they start dancing. Other voices join MAY's and JAMES crosses and invites her. WALLY falters.

Pardon me.

EVELYN. Oh, no, you're a natural. On a sprung floor in Freddie's pumps, you'd soon get the feel.
Sings with others for some moments. MAY, NANCY and LES provide music but other neighbours drift in from surrounding

vehicles, including GRANT *and* TRACY. *They join the singing, perhaps dance.* EVELYN *begins to imitate a TV Presenter.*

When she's not dancing, Evelyn's in the wig department of a large dragshop. Wally hails from British Columbia and used to be with the CPR.

The gazlamp splutters and goes out. Completely dark. Singing dies away. Dance stops.

Oh, no!

LES. That's the end of that.

MAY. Put the kitchen light on.

LES. Run the batteries down? Economy's even more essential now –

WALLY. Who cares? It's fine in the moonlight. Don't you think so? (*Sings.*) *By the light of the silvery moon –*

People join in again and the dancing resumes. They have hardly started when there is a sound of amplified tubular bells from speakers behind the audience.

VOICE (*speakers*). Attention, please! That signal is the curfew.

Groans and a few sheep bleats. Voice continues over.

Travellers should now return to their vehicles and when the sound is heard again, it will be the signal for Lights Out.

The party breaks up with some complaining. The furniture is folded and stowed by LES, WALLY *and* JAMES. GRANT *gets sleeping bag from bonnet-boot of his sports car, then goes off. Women clear food utensils.*

The grass verge should be cleared of furniture. The Linkroads Authority will not be responsible for loss or damage. Groups of transient workers are known to be plundering up and down the Freeway, so please ensure that doors and windows are fully secured.

EVELYN. Lord above! I said at the time they should never have let them in the country. They're so hard to see in the dark.

JAMES goes to boot of car, where NANCY is already looking for nightclothes. EVELYN and MAY go into bus.

VOICE. Reveille will be at six hundred hours. Inflammable material such as paper and plastic will be burnt before seven hundred. Immediate disposal of perishables will be delayed due to a work-to-rule in sympathy with the Wreckers' Union.

NANCY. That settles it! We *must* have martial law.

JAMES. Please, Mother –

NANCY. The alternative is epidemic! Which d'you want?

Angrily goes into bus, closing door. JAMES loads shell into his gun. The three men assemble, centre.

JAMES. Two rounds each, I believe you follow me, Les.

LES. Yes and Wally's last. The car open?

JAMES. Yes. I'll wake you at one. Good-night.

They say good-night and go off, up left. JAMES patrols the area.

VOICE (*speakers*). It is strictly forbidden to feed Alsatians patrolling the perimeter fence. Animal-lovers are reminded that guard-dogs are trained to appear hungry. Keep your distance and do not – repeat not – allow children to pat their muzzles. I am empowered by the Royal Freeway Authority to wish you pleasant dreams.

The curfew signal is repeated and dies away. The announcement is repeated at a distance. Spotlight flashes across and JAMES dodges behind the toilet tent, unseen. The spotlight examines the area then moves on.
   Man's voice raised in anger, siren on Freeway, last phrase of church bells from the village. JAMES comes from hiding as the light goes. TRACY and GRANT begin wearily singing

'Old MacDonald Had a Farm' and JAMES *goes into tent. The barrel of his gun protrudes between the flaps.*
  Lights out.

Scene Two

During the blackout, sound of animals and cockcrow. Then the cry of a woman in labour. Then two shots, some way off. Angry dog barks.

  Light up on empty stage: a dull, cold light without shadows, and as the scene proceeds, it becomes more clouded.

  LES *comes from up left, obviously from sleep.* JAMES *follows, unrolling shirt-sleeves.*

JAMES. Those shots sounded close.

LES. No sign of Wally.

  They approach the tent.

  Wally! You in there?

  WALLY *comes stealthily from up right, far side of road, carrying rifle and more food slung over shoulder in net bag. He looks an accustomed hunter.*

JAMES. Sleeping, d'you think?

  LES *unzips tent.* WALLY *approaches from behind, watching with interest. Raises gun to shoulder.*

WALLY. Get your arse outa there! That's a private toilet.

  They turn. He pulls trigger but it's not loaded.

LES. Where've you been?

WALLY. Village over the hill.

  Brings dead pigeon from jacket.

  Had to use both shells. I'm a little rusty.

JAMES. Well done!

LES. You left the teepee unattended.

WALLY. Come on Les. They're doing that in the open.

LES. We're not.

WALLY. Might as well. Being the only ones with a toilet is kind of silly, don't you think? James, what do you say? If nobody has any toilets, what have we got to lose?

JAMES. Nothing but our chains?

WALLY and JAMES laugh together.

LES (*resentfully*). Your idea to mount a guard.

JAMES. Situations alter. I rather incline to Wally's pragmatical approach.

Takes gun from WALLY.

Certainly the first time this has been used for poaching.

WALLY. Nearly had to shoot a guard-dog but he lost my scent.

JAMES. You shouldn't take such risks.

WALLY. The other side there ain't so many patrols. Ground's too rough. No crops. Not many rangers. This is from the village church.

Shows contents of bag: vegetables, bread, fruit.

JAMES. A Harvest Festival, I imagine.

LES. Stealing from a church? Blimey O'Riley!

JAMES. Such offerings go to the needy of the parish. I rather think we might qualify.

WALLY. Say grace over it.

LES. Don't know if they can pluck this bird. Looks like we're in for some rain at last.

Goes with food into bus. WALLY and JAMES go up left,

WALLY *to exit, JAMES to open boot and put in gun.*
NANCY *comes from left, goes to door of bus, shouts in. Now*
wearing trousers.

NANCY. Come along, you gels, there's work to do. Bring
blankets and all your water to the pink Pegasus six cars up.
Don't hang about. Young woman with a poor sense of
occasion has gone into labour. Even the voluntary ambulance
brigades have mutinied now so she's going to need all the help
we can give her.

JAMES. Good-morning, Mother. I'd no idea you were up.

NANCY. Didn't you hear those cries?

JAMES. Cries?

NANCY. Fine guards you make.

JAMES. Anything I can do?

NANCY. You! Good God!

Gives bark of laughter and goes. He comes down, considering
this as PAYNE enters from up left.

PAYNE. Morning, my lord. Just came ahead to make sure
you're here. Anyone else about, sir?

Brusquely searches area.

JAMES. They're in the Cherokee and at the car – why?

PAYNE *signals to COX who has come on upstage. He signals*
off and several camouflaged troopers come on with small
arms, checking out grounds, etc., followed by plainclothes
security man with walkie-talkie. He shuts door of bus, posts
troopers, signals to COX, who signals off.

PAYNE. Visitor for you, sir. The Minister of Movement.

BARRY enters by road, with photographer; fifty, ruddy face,
much of it hidden by joke moustache, a suburban squire in
tweedy checks, carrying shooting-stick.

JAMES. Barry!

BARRY. James! I couldn't believe you were really stuck in this bloody shambles! The Prime Minister couldn't believe it either, and, as he knew I was coming to do a traditional walkabout, he asked me to find you.

JAMES. A most agreeable surprise. However, my note was only to explain that Mother and I shan't be at Glencromarty to welcome him. The staff expect him and he knows my ghillie from my father's days so –

BARRY. Where *is* Nancy?

JAMES. Delivering a baby.

BARRY. She doesn't change.

JAMES. That would be against her principles.

BARRY *moves down to fence and breathes deeply.*

BARRY. Aah! That's better.

JAMES. One of your company's superphosphates.

BARRY. You ought to smell the Freeway!

JAMES. Is it bad?

BARRY. Three lanes of traffic jammed solid for eighty miles? For three days and nights? You wouldn't chuckle it's bad. I was longing to get away from Town and the Amir of Kuwindi's bean feast but when I got a whiff of that – !

JAMES. I haven't seen him for years. Since school, in fact.

BARRY. I might have guessed you'd know him.

JAMES. He fagged for me. Always wanting to be beaten. Nasty little turd.

BARRY. No change there, except he's grown a bit. But the Freeway was one worse.

JAMES. I'm glad you've seen for yourself. Now perhaps you'll get things moving.

BARRY. Any suggestions how?

JAMES. Surely a wage settlement with the Wreckers' Union?
Get Bill Brewer to rally the moderates for a show of strength
with the extremists. A swift return to work, open the
bottlenecks, get the traffic moving.

BARRY. Of course, you've had no private information. New
experience for you, knowing only what the public knows. The
chief blame lies with your friend Willie in Housing. Weren't
you at Eton with him too?

JAMES. Oxford.

BARRY. Those bottlenecks at the northern exits could only be
cleared by wholesale demolition. All those market crosses and
railway bridges kept up by crackpot preservationists, they'd
have been easy. But the main obstacles aren't village pumps,
they're post-war housing estates, geriatric homes, obsolete
blocks of flats. You can't knock them down because of the
people living there. Now this prize duffer Willie made such a
cock-up of the housing programme there isn't anywhere to
move them all. We can knock down a few Wesleyan chapels
to show our heart's in the right place but that's not going to
clear this lot! Which is the real issue, d'you agree, to get the
Freeway moving?

JAMES. Absolutely. The Freeway's more than a road, it's an
article of faith.

BARRY. There you are.

JAMES. The only single issue on which all parties are prepared
to sacrifice every principle.

BARRY. Which is why we must be grateful to the Wreckers' and
Breakers' Union. A jam like this could bring down the
government, if there wasn't someone standing by to hold the
country to ransom.

JAMES. You mean – act as scapegoat for the government?

BARRY. They'll get a whacking great wage increase.

JAMES. Sincere unionists would call that a bribe. I would myself.

Pause. BARRY *moves upstage a few steps, opens shooting-stick, sits.*

BARRY. James, I've never spoken out to you before. At your dinner-table and mine I've always had too much to learn from you about how the country's run and the people who run it. As a boy you rode piggy-back on Prime Ministers, kings blacked your boots at school. You're among the kindest, most civilised men I know. You're gifted with all the qualities one learns to value most highly: indiscriminate courtesy, unassuming confidence, unflinching patriotism, love of liberty, a total lack of regard for personal gain –

JAMES (*who has been trying to interrupt*). I simply cannot allow you to continue –

BARRY (*continuing forcibly*). Qualities bred by an almost invisible structure of privilege and sustained by an absence of responsibility. You love the Common People because you know fuck-all about them. At fourteen I left the elementary school and went as a tea-boy to the light engineering works.

JAMES. Most vividly described in your memoirs, yes.

BARRY. Don't turn this into a mutual admiration contest.

JAMES. Was I doing that?

BARRY. I only mention my early years to show you that I know the People at first hand. I was *one* of them. And my political life is devoted to improving the People's lot while making sure they never actually gain control. We daren't let them. And most of them don't want to. They want a bigger slice of the cake, not the bakery. The bright ones amongst them, like me, get out sharpish. And down on the floor you're left with a few militants, nasty little Hitlers, and the Men, the Majority. That's what it comes down to, James. Natural inequality.

JAMES. I prefer to say difference, variety.

BARRY. All right. There are two fundamentally 'different' kinds of people – Us, the ones in charge, and Them, the ones who clear the shit away. Now I'll do all I can to see they get decently paid for doing it but I'll make bloody sure they're not allowed any real say. So don't tell me we're bribing the unions . . .

A disturbance at the left. They turn to see a GUARD *struggling with* NANCY.

NANCY. Take your hands off me! Where's your officer?

COX. Let the lady pass, that man.

BARRY. Sorry, Nancy, I'll have that bloke on a fizzer.

JAMES. You remember Barry Potter, Mother?

NANCY. You caught in this jam as well?

BARRY. I'm on a walkabout. Since the last reshuffle I'm Minister of Movement.

NANCY. Time they shuffled again.

BARRY. I do apologise. But take what you need from the car and I'll lift you off.

NANCY. I'm not leaving now. This young woman's four fingers dilated. Where are my helping girls?

MAY *and* EVELYN *bang on door of bus.* NANCY *goes to it.*

Let them out this instant.

BARRY *nods to* GUARD *and he opens door.* MAY, EVELYN *and* LES *come out, the women with blankets,* LES *with kettle. They start explaining.*

No excuses now. If we don't look sharp, she'll manage this birth without us.

Leads off, left, others following. BARRY *smiles, then makes to go.*

BARRY. You'll persuade her to be ready in about ten to fifteen minutes?

JAMES. Most kind of you but we'd rather stay.

BARRY. I've got my orders. The Prime Minister told me --

JAMES. Then I must beg you to make our excuses. These people have become our friends – wage-slaves or not.

BARRY. Fact is, they'll all be leaving soon. By Shanks's Pony. I've already recorded an announcement. They'll be playing it as soon as we're airborne.

JAMES. This multitude by foot? Why?

BARRY. The welfare services aren't up to it. Jesus wept, you know what shape they're in. They can barely cope with the handicapped, the geriatric, people without cars, that class of person. But we've got the population of a sizeable town out here! With no plumbing!

JAMES. None of this affects our intention to stand by our friends. You may describe them as shit carriers, you may use the advantage of your lowly birth to denigrate their intelligence but –

BARRY. My dear fellow, I've enough problems –

LES comes from left, goes into tent and brings out bucket, with lid closed.

So much easier for us all if you collect your essential baggage and come with me. When the Freeway's cleared, an Autoguard will drive your car up to Glencromarty –

JAMES (*leading him to* LES). I don't believe you know each other. Barry Potter, Les Lorimer.

LES puts down bucket, wipes hand on trousers, shakes with BARRY.

BARRY. How are you?

LES. Bearing up.

BARRY. Jolly good. That's the spirit.

LES. I know your face. You're – what's his name – ?

JAMES. The Minister of Movement.

LES. That's him. Seen you often on TV. Seen you pop your head round the screen. Tally-ho!

BARRY (*wiping hand on handkerchief*). Keeping up the good work, I see?

LES. Someone's got to do it.

BARRY (*smiling at* JAMES). Exactly.

LES. Though my view is they ought to settle the dustmen's pay-claim or we shall have a sanitary problem.

BARRY. Then after that the Wreckers' hyper-claim and after that Charley Farnes-Barnes' hyper-claim and Uncle Tom Cobley-and-all's hyper-claim. That's the slippery slope, don't you think so?

LES. I couldn't agree with that altogether, not as a lifelong union man.

BARRY. It's your friends the unions that caused this bleeding shambles!

LES. I thought the Scrubbers had.

JAMES. Well said, Les.

BARRY. In the first place, yes, but now the Wreckers are taking advantage.

JAMES. But if the accident has been cleared, why can't we at least move northward as far as the bottlenecks?

BARRY. No point in that. At the London end there are massive queues of sightseers all coming up to look at the jam.

JAMES. Can't the police divert them, turn them back?

BARRY. Close the Freeway? Jesus wept!

LES. You can't do that, James.

JAMES. Stupid of me.

LES. We ought to start squeezing through the existing roads.

BARRY. Imagine it. Those Czechoslovakian juggernauts queueing in village streets, knocking prams over as they try to avoid the cathedrals! Pictures of carnage in the popular press! I'm not having that blood on *my* hands.

LES. Don't you worry. We've been through worse than this. Like Jerry found in the last lot, we can take it.

BARRY. Bang on!

JAMES. So you can assure us there's no question of evacuation?

BARRY (*annoyed*). We may have to act firmly but fairly to contain the danger to public health –

LES. Evacuation? How d'you mean? Reverse all the way back to the start of the linkroads?

BARRY. Reverse? Well –

LES. We'd never manage that, not with new people joining the queue every minute –

BARRY. Nothing of that sort, no.

JAMES. How would you feel about leaving the vehicles, Les?

LES. You're not going to try that? Blimey O'Riley, they'd skin you alive.

BARRY. Well, look, I mustn't keep you from your chores.

Makes to go but JAMES *detains him.*

JAMES. Skin you alive, you said, Les? Please enlarge.

LES. What was your election pledge? A car for every family and enough roads to drive them on? Not that I voted for you.

BARRY. Haven't we fulfilled that promise? We've crammed the streets with vehicles and covered the country with streets. All other public expenditure was cut back, truncated limbs of the social services were allowed to wither away –

LES. Granted. But one Scrubber demo, one justifiable wage
dispute, and look at us! A single Freeway's not enough.
There's got to be a whole interconnecting complex.

BARRY. Well, I shan't get them started nattering to you,
enjoyable though it may be –

Moves away, JAMES *follows.* LES *picks up bucket and moves
towards left with it.*

JAMES. Listen well to him, Barry. *Vox populi vox dei.* Or, as
Burke put it, the temper of the people amongst whom he
presides ought to be the first study of a statesman.

BARRY. Leave the people to me, James, you hold on to your
ideals –

Suddenly a recording of BARRY's *voice from behind
audience.*

BARRY (*speakers*). Tally-ho, all freewheelers! This is the
Minister of Movement, fresh from a traditional walkabout.

BARRY (*coming to fence*). Not yet!

JAMES. Oh, Lord!

LES *stands listening.*

BARRY (*speakers*). Now I've had a chance to see for myself the
sacrifices you're making to help us deal with the crisis. A crisis
brought about by two very different groups of extremists.

BARRY (*over this, moving to* SECURITY MAN). Get through
and tell them to turn that fucking thing off –

BARRY (*speakers*). And I know from what you've said to me
that when someone waves the big stick, you don't want us to
wave the white flag.

BARRY (*back to fence*). I'll have that man on a charge so fast
his feet won't touch the ground.

BARRY (*speakers*). And when I tell you that in the interests of
public health we must now begin to evacuate the Freeway, I'm
sure you'll accept –

LES (*same time*). What's that he's saying?

BARRY (*speakers*). – that it's one of those irksome things that sometimes have to be done.

BARRY. Potter here, are you receiving me? Over.

BARRY (*speakers*). Operation Dunkirk will begin immediately with Phase One; Leaving the linkroads. I can't promise that the Long March ahead will be without its hazards.

LES. Long March?

BARRY (*speakers*). But as you leave your keys in the vehicles and gather your essential hand baggage, you will know that –

Suddenly cut off. BARRY *comes down to fence and stares over at speakers.*

BARRY. I'll throw the book at that dopey bugger!

Neighbours have gathered on the road, attracted by the tannoy. From them and from offstage we hear rebellious noises.

LES. What's this about leaving our keys?

BARRY. As soon as the Freeway's clear, teams of Autoguards will drive the vehicles to some suitable car-park – say the Yorkshire Moors – and you chaps will be notified when you can go and collect –

LES. That may take months.

BARRY. I trust not.

LES. Months without a car! We're better off here.

BARRY. People are dying on the Freeway!

LES. People are always dying on the Freeway. That's part of the price.

MAY (*coming on from right*). Listen!

In silence hear a baby's cry.

He's a whopper. We reckon about four kilos.

JAMES. You see, Barry? People are being born as well.

MAY. I'm after some paper to make a parcel of the afterbirth.

LES. No paper left. All burnt. D'you hear that announcement?

MAY. What's it mean?

LES. They want us to leave our cars, start walking.

MAY. Who's they?

LES. Well, you know who this is, I expect?

MAY (*recognising* BARRY). Looks like Tally-ho.

LES. It *is*.

MAY. My daughter likes you. She says you speak your mind.

BARRY. I try to.

MAY. She reckons anyone that's as rude as you are on TV must be telling the truth.

BARRY. Oh, that's marvellous! Isn't that marvellous?

MAY. Well, tell me, how are we going to live without the Cherokee? How shall I get to the corner shop the far side of the motorway with the nearest bridge a mile off? If I want a bag of sugar or a dozen eggs, Les takes me on the flyover, drops me by the shop –

LES. There's nowhere to pull in, so I keep circling the roundabout while she's in the shop till I see her waiting at the kerb.

MAY. He slows down to let me jump on, we're home again in no time. I often fetch the groceries for neighbours who can't get out – widows without cars, pensioners – they daren't go out, a lot of them, not now the pavements are so narrow.

LES. What are *they* to do?

BARRY. You'll have it back in a few weeks' time.

LES. In what condition? How do we know a lot of scruffs and gippoes aren't going to get inside?

MAY. An Englishman's Motor Home is his castle.

EVELYN (*coming from left*). May, Lady Rhyne says not to bother. The father's going to bury the placenta on the verge.

MAY. Love, they want us to leave the Cherokee and walk back to London.

EVELYN. I heard. I turned round straightaway. I said, 'How am I to get to the Palais?' Now Freddie's gone I've no regular partner but I never miss a comp.

BARRY. A what?

MAY. A dancing competition. We pick her up.

EVELYN. With the one-way traffic non-stop round our crescent day and night the only other escape's by Underground. Well, picture me in a lurex bodice on the Bakerloo.

BARRY. It's appalling – and I speak for all parties when I say we're appalled at the hardship these dirty little scruffs are prepared to inflict on the people of Britain. And speaking for myself, if *I* ever meet a Scrubber up a dark alley, I'll have his guts for garters.

LES. What I'd like to ask is: your party's last election platform? Was it or was it not entirely based on keeping the Freeway moving?

BARRY. Like those of all other parties, yes.

LES. Well, we the car-makers played our part. The cars are still rolling off the line this very minute.

CROWD. Car workers? They can't grumble. Wish I could afford a Motor Home. They're only after what they can get (*etc.*).

MAY (*rounding on them*). You don't know what it's like on that assembly line. He used to come home, sit in the chair and go out like a light. When he was awake, it was more like sleep-walking. Months on end we hardly spoke to each other. The kiddies only saw him weekends and then his nerves were so bad he couldn't stand the sight of them. We weren't properly man and wife.

VOICES. Nobody forced them. It's a free country.

MAY. Well, it wasn't free when we were young. You worked where you were born and lucky to get it. And the day they took him off the line and gave him a white coat, we started living a decent life for the first time.

LES (gently). Well, that's all in the past now, love.

MAY. For you, but some poor devils are at it still.

LES. All transients though. No white European has worked on the line for nearly ten years. That was a big step forward for the British working man.

BARRY. Absolutely.

TRACY. Don't let's get into politics. If walking's the only way to get my children something to eat . . . d'you know what they had for breakfast? Playdoh.

Crowd murmurs sympathetically.

GRANT. Right! Modelling clay!

BARRY. Now that's victimisation, *if* you like. And on the main roads it's even worse.

MAY. And they've got farther to walk.

LES. Pay the Wreckers what they want and we can all drive home –

CROWD. They ought to be strung up! Put them up against a wall (*etc.*).

BARRY. Now, come on, ladies and gentlemen, this isn't Russia! Not yet! Nor is it some airy-fairy Utopia. This is what you voted for. It's what you want. It's what *I* want. A free-for-all.

MAY. Free for who exactly? Not us. We paid for every mortal thing.

LES. And all for what? To leave our life's work on the linkroads for gippoes to plunder?

JAMES has been at boot of car and now returns with gun under arm.

JAMES. Les, with respect, let us ask ourselves: what is the essence of a first-rate civilisation? The kind you and I earnestly crave? Surely it is that the greatest number of choices is given to the greatest number of citizens. Ever-proliferating democratic profusion. In other words, the free way. Now obviously such an infinity of options must remain an ideal; obviously too we must aim at nothing less. Neither the holy writ of the Marxist, nor the Luddite austerities of the Scrubber but the controlled chaos of parliamentary democracy. Not icy water but hot punch, not thin gruel but bouillabaisse.

BARRY. That's what I said. Or meant to.

JAMES. Now the Freeway has its weaknesses as well as its enemies and we may sometimes have to leave it to serve it. So that the fabric may be strengthened, the rules reappraised. And during the weeks ahead, while the Freeway is out of service, while the government exercises its emergency powers, there may be hardship, discomfort, danger, death. But, Les, you and I know it's only a skirmish in the battle for a free way that works. And knowing that, we who believe the Freeway to be the right way see no other course but to find our own ways home. The alternative is the dead end of despotism, a one-way street to a new age of darkness. (*To* LES.) I beg you –

LES. And what about the Wreckers?

JAMES. They'll get what they're asking, won't they, Minister?

BARRY. I dare say. We can't build without first knocking down.

Thunder. People look at the sky. One of the officers speaks aside to BARRY.

Yes, right. The helicopter's waiting, I must fly. *Arrividerci*, James. *A bientôt.*

JAMES. Very well.

BARRY. Bye, bye, ladies and gentlemen, chaps and chapesses. I'm going to tell the Prime Minister you may be down in the mouth but you're not downhearted. In fact, you're in jolly good nick. What are you?

CROWD(*feebly*). In jolly good nick.

BARRY goes to back, where SOLDIERS clear a way.

And remember the TV cameras will be following you on the Long March. So give us a smile and a wave and show them what kind of people you are, eh? Tally-ho!

CROWD. Tally-ho!

As he makes exit followed by his retinue, CROWD drifts away, including SCALES, who collect stuff from boot of car.

MAY (*to EVELYN*). All very well for him with his three Rolls-Royces.

JAMES. Appalling luck, though, this happening during his Ministry. And not really his fault. Indeed, looked at closely, nothing is ever anyone's fault.

MAY. Nobody's fault?

COX leads JAMES aside.

LES (*to MAY*). Don't interfere in politics, love.

MAY. Oh, lovely. (*To EVELYN.*) Stand in the corner with a dunce's cap on.

LES. I didn't mean that, but – d'you agree with James or not?

MAY. What you asking me for? You told me not to interfere.

EVELYN. I don't think you need to understand. It's more his way of talking.

JAMES has gone off, right, with COX. Only LES, MAY, EVELYN remain.

Thunder, LES looks up.

LES. I suppose I better strike this tent.

MAY. Wally!

WALLY has come along downstage of fence, stooping to avoid being seen, now he rolls under and they help him up. We see that his clothes are bloodstained and the sleeve of his jacket torn. Face bruised, muddy.

EVELYN. You're bleeding.

WALLY. Ain't my blood. Had to kill a dog. I was down the dairy unit, got us a bowl of cream . . . just coming away and one of those crazy Alsatians come at me. Got hold of my arm but I done for him with this –

Shows knife, stuck in belt.

MAY. My steak knife.

WALLY. Lost the cream but I got these.

Shows two green apples. EVELYN goes into bus.

MAY. Don't risk your life. We're not starving.

WALLY. Not yet, but this ain't gonna be no picnic from now on. There's armed Rangers all over. A couple of them come after me, that dog made so much noise dying.

MAY. Haven't you heard, though, love? We've got to take up our beds and walk.

WALLY. I heard, yeah. I been lying in the ditch waiting for the soldiers to go.

LES. Only reasonable, only way to solve the crisis. As you say, it wouldn't be any picnic staying here.

WALLY. You're selling out again, Les.

LES. What's that?

WALLY. You've got too much to lose, I guess. A photo
   album, a Motor Home, a toilet-tent –

LES. You're not going to start on that again? Blimey O'Riley!

EVELYN *comes back with Red Cross box and dresses wound.*

EVELYN. You're only grazed.

WALLY. Got him before he could sink his teeth in. Like a reflex
   action. Ain't had to kill since the war but seems I ain't forgot.

EVELYN. You never told me you were in the war.

LES. You get on my top-note, you do. Calling me a scab.

WALLY. Did I call you a –

LES. Accusing me of breaking solidarity with the lads in the
   other unions, then saying you don't give a monkey's for them
   anyway. What kind of solidarity's that? And you heard that
   Minister: they'll get their money.

WALLY. And what kind of victory's that? They'll get their
   money and buy all manner of crap and wreck the place they
   live and buy some goddam car and drive off and wreck some
   other place.

MAY. Oh, Wally, for goodness sake.

EVELYN. Nice language, I must say.

WALLY. Until they've wrecked the whole planet. And what
   then? Every family its own spacecraft?

LES. You're a bleeding malcontent, d'you know that?

MAY. Always has been. Even as a boy. Never learnt to march in
   step, did you?

WALLY. I watched the greedy bastards run the world. And I
   watched them turn the rest into greedy bastards too. Like a
   plague it's been, except not with rats but money.

EVELYN. If it's a plague, there's nothing to be done then, is
   there?

WALLY. Quit running. Stay where you are. Make it work, wherever you happen to be.

EVELYN. D'you mean stay here? This God-forsaken place? With all the nasty smells and insects in the food and no facilities?

Thunder. WALLY *looks at her, offers her an apple.*

I'll share it out. Thank you.

LES. Come on, before this breaks. And, Wally, you help. No skiving, I know you.

Goes into tent. EVELYN *packs away first aid, takes box into bus.* WALLY *stands, looking at his dressed wound.* MAY *goes to fold chairs, etc. During the next scene, these four clear: tent, pedal-bin, chairs, table, anything else that's left.* LES *goes upstage of bus with lavatory bucket.* RHYNES *return from right with* COX.

JAMES (*offering hand to* LES). Les, may I say what a tremendous pleasure and privilege it's been, sharing this experience with you. And do let's meet again before too long. The House will always find me.

LES. Which house is that?

JAMES. The one beside Big Ben.

PAYNE *emerges on top of Motor Home.* NANCY *and* COX *go behind.*

Where we conduct the friendly tug-of-war between the apparently different interests of your faction and mine. For wasn't it Burke who said that parties must ever exist in a free country? I think you'll find it was.

Bids good-bye to the others as NANCY *arrives on roof with* COX.

MAY. What are you doing on our roof?

NANCY. Good-bye. Thank you for all your splendid help. I only wish we could stay. But we've our duty as well.

*Helicopter approaches, arriving overhead with usual effects. A
rigid ladder or cradle descends from the flies over the bus and
COX and PAYNE help NANCY to climb up. JAMES has
followed them on to the roof, still with gun. Speaks down to
LES, watching on ground, raising his voice above the din.*

JAMES. Les!

LES. Hallo?

JAMES. May I commend to you one last observation? It is from
John Stuart Mill. 'The only freedom which deserves the name
is that of pursuing our own good in our own way, so long as
we do not attempt to deprive others of theirs, or impede their
efforts to obtain it.'

*He follows his mother into the sky. Helicopter flies off as
everyone waves. COX and PAYNE get off the roof and others
resume their packing. WALLY does not reappear.*

Thunder.

COX and PAYNE come to help.

COX. Give you a hand with the Big Top, sir?

LES. Thanks.

COX. So you can get off toot-sweet.

LES. We haven't been given the word yet, officially.

COX (*shrugs*). Sooner you move, the sooner you'll be there, the
better your position in the queue. Sooner you'll get home and
put the kettle on. Take only essential baggage of course, no
articles of sentimental value, which could represent a
temptation to roving lorry-drivers.

LES. D'you mean we're going on the motorways?

COX. I don't think you're going by Jumbo jet.

PAYNE. You'll be allocated to various pick-up points where
hundreds of voluntary helpers will take you in every available
form of transport to regional dispersal centres.

COX. They've been appealing on the radio for anything that moves on wheels . . . from a push-bike to a cattle-truck.

LES. Blimey O'Riley.

COX. You'll be all right. Remember nineteen-forty? The little craft?

LES. We had to leave the equipment behind on that occasion too.

COX and LES clear tent and stow it. Verge is as it was at start, but for the rubbish piled downstage. GRANT and TRACY have got their baggage and locked their boot. MAY and EVELYN come from bus wearing anoraks, etc., carrying bags, umbrella, radio, ciné-camera. SCALES wave good-bye.)

GRANT. Making an early start. Bye-bye. See you later perhaps.

MAY. Good-bye. See you on the ice.

TRACY (*to children, off*). Now don't fight, Sholto. Daddy's going to start us off. Right?

GRANT (*singing, as they go*). *I'll give you one-oh.*

BOTH. *Green grow the rushes-oh --*

MAY. Bless their hearts.

PAYNE (*to EVELYN*). Haven't you got more practical shoes? Or boots?

EVELYN. We only came for the day!

MAY. How far shall we have to walk then?

PAYNE. Anything up to ten miles.

EVELYN. Oh, my Lord!

LES has been round bus, locks door.

LES. Seen Wally?

MAY. He's the Missing Link.

LES. Ask him to do a stroke of work, he always does the vanishing trick.

COX. You'll meet him at the dispersal centre.

LES locks door of Motor Home.

LES. But he'd be useful on the road.

MAY. Perhaps we ought to wait for him.

COX. I shouldn't advise that. You'd best be cutting along. (*As LES makes to reply.*) Before the rain.

MAY. Your windcheater, love, and camera . . .

LES. Ta. Last shot of you against the Cherokee. Never know when we'll see it again. Come on, Evelyn, you know where to stand.

Women pose while LES runs camera.

COX. I should go now, if I were you, sir, not the middle of next week.

LES. Right you are.

LES brings keys to COX and gives him a banknote also.

See they take good care of her, will you, Sergeant?

COX. Do my best, sir. Thank you very much.

Women wait while LES goes to bus and rubs off a speck of dirt with his finger.

Bye-bye.

PAYNE. *Bon-voyage!*

LES, MAY and EVELYN go right. COX yawns, stretches, holds up other keys.

COX. Look. Lord Muck's keys. Nice little job lined up there. Driving to his game lodge. You on?

PAYNE. What about all that lot in front?

COX. Yes, well, after that lot's shunted into a car-park somewhere. See the Highlands before it disappears. Last countryside in Britain. We time it right, we might get dinner. You ever tasted venison?

They make off, left. More thunder.

WALLY looks through window of Cherokee. Opens door, comes out, shuts behind him. Wears parka, has knives which he stows about his person. Finishes one of the apples, throws down core, in pile of rubbish. He rearranges the wood pigeon in an airways bag round his neck.

WALLY (*sings, to himself*).
So what care I for my goose-feather bed
With the sheet turned down so bravely-oh –
Tonight I shall sleep in the cold open field –

Crash of thunder as WALLY puts up his hood and drops to roll under fence. Hear rain falling heavily.

Curtain

CPSIA information can be obtained at www.ICGtesting.com
Printed in the USA
LVOW08s2055310813

350455LV00001B/4/P